Justification by Faith

Lutherans
and Catholics
in Dialogue VII

Edited by
H. GEORGE ANDERSON
T. AUSTIN MURPHY
JOSEPH A. BURGESS

AUGSBURG Publishing House • Minneapolis

JUSTIFICATION BY FAITH
Lutherans and Catholics in Dialogue VII

Scripture quotations from the Revised Standard Version of the Bible are copyright 1946, 1952, and 1971 by the Division of Christian Education of the National Council of Churches.

Library of Congress Cataloging in Publication Data

Main entry under title:

JUSTIFICATION BY FAITH.

  (Lutherans and Catholics in dialogue; 7)
  Bibliography: p.
  1. Justification—Addresses, essays, lectures.
2. Lutheran Church—Relations—Catholic Church—
Addresses, essays, lectures.   3. Catholic Church—
Relations—Lutheran Church—Addresses, essays, lectures.
I. Anderson, H. George (Hugh George), 1932-   .
II. Murphy, T. Austin (Thomas Austin), 1911-   .
III. Burgess, Joseph A.   IV. Series.
BT764.J87   1985   234'.7   84-28412

Manufactured in the U.S.A.   APH 10-3626

1   2   3   4   5   6   7   8   9   0   1   2   3   4   5   6   7   8   9

CONTENTS

ABBREVIATIONS

Ap	Apology of the Augsburg Confession
BA	Bibliothèque augustinienne
BC	*The Book of Concord. The Confessions of the Evangelical Lutheran Church* (tr. and ed. T. Tappert; Philadelphia: Fortress, 1959)
BS	*Die Bekenntnisschriften der lutherischen Kirche*
CA	*Confessio Augustana* (Augsburg Confession)
CCL	Corpus Christianorum Series latina
CR	Corpus reformatorum
CSEL	Corpus scriptorum ecclesiasticorum latinorum
DS	*Enchiridion Symbolorum,* 33rd ed. (ed. H. Denzinger and A. Schönmetzer)
DThC	*Dictionnaire de théologie catholique*
FC Ep	Formula of Concord, Epitome
FC SD	Formula of Concord, Solid Declaration
FRLANT	Forschungen zur Religion und Literatur des Alten und Neuen Testaments
¶	Sections of documents on justification for or from the Fourth Assembly of the Lutheran World Federation, Helsinki, 1963
§	Sections of "Justification by Faith," part I of this volume
Loeb	*The Apostolic Fathers,* vol. 1. Loeb Classical Library
L/RC	Lutherans and Catholics in Dialogue (see part I, n. 1)
LW	*Luther's Works* (J. Pelikan and H. Lehmann, gen. eds.)
MR	Malta Report (see part I, n. 2)
PG	*Patrologiae cursus completus, Series Graeca* (ed. J. P. Migne)
PL	*Patrologiae cursus completus, Series Latina* (ed. J. P. Migne)

‡	Sections of *"Righteousness" in the New Testament,* by John Reumann, with responses by Joseph A. Fitzmyer, s.j. and Jerome D. Quinn (Philadelphia: Fortress; New York/Ramsey, N.J.: Paulist, 1982)
SA	Smalcald Articles
SC	Sources chrétiennes
S.T.	*Summa theologiae*
TDNT	*Theological Dictionary of the New Testament*
TWNT	*Theologisches Wörterbuch zum Neuen Testament*
WA	Martin Luther, *Werke* (Kritische Gesamtausgabe; "Weimarer Ausgabe"; Weimar: Böhlau, 1883 to the present)
WA Br	WA Briefwechsel
WA DB	WA Die Deutsche Bibel
WA TR	WA Tischreden

PREFACE

The present volume contains the results of the seventh round of theological discussions between scholars appointed respectively by the U.S. Roman Catholic Bishops' Committee for Ecumenical and Interreligious Affairs and Lutheran World Ministries, which is the USA National Committee of the Lutheran World Federation. Earlier rounds of this dialogue, begun in July 1965, have discussed "The Status of the Nicene Creed as Dogma of the Church," "One Baptism for the Remission of Sins," "The Eucharist as Sacrifice," "Eucharist and Ministry," "Papal Primacy and the Universal Church," and "Teaching Authority and Infallibility in the Church."

Although the topic of "Justification by Faith" has been touched upon or alluded to in previous sessions of the dialogue, it was not fully addressed until the present round. Its prominence in the development of the Reformation makes it a key factor for the climate of relationships between Roman Catholics and Lutherans. The time spent on investigating this topic, therefore, has been warranted.

During the nearly six years of discussion on this topic, the dialogue lost two of its experienced members to death. Dr. Paul Empie was the founding Lutheran co-chairman of the dialogue and provided a continual voice for clarity in expressing theological views. Dr. Warren Quanbeck, a systematic theologian, contributed a skill in formulation that speeded the dialogue's work. We are grateful for their gifts and for the time they were able to share in this common endeavor.

This statement is the result of a process of common search. It is not a compromise between initially opposing views. The group examined the separate traditions with care and with a sympathetic ear to the formulations of their partners in dialogue. Where they have been able to discern agreement, they have made a common statement. Where they have discovered differences, they have tried to state them clearly and to assess their effect on relationships between the two communions.

After the dialogue group completed its work, the task of final editing was delegated to Dr. Joseph Burgess. We thank him for the extra labor which this important task entailed. To all the participants we express thanks for uncommon diligence, patience, and skill in achieving this significant result. Although the dialogue group and its members do not speak officially for the churches they represent, their views as competent and responsible theologians may encourage parishes of their respective churches to respond in gratitude to the mercy of God which has been shed upon us all.

Co-Chairmen:
H. GEORGE ANDERSON
Lutheran World Ministries

✠ T. AUSTIN MURPHY
*Bishops' Committee for
Ecumenical and Interreligious Affairs*

CHRONOLOGICAL LISTING
OF SESSIONS AND PAPERS

September 1978, Minneapolis, Minnesota

Joseph A. Fitzmyer, s.j., "Brief Remarks on Luther's Interpretation of Pauline Justification" (unpublished).

Gerhard O. Forde, "Agreement on Justification? Some Reflections on the Systematic Problem" (incorporated into his essay in this volume).

Eric W. Gritsch, "The Historical Origins of the Lutheran Teaching on Justification. A Summary" (published in this volume).

George Lindbeck, "Justification in the Catholic-Lutheran Dialogues and in the Discussions of the Recognition of the Augsburg Confession" (unpublished).

George H. Tavard, "Luther's Understanding of Justification in Recent Catholic Theology" (incorporated into his book, *Justification: An Ecumenical Study* [New York/Ramsey, N.J.: Paulist, 1983]).

February 1979, Cincinnati, Ohio

Gerhard O. Forde, "Forensic Justification and the Christian Life: Triumph or Tragedy?" (incorporated into his essay in this volume).

Robert W. Jenson, "An Exegesis of the Apology of the Augsburg Confession" (unpublished).

September 1979, Princeton, New Jersey

Robert W. Bertram, " 'Faith Alone Justifies': Luther on *Iustitia Fidei*" (published in this volume).

Avery Dulles, s.j., "Vatican II and the Problem of Justification" (unpublished).

Gerhard O. Forde, "*Usus Legis*. The Functional Understanding of Law in Lutheran Theology" (incorporated into his essay in this volume).

Carl J. Peter, "Sin, Grace, and the Council of Trent" (unpublished).

March 1980, Atlanta, Georgia

Joseph A. Fitzmyer, s.j., "The Biblical Basis of Justification by Faith: Comments on the Paper of Professor Reumann" (incorporated into the volume, John Reumann, with responses by Joseph A. Fitzmyer and Jerome D. Quinn, *"Righteousness" in the New Testament* [Philadelphia: Fortress; New York/Ramsey, N.J.: Paulist, 1982]).

George Lindbeck, "Some Lutheran Reflections on Trent" (published in this volume).

Carl J. Peter, "The Tridentine Decree on Justification" (published in this volume).

John Reumann, " 'Justification by Grace Through Faith' as Expression of the Gospel: The Biblical Witness to the Reformation Emphasis" (incorporated into the volume, John Reumann, with responses by Joseph A. Fitzmyer and Jerome D. Quinn, *"Righteousness" in the New Testament* [Philadelphia: Fortress; New York/Ramsey, N.J.: Paulist, 1982]).

George H. Tavard, "Luther on Galatians" (incorporated into his book, *Justification: An Ecumenical Study* [New York/Ramsey, N.J.: Paulist, 1983]).

September 1980, Gettysburg, Pennsylvania

Avery Dulles, s.j., "Justification in Contemporary Catholic Theology" (published in this volume).

Robert B. Eno, s.s., "Some Patristic Views on the Relationship of Faith and Works in Justification" (published in this volume).

Joseph A. Fitzmyer, s.j., a further installment of his response to John Reumann, begun March 1980, at Atlanta, Georgia.

Karlfried Froehlich, "Aspects of Justification Language in the Middle Ages" (incorporated into his essay in this volume).

George Lindbeck, "A Lutheran Approach to the Limits of Diversity in the Understanding of Justification" (published as "Article IV and Lutheran/Roman Catholic Dialogue: The Limits of Diversity in the Understanding of Justification," *Lutheran Theological Seminary Bulletin*, Gettysburg, Pa., 61 (1981) 3-14.

Carl J. Peter, "Purgatory in the Decrees of Trent, the Teaching of the Second Vatican Council, and Some Recent Roman Catholic Theology" (unpublished).

John Reumann, a further installment of his paper begun March 1980, at Atlanta, Georgia.

February 1981, Cincinnati, Ohio

Joseph A. Burgess, "Rewards, but in a Very Different Sense" (published in this volume).

Gerhard O. Forde, "Review Critique of V. Pfnür" (unpublished).

Jerome D. Quinn, "The Scriptures on Merit" (published in this volume).

Jill Raitt, "The Value of Merit Talk" (unpublished).

John Reumann, the final installment of his paper, begun March 1980, at Atlanta, Georgia, and continued September 1980, at Gettysburg, Pennsylvania.

September 1981, Paoli, Pennsylvania
Robert W. Bertram, "Recent Lutheran Theologies on Justification by Faith: A Sampling" (published in this volume).

Eric W. Gritsch, "Notes on the Discussion of Justification between Lutherans and Catholics" (incorporated into his essay in this volume).

John F. Johnson, "Bultmann on Justification: A Brief Reflection" (unpublished).

Jill Raitt, "From Augsburg to Trent" (published in this volume).

William G. Rusch, "How the Eastern Fathers Understood What the Western Church Meant by Justification" (published in this volume).

February 1982, Biloxi, Mississippi
Karlfried Froehlich, "Justification in the Later Middle Ages" (incorporated into his essay in this volume).

September 1982, New York, New York
George Lindbeck, "What's New about Our Statement?" (unpublished).

February 1983, Belmont, North Carolina

September 1983, Milwaukee, Wisconsin

Others
John F. Johnson, "Justification according to the Apology of the Augsburg Confession and the Formula of Concord" (commissioned by the dialogue and discussed at the meeting in February 1984, Seguin, Texas).

Carl J. Peter, "Justification by Faith and the Need of Another Critical Principle" (commissioned by the dialogue and discussed in a conference telephone call by the systematic theologians on the dialogue).

PART I

JUSTIFICATION BY FAITH
(COMMON STATEMENT)

INTRODUCTION

§ **1.** Since 1965 a theological dialogue between Lutherans and Roman Catholics in the United States has been taking place concerning doctrines that have united or separated their churches from one another since the sixteenth century. The degree of consensus or convergence that exists on the Nicene Creed, Baptism, the Eucharist, the Ministry, Papal Primacy, and Teaching Authority and Infallibility has been expressed in summaries and joint statements[1] that have become important for relations between our churches and for wider ecumenical discussions.

§ **2.** The question of justification by faith, which is at the heart of the divisions inherited from the sixteenth century, has not yet, however, been directly addressed in the United States dialogue, although its implications for other topics have been noted in previous documents. The Malta Report of the International Lutheran/Catholic Study Commission said in the course of a short section on the doctrine that "today . . . a far-reaching consensus is developing in the interpretation of justification."[2] But a further treatment of the subject and its implications is needed.[3] The present relationship between the Catholic and Lutheran traditions calls for a greater clarity about the way to understand and speak of justification than has yet been achieved in official discussions, for the good news of God's justifying action in Jesus Christ stands at the center of Christian faith and life.

§ **3.** The present statement is a response to this need. It is based on discussions since 1978 of position papers drawing on a considerable body of biblical, historical, theological, and ecumenical literature.[4] It seeks to indicate how historic disagreements in the interpretation of the biblical doctrine of justification have developed and to what extent they can now be overcome. It attempts to remove obstacles to joint proclamation of the message of justification and includes a declaration proclaiming our common faith. For justification is above all a reality to be proclaimed in word and sacrament.

§ **4.** We emphatically agree that the good news of what God has done for us in Jesus Christ is the source and center of all Christian life and of the existence and work of the church. In view of this agreement, we have found it helpful to keep in mind in our reflections an affirmation which both Catholics and Lutherans can wholeheartedly accept: *our entire hope of justification and salvation rests on Christ Jesus and on the gospel whereby the good news of God's merciful action in Christ is made known; we do not place our ultimate trust in anything other than God's promise and saving work in Christ.* This excludes ultimate reliance on our faith, virtues, or merits, even though we acknowledge God working in these by grace alone (*sola gratia*). In brief, hope and trust for salvation are gifts of the Holy Spirit and finally rest solely on God in Christ. Agreement on this Christological affirmation does not necessarily involve full agreement between Catholics and Lutherans on justification by faith, but it does raise the question, as we shall see, whether the remaining differences on this doctrine need be church-dividing. Our intent in presenting this statement is to help our churches see how and why they can and should increasingly proclaim together the one, undivided gospel of God's saving mercy in Jesus Christ.

CHAPTER ONE

THE HISTORY OF THE QUESTION

§ 5. In order to understand how disagreements over justification that were once irresolvable may now not be church-dividing, it is important to have in mind certain features not only of the Reformation conflict itself but also of its medieval background and of later developments. In sketching these features in the following historical sections, we have utilized the work of many scholars of different traditions and outlooks who have done much to overcome the confessionally and polemically biased pictures of the past, but we do not claim to have done justice to the complexity of the material and the variety of interpretations. We have attempted simply to highlight those aspects of the total story which are of particular importance for the present Lutheran-Roman Catholic discussion.

A. Before the Sixteenth Century

§ 6. Historical research in recent generations has greatly increased our awareness of the degree to which the debate over justification in the sixteenth century was conditioned by a specifically Western and Augustinian understanding of the context of salvation which, in reliance on St. Paul, stressed the scriptural theme of *iustitia*, of righteousness. Eastern theologians, on the other hand, generally saw salvation within the framework of a cosmic process in which humanity occupies a place of honor.[5] Combining biblical allusions to divinization (e.g., Ps. 82:6; 2 Pet. 1:4; 2 Cor. 3:18) with an ascetically oriented, Neoplatonic understanding of the ascent of the soul, Eastern theologians described human salvation in terms of a return to God of a creation that had gone forth from God. This pattern is still found in Augustine's spirituality, in the Western mystical tradition influenced by Pseudo-Dionysius, and in the structures of Peter Lombard's *Sentences* and Thomas Aquinas' *Summa theologiae*.

§ **7.** Yet the basic pattern of thought in the West about salvation, especially as developed in Augustine's fifth-century confrontation with Pelagius, was distinctive. Not only did Augustine emphasize Paul's teaching on justification much more than was common in the East, but he understood this primarily in terms of the transformation of the individual, as suggested by the Latin etymology of the term *justificare*, to make righteous.[6] His concern was to stress that this transformation takes place by grace, and the specific theme of the present statement, justification by faith, was not at the center of his attention. Thus at issue in the debate with Pelagius and the Pelagians was the extent to which God's grace is necessary and sovereign in this soteriological process of individual transformation. Prominent Eastern theologians had different concerns, as is shown by the attention they gave to the cosmic dimension of salvation, the divinizing character of grace, the universality of corruptibility and death, as well as freedom and responsibility, in contrast to the prominence of fate and inevitability in some pagan and gnostic thought.[7] In some later treatments of sin, grace, and predestination, Augustine stressed the total need of grace on the part of human beings and the total sovereignty of God in regard to salvation. In so doing he set much of the agenda for both medieval and Reformation theology, and with his victory the name "Pelagianism" became the label for an infamous heresy (although the degree to which Pelagius was a Pelagian is now debated by historians).[8]

§ **8.** It is thus not surprising that virtually all medieval theologians claimed to be anti-Pelagian, but this did not prevent frequent charges of Pelagianism throughout the period,[9] and the Protestant critique suspected the entire sacramental system of the medieval church of this heresy. While Augustine's stress on the absolute priority of God's initiative and the primacy of grace was often reiterated, his transformational model of justification, when set within the context of new developments in intellectual outlook, church practice, and spirituality,[10] allowed for growing speculation about the human role in the process.[11] This development is particularly evident in (1) the treatment of grace, (2) the emphasis on merit, and (3) the changing attitude toward predestination.

§ **9.** *(1) Grace.* Augustine's intention in developing the doctrine of grace was to protect the absolute priority of God's action over all human endeavor: "What do you have that you did not receive?" (1 Cor. 4:7).[12] His distinctions between "operating" and "cooperating," "prevenient" and "subsequent" grace point in this direction.[13] Early Scholasticism added further categories such as first grace, grace freely given (*gratia gratis data*), and justifying grace (*gratia gratum faciens*) in order to clarify various stages of the process and was open, as is evident in Peter Lombard, to identifying infused love with the Holy Spirit.[14] In view, however, of a growing awareness that the difference between the natural and the supernatural is not simply identical with that between creatures and God,[15] a distinction came to be made between two types of supernatural grace, the uncreated grace (*gratia increata*, i.e., God himself or the indwelling of the Holy Spirit) and the created "habit" or disposition of grace (*gratia creata*).[16]

§ 10. Interest in the transforming effect of created grace led to discussion of the potentialities of human nature in the Aristotelian sense. For some theologians, such as Thomas Aquinas, God remained in total command as the initiator and perfecter of the movement (*motus*) from sinner to saint,[17] and for all theologians God retained the initiative in that the habit of grace is freely "infused" (cf. Rom. 5:5).[18] Yet for many the insistence on infused grace and on the presence of special assisting graces (*gratiae gratis datae*)[19] at every step of the way was combined with a strong emphasis on the ability of free will to contribute to salvation, not simply on the basis of grace, but independently, *ex suis naturalibus*.[20] This emphasis on human freedom was strong especially, though not exclusively, among those influenced by Ockham's nominalism and the *via moderna* at the end of the Middle Ages; yet there were others, including some nominalists, such as Gregory of Rimini, who attacked it as Pelagian despite the disclaimers of its proponents.[21]

§ 11. *(2) Merit.* A similar shift can be traced in the expanding thought on merit before the Reformation. Augustine took the term from the African tradition. For him it had its basis in the biblical language of reward, but again the mature Augustine wanted to vindicate God's absolute priority: "When God rewards our merits, he crowns his own gifts."[22] In time the shift of interest to the role of human nature led to the distinction between "congruous" and "condign" merit (*meritum de congruo* and *meritum de condigno*).[23] The former (*meritum de congruo*) in one of its meanings designated the basis for a hope that God "does not deny grace to those who do what is in them" (*facientibus quod in se est Deus non denegat gratiam*).[24] This assertion can be understood as affirming God's priority in the sense that merciful divine inspiration and direction are necessary for every good action of the human creature. It is in this sense that Thomas Aquinas speaks of doing what is in one's power (*facere quod in se est*). This preparation for justification is possible only because of the undeserved help of God's merciful providence.[25] Although Thomas describes the good works performed in the process of preparation as congruously meritorious, he does not fail to note that this involves an extended use of the term "merit." Indeed, he says one should, if pressed, concede that such works before justification do not merit any good rather than assert that they do.[26]

§ 12. The formula *facere quod in se est*, however, can also be used in a Pelagianizing sense if "doing what is in one" is thought of as a condition which on the one hand calls for the conferral of grace and which on the other hand human beings can and must fulfill by relying on the unaided powers of their fallen nature. In the late medieval *via moderna* such a condition was commonly regarded as involving a gracious accommodation on the part of God, who precisely by accepting human efforts that are unworthy chooses to grant the grace leading to justification and thus, in this broad sense, renders these efforts meritorious. While this explanation was intended to diminish the Pelagian danger,[27] it also allowed theologians to claim that God owes it to himself to be gracious if there is any attempt to seek him, and it could be used to urge people to try ever harder to prove themselves worthy of being accepted by good works. The precept, "to do what is in one's power" (*facere quod in se est*), according to some historians contributed to the rampant scrupulosity of the late Middle Ages, and it was viewed by the Reformers as a cause of the "terrified conscience."[28]

§ 13. *(3) Predestination*. A shift can also be observed in the treatment of predestination. Augustine's struggle in his later years to defend the primacy of grace against Pelagius led him also to stress the primacy of God's eternal will. He did not consistently teach a double predestination, but from his emphasis on God's election of some to glory it seemed logical to infer the predestination of others to eternal perdition. The regional Council of Orange, however, taught what is generally called single predestination (i.e., of the elect to glory)[29] and condemned double predestination.[30]

§ 14. Influenced by the new interest in the powers of nature, the Scholastic theologians of the twelfth and thirteenth centuries stressed that God, in predestining to salvation, sees to it that the person receives the grace that removes sin and sanctifies the soul. God, they insisted, imposes no constraint on human freedom; yet they continued to affirm the primacy of grace. Bonaventure, for example, held that in predestination there are an eternal divine plan, a conferral of God's grace in time, and an eternal glorification; in reprobation there are again an eternal plan, an obstinacy in time, and eternal punishment. One who has been given grace in this life merits the glory of heaven just as one who sins obstinately in this life merits the punishment of hell. Nevertheless, because both predestination and reprobation involve God's eternal plan, neither can, taken as a whole, be merited.[31] Why God wishes to justify this person rather than another has not been revealed because such knowledge is not necessary for our salvation.[32]

§ 15. Thomas Aquinas also emphasized the primacy of grace. Since eternal glory is the final gift that God bestows, it can be merited on the basis of earlier gifts of God's grace, but the grace of justification cannot itself be merited.[33] He says in the *Summa theologiae* that "it is impossible that the total effect of predestination in general have any cause on our part." Further, the reason why God has "elected some to glory and condemned" others is none other than "the divine will."[34]

§ 16. For John Duns Scotus predestination properly refers to an act of the divine will electing a rational or intellectual creature to grace and glory. With this in mind he asks whether one who is predestined can be damned. His answer is that God may predestine an individual or choose not to do so—not both simultaneously or successively but one or the other at the same instant of eternity.[35] Scotus made much of the distinction between what God could do by means of the divine power working in the present order (*de potentia ordinata*) and what God could do by absolute divine power (*de potentia absoluta*) in another order.[36]

§ 17. Some later theologians were less careful than Scotus in maintaining that predestination, as the entire effect of God's decree, is not based on foreseen merits. They held that even in the present order God can and does predestine those who do their best by their own natural powers.[37] Yet there were also late medieval theologians who taught that all preparation for grace is the effect of predestination as an act of God's will and who viewed this position as the touchstone of true Augustinianism against the "new Pelagians." In the Augustinian order, to which Luther later belonged, some argued this way, but others did not.[38]

§ 18. The late medieval scene was thus characterized by a bewildering variety in which Augustinian intentions combined with competing interests arising out of an emphasis on the power and freedom of human nature within the order established by God. Everyone professed to be Augustinian and anti-Pelagian, but there was little agreement on what these terms meant. Customary labels such as "*via antiqua*," "*via moderna*," "nominalism," and "Augustinian" do not correspond to specific types of the doctrine of justification,[39] and thus the Reformers of the sixteenth century, although influenced by their predecessors, cannot be aligned with any single medieval school of thought.

§ **19.** On the depravity of human nature, for example, there are parallels, recognized by Luther himself, between his teachings and those of theologians of the Augustinian order such as Giles of Rome and Gregory of Rimini.[40] The Reformers' rejection of the category of created grace may echo Peter Lombard's identification of infused love with the Holy Spirit.[41] In rejecting positions such as that of Gabriel Biel, that human beings have a natural capacity to merit grace, the Reformers resembled Aquinas and others. Their language of imputation, some scholars have argued, has similarities to the Scotist notion of acceptation and to the language of Bernardine mysticism.[42]

§ **20.** Yet, as we shall later see in more detail, fresh accents in the Reformation understanding of justification as by faith alone (*sola fide*), not simply grace alone (*sola gratia*), fundamentally challenged Augustine's transformationist thinking. The Reformation wanted to restore Augustinian emphases on sin and grace. With its stress on faith, however, it also went beyond these emphases and conceptualized salvation in a new way which, while retaining the focus on the individual, is in some respects as different from the older Augustinian and medieval patterns as these are from the ideas of divinization and cosmic redemption which prevailed in the East.

B. In the Sixteenth Century

§ **21.** In contrast to the medieval discussions, the debate over justification in the sixteenth century, with its focus on faith and not simply grace, embraced every aspect of Christian thought and practice. Further, what was central to the Reformers was often secondary to their opponents; perhaps neither side fully considered the claims of the other. In order to understand why this was so, we need to review in their historical setting the salient aspects of the Reformation doctrine[43] and the history of the controversy.[44]

1. *The Reformation Doctrine*

§ **22.** The two chief problems which occasioned the Reformers' appeal to St. Paul's teaching that human beings are "justified by faith apart from works of law" (Rom. 3:28 RSV) were, from their point of view, rampant Pelagianism or "works-righteousness," on the one hand, and the need to "console terrified consciences," on the other. Their attack on Pelagianism drew heavily on Augustine's theological stress on radical sinfulness, the loss of freedom, the primacy of grace, and, especially in Luther's *Bondage of the Will* (1525), predestination, but the focus of their attack was on medieval trends in piety as well as in theology. Salvation was widely viewed as something to be earned by good works, which included not only fulfillment of the moral law and the monastic counsels of perfection but also observance of a vast panoply of penitential disciplines and ecclesiastical rules and regulations. Moreover, money paid for Masses and indulgences was often thought of as automatically obtaining the remission of purgatorial penalties.

§ 23. By protesting against such practices and attitudes, the Reformers, without initially intending to do so, threatened the source of power and income of much of the clerical establishment. They thus became involved in a struggle against ecclesiastical moral corruption which was also a widespread concern among many who did not share their theological outlook. Before changes made by the Council of Trent (1545-1563), indulgences were a major source of papal revenues, and Masses for the dead and for other purposes provided the main support for a large proportion of priests. This system of "buying" salvation, furthermore, was administered by a frequently venal hierarchy. The higher ranks of clergy, among them Renaissance popes, included members of wealthy and noble families who had purchased lucrative church offices for large sums and used ecclesiastical income to live luxuriously, enrich relatives, build splendid public works, and fight wars. Monastic orders and the lower ranks of the clergy were also often in a decadent state and resistant to changes in practices from which they profited. Thus the Reformation emphasis on justification "apart from works of law" was a challenge not simply to trends in theology and religious practice but also to powerful special interest groups. It is also true that factors such as incipient nationalism and a desire for greater freedom from ecclesiastical control of life, expressed as anticlericalism and popular rationalism, influenced some supporters of the Reformation.[45]

§ 24. For the Reformers, however, the chief problem was neither moral laxity nor a Pelagianizing tendency to ascribe salvation partly to human effort apart from grace. In their situation the major function of justification by faith was, rather, to console anxious consciences terrified by the inability to do enough to earn or merit salvation. Even if grace is freely given "to do good works," one does not escape the perils of the anxious conscience. Thus for Luther the answer to the question "How do I get a gracious God?" must be "by faith alone," by trust in nothing but God's promises of mercy and forgiveness in Jesus Christ. Here Luther went beyond the Augustinian primacy of grace (*sola gratia*) to that of faith (*sola fide*). In reference to this problem of the terrified conscience and the assurance of salvation, it does not suffice to say that "when God rewards our merits, he crowns his own gifts."[46] One should add that it is not on the basis of his gifts of infused grace, of inherent righteousness, or of good works that God declares sinners just and grants them eternal life, but on the basis of Jesus Christ's righteousness, a righteousness which is "alien" or "extrinsic" to sinful human beings but is received by them through faith. Thus God justifies sinners simply for Christ's sake, not because of their performance, even with the help of divine grace, of the works commanded by the law and done in love.

§ 25. Justification by faith without the works of the law led Luther to a mode of thinking about Christian life and experience markedly different from traditional Augustinian and medieval transformationist models. Instead of a progressive transformation under the power of grace, the imputation of an alien righteousness received in faith implies a simultaneity; the justification is complete in the imputing of it so that the believer is "simultaneously a righteous person and a sinner" (*simul iustus et peccator*). All notions of "change" and "growth" in the life of the Christian therefore receive a quite different cast. The very imputation of Christ's righteousness also reveals to the believer the depth and persistence of sin. Sin, however, is then not merely the failure to do "good works" or the despair over such failure but is, above all, the human propensity to trust in one's own righteousness. The imputed alien righteousness of Christ creates a new situation in which sin is exposed as both presumption and despair and is attacked in its totality. Only when so exposed and confessed can sin no longer reign.

§ 26. It can be seen from this that justification *sola fide* (as Luther read Rom. 3:28)[47] is justification *propter Christum*. Nothing but faith in Christ alone makes sinners pleasing to God; their works are good in his sight only "on account of Christ" (*propter Christum*). Because faith itself is wholly the gracious work of the Spirit,[48] the Reformation teaches that God forgives and justifies by grace alone, through faith alone, on account of Christ alone.[49]

§ 27. The doctrine of justification with its Christological focus and trinitarian presuppositions was later described by Luther in the Smalcald Articles (1537) as the "first and chief article":

> . . . Jesus Christ, our God and Lord, "was put to death for our trespasses and raised again for our justification" (Rom. 4:25). He alone is "the lamb of God, who takes away the sin of the world" (John 1:29). "God has laid upon him the iniquities of us all" (Isa. 53:6). Moreover, "all have sinned,"

and "they are justified by his ⸜race as a gift, through the redemption which is in Christ Jesus, by his blood" (Rom. 3:23-25).

Inasmuch as this must be believed and cannot be obtained or apprehended by any work, law or merit, it is clear and certain that such faith alone justifies us. . . .

Nothing in this article can be given up or compromised, even if heaven and earth and things temporal should be destroyed. . . .

On this article rests all that we teach and practice against the pope, the devil, and the world.[50]

As Luther still later says, "If this article stands, the church stands; if it falls, the church falls."[51]

§ 28. To see justification by faith in this fashion as the *articulus stantis et cadentis ecclesiae* is, for the Reformers, to treat it as a criterion or corrective for all church practices, structures, and theology. They regard it as the heart of the gospel because the gospel message in its specific sense is the proclamation of God's free and merciful promises in Christ Jesus[52] which can be rightly received only through faith. All aspects of Christian life, worship, and preaching should lead to or flow from justifying faith in this gospel, and anything which opposes or substitutes for trust in God's promises alone should be abolished. The claim of the Lutheran confessional writings, especially in the Augsburg Confession and the Smalcald Articles, is that this criterion is the primary basis for the attacks on what the Reformers regarded as practical abuses and false theological teachings.

2. *The History of the Controversy*

§ 29. Turning now to the history of the sixteenth-century conflict, we shall see that the problem of justification was indeed the source of the Reformation protests but often was not central in the resultant controversies, especially not for the Roman Catholics. The starting point for Luther was his inability to find peace with God as an Augustinian hermit in the Erfurt monastery. Terrified in his own conscience, he became increasingly convinced that the theology in which he had been trained and the spiritual formation which he had received did not resolve the deep spiritual struggle (*Anfechtung*) of his quest for a gracious God. By 1517 he had made known his conclusion in published academic disputations as well as in intensive dialogue with his father confessor, the Augustinian vicar general John Staupitz; his conclusion was that the theology and piety of his time had fallen victim to Pelagianism, especially in relation to the sacrament of penance.[53]

§ **30.** It was in light of this conviction that Luther reacted against John Tetzel's preaching on the indulgences to be granted by Pope Leo X for contributions to the rebuilding of St. Peter's Basilica in Rome. Tetzel's sermons promised the remission of spiritual penalties of purgatory to those who gained the indulgences. They were, moreover, sanctioned by official instructions from Archbishop Albrecht of Mainz. Luther wrote to the archbishop, asking that preachers be given other directives:[54] people were not to be lulled into false security and an absence of fear but were to be instructed that "works of piety and love are infinitely better than indulgences" and to "learn the gospel and the love of Christ." Accompanying his letter were his *Ninety-Five Theses*,[55] which attacked abuses in the practice and doctrine of indulgences. Similarly, Luther protested against the instructions which people were receiving about the confession of sins in the sacrament of penance; they were being led to believe that their own contrition and satisfaction made the difference between forgiveness and rejection by God. In the context of these controversies over indulgences and penance, Luther already occasionally insisted that justification and forgiveness of sins came solely through faith in Jesus Christ, which was for him the heart of the gospel.[56]

§ **31.** Although Luther gained much popular support, he also met strong opposition. Some of it stemmed from nontheological concerns, such as the desire of those who profited from ecclesiastical benefices to retain their gains or the efforts of princes and the emperor to keep peace in the realm. The theological opposition, as indicated by the censures passed in 1518-1521 by the theological faculties of Mainz, Cologne, Louvain, and Paris, centered not directly on the doctrine of justification by faith alone taken as a doctrine by itself but rather on questions related to free will, the alleged sinfulness of all good works, the role of contrition, confession, and satisfaction in the sacrament of penance, the *ex opere operato* efficacy of the sacraments, the sinfulness of concupiscence, and the value of indulgences. During these years the various points under debate increasingly came to be linked with the question of the teaching authority of the church and especially the teaching authority of the pope.

§ **32.** The noted theologian Tommaso de Vio (Cardinal Cajetan) was sent by the pope to deal with Luther's case and met with him at Augsburg in 1518. Arguing on the basis of Scripture, Cajetan maintained that a person's reception of forgiveness is not an object of divine faith since faith bears only on what is revealed in the word of God; that forgiveness of sin is obtained by faith only if faith is animated by charity (*fides caritate formata*);[57] that the requisite charity is not among "the works of the law" which Paul rejected as a condition for justification; that those who do good works do so with the help of Christ's grace and truly merit under the terms of the new covenant, even though they never put God in their debt; and that good works done with Christ's grace do not satisfy for the guilt of sin, but for the temporal punishment due to sin.[58]

§ 33. Cajetan, unwilling to accuse Luther of heresy, charged him with having made rash assertions on two points. First, he rejected Luther's assertion in the *Ninety-Five Theses* (No. 58) that the merits of Christ do not constitute a treasury for indulgences. Since Pope Clement VI had affirmed in his bull *Unigenitus Dei Filius* (1343) that Christ has acquired for the church a treasure to be dispensed by it for the remission of the temporal punishment due to sins,[59] Cajetan demanded that Luther recant.[60] For Cajetan indulgences were not simply the removal of penalties imposed by the church; in granting indulgences, the church relied on a commission to heal the wounds left in the sinner after forgiveness had been given for Christ's sake and through his merits. Thus Cajetan and others feared that an emphasis on Christ's righteousness alone would lead to minimizing the church's role in communicating his merits to sinners. The second error indicated by Cajetan was what he took to be Luther's position on the kind of faith required by the sacrament of penance. For Cajetan it was excessive to demand that penitents have the certainty of faith that their sins are actually forgiven. "This is to construct a new church."[61]

§ 34. In November 1518 Pope Leo X, at the request of Cajetan, issued the bull *Cum postquam*, in which he set forth the current doctrine on indulgences and demanded that Luther retract any contrary opinions of his own. Before receiving the bull Luther had drafted a canonical appeal from the papacy to a future general council. Then in July 1519, in the course of a disputation with John Eck at Leipzig, he publicly refused to submit to *Cum postquam* on the ground that it failed to meet the arguments he had advanced from Scripture, the Fathers, and the canons. The debate at Leipzig, having begun with the issues of grace and predestination, climaxed with a disagreement over the teaching authority of popes and councils.[62] Eck believed that he had exposed the tendency of Luther's positions to overthrow the structure of the church.

§ 35. In view of these developments the Holy See determined to take further action. A papal commission, with the help of lists of Luther's errors compiled by the universities of Cologne and Louvain, began to draw up a condemnation. As a result of the commission's work in February and March 1520, Pope Leo X on June 15 issued the bull *Exsurge Domine*. Threatening excommunication, it censured forty-one of Luther's assertions on penance, indulgences, purgatory, sacramental grace, and papal teaching authority as "heretical or scandalous or false or offensive to pious ears, or seductive to simple minds and standing in the way of Catholic faith." [63] Luther's conflict with the late medieval church came to a head later in the same year when he published four reform treatises (*Treatise on Good Works, To the Christian Nobility of the German Nation, The Babylonian Captivity of the Church*, and *The Freedom of a Christian*). [64] Further Roman reaction followed in the bull of excommunication, *Decet Romanum Pontificem* (January 3, 1521). At the subsequent Diet of Worms (January 27–May 25), to which Luther had been summoned to defend his theses before the Emperor Charles V, an imperial ban was imposed on him (Edict of Worms, May 25). In that edict Luther was declared a heretic for teaching a pagan determinism which denied the doctrine of free will. [65]

§ 36. By 1525 the Reformation movement had gained sufficient political support to threaten the unity of the Holy Roman Empire. At the Diet of Speyer in 1526 Emperor Charles V postponed the enforcement of the Edict of Worms in Lutheran territories until a general council could be called to deal with the religious conflict. Consequently the Lutheran movement expanded its influence in Germany and strengthened its foothold through catechetical and liturgical reforms, especially in electoral Saxony. [66]

§ 37. When Charles V invited the Lutherans to present their case at the Diet of Augsburg in 1530, Philip Melanchthon was chosen to draft the Augsburg Confession, which was subsequently approved by Luther, who because of the ban was unable to attend the Diet. Read before the emperor on June 25, 1530, this Confession sought to present the Lutheran position in an irenic form, acceptable to the Roman party. Twenty-one of its articles were devoted to doctrinal questions and seven to church practices. After the first three articles on God, sin, and Christ, the fourth article asserts:

> Our churches also teach that men cannot be justified before God by their own strength, merits, or works but are freely justified for Christ's sake through faith when they believe that they are received into favor and that their sins are forgiven on account of Christ, who by his death made satisfaction for our sins. This faith God imputes for righteousness in his sight (Rom. 3, 4). [67]

Stressing the problem of abuses, the Confession claimed to uphold rather than denigrate ancient traditions and called for further dialogue on controverted matters in the hope of avoiding a schism between Lutherans and Catholics.[68] However, the Confession did not attain its goal.

§ **38.** A commission of theologians appointed by the emperor found difficulties in some of the affirmations of the Augsburg Confession. In their report of August 3, 1530, the *Confutatio*,[69] they approved ten of the doctrinal articles, accepted five others with qualifications, and rejected six as deficient. Their objections concerned Lutheran denials of Roman Catholic teachings on original sin, concupiscence, merit, faith animated by love, the necessity of confessing all serious sins one remembers, the value of satisfaction in the sacrament of penance, divinely instituted ecclesiastical order, good works, and invocation of the saints. The doctrine of justification by faith alone was, moreover, described as "diametrically opposed to the evangelical truth, which does not exclude works."[70] The differences were not, however, solely doctrinal, for they also involved church practices (e.g., celibacy, communion under two forms). Although the emperor insisted that theologians from both sides meet in order to overcome the impasse and some rapprochement ensued,[71] no full agreement was reached, and the conflict intensified.

§ **39.** Melanchthon was once again commissioned to defend the Lutheran cause. In his Apology of the Augsburg Confession (1530) he argued that "in this controversy the main doctrine of Christianity is involved," viz., the proper distinction between law and gospel grounded in Scripture.[72] Following Luther, who had called this distinction "the greatest skill in Christendom,"[73] Melanchthon explained that justification is the cornerstone of a theology which must always properly distinguish between the two ways in which God deals with the human creature: in the demands of the law God reveals human sin, whereas in his gift of the gospel he promises the righteousness of faith in Christ. Justification must be exclusively attributed to faith, not to the law. "If the doctrine of faith is omitted, it is vain to say that our works are valid by virtue of the suffering of Christ."[74] Ultimately "God pronounces righteous those who believe him from their heart and then have good fruits, which please him because of faith and therefore are a keeping of the law."[75] Frightened consciences are consoled by faith in the benefits of Christ's suffering. "Faith is not merely knowledge but rather a desire to accept and grasp what is offered in the promise of Christ."[76]

§ **40.** Melanchthon's detailed argumentation constituted an attack on what he considered to be the Scholastic doctrine, namely, that faith is saving because it is animated by love (*fides caritate formata*). Rather, faith is saving because it clings to its object, God's promise of forgiveness in the death and resurrection of Jesus Christ. Saving or justifying faith, to be sure, is never alone, never without good works; but it does not justify for that reason. Melanchthon, in contrast to much Scholastic teaching, held that love is a work, indeed "the highest work of the law."[77] Thus the Reformers maintained that love and good works are the necessary fruits of faith, though not its perfecting form, and are the inevitable consequences of forgiveness rather than prior conditions for it. Such assertions were a reply to the accusation that justification by faith alone is an antinomian doctrine which undermines morality.

§ **41.** In contrast to a "spiritualist" (*schwärmerisch*) exaltation of the internal word (*verbum internum*), the Lutheran understanding of justification maintained the priority of the external word (*verbum externum*) and the indispensability of the means of grace through which this faith-creating word is communicated.[78] This principle of the dependence of faith on the external word and the means of grace also enabled Lutherans to defend their retention of postbiblical traditional practices and their refusal to engage in the iconoclasm characteristic of many Protestants. Lutherans contended that some practices such as private confession and absolution should be preserved, since they can be helpful in proclaiming the word and arousing faith. Other practices, such as the use of vestments and the presence of pictures and statues in churches, are in principle *adiaphora*[79] or matters of indifference which need not be abandoned so long as they do not detract from trust in God alone. To insist on their elimination, as the iconoclasts did, was from this Lutheran perspective to fall victim to new forms of legalism and works-righteousness. Similarly, fasting and other ascetic practices and vocations, including celibacy, should not be imposed as law or thought of as earning grace but were nevertheless appropriate as voluntary responses of faith to discipline the body to "perform the duties required by one's calling."[80] Thus because justification by faith served as a criterion against puritan radicalism and not only against rigid traditionalism, Lutheranism was in some respects, as has often been observed, a conservative reforming movement. In the polemical atmosphere of the sixteenth century, however, this openness to tradition was often not emphasized by Lutherans and usually not recognized by Catholics.

§ **42.** It would be erroneous, however, to conclude that all Catholic reactions to Luther were negative. There were Catholics who, while accepting papal decisions and authority, also shared some of Luther's ideas. His call for reform of the church was in tune with the wishes of many in the early sixteenth century. The reforming movement was itself no stranger to the papal court, as one may see in the election of Adrian VI (1522-1523) to the papacy and in the creation by Paul III (1534-1549) of a commission of cardinals which made bold though unsuccessful proposals for reform in its *Consilium de emendanda ecclesia*.[81] Furthermore, Luther's conception of justification by faith found a favorable echo in spiritual movements such as those centered in the "oratories of divine love" of Italy and in circles influenced by some of the early Christian humanists. His way of reading Scripture was not uniformly rejected. There were theologians, still faithful to the pope, whose emphasis on the sufficiency of Scripture was similar to his.[82]

§ 43. Yet this was not enough to stem a deterioration of the relationships between Lutherans and Catholics, a deterioration which was powerfully abetted by nontheological factors. In the Reformation lands princes and the rising middle classes profited from the expropriation of monastic and church property and were resistant to any reconciliation which would endanger their financial and political advantages. Violence was used by Lutherans as well as by Catholics in advancing and defending their causes. Such an outcome was perhaps inevitable in a society which had no experience of religious pluralism, in which civil authorities, no matter what their church allegiance, considered it necessary to enforce religious uniformity, and in which much political as well as ecclesiastical power was still held by churchmen. Luther's movement suffered from the traumatic disorders provoked by extremist groups and by the peasant revolts, which often claimed to implement justification by faith by rejecting any kind of church authority, all sacraments, and all political authority.[83] It is not surprising that a Catholic opponent of the Reformation, Johannes Mensing, wrote thus to Melanchthon:

> You, however, with your countless errors, tumult, and false teaching, have brought it to the point where no one believes you, even if once in a while a truthful word escapes you. . . . And truthfully, as was said, that is why we trust you so little when you say something which otherwise could perhaps be tolerated and benevolently interpreted, just as we also understand many sayings of the holy teachers in the best sense.[84]

§ 44. After 1530 the schism between Lutherans and Catholics began to threaten Germany's political stability, and the Lutheran princes formed the Smalcald League (1531) in anticipation of the possible need to defend the Lutheran cause in a religious war. Luther himself believed that reconciliation had become impossible. Instructed by the Saxon court to state the articles of faith which could not be compromised and those which could, Luther drafted the Smalcald Articles for review by the Smalcald League at its meeting in 1537. He declared, as we have already noted,[85] that no concessions could be made on justification by faith. The Mass, practiced as a sacrificial work to earn God's favor, must be rejected, Luther held, because it was a fundamental denial of justification by faith. He further argued that "if the Mass falls, the papacy will fall with it"[86] and that the papal office could never be reformed or made acceptable.[87] On this last point Melanchthon and some of his associates disagreed, saying that they could concede to the pope "that superiority over the bishops which he possesses by human right" provided "he would allow the gospel," that is, justification by faith.[88] Thus although there were differences at Smalcald over the application of the criterion of justification by faith, there was agreement that this doctrine is the ultimate test for church unity.

§ **45.** Despite Luther's stance some Lutherans and Catholics continued their efforts at rapprochement. At least on one occasion, at the meeting arranged by Emperor Charles V during the Diet of Regensburg in the spring of 1541, they seemed to reach an understanding on justification. Catholic and Protestant teams, each consisting of three theologians, two princes, and two jurists, agreed on common statements concerning the human condition before the fall, free will, the cause of sin, and original sin. After they had discussed justification, they announced on May 2, 1541, that they had agreed on this crucial doctrine.[89]

§ **46.** The agreement at Regensburg on justification asserted that no one can be reconciled to God and freed from sin except by the unique mediator Christ who makes individuals sharers (*consortes*) of the divine nature and children of God. These benefits of Christ are not available except by a prevenient motion of the Holy Spirit, moving one to detest sin. This motion is through faith by which the mind, surely believing everything revealed (*tradita*) by God, also most certainly and without doubt assents to the promises given by God.

§ **47.** The participants in the Regensburg Colloquy forged a double justification formula, speaking of "inherent righteousness" (*iustitia inhaerens*) or the infusion of charity by which the will is healed, and an "imputed righteousness" (*iustitia imputata*) which is given solely because of Christ's merits. But one may not depend upon communicated, inherent righteousness. Assurance of salvation lies only in the righteousness of Christ by which one is accounted righteous and in the promise of God by which the reborn from the moment of their rebirth are owed eternal life. Although the good works of these children of God merit a reward in this life and in the life to come, nevertheless these good works cannot earn justification. Also with regard to good works, therefore, a form of double justification is involved, for rewards are not given "according to the substance of the works, nor insofar as they are human works, but insofar as they are done in faith and are from the Holy Spirit who dwells in the faithful while our free will concurs as a partial agent."[90]

§ 48. The Regensburg participants disagreed on teaching authority, transubstantiation, confession, and the relation of justification to hierarchical authority. Rome and Luther, however, rejected the results of the Regensburg Colloquy. A papal consistory disapproved of the double justification formula because of its ambiguity; the faithful as well as preachers could be misled.[91] Luther rejected the formula because it attempted to "glue together" (*zusammenleimen*) biblical justification and the Scholastic doctrine of "faith animated by love"; moreover, he still found in the formula traces of free will and other objectionable matters.[92] But while the Regensburg formula failed to reunite Roman Catholics and Lutherans, both the effort and the momentary agreement of theologians and princes on both sides indicate that the two ways of explaining justification are not necessarily exclusive.

§ 49. Luther, who had appealed several times for a general council, wanted one free of papal control. The spread of Lutheran influence in Europe and the fact that many people loyal to Rome sensed the need for drastic reform in doctrinal, moral, and administrative areas eventually led to a widespread demand for a general council. Wars among Catholic rulers and the hesitations of various popes, however, continued to delay the convocation of such a council. After several frustrated attempts and postponements and to avoid an impending war between Lutheran and Catholic territories in Germany, Paul III in 1542 called a council to meet at Trent, south of the Alps. It was actually convened on December 13, 1545. The Lutherans were absent, however, because their condition that it should be "free, general, and not a papal council" had not been met.[93] Luther's death, which occurred on February 18, 1546, and the Smalcald War, which erupted in the same year, made prospects for rapprochement even less likely.

§ 50. Twenty-five sessions were held at Trent in three periods and under three popes: 1545-1547 (sess. I-X), 1551-1552 (XI-XVI), and 1562-1563 (XVII-XXV). Addressing themselves simultaneously to right doctrine and church reform, the council fathers reaffirmed the Nicene-Constantinopolitan Creed as the basis of Catholic faith and dealt extensively with such topics as the canon of Scripture and its relation to apostolic traditions, original sin, justification, grace and merit, the sacraments, eucharistic presence, communion under both forms, the sacrifice of the Mass, purgatory, the cult of saints, and indulgences. The debate on justification began on June 22, 1546, and the decree was promulgated on January 13, 1547.

§ 51. The Council of Trent taught that original sin is a condition affecting "the whole human race" and that such sin, and the punishment due to it, are remitted by the grace of baptism. The council fathers distinguished original sin from concupiscence, which remains in those baptized. Concupiscence "comes from sin and leads to sin," but it is not by its mere presence a sin before it is freely consented to. Here Trent thought it was standing with Augustine and against Luther.[94]

§ 52. In its teaching on justification the Council of Trent reaffirmed the unique role of Christ who died for all and who grants grace "through the merits of his passion" to those reborn in him, and without rebirth in him one can never be justified.[95] The Council further taught that "nothing prior to justification, whether faith or works, truly merits (*promeretur*) the grace of justification."[96] Moreover, in the process leading to the justification of the adult sinner, priority belongs to "the predisposing grace of God [given] through Christ Jesus."[97] The sinner indeed cooperates with this grace, at least in the sense of not sinfully rejecting it. Influenced by grace and enlightened by the Holy Spirit, the sinner believes the truth of God's revelation and God's promises, especially that the unjustified are justified by the grace of God in Jesus Christ.[98]

§ 53. In a central paragraph the Council of Trent expounded the nature of justification with the help of Scholastic causal categories.[99] The final cause is the glory of God and of Christ, and eternal life. The efficient cause is the merciful God who freely cleanses and sanctifies, sealing and anointing by the Holy Spirit. The meritorious cause is Jesus Christ, who by his passion merited our justification and made satisfaction for us to God the Father. The formal cause is "the righteousness of God—not that whereby God is righteous but that whereby he makes us righteous."[100] The justified sinner is not only reckoned righteous but is truly called righteous and is righteous, since one receives righteousness according to the free generosity of the Holy Spirit and in proportion to one's own dispositions and cooperation.

§ **54.** In its description of justification Trent insisted on the primacy of faith. " 'Faith is the beginning of human salvation,' the foundation and root of all justification, 'without which it is impossible to please God,' "[101] but faith, although unconditionally necessary for justification, is not living unless

> through the Holy Spirit the charity of God is poured into their hearts . . . and inheres in them. Hence in justification itself one receives through Christ, into whom one is engrafted, along with the forgiveness of sins, all these [gifts] infused at the same time: faith, hope and charity. For faith, unless hope and charity be added to it, neither unites one perfectly with Christ, nor makes one a living member of his body.[102]

Thanks to this justification, received through the grace of Christ, human beings are renewed, and "as faith cooperates with good works [cf. Jas. 2:22], they grow and are further justified."[103]

§ **55.** The council went on to affirm that a person who is justified can still fall into sin and, having sinned, cannot be sure of future repentance.[104] The identity of the predestined remains a mystery hidden in God.[105] Finally, to avoid the suspicion that stress on faith and on works performed in grace might derogate from the saving power of Christ, Trent asserted: "Far be it from Christians to trust or glory in themselves and not in the Lord [cf. 1 Cor. 1:31; 2 Cor. 10:17], whose bounty toward all is so great that he wishes his own gifts to be their merits."[106]

§ **56.** The first part of the last statement can be read as open to the central insistence of the Reformers that believers should look entirely to God and not at all to their own accumulation of merits for salvation, while the second implies (as the decree on justification elsewhere explicitly states)[107] that, faithful to his promise, God finally judges human beings "not apart from" the merits he gives them. Nonetheless Trent and later Roman Catholicism frequently failed to stress the first concern (that of the Reformation), whereas Lutherans regarded the Catholic doctrine of merit as undermining trust in God alone for salvation. The Tridentine decree on justification, with its own way of insisting on the primacy of grace (*quae virtus [Christi] bona eorum opera semper antecedit*),[108] is not necessarily incompatible with the Lutheran doctrine of *sola fide*, even though Trent excluded this phrase. Part of the reason for this exclusion was, it seems, to deny that human beings can rely for assurance of salvation on knowledge or experience of their own faith rather than on Christ. Moreover, Trent insisted that "the good deeds of one justified are gifts of God'' in such a way that they are also "the good merits of that same justified person" and that the justified person "by the good deeds which are done by him, through the grace of God, and the merit of Jesus Christ (of whom he is a living member) truly merits an increase of grace, eternal life, and the attainment of that eternal life (if indeed he die in grace), as well as an increase in glory.''[109]

§ 57. In its doctrinal as well as in its reform decrees, the Council of Trent recognized that the Reformation critique of the state of the church was at least partly justified. In particular, its reaffirmation of the primacy of grace in the role of justification and salvation assured that the anti-Pelagian intention of the classic Augustinian tradition not be lost.

§ 58. After the Council of Trent the final statements on justification and related issues in the Lutheran Confessions were not replies to that council but were concerned with intra-Lutheran problems. Following Luther's death in 1546, Lutherans in Germany were torn by conflicts over the proper interpretation of Luther's "chief article."[110] In a series of theological controversies "Gnesio-Lutherans" (disciples of the "authentic" Luther) and "Philippists" (disciples of Melanchthon) struggled for formulations which would preserve the preeminence of justification and at the same time make it of controlling importance for other doctrines, especially original sin, human freedom, good works, and the proper distinction between law and gospel. The Formula of Concord (1577) tried to settle these controversies.[111]

§ 59. In their attempt to establish Lutheran unity, the authors of the Formula increasingly moved towards a purely forensic[112] understanding of justification as the divine reckoning which must be carefully distinguished from any intrinsic human righteousness. This was not done primarily in opposition to Roman Catholics but against some Lutherans who understood justification as the indwelling of Christ's divine nature in the believer. The Formula, on the other hand, insisted strongly on the distinction between the "imputed righteousness of faith" (*imputata fidei iustitia*) and the "inchoate righteousness of the new obedience of faith" (*inchoata iustitia novae obedientiae seu bonorum operum*). Only the former counts before God, whereas the latter follows justification. Although the latter should be preached to Christians, it is too imperfect and impure to stand before the divine tribunal.[113] Although the primary intention of the distinction was not to attack Trent, the opposition is unmistakable.

§ 60. This tendency to objectify justification as a forensic act created difficulties for the framers of the Formula when they attempted to recast traditional teachings on original sin, human freedom, and good works. When radical Gnesio-Lutherans contended that justification by faith alone excluded any notion of natural human good, or when some Philippists, at the opposite end of the spectrum, argued that free will cooperates with the justifying and faith-creating work of the Holy Spirit, the Formula had recourse to medieval Scholastic terminology and Aristotelian philosophical categories in order to mediate this controversy over synergism. Distinctions similar to those employed by medieval theologians were made between the human "substance" (*substantia*), created in the image of God, and original sin inhering in fallen human nature as "accident" (*accidens*). In this way the Formula sought to assert a deep and unspeakable corruption of human nature in all its parts and powers but not a destruction or substantial transformation of human nature in the fall.[114] Quite aware of their inability to settle all controversies through new formulations, the authors of the Formula kept reminding the feuding factions that Lutheran theology was to be guided by Luther's injunction to distinguish between law and gospel so that Christians find true comfort in the benefits of Christ rather than in their own righteousness.[115]

§ 61. The theological distinction between law and gospel raised questions about the relation of law to the chronology of the life of the justified. Does the distinction between divine demand and divine promise lead to an end of the law at some point in time? Luther, holding to his view of the justified person as simultaneously righteous and sinful (*simul iustus et peccator*), stressed only two uses of the law: one is for the restraint of sin through political authority (*usus legis politicus*); the other is for the disclosure of sin through accusation and exhortation (*usus legis theologicus* or *paedagogicus*, which is also called *elenchticus*). Under the pressure of antinomian controversies, the Formula of Concord, apparently fearing a separation between law and gospel, which would lead to individualistic "enthusiasm" (*Schwärmerei*), held that believers "require the teaching of the law"; under the heading of "the third function of the law," it insisted on the preaching of the law to believers "so that they will not be thrown back on their own holiness and piety and under the pretext of the Holy Spirit's guidance set up a self-elected service of God without his Word and command."[116]

§ 62. The Formula also took a stand against what its authors understood to be the Calvinist doctrine of predestination to damnation as well as to salvation. It speaks only of "our eternal election to salvation" and insists that this should be preached only in order to console consciences: "If anyone so sets forth this teaching concerning God's gracious election that sorrowing Christians can find no comfort in it but are driven to despair, . . . then it is clearly evident that this teaching is not being set forth according to the Word and will of God."[117] Because of this focus on pastoral concerns, on consoling consciences, the Formula viewed itself as in agreement with Luther, even though it avoided the strongly predestinarian language which he employed in such treatises as the *Bondage of the Will*.[118]

§ 63. Thus the Formula of Concord and Trent seem closer to each other on the role of morality and law in Christian life, the nature of sin, the primacy of grace, and even the role of faith than were Luther and the "Pelagianizers" whom he chiefly attacked. Yet the interconfessional polemics remained much the same. Lutheran controversialists argued that Pelagianism and works-righteousness were in fact concealed under what they regarded as Trent's specious use of biblical and Augustinian language,[119] while the Catholics, on their side, generally ignored the careful formulations of the Lutheran Confessions and continued to repeat unchanged the earlier charges of antinomianism, Manichaeism, determinism, and the denial of sacraments.[120]

C. After the Sixteenth Century

§ 64. In the last four hundred years both the Roman Catholic and the Lutheran churches have continued to affirm their sixteenth-century pronouncements on justification. Since the Council of Trent and the *Book of Concord*, Lutheran theologians have usually claimed that the doctrine is of central importance but have interpreted it in a variety of ways; Roman Catholics, although debating the issues of sin, freedom, nature, and grace, have for the most part not made justification itself a primary object of attention. In both cases, furthermore, the discussions have been chiefly within, rather than between, the two communions.

§ 65. Seventeenth-century Lutheran Orthodoxy attempted to bring systematic clarity to the Lutheran Confessions included in the *Book of Concord* (1580). To solve the problem of the relationship between justification as an objective forensic act and the individual's apprehension of it (subjective justification), Lutheran dogmaticians developed various theories about the "order of salvation" (*ordo salutis*). While justification retained its forensic character, at least in theory, attention tended to shift to more subjective aspects of the process of salvation. Melanchthon's description of faith, involving knowledge of objective truth, assent to that truth, and trust of the heart (*notitia, assensus*, and *fiducia*) was now analytically expanded into an order which introduced such categories as gospel call, illumination, conversion, regeneration, renewal, mystical union, sanctification, good works, preservation, and glorification. The teaching about justification by faith was shifted to the section in dogmatics on practical theology (*gratia applicatrix*). In the opinion of some interpreters, Lutheran Orthodoxy came to think of justification in a framework similar to that of Trent in that Orthodoxy used Scholastic terminology and viewed justification in the context of an order of salvation.[121] This was a partial return to transformationist modes of thought, but it tended to sharpen the remaining differences over the specifically forensic character of justification as an act distinct from sanctification.

§ **66.** A few Catholic theologians in the seventeenth century (e.g., Lessius, Petavius, Thomassinus), assisted by their studies in the Greek patristic tradition, expanded on Trent's teaching regarding the divinizing presence of the Holy Spirit in justification. In general, however, Catholic theology in the post-Tridentine period concentrated on the nature and causes of created grace. Prolonged and bitter disputes broke out regarding the question how grace, while being infallibly efficacious, could leave intact the freedom of the recipient. Some, such as Luis de Molina, S.J., maintained that the decree of predestination to glory (*praedestinatio praecise ad gloriam*) is logically subsequent to divine foreknowledge of a person's merits, while others, such as Domingo Báñez, O.P., held that this decree is prior to any foreseen merits. The opposing schools accused one another of Pelagian and Lutheran tendencies, but Rome intervened and forbade either of these positions to be branded as heretical.[122]

§ **67.** Yet there were positions that Rome would not tolerate. Michel de Bay (Baius) and Cornelius Jansen (Jansenius), taking a very pessimistic view of the effects of the fall, emphasized divine predestination almost to the exclusion of human cooperation. Their positions were condemned by Rome in 1567 and 1653 respectively. In so doing, Rome rejected as heretical the view that Christ died only for the predestined.[123] This condemnation was an emphatic reassertion of the reality of God's universal salvific will. In 1713 Rome condemned one hundred and one propositions taken from the writings of the Jansenist Pasquier Quesnel. Some of these propositions relating to justification can be seen as similar to Lutheran statements, for example, "Without the grace of the Liberator, the sinner is not free except to do evil" and "Under the curse of the law, good is never done, for one sins either by doing evil or by avoiding it simply out of fear (Gal. 5:18)."[124]

§ 68. Partly as a result of the voyages of discovery to the Americas and to the East, the question of the salvation of infidels became acute. The adversaries of Jansenism reached a consensus that justification lay within reach of the unevangelized, who were included in God's saving will. Agreeing that faith was necessary for salvation, theologians disputed about the kind of saving faith pagans could have. In opposition to certain liberal views, the Holy Office in 1679 denied that "faith in the broad sense (*fides late dicta*), based on the witness of creatures or some such motive, is sufficient for justification."[125]

§ 69. Much of the spiritual literature of the seventeenth and eighteenth centuries continued to emphasize both the primacy of faith as "the only proximate means of union with God" (St. John of the Cross) and, especially in the circles influenced by Cardinal de Bérulle, the centrality of Christ.[126] Even authors who had no connection with "quietism" stressed self-abandonment to divine providence and renunciation of self, of spiritual consolations, and of personal merits. "Trust in God alone" (Henri-Marie Boudon) and "It is God who does everything" (Jean-Martin Moye)[127] often acted as correctives to an exuberant piety which sometimes took peculiar forms not unlike the decoration of rococo churches. Thus despite the prevalence of anti-Reformation themes in the dominant official theology of the period, there remained currents within Catholicism which had affinities with several of the basic ideas of the Reformers.

§ 70. In the same centuries Lutheran Pietism called for major changes in the understanding of justification in Lutheran Orthodoxy. Thus the movement in Germany and later in Scandinavia was more concerned with the experiential impact of justification on the individual person than with a systematic description of justification in an *ordo salutis*. Emphasizing rebirth, evidenced by a conversion experience, and sanctification, measured by external tests of conduct, the Pietists in effect de-emphasized forensic justification in which an individual is *declared* righteous in favor of stressing how an individual is *made* righteous. Justification therefore was seen as identical with the rebirth of the sinner who has experienced the "penitential struggle" (*Busskampf*) precipitated by the saving work of God.[128]

§ 71. Whereas Pietism emphasized the individual experience of justification in rebirth and sanctification, Enlightenment theologians of the eighteenth century, such as Semler, no longer viewed justification as an essential Christian doctrine. Reflecting a rationalistic anthropology which minimized sin and stressed the prowess of the natural creature and the ability of individuals to control their destiny, these theologians taught that righteous conduct, in accord with natural morality and the teaching of Jesus, brings salvation. It seemed sufficient to acknowledge God as the father of humankind, to follow Jesus as the teacher of universal moral values, and to experience the Holy Spirit as the power which prompts human beings to lead a better moral life.[129]

§ 72. In the nineteenth and twentieth centuries, however, there has been renewed attention to the Reformation docrine of justification with its concern for sin and forgiveness. Schleiermacher, Ritschl, Kähler, Althaus, Elert, Prenter, Aulén, Tillich, and Barth, among other Protestants, have dealt extensively with the doctrine in a wide variety of ways.[130] Meanwhile, Möhler, Newman, Scheeben, Rahner, and Küng, among others, contributed to the development of Catholic thought on this topic.[131] Further, exegetes such as Schlatter, Bultmann, and Käsemann have emphasized the biblical importance of the doctrine,[132] and the renaissance of Luther studies in the last hundred years has made Catholics and Protestants increasingly aware that at the heart of the Lutheran Reformation was not a value such as freedom of conscience or individual autonomy, or even the principle *sola scriptura*, but rather justification by faith. Finally, the growth of dialogue in recent decades between Catholics and the heirs of the Reformation has stimulated research into the interconfessional aspects of justification. Each of these developments could be profitably explored at length, but for our purposes it is the recent statements of the churches and certain emphases in contemporary theology which are of primary importance. The problem of justification was addressed in indirect ways by the Second Vatican Council; the Assembly of the Lutheran World Federation in 1963 took up justification as a major theme. Some comments on these treatments and on the current theological situation are in order before we turn to our own reflections.

D. Recent History

1. Vatican Council II

§ 73. Vatican II gave little explicit attention to the theme of justification, but it touched on the subject indirectly in its teachings on matters such as faith, grace, salvation, and the ministry of the church. By broadening the definition of faith beyond intellectualistic concepts that had been prevalent in modern Scholasticism, the council left open the possibility that faith might include the entire response of the faithful to justifying grace.[133] In its references to cooperation and merit, the council showed sensitivity to Protestant concerns and to the need of resisting any Pelagianizing tendencies that might exist among Catholics.

§ 74. In its Constitution on the Church the council set the traditional doctrines of grace, hope, cooperation, merit, and prayer for the dead in an ecclesiological and eschatological framework. The renewal of creation is seen as anticipated in a real way, so that even in its pilgrim state the church is marked by "genuine though imperfect holiness."[134] Christians should remember, however, that their dignity is "to be attributed not to their own merits, but to the special grace of Christ."[135] Thanks to the gift of the Holy Spirit, the baptized can look forward to their salvation in hope. They are linked to the heavenly church in the hope that, when "judged according to their works," they may be numbered among the blessed.[136] The saints in heaven "show forth the merits which they won on earth through the one Mediator between God and man, Christ Jesus (cf. 1 Tim. 2:5)."[137]

§ 75. Vatican II stressed that Christ is the one mediator[138] who made "the perfect satisfaction needed for our reconciliation."[139] Christ associates the work of the church with himself and is present by his power in the sacraments, so that the liturgy is an exercise of Christ's own priesthood.[140] He is present likewise in the proclamation of the gospel, which is seen as the principal ministry of bishops and of priests.[141] This understanding of Christ as the one who above all acts in the liturgy involves a different view of the Eucharist from the one the Reformers had in mind when they attacked the sacrifice of the Mass as a human work.

§ 76. Further, to participate in the liturgy one must have accepted the gospel in faith and repentance.[142] The sacraments, inseparable from the ministry of the word,[143] are rightly called "sacraments of faith," for they presuppose faith and nourish, strengthen, and express it.[144] By taking part in the praise and worship offered by the church, the faithful receive the grace of Christ.[145] They are required to cooperate with that grace "lest they receive it in vain (cf. 2 Cor. 6:1)."[146] This stress on cooperation or "active participation" in worship is in some respects similar to Luther's concern for personal faith in connection with the reception of the Lord's Supper.[147] For purposes of the present dialogue it is also significant that Vatican II envisaged the church as "embracing sinners in her bosom'' and as "always in need of being purified." [148] It pursues "the path of penance and renewal," [149] for, as an earthly and human institution, it stands in need of "continual reformation," whether in conduct, in discipline, or in the formulation of doctrine. [150]

§ 77. Of no less significance is the emphasis placed by Vatican II on the word of God and especially on Scripture as sources of life and energy for the church. [151] Paul is quoted as teaching that the gospel "is the power of God unto salvation to everyone who believes, to Jew first and then to Greek (Rom. 1:16)." [152] The church and its *magisterium* are held to be under the word of God. [153] Holy Scripture, as the word of God "consigned to writing under the inspiration of the Holy Spirit," [154] is accorded a certain priority over tradition. While acknowledging the supremacy of Christ and the gospel over all that could be set against them, the council did not anticipate that there could be ultimate conflicts between gospel and church. Vatican II embodies the traditional Catholic position that Christ, by the assistance promised in the gospel, keeps the teaching of the church faithful to revelation by the power of the Holy Spirit. [155]

2. Catholic Theology since World War II

§ 78. In the features just noted Vatican II reflects the general character of Catholic theology since the Second World War. Without making any radical break with earlier Catholic tradition and the doctrine of Trent, recent Catholic theologians have sought to distance themselves from the thought forms of late Scholasticism as being too individualistic, intellectualistic, abstract, and legalistic. Catholic theology has been seeking to renew itself through a return to biblical categories together with a more personalistic and historical emphasis. The contemporary tendency is to look upon conversion as a conscious response of the whole person to God's gracious call in Christ; to view grace primarily as the loving self-communication of the triune God; to stress that in sacramental worship the faithful share in the communal life of Christ's mystical body; and to regard merit and satisfaction as features of the pilgrim existence of believers as they are drawn by God to eternal life. This changing climate in Catholic theology has opened up new possibilities of encountering, and profiting from, the Reformation theology of justification. [156] The adequacy of polemical statements made in the atmosphere of the Counter Reformation can no longer be taken for granted.

§ 79. Among influential contemporary Catholic theologians, Karl Rahner may be given special mention. His theology emphasizes the primacy and centrality of Christ in the whole order of creation and redemption. Grace is not to be understood primarily as a created quality (i.e., as sanctifying grace), but rather as God making himself personally present in the Spirit in merciful love (and thus as "uncreated grace"). Insofar as the human subject is never fully delivered from the deleterious effects of the fall, there is a sense in which one may speak of the justified as *simul iustus et peccator*. The free human response to grace, for Rahner, does not diminish the primacy of grace, for the act whereby grace is accepted is itself a gift of grace.[157] Without holding that explicit faith in the gospel is essential for the justification of adults, he maintains that every movement toward justification, sanctification, or salvation is a free gift of God through Christ, transforming human consciousness and thus involving the active receptivity of faith. Proceeding from a *solus Christus*, Rahner believes that he has affirmed in a Catholic context much of what has traditionally been understood by the Reformation principles of *sola gratia* and *sola fide*.[158] His Christocentric approach offers some parallels to the Reformation view that the article of justification is nothing other than "applied Christology" and contributes to significant convergences between Lutheran and Catholic theologians.

§ **80.** A number of Catholic theologians, including Rahner, have attempted to build into Catholic theology a more vivid appreciation of the word of God. They depict the word not simply as a preliminary condition for the sacramental conferral of grace, but as a dialogic event in which God's justifying power is made present and active under the conditions of history.[159] This position represents a conscious rapprochement with certain strands in Lutheran theology.

§ **81.** The most recent Catholic theology is marked by a growing concern to overcome any suspicion of individualism or privatism in the theology of grace. The free and gracious gift of justification, according to Edward Schillebeeckx, cannot be experienced except by those who lose themselves for the sake of others.[160] The Uruguayan liberation theologian, Juan Luis Segundo, warns that a paralyzing concern for one's personal justification could distract one from the communal task of building the kingdom.[161] The Brazilian Leonardo Boff, although concerned to remain in continuity with the Council of Trent, prefers to speak of liberation rather than justification. The term *liberation*, he holds, designates the same reality, but "now elaborated in terms of its dynamic, historical dimensions."[162] These themes from contemporary Catholic political theology and liberation theology converge, as we shall presently see, with the stress on corporate service in certain recent Lutheran theologies of justification.

3. The Helsinki Assembly of the Lutheran World Federation

§ 82. World Lutheranism has had no counterpart to Vatican II, but the Fourth Assembly of the Lutheran World Federation in Helsinki, Finland (1963), gave particular attention to justification. Considerable work was done by its Commission of Theology from 1952 on, and the Assembly itself dealt with the topic in addresses, discussions, and its report.

§ 83. Although official dialogue between the Lutheran and Roman Catholic churches had not begun,[163] a preparatory *Study Document "On Justification"*[164] noted that, while the Reformation doctrine had been hammered out in debate with the Church of Rome, Rome was now changing, as can be seen in "the renewal of biblical studies" and the "liturgical movement." Furthermore, problems were posed for traditional Lutheran understandings, it was said, by historical study of the Bible, the "greater variety and diversity among the biblical writers" which "we now see," erosion of theological terms, changes in cultural climate (including a more anthropocentric emphasis and the loss of eschatology), and the fact that "the Gospel can be proclaimed without . . . the word Justification." Exposition of the doctrine followed the approach of the Augsburg Confession; new accents were provided by the stress on the Old Testament (¶¶ 46-48), Jesus (¶¶ 49-51), and "use of the terms 'justify' and 'justification' in the earliest period of the Christian community" prior to Paul (¶ 52). The theological analysis showed that Lutherans now, as in the sixteenth century, do not understand the *sola fide* as minimizing the means of grace; faith takes shape in a church with Ministry and sacraments. Not surprisingly, the social dimension of the good works which flow from faith was emphasized more than in the past; the "new obedience" includes opposition to the materialism of modern culture, to nationalism, and to divisions of race and caste.

§ 84. At Helsinki addresses and discussion groups took up the theme.[165] The Reformation witness to justification was said to have been in a threefold "Babylonian captivity" of "doctrinalization, individualization, and spiritualization." Hence justification should be understood as focusing on the entire human race and on "amnesty for all." God's power "takes hold of the whole world . . . and subjects it to his righteousness." This universalist emphasis parallels a similar concern on the Catholic side (see above, § 78). The opposition between forensic and transformationist views of justification was questioned: "The old alternative whether the sinner is considered justified . . . 'forensical-ly'—or . . . 'effectively'—is begging the question,'' for God's action brings about ''rebirth.'' Another address insisted that the ''act through which God forgives is at the same time that act through which God renews.''[166]

§ 85. It has sometimes been concluded that at Helsinki Lutherans failed to agree or say anything significant about justification. A summary statement prepared during the sessions was presented to the Assembly but was merely ''received'' rather than approved, though the next year it was published by the Commission with only minor revisions.[167] In part, the negative reactions at the Assembly stemmed from procedural matters, over what the status of such a statement would be (the *magisterium* question), and whether this particular draft represented fully the twenty-six group discussions. In part, the concern was also with structure and tone.[168] Some found fault with the traditional language, the absence of attention to the Old Testament,[169] or the lack of emphasis on fresh approaches from the New Testament exegetes.

§ 86. The resulting document from Helsinki, *Justification Today*, suggests that the world's current question is no longer about ''a gracious God'' but about the ''meaning of life'' (¶¶ 1-4). Yet justification is still said to be central, for the fact ''that Christ is with sinners and lives as true man in the midst of the godless, . . . gives courage to believe in the justification of man before God'' (¶¶ 5-8). The church with its sacraments is built upon such faith (¶¶ 9-10). Justification creates fellowship, a church in service to the world (¶¶ 11-15). A new life lived in faith must follow (¶¶ 16-24), ''a new courage to be'' which conquers meaninglessness (¶¶ 25-29).

§ 87. Some of the insights expressed at Helsinki have proved fruitful in later discussions, including our own, but perhaps the main importance of the Assembly is that it alerted Lutherans to a need for further consideration of the cardinal theme of justification. This need was apparent from the ''free and persistent expressions of differences of opinion'' by voices from around the world, especially ''Africa and Asia, desirous of bridging immediately the gap between the timely Augsburg Confession of 430 years ago and an explication of the faith of Lutherans for the man of today.''[170] What ''made it impossible to write a satisfactory theological document on such an important subject in a mere ten days'' was the very ''vigor and involvement of the assembly.'' ''A healthy discussion had begun'' and, according to one prediction, ''It will continue. . . . '' One may regard the present dialogue between Lutherans and Catholics as part of that continuation.

4. A Lutheran Hermeneutical Perspective

§ 88. A further development in the understanding of the Reformation doctrine of justification is rooted in such historical studies of Luther's hermeneutics as those of Karl Holl and Gerhard Ebeling.[171] Although of little direct importance at Helsinki, this development has since become increasingly influential. It focuses on the hermeneutical insights which lay at the root of Luther's proposal of justification by faith alone and helps clarify why this doctrine functions as a critical principle in judging all thought and practice. The central point is that the proclamation of God's grace in word and sacrament is itself the saving event in that it announces the death and resurrection of Jesus Christ. God's word does what it proclaims or, in modern terminology, the gospel message is performative; it effects the reality of which it speaks. The preaching of the gospel has the force of decreeing the forgiveness of sins for Christ's sake. Like a will or testament, it makes human beings heirs of the promise quite apart from what they deserve. God's word accomplishes what it says in the very act of being proclaimed.

§ 89. In this hermeneutical perspective even the faith which receives the promise is not a condition for justification. It is not a human achievement, but it is rather a free gift created and bestowed in the power of the Holy Spirit by the justifying word to which it clings. Justification is unconditional in the sense that the justifying word effects its own reception. In a similar vein, the Apology says: "For if the promise were conditional upon our merits and the law, which we never keep, it would follow that the promise is useless. Since we obtain justification through a free promise, however, it follows that we cannot justify ourselves. Otherwise, why would a promise be necessary?"[172]

§ 90. This hermeneutical understanding of justification can be termed forensic but not in the sense that it gives exclusive primacy to one image for the saving action of God in Christ over others. Particular images, however, are of special usefulness for particular purposes, and judicial or forensic ones are of prime importance when emphasizing the proclamatory character of justification. There are various ways of expressing that God's promises are themselves unconditional, but this is done with particular pointedness by saying that God declares or imputes an alien righteousness, that of Christ, to wholly undeserving sinners.

§ 91. Whatever the imagery, the affirmation that God's word saves by being declared introduces sharp discontinuities into theologies that are centered on justification by faith. When, for example, justification is seen wholly as a liberating gift bestowed in proclamation, the will cannot be said to have any freedom in itself; it is in bondage, as Luther says, in relation "to those things which are above us."[173] Similarly, it is in hearing the gospel that believers recognize the gravity of sin and their situation as *simul iusti et peccatores*. Because they look only to the promise of forgiveness in Christ, they can see nothing in themselves that is good before God (*coram deo*). To be sure, when human beings are viewed in comparison with one other (*coram hominibus*), it is appropriate to speak of them as having free will and varying degrees of goodness, but before God all "righteousnesses are filthy rags" (Isa. 64:6 KJV). Thus salvation as a product of God's creative word is, in this perspective, radically discontinuous with fallen nature.[174] It is a new creation, not a transformation or perfecting of the old.

§ **92.** This emphasis on the proclamatory character of justification does not result in an uncatholic narrowing of the Christian reality. Faith is not excluded, for the justifying promise is received by faith alone. The word and sacraments are not excluded, for it is through them that the promise is declared. "Love and good works must also follow faith. So they are not excluded. . . ."[175]

The doctrines of justification, of the word and sacraments, and of the church (which for Luther was a "mouth house" that exists to proclaim the gospel)[176] are inseparable. Justification by faith is emphasized not primarily by speaking of the doctrine but by so teaching and acting within the church that Christians are constantly directed to God's promises in word and sacrament from which all else flows. Thus Luther says little directly about the doctrine of justification in his sermons and catechisms, but the doctrine is nevertheless constantly present as the hermeneutical guide for the presentation of all other teachings. This hermeneutical guide, furthermore, may be operative even when the doctrine of justification by faith alone is not articulated. Such saints as Gregory, Bernard, Francis, and Bonaventure, Luther says, ultimately relied wholly on God for salvation despite their errors in theology and practice.[177]

§ **93.** While this hermeneutical interpretation of the doctrine of justification is suggested especially by Luther's early writings, it was largely forgotten in later Lutheranism and even now is often not understood. Yet it is important for our purposes because, while it conflicts with Scholastic approaches, whether Catholic or Lutheran, it also converges in part with certain recent trends in Catholic sacramental and kerygmatic theology (cf. §§ 77 and 80, above).

CHAPTER TWO:

REFLECTION AND INTERPRETATION

§ **94.** As we now turn from historical considerations to an examination of the contemporary relations of Roman Catholics and Lutherans on the question of justification, it is evident that many of the difficulties have arisen from the contrasting concerns and patterns of thought in the two traditions. In the polemical atmosphere of the past, these differences gave rise to fears and were interpreted as conflicts, but the development of ecumenical dialogue, historical research, and new modes of theological thinking enable us to consider the possibility that these patterns may in part be complementary and, even if at times in unavoidable tension, not necessarily divisive. In this second part of the report, therefore, we shall describe and interpret the historic concerns and thought patterns of Lutheran and Catholic understandings of justification before we turn in the third part to a consideration of convergences in biblical exegesis and theological understanding.

§ **95.** Lutherans generally emphasize God's address to sinners in the good news of Christ's life, death, and resurrection; theology and doctrine should serve proclamation so as to exclude reliance on self for salvation. They therefore focus on safeguarding the absolute priority of God's redeeming word in Jesus Christ. The unconditionality of God's love for fallen humankind implies that the fulfillment of the promise of salvation depends on nothing else but the gift of faith by which believers trust in God. Catholics, while not rejecting the absolute priority of God's saving action, are generally speaking more concerned with acknowledging the efficacy of God's saving work in the renewal and sanctification of the created order, an efficacy which Lutherans, for their part, do not deny.

§ **96.** These different concerns entail notably different patterns of thought and discourse. The Catholic concerns are most easily expressed in the transformationist language appropriate to describing a process in which human beings, created good but now sinful, are brought to new life through God's infusion of saving grace.[178] Grace, as the medieval adage has it, does not destroy but perfects nature.[179] Lutheran ways of speaking, on the other hand, are shaped by the situation of sinners standing before God (*coram deo*) and hearing at one and the same time God's words of judgment and forgiveness in law and gospel. Attention is here focused on this discontinuous, paradoxical, and simultaneous double relation of God to the justified, not on the continuous process of God's transforming work.

§ 97. These different concerns and thought patterns entail different ways of speaking and thinking about points such as (1) the imputational or forensic character of justification, (2) the sinfulness of the justified, (3) the sufficiency of faith, (4) merit, (5) satisfaction, and (6) the criteria by which Christian life and doctrine are to be judged. On each of these questions we shall make brief observations, while fully recognizing that our generalizations cannot do justice to the complexity of the questions and the variety of theological positions that are possible within each tradition.

§ 98. *1. Forensic Justification.* Lutherans describe justification as the imputation to sinners of a righteousness which is that of Christ himself (*iustitia aliena*), received in faith. Justification therefore is the forensic act whereby God declares the sinner just; it is an act performed outside of us (*extra nos*) by which faith is accounted as righteousness. Looking on God's declaration as efficacious, Lutherans also affirm the reality of sanctification and good works, but they regard these effects as fruits rather than parts of justification itself. In this sense the Lutheran doctrine of imputed righteousness is intended to safeguard the unconditional character of God's promises in Christ.

§ 99. Catholics agree that God's saving will has no cause outside himself and that therefore salvation in its totality, as an effect of that will, is unconditional.[180] But they see this totality as including a number of elements, some of which are conditional upon others. Thus justification depends on faith, which in turn depends on the word of God, mediated through the Scriptures and the church (cf. Rom. 10:13-17). Receptivity to God's saving word requires that the seed fall on good soil and that the hearer be not deaf (cf. Matt. 13:1-9 par.). In the execution of God's saving plan, therefore, there may be conditions, which, without restricting God's power and freedom, condition the created effects of his powerful decrees. In efficaciously willing the effect, of course, God also wills the conditions and provides for their realization. With regard to the centrality of justification, Catholics agree with the Lutheran insistence that the truth of the gospel is saving truth and that Christology must be seen not statically but dynamically as God's deed "for us and for our salvation." But Catholics hesitate to trace everything to justification considered simply as a forensic act. They are often inclined to emphasize other images or concepts such as the remission of sin, adoption, redemption, regeneration, healing, sanctification, reconciliation, new creation, and salvation.

§ **100.** Although Catholics recognize the possibility of organizing one's theology about the theme of justification, they commonly fear that emphasis on forensic justification or imputed righteousness, if not accompanied by other themes, could unintentionally encourage a certain disregard of the benefits actually imparted through God's loving deed in Christ. Lutherans, conversely, fear that the Catholic emphasis on the non-forensic aspects could tend to throw believers back on their own resources. On this, as on other points, each tradition wishes to guard against what the other sees as weaknesses and is convinced that it can do so within its own framework.

§ **101.** Characteristic of the two traditions are different approaches to the relationship between the remission of sins and the transformation wrought by grace. Catholics have tended to look on the infusion of grace as a cause of the forgiveness of sins and sanctification.[181] Lutherans can admit that this Catholic understanding of the infusion of grace does not necessarily imply that justification is dependent on sanctification in such a way as to undermine confidence in God and induce an anxiety-ridden reliance on the uncertain signs of grace in one's own life. Yet they are likely to think that the traditional Catholic emphasis on the infusion of grace makes it difficult to express adequately the unmerited character of God's forgiving mercy. For them God's justifying act of forgiveness is itself the cause or constant power of renewal throughout the life of the believer. Catholics, conversely, may think that the Lutheran position is too narrowly focused on the "consolation of terrified consciences" and does not take sufficient account of the doxological dimension of the response of faith, i.e., of the praise of God for his transformative indwelling.

§ **102.** *2. Sinfulness of the Justified.* Lutherans maintain that the sinfulness of the justified is revealed simultaneously with the forensic act of justification. Thus the justified see themselves as in a true sense sinners (*simul iusti et peccatores*). While granting that justification unfailingly effects inner renewal (including the gifts of the Holy Spirit, sanctification, and good works), Lutherans see this renewal as a lifelong struggle against sin both as unrighteousness and self-righteousness. Because God's justifying act is itself the attack on the sin it exposes, original sin and its effects can no longer reign in those who continue to hear and trust the justifying proclamation. Sin nevertheless remains and is in need of continued forgiveness.[182] Catholics, on the other hand, hold that the sanctifying action of the Holy Spirit removes the guilt of sin (*reatus culpae*) and renders the justified pleasing in God's sight.

The concupiscence which remains is not "truly and properly sin in those born again."[183] As a result it is possible, Catholics maintain, for the justified to avoid mortal sins, which involve the loss of the Holy Spirit. Grace enables the justified to avoid venial sins as well, although lifelong success in this struggle can be achieved only by a special divine favor.[184] For however just and holy, they fall from time to time into the sins that are those of daily existence.[185] What is more, the Spirit's action does not exempt believers from the lifelong struggle against sinful tendencies. Concupiscence and other effects of original and personal sin, according to Catholic doctrine, remain in the justified, who therefore must pray daily to God for forgiveness.[186]

§ 103. Lutherans fear that the Catholic doctrine of inherent righteousness may cause the Christian to be anxious or complacent, and in either case insufficiently reliant on God's promise of mercy. Catholics fear that the Lutheran position may lead to a certain neglect of good works or may not adequately motivate the believer to give praise and thanks to God for the healing and transforming effects of his redemptive action in us. To describe this transformation, Catholics sometimes appeal to the concept of divinization (*theosis*), which occupied such an important place in the Greek patristic tradition, and thereby stress that the "inherent righteousness" of believers is primarily God's gift of himself, i.e., primarily *gratia increata* and only secondarily *gratia creata*.[187] Ordinarily Lutherans have not employed the language of divinization, though at times Luther approximated it. But they do follow him in speaking of the believer's participation in the glory of the resurrected Christ and of the continuously operative presence in believers of the Holy Spirit, who "calls, gathers, enlightens, and sanctifies the whole Christian church on earth and preserves it in union with Jesus Christ in the one true faith."[188]

§ 104. Recent ecumenical discussion, by calling attention to the common elements within different structures of thought, makes it difficult for Catholics to accuse Lutherans of diminishing the importance of sanctification or of the Holy Spirit and at the same time makes it difficult for Lutherans to accuse Catholics of overlooking the abiding effects of sin in the baptized. Nonetheless, the divergent ways in which the two traditions usually talk about the sinfulness of the justified are symptoms of continuing differences in their concerns.

§ 105. *3. Sufficiency of Faith.* Catholics can speak of justification by faith or even of justification by faith alone insofar as they teach, as do Lutherans, that nothing prior to the free gift of faith merits justification and that all of God's saving gifts come through Christ alone.

Catholics stress, however, that the indwelling Holy Spirit brings about in believers not only assent and trust but also a loving commitment that issues in good works. In Catholic theology it has therefore been customary to hold that faith, to be justifying, must be accompanied (or, perhaps better, intrinsically qualified) by the gift of love (*caritas*). This traditional position is somewhat technically summed up in the Scholastic formula, "faith animated by love" (*fides caritate formata*). Only when love qualifies faith does faith unite believers perfectly to Christ and make them living members of his body.[189] By consenting to sin and allowing it to reign in oneself, it is possible, according to the Catholic view, to be outside the realm of righteousness even while continuing to believe and hope in Christ; in this sense faith can exist without love and without justifying grace.

§ 106. Lutherans, for their part, recognize without difficulty that the faith that justifies is living and operative. They also deny that faith as mere assent (called in their theological tradition *fides historica*) can be justifying. They stress that faith is living, and it alone justifies because it clings to Christ and the promise of the gospel. Love always springs from such faith, but is among the works of the law, which do not justify. Thus Lutherans are dissatisfied with the Catholic teaching that infused faith (i.e., faith as a gift produced in the soul by God) can be dead and sterile. They suspect that in making a distinction between dead faith and living faith Catholics teach by implication that believers can move themselves from a state of sin to righteousness, thus in effect justifying themselves. Lutherans' fears are increased when they find Catholics speaking of sinners actively cooperating in their own justification. Although Catholics maintain that cooperation is itself a gift of grace and that the love which makes faith live is totally God's gift, Lutherans find that thinking in terms of such a process is liable to Pelagian distortions.[190] The Catholic doctrine that faith alone is insufficient, some Lutherans maintain, tempts Christians to rely on their own activity rather than on the saving work of Christ.

§ 107. The past controversies about the sufficiency of faith alone were aggravated by differences in terminology emerging from late medieval Scholasticism and by the then prevalent tendency to read the New Testament in the light of Scholastic problems and concepts. In recent decades the common approach to exegesis and the shift from Scholastic to modern categories of thought (personal and existential rather than physical or metaphysical) have greatly narrowed the differences. But the theological differences regarding the relation of faith to love have not been fully transcended, even though faith is now recognized on both sides as incomplete without trust in Christ and loving obedience to him.

§ **108.**   *4. Merit.*   Both Lutherans and Catholics hold that, thanks to the inner renewal that comes from justification, the justified can, do, and must perform good works. Lutherans, however, associate merit with law. Asserting that Christians "are justified before they keep the law,"[191] they deny that good works merit salvation. They grant in their Confessions, on the other hand, that the good works of the justified are meritorious "not for the forgiveness of sins, grace, and justification (for we obtain these only by faith) but for other spiritual and physical rewards in this life and in that which is to come."[192] Lutherans, however, have generally considered it misleading to speak of any rewards as "merited."

§ **109.** Catholics, convinced that justification removes whatever is hateful to God in the justified, hold that the good works of the righteous give a title to salvation itself in the sense that God has covenanted to save those who, prompted by grace, obey his will. Catholics recognize, to be sure, that the merit of the creature before God differs radically from that whereby one human being merits from another. Any merit which the creature can have in the sight of God, they point out, is predicated on God's free promises in Christ. Meritorious works, moreover, necessarily presuppose grace and bring to fruition what God's grace has initiated. They have their meritorious value because the Holy Spirit is present and active in those who do such works.

§ **110.** Even when these reservations are made, Lutherans are inclined to hold that Catholic ways of thinking and speaking about merit can lead to a legalism that derogates from the unconditional character of God's justifying word. They speak of reward, new obedience, and good fruits, but avoid the language of merit.

§ **111.** Catholics readily admit that merit has often been preached in a self-righteous way bordering on legalism, but they deny that the abuse of the doctrine invalidates the doctrine itself. To minimize God's gifts, Catholics assert, is not a way of magnifying the giver. It must never be forgotten, they observe, that in crowning our merits God crowns his own gifts. Meritorious works, moreover, cannot derive from a mere desire to accumulate spiritual treasures for oneself. Such works presuppose a charity that proceeds from God and goes out to God. For any assurance of final perseverance and salvation, Catholics believe, one must not trust in one's own merits but rather hope in God's continued mercy.

§ **112.** Thus the essential intentions behind both the Catholic doctrine of merit *ex gratia* and the Lutheran doctrine of promise may be compatible, but the two sides have difficulty in finding a common language. The differences of language here again reflect differences in concern. Lutherans are primarily intent on stressing the saving character of the unconditional promises God addresses to human beings and on preventing Christians from being left to their own resources, whereas the Catholic preoccupation is to make sure that the full range of God's gifts, even the crowning gift of a merited destiny, is acknowledged. Both concerns reflect aspects of the gospel, but the tension nevertheless remains.

§ **113.** *5. Satisfaction.* The disagreements regarding satisfaction are hard to specify since this theme has been less prominent in modern theological discussion than the other themes mentioned here. In the sixteenth century both Lutherans and Catholics were convinced that, as far as eternal punishments were concerned, Christ through his sufferings and death gave full satisfaction for all sin, original or personal. Lutherans, furthermore, agreed that the good works which are the fruit of repentance and of faith include mortification of the flesh, i.e., "the amendment of life and the forsaking of sin." [193] While they did not themselves call this mortification of the flesh "satisfaction," they agreed with the statement ascribed to Augustine that "true satisfaction means cutting off the causes of sin, that is, mortifying and restraining the flesh, not to pay for eternal punishments but to keep the flesh from alluring us to sin." [194]

§ **114.** Catholics, however, held that the sufferings of the saints, united in a mysterious way with those of Christ himself, could "fill up" what was lacking in Christ's sufferings (cf. Col. 1:24), not as regards intrinsic value but as regards the application to particular times, places, and persons. They held that believers who were living in the grace of God could participate in the sufferings of Christ, in his expiation of their sins, and in his intercession for the spiritual needs of others.

§ **115.** The Catholic doctrine, often poorly presented and wrongly understood, was used in support of a variety of abuses that were rightly denounced by the Lutherans and by many reforming Catholics. Many of these abuses were corrected by the reforms of the Council of Trent; others have gradually died out, but some, no doubt, still remain.

§ **116.** In spite of these abuses, Catholics generally continue to hold that the sufferings of penitent sinners and of the innocent can be prayerfully applied, in union with the immeasurable satisfaction given by

Christ, to beseech God's mercy and pardon. Although it may be impossible to know exactly what such an entreaty implies, it need not involve the "works-righteousness" attacked by the Reformers. Properly interpreted, the Catholic doctrine of satisfaction can give a Christian meaning to suffering and to solidarity in the communion of saints. Further study will be needed to determine whether and how far Lutherans and Catholics can agree on these points, which have far-reaching ramifications for traditionally disputed doctrines such as the sacrament of penance, Masses for special intentions, indulgences, and purgatory. These questions demand more thorough exploration than they have yet received in this or other dialogues.[195]

§ 117. 6. *Criteria of Authenticity.* The Lutheran movement, founded at a time when superstition and corruption were rampant, was legitimately concerned to find a critical principle by which to test what is authentically Christian. The principle of justification by faith, understood as the correlative of the sole mediatorship of Christ, was accepted as the article by which the church must stand or fall. Lutherans believe that this principle has continuing validity, since the tendency of Christians to rely on their own devices rather than on Christ is unabating. While granting that the principle of justification by faith alone must not be employed to erode the fullness of the apostolic heritage and of the means whereby this heritage is to be mediated in any given time and place, they believe that this principle retains its critical importance.

§ 118. Catholics, on their side, are wary of using any one doctrine as the absolute principle by which to purify from outside, so to speak, the catholic heritage. They recognize, to be sure, the danger of absolutizing merely human ecclesiastical structures. While conceding that the church stands under the gospel and is to be judged by it, Catholics insist that the gospel cannot be rightly interpreted without drawing on the full resources available within the church. To speak of "Christ alone" or "faith alone," they contend, could lead, contrary to the intentions of Lutherans themselves, to the position that the grace of Christ is given apart from the external word of Scripture, Christian preaching, the sacraments, and the ordained ministry.

§ 119. Here, as on other points, there is much common ground. Lutherans are aware of the dangers of neglecting the means of grace and of fostering individualism in the church. They recognize the importance of the canonical Scripture, sacraments, ritual, devotion, and of the ordained ministry.[196] They have recently been recovering valuable elements in the ancient liturgical tradition of the church. But they continue to ask whether, even in modern Catholicism, it has been made sufficiently evident that (as the Malta Report expressed the Lutheran position) "the rites and orders of the church are not to be imposed as conditions for salvation, but are valid only as the free unfolding of the obedience of faith."[197] They suspect that the papacy and magisterial infallibility remain in need of reinterpretation and restructuring in order to make them ummistakably subordinate to the gospel.[198] Finally, to mention a problem this dialogue has not discussed, they wonder whether official teachings on Mary and the cult of the saints, despite protestations to the contrary, do not detract from the principle that Christ alone is to be trusted for salvation because all God's saving gifts come through him alone.

§ 120. In the existing divergences concerning the principles and methods of church reform, we see once again the consequences of two different sets of concerns. Lutherans, primarily intent upon emphasizing God's unconditional saving promises and upon purifying the church from superstition, corruption, and self-glorification, continue to press for a more thoroughgoing application of justification by faith as a critical principle. Catholics, concerned with protecting the fullness of God's gifts as granted through Christ in the Holy Spirit, are on guard against criticism that might erode the catholic heritage. In spite of their different concerns, both traditions agree that the church is subject to criticism and judgment in light of the gospel and that the gospel is always to be heard and interpreted by Christians in the church, where God's word is explicitly proclaimed.

§ 121. *Conclusion.* If this interpretation is correct, Lutherans and Catholics can share in each others' concerns in regard to justification and can to some degree acknowledge the legitimacy of the contrasting theological perspectives and structures of thought. Yet, on the other hand, some of the consequences of the different outlooks seem irreconcilable, especially in reference to particular applications of justification by faith as a criterion of all church proclamation and practice. In order to move beyond this impasse, it is necessary for both sides to take seriously the concerns of the other and to strive to think jointly about the problems. It is to such an effort that we now turn, first, by looking at the biblical data on justification, and, second, by summarizing and reflecting on the convergences of past and present.

CHAPTER THREE

PERSPECTIVES FOR RECONSTRUCTION

A. The Biblical Data

§ 122. In recent decades developments in the study of Scripture have brought Catholics and Lutherans to a fuller agreement about the meaning of many passages controverted at least since the sixteenth century. Of special importance has been, within general Roman Catholic biblical emphasis, the encouragement given by church authority to Catholic interpreters in the last fifty years to make use of historical-critical methods, thus sharing in a mode of interpretation employed by Protestants for a longer time. In particular, this approach to the Bible lays emphasis on the context of each book or passage and on the theology of each individual writer. In that way readers are encouraged to avoid misusing isolated verses out of context as "proof-texts" in a bad sense and so to respect the meanings of the biblical authors. This common concern for what the biblical texts in their situations affirm has also influenced Lutheran and Catholic systematic theologians in their work.

§ 123. As part of our dialogue, extensive attention has been given to biblical passages bearing on righteousness/justification by faith and its relation to the love and good works expected of a Christian. A detailed and comprehensive survey, impossible to summarize fully here, is available in a separate volume entitled *"Righteousness" in the New Testament* as well as in related essays on merit.[199] Here we shall accent the contributions from our joint study that bear on the historically divisive issue of how to interpret the biblical data on justification by faith. Overall it may be said that Catholics have come to acknowledge that "righteousness/justification is more prevalent in NT teaching than has normally been suspected in earlier centuries or among earlier commentators, and that it is an image of prime importance for our expression of the Christ-event or even the gospel" (*Righteousness*, ‡ 423); and Lutherans acknowledge that this theme has more nuances and, some would say, limitations in expressing the gospel (‡‡ 347-49) than has been generally supposed in their tradition.

§ 124. Our examination of the scriptural evidence has brought out not merely a number of convergences and outright agreements already existing in the work of Catholic and non-Catholic exegetes[200] but also

58

some particular emphases and new insights not previously highlighted in ecumenical discussions on righteousness/justification. The *first* of these involves the fact that it is the Hebrew Scriptures (or Old Testament) which provide the proper setting for any such discussion (‡‡ 27-48; 358-64). That point is readily apparent even from a casual perusal of Paul, for Paul's appeal, in his dispute with his opponents, is to Hab. 2:4 (cf. Gal. 3:11; Rom. 1:17, "he who through faith is righteous shall live") and to Gen. 15:6 (Gal. 3:6; Rom. 4:3, "Abraham 'believed God, and it was reckoned to him as righteousness' "; cf. also Rom. 3:21, "the law and the prophets bear witness"). Many of the varied meanings of the New Testament Greek term *dikaiosynē* (and related words) stem from the nuances of the Hebrew root *ṣdq*.

§ **125.** The biblical terms "righteousness" and "justification" have a rich background and a wide variety of uses. As images they are drawn from juridical, forensic (law court) settings and are employed to describe the right relationship of human beings to God or to one another and the mode or process by which such a relationship comes about. Thus the term "righteous" may denote a human being as innocent or acquitted before a judge's tribunal. It may also suggest a complex of right relationships and, according to many interpreters, covenant behavior and loyalty, and, according to some, even a relation to the cosmic order.

§ **126.** When predicated of human beings, biblical "righteousness" is understood as justice in ruling or judging, ethical uprightness, covenantal loyalty, obedience to the Torah, or forensic innocence. The descriptions of the way in which a person is brought to righteousness in the sight of God vary among the OT authors and in the NT, especially in the writings of Paul.

§ **127.** When predicated of God, "righteousness" is understood as his fundamental uprightness; his triumph(s) in a holy war, in a law-court dispute (*rîb*) with Israel, or in legal decisions (Ps. 9:5); but above all, especially in the postexilic period, as his gracious salvific activity, manifest in a just judgment (Isa. 46:3; 51:5-8; 56:1; cf. Hos. 2:18-19; Pss. 40:9-10; 98:2). We are made especially aware of such nuances associated with God's "righteousness" when the Hebrew for that term (*sdq*) appears in the Greek translation of the Old Testament as his "mercy" (Isa. 56:1; RSV "deliverance") or when his "steadfast love" (Hebrew *ḥesed*) is rendered as his "righteousness" (*dikaiosynē*; LXX Ex. 34:7; Isa. 63:7).

§ **128.** The *second* area of discovery for the present dialogue lay in the possibility of determining the earliest Christian use of righteousness/

justification terminology. While Jesus himself is not normally attested as having employed such language (‡‡ 49-54, 365-67), the words and associated forensic imagery seem first to have appeared in creedal summaries or confessions of faith now embedded in the Pauline and other epistles but pre-Pauline in origin (‡‡ 55-76, 368-75). Examples include 1 Cor. 6:11 ("justified in the name of the Lord Jesus Christ"); Rom. 4:24-25 ("Jesus our Lord, who was put to death for our trespasses and raised for our justification"); and Rom. 3:24-26a (cf. also 1 Cor. 1:30; 1 Pet. 3:18; 1 Tim. 3:16; and possibly 2 Cor. 5:21). Clearly in the thirties and forties of the first century the early Christian community was making use of this Old Testament imagery to express the claim that by Christ's death and resurrection human beings stand righteous before God's tribunal. These formulations do not specifically mention "faith" or "works," but they show, as part of a common expression of the apostolic faith, that Paul was not the first to formulate the meaning of the Christ event in terms of righteousness/justification.

§ 129. What Paul did do, in inheriting the righteousness/justification language of the Old Testament and its previous applications to Christ, was to sharpen the meaning, especially though not exclusively, in Galatians, Romans, and Philippians. He related the process of justification to "grace" and set forth the theme of "justified through faith, not by works of the law," though he also insisted on "the obedience of faith" (Rom. 1:5) and response to the gospel in believers' lives (see §§ 132-36 below). The Pauline data became for us a *third* area containing a number of new insights (‡‡ 77-162, 376-99).

§ 130.   *(a)* In the face of disputes since the Reformation, our understanding of what Paul meant when he wrote that his gospel revealed "the righteousness of God . . . through faith for faith" (Rom. 1:17) has been greatly helped first of all by consideration of the rich Old Testament and pre-Pauline background which has opened up concerning "the righteousness of God."

§ 131. Luther at times attributed to his predecessors an identification of the biblical "justice of God" (Vulgate, *iustitia dei*) with God's punitive, vindictive justice.[201] He himself preferred to speak of "the righteousness of God" as an alien righteousness (*iustitia aliena*) that God gives on account of faith in Christ. It alone is *"die Gerechtigkeit die vor Gott gilt."*[202] Historians of doctrine today usually admit that Luther's medieval predecessors did not as a rule identify *iustitia dei* with a punitive justice.[203] In any case, recent biblical scholarship sees the righteousness of which Paul speaks both as a gift from God[204] and, in some passages, as an attribute or quality of God, a power exercised on behalf of sinful humanity to save and justify (*heilsetzende Macht*).[205] This widespread consensus in the modern understanding of *dikaiosynē theou*, according to which it is an attribute of God, but also his power present in his gift, should help us further to go beyond the divisive issues of the sixteenth century. At that time Paul's texts were interpreted in polemical debates about sin and grace, faith and good works; his use of the notion of "righteousness of God" was often translated into categories other than his own and categories that were mutually exclusive. Moreover, each side then suspected the other's intentions when appealing to Paul.

§ **132.** *(b)* A second way in which we have been helped in grasping what Paul says on justification is by relating this theme to other images which he employed to describe God's salvific activity toward human beings. While righteousness/justification is the primary way the apostle describes what God has done for us in Christ, it is complemented by other images which express aspects of God's activity in a nonforensic terminology that refers to personal and corporate transformation. Paul recognized that Christ had "once for all" (Rom. 6:10) died to sin and had justified human beings (Gal. 2:16; Rom. 3:26-28; 4:25; 5:18), but he freely described what this involves under such other images as salvation (2 Cor. 7:10; Rom. 1:16; 10:10; 13:11), expiation of sins (Rom. 3:25), redemption of sinners (1 Cor. 1:30; Rom. 3:24; 8:32), reconciliation of sinners to God (2 Cor. 5:18-20; Rom. 5:10-11; 11:15), adoption (Gal. 4:5; Rom. 8:15, 23), sanctification (1 Cor. 1:2,30; 6:11), freedom (Gal. 5:1,13; Rom. 8:1-2,21), transformation (2 Cor. 3:18; Rom. 12:20), glorification (2 Cor. 3:10; Rom. 8:30), and a new creation (Gal. 6:15; 2 Cor. 5:17; cf. 1 Cor. 15:45). Though sometimes intertwined with righteousness/justification, these images point to dimensions of God's saving activity that cannot easily be denoted by forensic terminology, even though the forensic emphasis may be needed for their proper interpretation.

§ **133.** *(c)* While, as already noted, Paul inherited righteousness/justification terminology as a biblical way of describing what Christ Jesus had done for human beings, he also more clearly related it to grace and faith than had been done previously. Yet in all seven of his uncontested letters he makes use of righteousness terms in a generic sense as though their meaning could be presumed. Hence it appears that this way of articulating what Christ's death and resurrection means is not merely the result of debates with Judaizers in Galatia, though such

confrontation may have been the occasion for sharpening his formulation
in terms of "faith" and in contrast to "works of the law." Paul's classic
thesis is set forth in Gal. 2:16: "a human being is not justified [*di-
kaioutai*] because of deeds [i.e., observances] of [the] law, but rather
through faith in Jesus Christ" (cf. Rom. 3:21). The verb "is justified"
is surely used in a declarative, forensic sense; whether there is also an
effective sense here (i.e., that the person is made, as well as declared,
righteous) is not resolvable by philological analysis alone. Yet since
justification has not only a forensic sense but also represents God's
power at work, sinners are "rendered righteous" (cf. Rom. 5:19); this
involves righteousness both in an ethical sense and before God (‡‡ 100,
382).

§ 134. In any case, according to Paul, this justification takes place
by "the grace of God," through faith, not through the law (Gal. 2:21;
Rom. 3:22, 24), as Paul's argument from the Abraham story in Galatians
3–4 and Romans 4 shows. For Paul faith in Christ is a response to the
gospel; it comes from hearing the gospel (Gal. 3:2, 8; Rom. 10:17) and
results in personal "obedience" (Rom. 1:5; cf. 16:26). Faith is also
something "which works itself out through love" (Gal. 5:6), a concise
Pauline phrase expressing the relation of faith and loving Christian
service (unless *agape* might here refer to God's love for us). Such an
understanding (‡‡ 105, 106, 384) avoids much of the sixteenth-century
acrimony over the interpretation of Gal. 5:6.[206]

§ 135. Without doubt Paul emphasizes in the Letter to the Romans
the argument that righteousness comes through faith and by grace (1:17;
3:21ff.). Yet even in this letter there have been problems over "judgment" and "works." For Paul states that "God's righteous judgment"
(Rom. 2:5; *dikaiokrisia* as distinct from his *dikaiosynē*) will be revealed;
"[God] 'will render to everyone according to his works' (Ps. 62:12);
to those who by persistence in a good deed seek glory and honor and
immortality [he will give] eternal life''; for those who sin, his furious
wrath waits (Rom. 2:6-8). Whether Rom. 2:6-11 refers to Christians or
not is debated by exegetes (‡‡ 125-29, 390-91). Compare also 2 Cor.
5:10, "For we must all appear before the judgment seat of Christ, so
that each one may receive good or evil, according to what he has done
in the body." We note that from such passages some Protestant interpreters have come to reckon more fully in Paul with a judgment based
on works and some Catholics with the likelihood that this need not be
understood as contrary to justification by faith (‡ 129).

§ 136. *(d)* With regard to such passages, we realize today that Paul's
statements about the appearance of human beings before God's tribunal

have to be understood in the larger context of his insistence on God's gracious justification offered to all men and women through faith in Christ Jesus, a justification accomplished through Christ's death for sins "once for all," yet one for which believers wait in "the hope of righteousness" through the Spirit (Gal. 5:5; cf. Rom. 8:23, 25). It is moreover an effective declaration, happening now, when one is justified and lives at peace in Christ, having in effect heard the judgment of God and his justifying word (Gal. 2:15-20; Rom. 5:1-2; 8:28-37). Thus justification is not simply a future or past event, but is an eschatological reality which stretches from the past through the present and into the future (‡‡ 147, 398). Hence Paul, in writing to the Philippians, can enjoin, "Work out your own salvation with fear and trembling," and then immediately add, "For God is at work in you, both to will and to work for his good pleasure" (2:12-13). "God does everything, therefore we have to do everything. And we shall receive everything."[207] The "good deed" (cf. Rom. 2:7; 1 Thess. 1:3) that Christians, justified by faith in Christ Jesus, will bring to the tribunal of God will be done because God is at work in them (‡‡ 83, 125, 377, 390). In brief, it seems that Paul's eschatological outlook enabled him to speak of both judgment in accordance with works and justification by faith apart from works of the law.

§ 137. A *fourth* area where there is now greater agreement because of modern scholarly attention to the specific contexts within which biblical passages need to be interpreted concerns those Pauline epistles widely conceded to be the product of Paul's pupils and the Pauline school. The emphasis in Paul's own letters on justification by faith becomes less pronounced in the changed situations of the Deutero-Paulines and Pastorals. There is less interest in the mode by which believers are justified and a rising emphasis upon the effects of justification in their lives. Thus Col. 4:1 and Eph. 5:9; 6:14 take up righteousness terminology in urging the ethical effects of justification. Even Eph. 4:24 presupposes rather than argues that justification causes holiness. Eph. 2:4-10 echoes Pauline teaching about being "*saved* by grace through faith," but Ephesians does not use "righteousness/justification" terminology to make this point. Moreover, the eschatology changes, for there is no future reference, and while salvation is "not by works" (2:9), the "good works" in which Christians are to walk have been "prepared beforehand" by God (2:10; cf. ‡‡ 171-74, 401).

§ 138. The Pastoral Epistles are similar in tone. On one occasion (Titus 3:5-7) the mode of justification is expounded in connection with baptism ("justified by his grace," "not because of deeds done by us in righteousness"). Elsewhere the three letters emphasize the effects of God's grace and mercy (undeserved by merely human works) in terms of the "good (*agatha*) deeds" or the "fine (*kala*) deeds" of believers. The latter phrase, unprecedented in Paul and very rare in the Greek biblical tradition, lends a missionary orientation to the effects of justification (‡‡ 178-91, esp. 185; 402; 428-37, esp. 432 and 434). As a body of literature the Deutero-Paulines (and the Pastorals specifically) illustrate the living reality that justification introduces into the believer's existence. Thus methods of analysis unavailable in the sixteenth century show to a greater degree than has been possible in the past how Paul's doctrine was further developed in the Pastoral Epistles.

§ **139.** The *fifth* area of insights is provided by a full survey of the other New Testament writings on righteousness/justification, the Synoptics and Acts, the Johannine literature, Hebrews, and the Petrine epistles (‡‡ 223-318, 409-20), and gives further support to the overall trends noted above (§ 123): righteousness terminology and expressions of the concept of justification are more prevalent than has often been suspected, but the usages vary, differing especially from Paul's. Some examples follow.

§ **140.** Among the Synoptic evangelists Matthew has especially used the noun *dikaiosynē* to refer to God's way of salvation (e.g., 5:6; 6:33) or human ethical response (e.g., 5:10; 6:1) or both (cf. 21:32; ‡‡ 226-43; 410). Whereas Paul regarded "righteousness" as God's gift and "faith" as human response, Matthew speaks at times of "the kingdom" as the gift from God and "righteousness" especially as the response. The few occurrences of the terms in Luke (18:14) and Acts (15:10-11; 13:38-39) are akin but not identical to Paul's usages and represent another type of development (‡‡ 244-53, 411).

§ **141.** What examples there are of righteousness terminology in John, 1 John, and Revelation reflect Old Testament, especially ethical nuances, though Christ is "the Righteous One" who is the expiation for sins (1 John 2:1-2; ‡‡ 254-65; 412). Hebrews interprets the Christ event at times in terms of righteousness (1:9; 5:13; 10:37-38) but scarcely with the Pauline sense of justification and with a different sense for faith (11:1ff.; ‡‡ 285-99, 415-17). The modest use of righteousness terms in 1 Peter puts that document in the Pauline or, better, pre-Pauline apostolic Christian orbit; in 2 Peter, "the righteousness of our God and Savior, Jesus Christ" (1:1) suggests use of inherited language to meet a new threat from false teaching in a pluralistic Hellenistic environment (‡‡ 305-14, 418-20).

§ **142.** The Letter of James constitutes a *sixth* area of exegetical understanding (‡‡ 266-83, 413-14), an area which has been of neuralgic significance in Lutheran-Catholic debates. Some usages are not controversial: Jas. 1:20 speaks of the "righteousness of God" in the sense of God's unshakable fidelity understood as a norm for Christian conduct, and "righteous(ness)" in an ethical sense also occurs (3:18; 5:6,16). In Jas. 2:14-26, however, we encounter the famous discussion of faith and works, which argues that justification is not by faith alone but by works that complete it. One widespread contemporary interpretation sees this part of the letter as not directed against Paul himself or his teaching on justification by faith.[208] It is rather an attempt to correct a caricature of his teaching which seemingly advocated some form of libertinism, a caricature with which Paul himself at times had to contend (see Rom. 3:8; 6:1,15). "You see that a human being is justified by works and not by faith alone" (Jas. 2:24) may seem to contradict Gal. 2:16 or Rom. 3:28. Yet we recognize that for Paul "works" regularly means "works of the [Mosaic] law" (see Rom. 3:21) and "faith" means a faith which "works itself out through love" (Gal. 5:6, see § 134). Such faith is for Paul no "dead" faith; it is akin to that "faith which is completed by works" (Jas. 2:22b). Moreover, for Paul the pregnant sense of faith includes both allegiance to God in Christ and the inescapability of good deeds flowing therefrom. It thus differs greatly from what "faith" denotes in Jas. 2:19—acceptance of revelation without corresponding behavior. (It may be noted that in the New Testament the phrase *sola fide* occurs in Jas. 2:24, not in a Pauline writing.) Thus it can now be agreed that James did not directly attack Paul's concept of faith or of justification by faith, although it may be difficult to reconcile James' overall understanding of law, works, and sin with Paul's teaching on the same themes.

§ **143.** The topic of merit provides a *seventh* area where modern examination of the biblical data sheds some light on what was another divisive issue in the sixteenth-century controversies of Rome with Luther and his colleagues. "Merit" is a technical Western theological term for a concept that has no single terminological equivalent in the original texts of the Bible. Even in the Vulgate *meritum* occurs at only two or three places in Ecclesiasticus (10:31; 16:15; 38:18 [?]), translating a variety of Greek or Hebrew terms (see LXX Sirach 10:28; 16:14; 38:17), none of which has much to do with "merit."

§ **144.** However, the notion can be related to, though it is not exactly the same as, the biblical idea of the "recompense" or "retribution" that the God of Israel gives for human conduct. Under a variety of images drawn from nature (e.g., "produce," "fruit," "harvest") and from human relationships (particularly of a contractual or competitive character, e.g., "wages" and "prizes"), the Old Testament literature, from the Torah through the prophets, psalms, and sapiential books, often sets forth this aspect of life and conduct, the relationship between what men and women do for (or against) God and what they in turn receive from him (see Gen. 2–12; Deut. 28; Jer. 31:29-30; Ezek. 18:1-32; Pss. 1; 37:25-26; Prov. 13:13; 19:16-17; the Book of Job; cf. Tob. 4:7-11; 12:5-6; Wis. 2:22; 3:14-15; 5:15-16; Sir. 51:30). Paul can write of death as "the wages of sin," but he does so in contrast to eternal life as "God's free gift" (*charisma*; never "wages of good works," Rom. 6:23; cf. Gal. 6:7-9) which has been effected by the all-sufficing act of the Christ who died for us (cf. Rom. 5:9-11 with vv. 15-17). Eph. 2:1-10 (see § 137 above) describes this act of Christ in terms of the immeasurable riches that the Father has freely given through his Son (cf. 1 Pet. 1:18-19, on believers ransomed "with the precious blood of Christ"). Using such biblical data, the Latin theological and liturgical tradition interpreted the immeasurable riches of Christ's work as his "infinite merits" and compared them with the lesser or nonexistent "merit" of merely human or Christian works;[209] in Lutheran and Protestant hymnody the merits of Christ, in contrast to human lack of merits, are often mentioned.[210]

§ **145.** The images and parables that the New Testament uses to designate the recompense that God gives to each person for his conduct (e.g., Mark 10:29-30 and parallels: Matt. 19:29; Luke 18:29-30)[211] when considered together with those which stress the "unprofitableness" of works (Matt. 20:1-10; Luke 17:7-10) remind us how complex are the questions that stand under the heading of "merit." There is no easy, systematic transfer of our human ethical schemata (including those of natural or commutative justice) into the divine judgment. Matthew, to take one example, depicts the Son of man separating sheep from goats and granting rewards for human conduct (Matt. 25:31-46; cf. 16:27). John, to take another, portrays the consequences of faithful and unfaithful discipleship through the image of the vine and the branches (John 15:1-11; cf. John 3:19-21; 5:25-29). In still other ways Hebrews (4:1; 6:7-8, 10-12; 10:26-36) and the book of Revelation (14:13; 22:11-12) articulate the same teaching, illustrating the paradoxical incalculability of a divine recompense which, in the last analysis, is, for those who do good, God himself, and for those who do evil, the eternal loss of God. One dare not overlook this aspect of biblical teaching, though it must always be set within the framework of God's merciful action on behalf of humankind in Christ.

§ 146. Yet it is righteousness/justification which emerges in Paul and elsewhere as an image and concept of prime importance, at times, as in Romans, the central or dominant image, for expressing what God has done in Christ and thus for expressing the gospel. Along with this emphasis there is also found in the New Testament writings a stress, though on the whole not as great, on the consequent deeds of the righteous Christian and on the recompense that awaits them. "Righteousness" and "justification" in other New Testament writings are not always qualified, as they are in the Pauline writings, with the phrases "by grace" and "through faith." Yet the classic formulation of the doctrine of *iustitia dei* has come to us through Paul. It is he among biblical authors who most fully and carefully discussed "righteousness" and "faith" and who, in the light of his understanding of these terms, thinks of justification as simply "by grace" and "through faith" without additions or qualifications. Paul was not, he tells us, "ashamed of the gospel," because "in it the righteousness of God is revealed through faith for faith" and "it is the power of God for the salvation of everyone who believes" (Rom. 1:16-17). In brief, a faith centered and forensically conceived picture of justification is of major importance for Paul and, in a sense, for the Bible as a whole, although it is by no means the only biblical or Pauline way of representing God's saving work.

§ 147. The significance of these exegetical findings depends in part on the attitude adopted toward the theological problem of "the center of Scripture," which is related to that of a "canon within the canon." When a principle such as justification by faith is taken as the key to the interpretation of all Scripture, those biblical books, especially Paul's major letters, which stress this doctrine are sometimes regarded as canonical in a special sense, while others (e.g., James) may be viewed as of secondary or even doubtful canonicity. Luther sometimes spoke in this way, but the issue of a canon within the canon has become a major one chiefly in recent times, in part because of our greater awareness of the theological differences among biblical authors.

§ 148. The problem is not entirely new. Medieval authors commonly agreed that there was a hierarchy among the books of the New Testament, the four Gospels coming first in importance (a view reiterated by Vatican Council II).[212] The "spiritual" senses of Scripture often led to a Christocentric reading of it, as is patent in this formula of Bonaventure: " . . . by faith Christ dwells in our hearts. Such is the knowledge of

Jesus Christ, from which the certainty and understanding of all the Holy Scripture derives."[213] This Bonaventurean statement may be compared to Luther's view that Scripture is *was Christum treibet*,[214] an approach which for Luther meant, among other things, that Scripture should be interpreted in terms of justification by faith.

§ 149. In view of this history it is possible for Lutherans and Catholics to agree that for purposes of theological interpretation Scripture has a Christological center which should control the interpretation of those parts of the Bible which focus on matters other than the center itself and which are therefore of secondary rank in the canonical hierarchy. Their lesser rank, however, does not mean that they lack all importance or authority; on that both Lutheran and Catholic confessional traditions are agreed.[215] When it is thus granted that all Scripture must be taken seriously, it becomes clear from the exegetical findings we have summarized that the biblical witness to the gospel of God's saving work in Christ is richer and more varied than has been encompassed in either traditional Catholic or Lutheran approaches to justification. Both sides need to treat each other's concerns and ways of interpreting Scripture with greater respect and willingness to learn than has been done in the past.

B. Growing Convergences

§ 150. The interpretation of Scripture is crucial, but it is not the only factor which contributes to the theological convergences we shall now review. These convergences have been facilitated by the widespread disappearance of nontheological sources of division. The crowns of princes, the incomes of priests and pastors, the standings of social classes are no longer intertwined, as they were in the sixteenth century, with the conflict over justification. The disestablishment of the churches and their detachment from the struggle for worldly power make it easier to discern and acknowledge agreements between them.

§ 151. In light of these developments Lutherans and Catholics have drawn closer together. Theology in both churches is influenced by modern scriptural studies and intellectual developments in the humanities, social studies, and the natural sciences. Both churches are affected by the liturgical renewal, with its emphasis on early Christian patterns of worship different from those of the Middle Ages and post-Reformation Protestantism. The abuses which occasioned the Reformation have for the most part been condemned by Trent and by the Second Vatican

Council; in four hundred years of history Lutherans on their side have acquired their own burden of unfaithfulness to the gospel. Both communions acknowledge the need for continual reformation, and both are learning to work together towards that end. They increasingly cooperate in the service of human needs and, to a lesser though important extent, in educational efforts and in bringing the gospel to the world. Lutherans and Catholics are at home with each other and in each other's churches as never before in their divided histories. It is scarely surprising that they are now closer on the doctrine of justification than at any time since the collapse of their last extended official discussion of the topic at Regensburg in 1541 (§§ 45-48 above).

§ **152.** What has emerged from the present study is a convergence (though not uniformity) on justification by faith considered in and of itself, and a significant though lesser convergence on the applications of the doctrine as a criterion of authenticity for the church's proclamation and practice (§ 121). We shall comment first (1) on the incomplete convergence on the use of the criterion and then (2) on the material convergence.

1. Use of the Criterion

§ **153.** Catholics as well as Lutherans can acknowledge the need to test the practices, structures, and theologies of the church by the extent to which they help or hinder "the proclamation of God's free and merciful promises in Christ Jesus which can be rightly received only through faith" (§ 28). This accord, however, does not always imply agreement on the applications of the criterion, i.e., which beliefs, practices, and structures pass the test. Catholics and Lutherans, for example, traditionally differ on purgatory, the papacy, and the cult of the saints (§§ 116, 119). Lutherans, however, do not exclude the possibility that such teachings can be understood and used in ways consistent with justification by faith; if such teachings are preached and practiced in accord with this doctrine, they need not, from this Lutheran perspective, divide the churches even though Lutherans do not accept them. Catholics, on their side, admit the legitimacy of the test and hold that their doctrines do foster the "obedience of faith" (cf. Rom. 1:5), but they are open to different opinions regarding the degree to which these traditionally Catholic positions must be accepted by others on the way to closer communion. The ecumenical rapprochement that has already occurred during and since Vatican II is evidence that greater church union, including a limited admission to the Eucharist, is possible without explicit adherence to all Roman Catholic dogmas.[216] The problems regarding the acceptability of post-Reformation developments in each tradition cannot be solved simply by reference to justification by faith as a doctrine per se. Each development must be assessed in its own right and in connection with other outstanding issues such as the relation between Scripture and tradition.

§ 154. It is apparent from our discussion that differences in thought structures play a considerable role in causing tension between Catholic and Lutheran views on justification. Reference has been made (§ 25) to Augustinian and medieval "transformationist models" in contrast to "a model of simultaneity" that reinterprets all notions of change and growth. The Lutheran hermeneutical understanding of justification by faith (§§ 88-93) in some ways heightens the tension with Catholic positions. It does so by excluding from the gospel proclamation all reference to the freedom and goodness of fallen human beings on the ground that this would undermine the unconditionality of God's promises in Christ. Such interpretation raises even more questions from Lutherans regarding Catholic descriptions of justification as a process of ontological transformation. Catholics, on their side, continue to ask whether Lutheran formulations of this kind do justice to God's respect for human freedom and to the idea of a real change wrought by the Holy Spirit (§§ 98-104). These problems are complicated, no doubt, by differing thought structures within Lutheran and Catholic theological "camps" as well as between them. The conflict between thought structures raises a number of issues we have not resolved and points to the need for further dialogue. We believe, however, that here too Lutherans and Catholics can acknowledge the legitimacy of concerns that come to expression in different ways. In view of the convergences to which we now turn, theological disagreements about structures of thought in relation to the proclamation of the gospel, though serious, need not be church-dividing.

2. Material Convergences

§ 155. The convergence on the use of justification by faith as a criterion depends on prior and fuller material convergences on the doctrine itself. It is only because Catholics and Lutherans share fundamental convictions regarding justification and faith that they can be in increasing accord on criteria of Christian authenticity and accept justification as an *articulus stantis et cadentis ecclesiae* protective of the *solus Christus* (cf. § 160). Some of their common convictions are long-standing, others have come to light more recently, and all remain subject to different interpretations and formulations in each tradition. Yet, when looked at as a whole, they constitute a very significant agreement.

§ **156.** Elements in this agreement may be formulated as follows:

1) Christ and his gospel are the source, center, and norm of Christian life, individual and corporate, in church and world. Christians have no other basis for eternal life and hope of final salvation than God's free gift in Jesus Christ, extended to them in the Holy Spirit.

2) The prerequisite of final salvation is righteousness. To be saved one must be judged righteous and be righteous.

3) As a consequence of original sin all human beings stand in need of justification even before they commit personal sins. Those in whom sin reigns can do nothing to merit justification, which is the free gift of God's grace. Even the beginnings of justification, for example, repentance, prayer for grace, and desire for forgiveness, must be God's work in us.

4) We remain God's creatures even when ruled by sin. We retain the human freedom to make choices among created goods, but we lack the capacity to turn to God without divine help.

5) Justification, as a transition from disfavor and unrighteousness to favor and righteousness in God's sight, is totally God's work. By justification we are both declared and made righteous. Justification, therefore, is not a legal fiction. God, in justifying, effects what he promises; he forgives sin and makes us truly righteous.

6) Scripture, the proclamation of the word, and the sacraments are means whereby the gospel, as the power of God for salvation, comes concretely to individuals to awaken and strengthen justifying faith.

7) In justification we receive by faith the effects of Christ's action on our behalf. Justifying faith is not merely historical knowledge or intellectual conviction, but a trustful, self-involving response to the gospel.

8) Justifying faith cannot exist without hope and love; it necessarily issues in good works. Yet the justified cannot rely on their own good works or boast of their own merits as though they were not still in need of mercy.

9) Sin no longer reigns in the justified, yet they remain subject to sinful inclinations and the assaults of sin so that, when left to their own powers, they fall repeatedly. Of themselves they remain capable of losing justification, but, because of the great mercy of God in Christ, they may firmly trust and hope that God will bring them to final salvation.

10) The eternal reward promised to the righteous is a gift, for it depends wholly on God's grace in Christ, the one mediator between God and fallen humanity.

11) The good works of the justified, performed in grace, will be recompensed by God, the righteous judge, who, true to his promises, "will render to everyone according to his works" (Rom. 2:6) (cf. § 108).

12) The priority of God's redeeming will over every human action in bringing about ultimate salvation is recognized in both our traditions by the classic doctrine of predestination.

§ 157. Involved in this agreement, as is apparent from §§ 6, 7, and 8 , is a fundamental affirmation which was noted in the introduction (§4) as particularly helpful for our discussions: *our entire hope of justification and salvation rests on Christ Jesus and on the gospel whereby the good news of God's merciful action in Christ is made known; we do not place our ultimate trust in anything other than God's promise and saving work in Christ.* Such an affirmation is not fully equivalent to the Reformation teaching on justification according to which God accepts sinners as righteous for Christ's sake on the basis of faith alone; but by its insistence that reliance for salvation should be placed entirely on God, it expresses a central concern of that doctrine. Yet it does not exclude the traditional Catholic position that the grace-wrought transformation of sinners is a necessary preparation for final salvation. The agreement, in short, is on the nature of trust or assurance of salvation, on the fundamental experiential attitude of the justified in relation to God (*coram deo*). There are, however, remaining differences on theological formulations and on the relation between theology and proclamation (cf. §§ 88, 154).

§ 158. It must be emphasized that our common affirmation that it is God in Christ alone whom believers ultimately trust does not necessitate any one particular way of conceptualizing or picturing God's saving work. That work can be expressed in the imagery of God as judge who pronounces sinners innocent and righteous (cf. §90), and also in a transformist view which emphasizes the change wrought in sinners by infused grace. Further, as the Malta Report puts it, "The event of salvation to which the gospel testifies can also be expressed comprehensively in other representations derived from the New Testament, such as reconciliation, freedom, redemption, new life and new creation."[217] Yet whatever the aspect of God's saving action one is led to highlight by the needs of gospel proclamation in each age, the affirmation holds that ultimate hope and trust for salvation are to be placed in the God of our Lord Jesus Christ, and not in our own goodness, even when this is God-given, or in our religious experience, even when this is the experience of faith.

§ 159. Wherever this affirmation is maintained, it is possible to allow great variety in describing salvation and in interpreting God's justifying declaration without destroying unity. There may still be debate over the best way to proclaim or evoke reliance on God's gift of himself in Christ Jesus. The belief that the assurance of salvation and the certainty of hope are to be found (as Thomas Aquinas puts it) "chiefly" (*principaliter*) by looking at God's mercy, not at oneself, does not decide such disputes.[218] But where the affirmation is accepted, Lutherans and Catholics can recognize each other as sharing a commitment to the same gospel of redemptive love received in faith.

§ 160. This affirmation, like the Reformation doctrine of justification by faith alone, serves as a criterion for judging all church practices, structures, and traditions precisely because its counterpart is "Christ alone" (*solus Christus*). He alone is to be ultimately trusted as the one mediator through whom God in the Holy Spirit pours out his saving gifts. All of us in this dialogue affirm that all Christian teachings, practices, and offices should so function as to foster "the obedience of faith" (Rom. 1:5) in God's saving action in Christ Jesus alone through the Holy Spirit, for the salvation of the faithful and the praise and honor of the heavenly Father.

Declaration

§ 161. Thus we can make together, in fidelity to the gospel we share, the following declaration:

We believe that God's creative graciousness is offered to us and to everyone for healing and reconciliation so that through the Word made flesh, Jesus Christ, "who was put to death for our transgressions and raised for our justification" (Rom. 4:25), we are all called to pass from the alienation and oppression of sin to freedom and fellowship with God in the Holy Spirit. It is not through our own initiative that we respond to this call, but only through an undeserved gift which is granted and made known in faith, and which comes to fruition in our love of God and neighbor, as we are led by the Spirit in faith to bear witness to the divine gift in all aspects of our lives. This faith gives us hope for ourselves and for all humanity and gives us confidence that salvation in Christ will always be proclaimed as the gospel, the good news for which the world is searching.

§ **162.** This gospel frees us in God's sight from slavery to sin and self (Rom. 6:6). We are willing to be judged by it in all our thoughts and actions, our philosophies and projects, our theologies and religious practices. Since there is no aspect of the Christian community or of its life in the world that is not challenged by this gospel, there is none that cannot be renewed or reformed in its light or by its power.

§ **163.** We have encountered this gospel in our churches' sacraments and liturgies, in their preaching and teaching, in their doctrines and exhortations. Yet we also recognize that in both our churches the gospel has not always been proclaimed, that it has been blunted by reinterpretation, that it has been transformed by various means into self-satisfying systems of commands and prohibitions.

§ **164.** We are grateful at this time to be able to confess together what our Catholic and Lutheran ancestors tried to affirm as they responded in different ways to the biblical message of justification. A fundamental consensus on the gospel is necessary to give credibility to our previous agreed statements on baptism, on the Eucharist, and on forms of church authority. We believe that we have reached such a consensus.

§ **165.** We submit this statement to our churches for study, with the hope that it will serve them as they face the need to make appropriate decisions for the purpose of confessing their faith as one. We also trust that Christian believers of all traditions may find in it an invitation to new hope and new love in the grace that is offered to humanity by God through his Word, Jesus Christ, in the Holy Spirit.

PART II
BACKGROUND PAPERS

1

JUSTIFICATION BY FAITH AND "RIGHTEOUSNESS" IN THE NEW TESTAMENT

Joseph A. Fitzmyer, S.J.

Of all the topics discussed so far in the seven rounds of the national dialogue of Lutherans and Roman Catholics in the United States none has been so closely related to a biblical topic as "justification by faith." When one hears this phrase, it conjures up not only memories of the basic thrust of the sixteenth-century Reformation, but also of a prime teaching of Pauline theology in the New Testament. It is not a topic limited in the Bible to the major Pauline writings, but one which many Old and New Testament writers have treated with varying nuances. When the dialogue members took up this topic for discussion, it was with a keen awareness of how fundamental an issue was being broached, an issue not only of division between our churches for four and a half centuries but of its close relationship to the Christian gospel itself. Differences between Lutheran and Catholic interpretations of this biblical teaching had developed over the centuries. Yet it was felt that the modern climate of biblical studies and interpretation had changed so much that a convergence, if not a consensus, could be reached on this major and basic topic, at least from the viewpoint of biblical interpretation.

The common statement on "Justification by Faith" presented in this volume would undoubtedly never have seen the light of day were it not for the modern Catholic biblical movement and its advocacy of a mode of biblical interpretation that had been dear to the hearts of many Lutheran interpreters for decades. In the last forty years Lutheran and Roman Catholic modes of biblical interpretation—if it is even right to use the plural!—have become so similar that the differences are no longer drawn along confessional lines but rather along those of individual or group exegetical preferences. This shift in biblical interpretation made it possible for the late Cardinal Augustin Bea to recommend and advocate the use of G. Kittel and G. Friedrich, *Theologisches Wörterbuch zum Neuen Testament*, which had been produced almost exclusively by German Lutheran scholars,[1] for Lutheran and Catholic interpreters in Germany to launch an ecumenical series of technical commentaries on the New Testament, *Evangelisch-katholischer Kommentar zum Neuen Testament*,[2] and for Lutheran and Catholic editors to produce together the invaluable dictionaries, *Theologisches Wörterbuch zum Alten Testament*[3] and *Exegetisches Wörterbuch zum Neuen Testament*.[4] One could cite other such cooperation in the area of modern biblical interpretation, but what is noteworthy is that such common endeavors have been based in large part on the use of the historical-critical method of biblical interpretation as a tool to arrive at the genuine religious or spiritual sense of the biblical writings that constitute our common heritage. The historical-critical method has often been misunderstood, sometimes being seen only as an end in itself, but when rightly used it has no peer. It is the common use of this method by Catholic and Lutheran members of the dialogue which lies at the root of the biblical section of the statement on "Justification by Faith" presented in this volume.

For the presentation and discussion of the biblical basis of "Justification by Faith" in this seventh round of dialogue a procedure was followed that resembles the one used in the discussion of the New Testament data bearing on "teaching authority and infallibility in the church," the topic of the sixth round. In that instance I, as a Roman Catholic member, was asked to marshal and present what the New Testament might have to say about what was regarded as a peculiarly Catholic concern, teaching authority and infallibility.[5] John Reumann was asked to respond to my presentation,[6] and Msgr. Jerome D. Quinn contributed a further short paper on related topics in the Pastoral Epistles.[7] In this seventh round of the dialogue Reumann was similarly asked to address himself to the biblical basis of what was regarded as a peculiarly Lutheran concern, justification by grace through faith. Whereas the biblical data on teaching authority in the church were somewhat limited and easily handled in one session, the task that confronted Reumann was quite different, for the biblical data on righteousness/justification are of mammoth proportions. Yet he completed his assignment and presented his material in three stages, beginning at Atlanta, Ga., in March 1980, continuing at Gettysburg, Pa., in September 1980, and finishing at Cincinnati, Ohio, in February 1981.[8] I was asked to respond to his presentation, and at each stage I offered a Catholic reaction, but agreed in large part with Reumann's presentation.[9] At the Gettysburg meeting Quinn also made comments on righteousness in the Pastoral Epistles,[10] and Joseph A. Burgess, who was present at all three stages of the discussion, also commented on Reumann's presentation.

Two subsequent papers on aspects of the New Testament data not covered by Reumann were also prepared, and they are incorporated in this volume: J. D. Quinn, "The Scriptures on Merit,"[11] and J. A. Burgess, "Rewards, but in a Very Different Sense."[12]

Because of the length of Reumann's material it became evident that it would not be possible to use it *in extenso* in the common statement on justification eventually to be drafted. After no little discussion in the plenary sessions, it was decided that the highlights of his material would be incorporated into the common statement. They are found in the biblical section of it (§§ 122-49). Consequently, it was agreed that the biblical background for this statement, being so important because of the role that it had played in the historic sixteenth-century debate on justification, should be published separately in its entirety. That is to be found in *"Righteousness" in the New Testament: "Justification" in the United States Lutheran-Roman Catholic Dialogue,* by John Reumann, with responses by Joseph A. Fitzmyer and Jerome D. Quinn.[13] Hence the reader of this present volume will not find herein all the position papers that treated the biblical aspects of the common statement on justification by faith. This brief essay is intended only to explain the connection between the two books, *Justification by Faith* and *"Righteousness" in the New Testament.*

Readers of this volume may recall that in the fifth round of the national dialogue, which issued *Papal Primacy and the Universal Church,*[14] a subsidiary text was published on the New Testament data pertaining to the Petrine role, which was very important for the topic of that round of discussions. It was entitled *Peter in the New Testament: A Collaborative Assessment by Protestant and Roman Catholic Scholars.*[15] Because of the technical nature of the discussions involved it had been decided to leave the preparation of such a study to a special task force. Members of this task force were eleven American New Testament scholars, five Lutheran (J. A. Burgess, K. P. Donfried, K. Froehlich, G. Krodel, and J. Reumann), four Roman Catholic (M. M. Bourke, R. E. Brown, S. Brown, and J. A. Fitzmyer), one Reformed (P. J. Achtemeier), and one Anglican (R. H. Fuller). Only five of these eleven were at the time members of the national Lutheran-Roman Catholic dialogue, but all eleven functioned as members of the task force sponsored by the dialogue itself. Though the materials gathered and discussed in *Peter in the New Testament* were subsequently used by the dialogue members for the common statement on *Papal Primacy and Universal Church*, they were not all discussed in detail at the plenary sessions to the same extent as Reumann's material in *"Righteousness" in the New Testament*. It is important to note this difference of approach in the handling of the New Testament data relevant to the two topics. It was the sentiment of the dialogue group as a whole in this round that the biblical basis of justification, being so important, should not be handled only by a sponsored task force. This accounts, then, for the procedure followed in this round of the dialogue and for the separate publication of *"Righteousness" in the New Testament*. This book, written by Reumann with responses by Quinn and myself, does not represent a collaborative assessment, as did *Peter in the New Testament*. In chapter 1 of the latter book the task force stated, ". . . we must emphasize that it [the book] has emerged as *a collective study*, i.e. a study truly representative of discussions by a group of scholars. Each member of the task force contributed to it in different ways, but the end product is not what any one of us would have written personally."[16] Here it is necessary to draw attention to this difference of approach.[17]

Sections 122-49 of the common statement, "Justification by Faith," give a summary of Reumann's research and of our full debate about it. He and I worked over various drafts of that summary, which were eventually discussed in detail in plenary sessions by all the members of the dialogue. It is, then, a collaborative summary worked out by both exegetes and theologians and serves as an important factor in the common statement. For it builds on the use of the historical-critical method of studying the biblical texts dealing with justification by faith and its relation to the love and good conduct expected of a Christian. It also provides the springboard for our "growing convergences" and the common "declaration."

The summary of the biblical data calls attention to seven areas of common Lutheran and Catholic interpretation that have enabled us to transcend the sixteenth-century polemical stances. First, the summary emphasizes the Old Testament background of the New Testament concept of justification, exploring its varying nuances or uses and setting forth its specific image, forensic or judicial, which Paul and other New Testament writers used to describe the right relationship of human beings to God or to one another. Second, this summary insists on justification

as an early Christian way of summing up a prime effect of Christ's death and resurrection. It is found in the pre-Pauline formulas, creedal and confessional, embedded in various New Testament writings. Third, the biblical summary highlights Paul's adoption of this early formula and also his own specific conception of it. For he not only related justification through Christ Jesus to "the righteousness of God," but saw it as a primary figure among many other images which could be used to express in nonforensic terminology God's salvific activity in Christ Jesus. Paul insisted in a very specific way on justification by grace through faith, on the obedience of faith, and on faith working itself out through love. Though Paul's recognition that human beings will one day have to stand before the judgment seat of Christ to receive good or evil according to what they have done in the body (2 Cor. 5:10) is acknowledged, the summary carefully puts that recognition in the fuller Pauline context of God's gracious justification of human beings that was accomplished "once for all" in Christ Jesus and that is available to those who apprehend its effect through faith. Fourth, these sections of the common statement reckon also with the development of Pauline teaching in the Deutero-Pauline letters, Colossians, Ephesians, and the Pastorals, in which the effects of justification on Christian life are given greater emphasis, "salvation" tends to be substituted for "justification," and the "good works" of believers are put in a new relationship. Fifth, the use of righteousness/justification in other New Testament writings (the Synoptic Gospels, Acts, the Johannine literature, Hebrews, the Petrine letters, and especially Matthew) is briefly summarized. Sixth, the crucial passage in the Letter of James (2:14-26) is put in its proper relationship, not only with the rest of the teaching in James, but also with Paul's teaching, of which it has often been seen as a contradiction. An interpretation of it that is widely used today is adopted as a way of transcending the sixteenth-century debate. Seventh, the notions of merit, recompense, and retribution are explored for the possible relation that they may have to various biblical passages.

In conclusion, it is recognized in this summary that righteousness/justification emerges in Paul not only as an image and concept of prime importance for expressing what God has done in Christ Jesus for the sake of humanity, but even for expressing the gospel. This is not asserted in the sense of affirming some sort of "canon within the canon" but with the recognition "from the exegetical findings we have summarized that the biblical witness to the gospel of God's saving work in Christ is richer and more varied than has been encompassed in either traditional Catholic or Lutheran approaches to justification" (§149).

2

THE SCRIPTURES ON MERIT

Jerome D. Quinn

I. Foreword

It is useful to know in advance the senses in which the terminology for merit can be employed, even though the definitions anticipate to some extent the conclusions of this study. The term *merit* can designate the simply human worth or value of our human acts, a value that can be calculated, sometimes according to human standards of commutative justice. This merit in the eyes of human beings and quite apart from faith and grace occurs throughout the whole secular order, with its wages, prizes, rewards, and the like. It is an object for philosophical study in human ethics. A second, more properly theological use of merit refers to the value or worth in God's eyes of human acts that are the fruit of faith and grace, human acts that receive God's recompense according to his criteria.

In the following study, *merit* and its cognates occur in the latter sense. When the term occurs in the former sense, it will be qualified as "simply" or "merely" or "our own" human merit.

There is no way to assemble a straightforward, terminological profile of *merit* in the Scriptures. As with our modern theological terminology for miracle or conscience, so with *merit* there is no single term and no single concept in the biblical literature that coincide precisely with what Western theologians speak of in terms of merit. The Vulgate itself illustrates why theological analysis and definition of merit are hard to come by. The case with *meritum* is precisely analogous to *miraculum*, not to mention *praemium*. Neither term appears in the Vulgate New Testament. Both occur very rarely in the Latin Old Testament.

In the Vulgate *meritum* occurs only in Sirach and then only three times. However, these occurrences are to be noted, for they indicate the Greek and Hebrew expressions that dictated the Latin *meritum*. In the Latin Sir. 10:31 and 38:17, *secundum meritum* corresponds to what a human being considers *kata tēn axian* (LXX Sir. 10:28; 38:17). The extant Hebrew suggests *produce, fruit,* or *progeny.* In Sir. 16:15, *secundum meritum operum suorum* renders LXX 16:14 *kata ta erga autou* (cf. 16:12). Here God is repaying men for their works (thus the Hebrew). The problem for theologians begins to surface in the Latin version of the Septuagint. Merit is linked to works. A discussion of the relation between works and justification involves whatever we mean by merit. As the Greek *axi-* suggests, what do we really mean by the *worth* or *worthiness* of the acts of human beings? What weight can human deeds have in God's eyes?[1]

The materials for discussion of the Scriptures on merit will be marshaled under three headings. First, there will be a survey of the Scriptures as a whole on merit. Because the witness of the whole collection is to be reviewed, the deuterocanonical books will be included. Second, the specifically Old Testament teaching on merit will be reviewed briefly, with attention as space allows to historical developments (insofar as they are ascertainable and pertinent). Finally, New Testament data pertaining to merit will be considered, again with some attention to the historical setting of these documents and to the other early Christian literature.

II. The Scriptures on Retribution

In the Scriptures as a whole the setting for questions about merit is the broader context of God's recompense or retribution for all human conduct. In this perspective merit and its reward are the obverse of demerit and punishment. A basic conviction that grounds the whole scriptural teaching is that the one God ultimately punishes those who do evil and rewards those who do good. The God who gives human beings commands to act upon reserves ultimately to himself retribution for the actions that he has ordered. Thus the whole question of merit and demerit takes on an eschatological character. The divine recompense for what persons do and fail to do appears fully in the final judgment. The recompense thus involves the whole of human life which in turn cannot be separated from the death which closes off human activities as we know them (see Heb. 9:27-28). Yet proleptic glimpses of eschatological retribution do appear in human history and in the history of believers.

A critical presupposition of the scriptural authors as they discuss recompense is their conviction of the unitary, integral character of human action. The purposeful, internal conception of an activity; the external implementation of that intent; and the effects produced—all are conceived of as a whole with an inner coherence and interdependence that does not permit one really to separate intention, activity, and effects (purpose, practice, and product) any more than one can really separate a birth from a previous conception or a subsequent life (cf. Ps. 7:14 with Jas. 1:14-15). In this problematic, retribution must somehow inhere in the activity itself. Thus the question of merit and demerit cannot be isolated from human purpose and practice. Moreover, that practice cannot be isolated from the different legal systems presupposed by the societies which the biblical authors addressed, not to mention the variety of systems that have proliferated to our own times.

That God ultimately punishes the wicked and rewards the good is the conviction of the Scriptures as a whole. When God does this and how he does it are consequent questions to which biblical authors address themselves. The variety of answers is bewildering. Two principles bring some focus into the analysis of these answers. First and most important, the scriptural language for answering the questions about divine retribution (and thus about merit and demerit) is a notably figurative, metaphorical, and parabolic language. God has a treasury, keeps books, hires and fires, pays wages, harvests crops, herds animals, hands down sentences, gives rewards, prizes, and crowns in athletic contests, bestows inheritances, and the like.[2] The whole complex of human relationships that involve retribution and our human merits and demerits is taken seriously as giving some insight into our personal relationship with one who gives retribution in another order of merit and demerit. The variety and complexity of the comparisons already signal that no one situation in which human retribution is at stake can fully explain how God gives retribution to persons who act for him or against him. Human merit is not always merit in God's eyes; human demerit is not always demerit before God.[3]

The second principle for analyzing the Scriptures as a whole on retribution is a readiness to accept historical developments in the teaching on how God rewards and punishes. Not only are there developments but the Scriptures have preserved evidence for them as well as their patterns or trajectories. To hear the Scriptures historically is also to take seriously the varied geographical and temporal milieux, Semitic, Hellenistic, or Roman, from which the documents came and within which their addressees lived.

III. The Old Testament on Retribution

What does the Old Testament teach about divine recompense? The oldest strata contain the concept in its negative form, i.e., in a context of the punishment that lies in wait for human desires and acts that run counter to God's will and commands for human beings.[4] The *lex talionis* of Israelite civil law, found elsewhere in the ancient Near East,[5] served as a standard and precedent for explaining when and how God's punishment came upon human deeds. Thus recompense is *post factum* in a way that is recognizably equitable and even merciful by some standards, tempering the wildly disproportionate vengeance of Lamech (cf. Gen. 4:23-24 with 4:15). The *lex talionis* also sought to express the inner unity and coherence of a human deed with the divine retribution for it.

With the prophets of the eighth century B.C. and thereafter, the disasters that overtook Israel and Judah were explained as retribution for the sins of the nation (Amos 2:3-16; Tob. 3:3-5). Evil deeds involve the whole community in which they occur and divine retribution accordingly has a corporate aspect. With the Deuteronomic school in particular the conditional character of the divine retribution becomes clearer and with that, the fact that God's retribution is positive as well as negative. He rewards the fulfillment of his commands as he punishes their contravention. Already in the Deuteronomic conceptualization, with carefully balanced blessings for good works and curses for evil deeds, there is a certain scaling back of punishment and an escalation of mercy in divine retribution. Punishment extends over three generations; merciful love for a thousand.[6]

A further refinement of the Old Testament teaching occurs with the dissolution of the kingdoms of Israel and Judah as political entities. It is not only the community, the nation, which receives divine retribution. Individual believers must now come to terms with this teaching. Ontogeny recapitulates phylogeny. The sapiential literature of Israel, particularly the Psalms (*passim*), and the prophet-priest, Ezekiel (18:1-32; cf. Jer. 31:29-30), rearticulate the retribution schema for the deeds of

individual persons, deeds that have their inherent, ineluctable consequences for these same persons. With this concentration upon divine
retribution for individuals, a further problem becomes acute. Why do
individuals who have done good later suffer? Why do those who did
evil later prosper? Job, Psalms, and apocalyptic literature submit answers for this cruel riddle. The solutions range from, "I have never
seen a just man forsaken or his children begging bread" (Ps. 37:25),
through Tobit on the ephemeral character of adversity, Job on a divine
plan and wisdom quite beyond human grasp, the resigned, agnostic
skepticism of Qohelet, the insistence of Sirach upon a future, unspecified
reward, up to an explicit transfer of full divine retribution for human
deeds into the ultimate *post factum*, the order of human existence that
lies beyond the grave.[7] This last development constitutes a "change
into another kind" (*metabasis eis allo genos*), a quantum leap for the
understanding of the *when* and *how* of divine reward or punishment for
the merit or demerit of a person's deeds. On this understanding, human
calculation of merit and demerit becomes impossible. Retribution is in
the hands of God alone. The reward completely transcends all human
merits (cf. Ps. 49:5-9 with 15). Yet this ultimate gift or grace of immortality is the fruit of good acts (Wis. 3:14-15). In fact, it is precisely
the godless who have no grasp of the mystery of immortality, who have
no anticipation of "the wages of holiness" (*misthon*), who do not reckon
with "the prize for stainless souls." "But the righteous live forever,
and their reward (*misthos*) is with the Lord, and the Most High takes
care of them. Therefore they will receive a glorious crown and a beautiful diadem from the hand of the Lord, because with his right hand he
will cover them, and with his arm he will shield them."[8]

If immortality substantially answers the question about when the *post
factum* of divine recompense occurs, it leaves open the question of how.
To that question some in Israel responded by affirming that the flesh,
in which human beings did good and suffered for doing it, will be
rewarded by resurrection in the order of existence that follows human
life in this world. In that order, "some [will rise] to eternal life and
some to shame and eternal contempt" (Dan. 12:2; 2 Macc. 7:9-14, 23).

IV. The New Testament on Retribution

In the New Testament the perspective on merit broadens still further.
Belief in the fact of divine recompense for human acts remains an intact
constant. The acts of Jesus and in particular his death reveal that human

acts can bear a value and instrumental power before God that was hardly suspected previously. The Son of God assumed the *"schema"* of human nature ("being found in form [*schemati*] as a human being," Phil. 2:7c), and thus he was enabled to "merit." The Father accepted the death of his Son as the source of life for believers. The crucified Jesus has been made "our wisdom, our righteousness and sanctification and redemption" (1 Cor. 1:30).[9]

This Pauline theme is reorchestrated in Eph. 2:1-10 with an emphasis on the figurative language of wealth for describing what "the God who is rich in mercy" has done for sinners by Christ's death and rising, "that in the ages to come he might show the immeasurable wealth of his grace in kindness toward us in Christ Jesus."[10] The merciful and immeasurably precious acts of Christ were not called forth by our own merits but presupposed in fact our demerits.[11] Those same acts of Christ in God's plan make possible "good works" (Eph. 2:10).

Granted that human merits did not elicit the redemptive acts of Jesus and granted the effect of those acts on those who put their faith in him, how is one to evaluate the human activities that follow upon baptismal faith and that precede individual human death? Do a Christian's acts after baptism have a genuine, serious relationship to his lot after death? The New Testament and Paul specifically see no mutually exclusive contradiction between justification by faith in Christ and a final divine recompense that takes very seriously indeed the good and evil works of the believer.

Rom. 2:1-11, with full deliberation, puts the retribution schema (2:6-7) into the presuppositions for understanding the apostolic exposition of justification by faith. The parenesis of Rom. 14:10-12 proposes the principle of ultimate divine recompense as an irrefutable argument.[12] 2 Cor. 5:10 teaches: "For we must all appear before the judgment seat of Christ, so that each one may receive good or evil according to what he has done in the body" (cf. 1 Cor. 4:4-5; 2 Cor. 11:15). The Lord has a reward for the good work of a believer (1 Cor. 15:58), but there are no grounds for human pride and boasting here (1 Cor. 1:31; 2 Cor. 10:17) since this work is done "in the Lord" who gives both the inclination and the power to do it (Phil. 2:12b-13). All such work, even that of an apostle, is destined for God's judgment and differing rewards and punishments (1 Cor. 3:10-15). The apostle as well as those who have believed in his gospel work out their salvation in sober realization of the ultimate seriousness of that work (cf. Phil. 2:12b with 1 Cor. 9:27). If from one aspect the final reward differs as the lives of those who receive it differ (cf. 1 Cor. 15:41; Eph. 6:8), from another point of view the reward for good works is simply eternal life. Rom. 6:23 does not contradict that in saying: "The wages of sin is death but the free gift (*charisma*) of God is eternal life in Christ Jesus our Lord." The *charis* described here is nothing less than the antecedent, all-sufficient, invaluable act of Christ; the ultimate effect of this *charis*, i.e., the *charisma*,[13] is the life into which the final resurrection ushers the believer; and that final effect involves the whole existence of the justified believer, including his good acts performed in the flesh before his death.

Can more be said about the intrinsic link between the believer's good acts and the antecedent and sustaining gracious acts of Christ? How do the believer's acts issue from justifying grace and into eternal life? It is in this connection that the New Testament uses parabolic language from biological growth. For Paul, "Whatever a man sows, that he will also reap. . . . He who sows into the Spirit will reap from the Spirit eternal life. And let us not grow weary in well-doing, for in due season we shall reap, if we do not lose heart" (Gal. 6:7-9). "The fruit (*karpos*, harvest) of the Spirit is love, joy, peace. . ." (Gal. 5:22).[14] The Spirit of Christ thus initiates, sustains, and perfects the good human acts which issue in resurrection and eternal life. Another figure of growth in union with Christ appears in Eph. 4:15 and Col. 2:19. In this figurative type of exposition, the act of Christ and the acts of believers are understood as a living, organic whole in which the believer's personal, individual history is integrated into the history of his Lord who has come and will return.[15]

How is one to conceive the reward in which good acts issue? Again the New Testament terminology is figurative and connotative rather than denotative and literalistic. One of the most notable comparisons already appears in the Pauline tradition and presumes the games and contests of the Hellenistic world. The Greeks introduced a fiercely competitive atmosphere into their community life, "ever to be best and to surpass others" (*Iliad* 6.208 = 11.784). There were competitions and prizes for races, wrestling, and discus throwing; for speeches, songs, dances, and plays; for beauty; for everything one wanted to encourage, if Xenophon is to be believed.[16] The risks that this poses for human harmony were acknowledged, but there was no inclination to cut back.[17] Such competitions occurred under the eyes of judges and with strict rules. They were always religious events and under religious auspices in the Hellenistic world.

Paul saw himself, as a Jew and as a Christian, as fiercely competitive (cf. Gal. 1:13-14; Phil. 3:4-7 with 1 Cor. 15:10; 2 Cor. 11:22-29). He took up the Hellenistic language of the contest without a qualm and exploited it for describing how believers, including the apostle himself, competed for the goal and prize and crown that lay in wait at the end of the Christian contest (1 Cor. 9:24-27; Phil. 3:12-14; Rom. 9:16). In one sense the apostle had already received his crown, his reward, in this life in his converts (1 Thess. 2:19; Phil. 4:1). In another sense these churches were the proleptic sign and pledge of the crown that remained in the judge's hands until the race was over.

The Pauline tradition of 2 Tim. 4:6-8 has the apostle, on the verge of death, assert: "I have contended in the contest that matters. I have run the whole track. I have kept faith. Whatever happens there lies in store for me the crown of the upright life with which the upright judge, the Lord, will recompense me on that Day—and of course not only me but all who have their hearts set on his revelation." The athletic imagery here ought to be correlated with 2 Tim. 2:3-6 where the apostolic work is compared to the tasks of the soldier (cf. 1 Tim. 1:18) and farmer as well as the athlete. "The crown of the upright life" has an ambivalence that suggests the mystery of the passage of uprightness in this life into another order in which the risen Lord crowns it.[18]

The parenesis of 1 Tim. 6:17-19 charges wealthy Christians to set their hearts on God, "to do good, to become wealthy in fine deeds, to be munificent, sharing all around, making their deposits in an excellent fund [or foundation] for the future, so that they can lay hold on the life which deserves that name." The retribution schema in Rom. 2:5 has the evil man treasuring up eschatological judgment for himself as here in 1 Timothy the generous believer's acts become an investment for another life.

As second generation Christians gathered and recorded their traditions about the words and deeds of Jesus in the gospel documents, there is no lack of teaching about the divine retribution that awaits human acts. The documents retain the vivid apocalyptic atmosphere and imagery of early first-century Palestine, with their unquestioning commitment to the ultimate vindication of God's justice in his final punishment of the wicked and his reward of those who have suffered and lost all for his sake. Jesus takes up and teases out this schema in paradoxical ways. The beatitudes illustrate one of his approaches (Matt. 5:3-12; Luke 6:20-26). Another is the reversal of the wildly hyperbolic revenge schema of Lamech (Gen. 4:24) in the equally overwhelming and more than human forgiveness schema of Matt. 18:22 (cf. Luke 17:4). Moreover, the disciples who have left anything for the sake of Jesus will receive a hundredfold of everything "and in the age to come eternal life" (Mark 10:29-30 and parallels). The judgment scene in Matt. 25:31-46 probes even more deeply the real link between human acts and divine recompense yet with no proportion measurable in terms of strict justice. Retribution is broached from several different angles in the Matthean parables of the unforgiving servant (Matt. 18:23-35), the laborers in the vineyard (Matt. 20:1-16), and the talents (Matt. 25:14-30). The comparison of the future reward with money surfaces in another form in Mark 10:21 (and parallels), where the prospective disciple is to sell his possessions to have "treasure in heaven" (cf. Matt. 6:19-20; Luke 12:33-34). The exchange of the visible for the invisible is notable in this connection, for it leads one beyond the order in which human competition and calculation can occur into an order that is directly and totally at God's disposal. The parables of growth and harvest from a variety of aspects illustrate the ways in which human acts constitute an inseparable and serious aspect of the divine act that brings God's kingdom (thus Mark 4:1-32; Matt. 13:3-43; Luke 8:4-15; 13:18-19; cf. Rev. 14:15).

The Johannine corpus differs from the synoptic tradition in its articulation of divine judgment and the retribution schema for human deeds. Thus the traditional schema surfaces in John 5:25-29 (cf. 1 John 2:28-29) but it must be interpreted in the light of John 3:19-21, where good deeds "have been wrought in God." The passing contrast between "working" for the bread that one eats for human nourishment and working for "the food which endures to eternal life, which the Son of man will give you" (John 6:27; cf. 2 John 8) is not as significant for the Johannine understanding of merit as the great parable of the vine and the branches where the disciples really bear and ought to bear fruit, but never apart from Jesus, the vine (John 15:1-8).

The Letter to the Hebrews has no illusions about the relation of "dead works" (Heb. 6:1; 9:14)[19] to "the rest" that God has promised to believers, a rest that nevertheless they may fail to attain (Heb. 4:1; cf. 2:2-3; 3:12; 10:26-31). The language of growth and bearing fruit is used as in the synoptic tradition (Heb. 6:7-8; 12:11). More striking is: "For God is not so unjust as to overlook your work and the love which you showed for his name when you ministered to the saints, as you still are doing" (Heb. 6:10). In Heb. 10:32-36 believers do good works and endure losses with a view to "a better possession and an abiding one." This confidence has "a great reward. . . . For you have need of endurance, so that you do the will of God and receive [*komisēsthe*; cf.

11:13,19,39-40; 2 Cor. 5:10] the promise.'' In his great panegyric of the faith of Moses, the author asserts: ''He considered abuse suffered for Christ greater wealth than the treasures of Egypt, for he looked to the reward'' (Heb. 11:26). Faith demands that one believes there is a God and that he is the rewarder of those who seek him (Heb. 11:6).

The final volume of the Christian canon is an apocalyptic compendium of Christian belief in and hope for the final judgment and the retribution that ineluctably accompanies the ultimate divine intervention in the world as we know it. The succession of visionary images that resist our understanding and elude our grasp while remaining haunting and evocative is an attempt to articulate the ineffable divine recompense that awaits every human person and the whole society that we constitute. Within that society Christians have been caught as if in a spider's web which only God can and will tear apart. In the meantime the sufferings of believers, even to death, are not meaningless or empty: ''I heard a voice saying, 'Write this: Blessed are the dead who die in the Lord henceforth.' 'Blessed indeed,' says the Spirit, 'that they may rest from their labors, for their works follow them' '' (Rev. 14:13). After the closing vision of the heavenly city that lies beyond the present human order, the prophecy returns to this present society in which the wicked are still to act wickedly and the just to act justly (Rev. 22:11). In this order the risen Jesus, origin and end of all, announces: ''Behold, I am coming soon and my retribution [*ho misthos mou*; cf. 11:18] is with me, to repay each one as his work is'' (Rev. 22:12).[20]

V. Summary

The language for merit cannot be divorced from the scriptural language for the retribution that God gives to human works. God's revealed will for human beings is intended to evoke a human response, external as well as internal, corporate as well as individual. This human response, in all its aspects, comes finally under God's judgment for the reward or punishment that God has also willed.

This retribution schema becomes incarnate in Jesus, to whom the Father reveals his good will and to which Jesus responds by obedience ''to him who judges justly'' (1 Pet. 2:23), even to death on the cross. This was not simply the response of an individual human being but that of the head of a group, one ''who for the joy that was set before him, endured the cross, despising the shame'' (Heb. 12:2). The resurrection and exaltation of Jesus are the divine recompense for his sacrifice (cf.

Heb. 11:19), and his members who share his attitude (cf. Phil. 2:5) will share his recompense (cf. Phil. 3:10-11; 1 Pet. 4:13). In this perspective, when one turns to the works of believers and members of Christ, the head, there is no longer a question of dead works and merely human merit. Christian acts are done in Christ and thus are living works, which have their life from Christ and his Spirit (cf. Gal. 6:7-8; Rom. 8:1-17). The value of such works, and thus their merit, is rooted in the vital gifts of Jesus and the Spirit. To the extent that these acts do not derive from Christ and the Spirit, they bring not reward but punishment.

Human acts have an integrity and unity that proceeds from their internal conception through their execution into the result obtained. This inner coherence and order appear also in the human acts which God wills and which he recompenses. Just as the divine will and word are in some sense always antecedent to the human response, so the recompense is always in some way *post factum*. Because it is so, questions of recompense, and thus of merit and demerit, become eschatological questions about death, judgment, resurrection, and eternal reward or punishment. Like other eschatological questions, those about merit ultimately transcend human calculations and categories. As the precise day and hour and mode of judgment are unknown to us while the fact remains certain, so beyond the fact of God's recompense for the works that he commands and sustains, precise knowledge is hard to come by. What can be known comes through a broad spectrum of figures, comparisons, and parabolic images that are by definition concerned with an order that lies beyond human science. The many images suggest that the reality being described is both very much part of the fabric of human existence as we know it and still ultimately incalculable by human means. The way we take merit out of this life bears more than a passing resemblance to the way in which the kingdom of God has come into our life.

From one point of view, all human activity, including Christian activity in the order of grace, begins in, is sustained by, and ends in God. The parabolic language of seeding, growth, fruition, and harvest illuminates this aspect of merit and reward, for the emphasis lies primarily on the creative power and plan of God in the whole range of human acts.

From a second, complementary point of view that stands always in function of the preceding, a human person intends, does, and gains something by his activity. In this connection the figurative language of competitions, contractual relations, commutative justice, wages, and prizes is particularly helpful. Personal, responsible, reciprocal relationships between Christians and their God are thus emphasized. Christian works are recognized as serious, consequential, weighty matters and rescued from frivolity and pointless triviality. The justice of God is vindicated in the reward that he bestows on the action that he commands.

The parabolic language prepares one for a certain paradoxical incalculability at every level. All that human beings consider their own merit is not necessarily merit in God's eyes. Not all that persons reckon as unworthy and punishable is necessarily demerit before God. Finally, the mercy and love of God issue in a recompense that is as far beyond human calculation as is the person who bestows it. In fact that recompense is, in the last analysis, God himself and his Son (cf. Pss. 16:5-6; 73:23-28; 142:5; Phil. 1:20-23).

3

REWARDS, BUT IN A VERY DIFFERENT SENSE

Joseph A. Burgess

Is it not true that the Bible states that judgment will be according to the works a person has done? Is not the "iniquity of the fathers" visited "upon the children to the third and fourth generation" (Deut. 5:9)? Will God "not requite man according to his work" (Prov. 24:12)? Do not the two servants who use their talents receive rewards, and does not the servant who has only one talent and does not use it receive punishment (Matt. 25:14-30)? Does not the Lord at the judgment "repay every one for what he has done" (Rev. 22:12)? Even Paul writes: "For he will render to every man according to his works" (Rom. 2:6; cf. 14:10-12; 1 Cor. 3:1-11; 4:4-5; 15:41, 58; 2 Cor. 3:18; 4:17; 5:10; 9:6; 11:15; Gal. 6:7-8). Is it not therefore obvious that the Bible, taken as a whole, says that ultimately God rewards the good and punishes the wicked?

Lutherans would seem to have a particular problem at this point. They have been renowned for firmly believing that justification is by faith alone, not by works. Faith has results, to be sure, which are works, but such works do not "merit" salvation. Yet at the same time, according to the Lutheran Confessions, "rewards," a term closely associated with "merit," clearly accrue to the Christian. In fact, rewards can be expected by the non-Christian in this life. And for the Christian "good works are meritorious," although not for salvation, leading to physical and spiritual rewards in this life and in the life to come. "There will be distinctions in the glory of the saints."[1]

Is this not simply common sense? "Laws being useless without a sanction," in a world of laws rewards and punishments are not only expected but demanded. "Both on religious grounds and on grounds of expediency it is eminently desirable that he who has been faithful in a few things should be made ruler over many things."[2] It has therefore seemed self-evident to most that in the afterlife there will be degrees of reward and punishment in heaven and hell corresponding to what a person has done on earth.

But is the Bible simply common sense or perhaps common sense spiritualized? Does the Bible not have a unique message to offer, a message not based on common sense or even on claims made by any other religion? What has happened to justification by faith? Can judgment according to works and justification by faith be reconciled? Or is no reconciliation possible?

I. The Old Testament

The Old Testament needs to be seen in all of its variety and complexity. On the one hand, it does at times state that God ultimately punishes those who do evil and rewards those who do good. On the other hand, at times the law of recompense is at least questioned. For this reason the law of recompense cannot be said to pervade the Old Testament but must be understood as part of a broader context.

What is this broader context? To be sure, Deuteronomy states that the "iniquity of the fathers" would be visited "upon the children to the third and fourth generation" (Deut. 5:9), although this tradition was corrected by Ezekiel in order to uphold God's justice: "The person who sins shall die" (18:2), not someone who had not sinned personally. Yet neither the individual nor the individual's children seemed in fact to be rewarded or punished according to the law of recompense. Evil seemed to prosper, and good seemed to go unrewarded. Old Testament writers struggled with this difficulty in a variety of ways.

Klaus Koch[3] theorizes that "recompensatory" thinking only entered Old Testament theology with the Septuagint translators. The law of recompense is based on the schema that there exists an objective norm which measures one's actions and then a "judge" who doles out rewards and punishments according to what one has done. Instead, Koch points out, in the Old Testament one is entrapped in a powerful sphere created by one's deeds. The deed is the seed which inevitably, fatefully bears fruit. This does not involve juridical conceptions. Yahweh simply leaves one to the results of one's deeds. For example: "He who digs a pit will fall into it, and a stone will come back upon him who starts it rolling" (Prov. 26:27; cf. 28:10,18; 29:6; Gen. 9:6; Rev. 13:10). This is a widely held perception outside of Scripture as well: "We but teach bloody instructions, which, being taught, return to plague the inventor" (Shakespeare, *Macbeth*, I, 7).

Koch's thesis has unleashed wide debate.[4] It is objected that Koch has not brought out that in the Old Testament the personal God plays a decisive role even in those actions which are left to work out their own results and that everything in the Old Testament centers on and is influenced by the cult. Koch has modified his point to some degree,[5] but through this debate the diversity of Old Testament material dealing with "recompense" has come to be more widely recognized.

The original version of Ecclesiastes is skeptical about the conviction that God ultimately punishes those who do evil and rewards those who do good. For example: "There is a vanity which takes place on earth, that there are righteous men to whom it happens according to the deeds of the wicked, and there are wicked men to whom it happens according to the deeds of the righteous. I said that this also is vanity" (8:14; cf. 7:15; 9:1-6). As Hengel puts it, death " . . . brings all the speculations of earlier wisdom about a just retribution to nothing. . . . All that is left for man, therefore, is a 'resigned' attitude of *'fear of God'* in face of the incomprehensible rule of the divine plan. . ." (cf. 2:12-17; 3:19-21, 14-15).[6] Later redactors, to be sure, added two epilogues (12:9-11, 12-14) and perhaps other material in order to try to make Ecclesiastes orthodox, but the resigned skepticism of the original author remains.

A very different kind of questioning of the law of recompense is found in the book of Job. God's ways are beyond human understanding, and even a blameless person such as Job may not be rewarded, but the faithful person can still know God personally (40:8-9; 42:2-6). In a similar fashion several wisdom psalms struggle with the fact that the evil prosper and the good suffer, concluding finally with confidence in God's justice and even with hope that those who trust in God will continue to be with him after death (Pss. 37:27-8; 49:15; 73:26). Only in late, apocalyptic passages, however, is there a clear indication of a resurrection in which the good will be rewarded and the evil punished (Isa. 26:19; Dan. 12:2).

More important is the fact that the broader context is shaped by God's electing love, for example, as seen in choosing Abraham and in rescuing the people of Israel from Egypt. From a human point of view no reason can be given for God's election. Abraham and the people of Israel had done nothing to merit being elected. Nor are they, once elected, rewarded according to the law of recompense, at least not as understood from a human point of view. "He does not deal with us according to our sins" (Ps. 103:10; cf. Hos. 11:1-9). God's electing love not only surpasses but bursts every human attempt to calculate what the law of recompense means for God.

What then is to be done with passages clearly stating God will "requite man according to his work" (Prov. 24:12)? Such passages must be taken seriously and understood in their historical contexts because they are part of the canon. Obviously the same must be said for Ecclesiastes, Job, and Psalm 49:15 in their historical contexts. Not only does the Old Testament include the law of recompense, but it also includes material questioning the law of recompense and describing God's electing love. How is it possible to respect the variety and diversity of Old Testament materials and yet to discern a theological unity within the Old Testament? Presuppositions about development and the unitary nature of human action in the Old Testament must not displace Old Testament variety and diversity. Is there not also a danger that the "canonical" validity of material questioning the law of recompense depends on the fact that such material is no longer historically understood?[7] Nor is this a uniquely Lutheran problem. As Beumer has pointed out, Catholics are also faced with difficult questions when determining whether material is canonical.[8] In any case, it hardly seems possible to say without major qualification that the law of recompense pervades the Old Testament. On the other hand, Christians have traditionally held that God's electing love in the Old Testament is central because it foreshadows God's love in Christ, which grounds all revelation.

II. The New Testament

But is not, as is sometimes claimed, Christ's love, particularly his obedient love even unto death, rewarded by resurrection and exaltation, thus showing that good human actions can be meritorious in an astounding fashion? Does this not prove that the law of divine recompense continues into the New Testament?

One theory of atonement is the satisfaction theory, associated historically with Pope Gregory I and Anselm of Canterbury. Attempts have been made to establish a New Testament basis for this theory, but usually such attempts confuse it with New Testament ideas of propitiatory atonement. The problem with the satisfaction theory is that it is docetic. Nothing that a human being does, even the greatest sacrifice, is more than what is owed God, and therefore God does not have to reward anything a person does. Nor can anything a person does be transferred to someone else, for God wants a person's own obedience, not someone else's. Jesus, since he is truly human, gives his father the loving obedience that he as son owes his father. It is true that in the centuries immediately following the Reformation Lutheran theologians continued to make use of the satisfaction theory even though it was inappropriate to combine it with justification by faith. More recent Lutheran theologians use language describing Christ taking our place (*propter Christum*), but such language does not imply Christ meriting our salvation.[9] Furthermore, as Schmaus, a Catholic theologian, puts it: "Because of God's transcendence and the resultant inequality between God and man, merit in the strict sense of the word cannot occur in man in his relationship to God."[10] And any parallel between reward for Jesus' actions and reward for actions by all other human beings disappears because Jesus was without sin. All other human beings sin, and everything they do is contaminated by sin.

Paul

Even Paul, it is claimed, holds that judgment will be according to the works a person has done. The first paragraph of this essay contains a list of the disputed passages. How is it possible to reconcile these passages with his clear statement that justification is by faith, not works (Rom. 4:5)? This question has been answered in at least ten different ways:

1. This is simply an unresolved contradiction in Paul which we today have to accept. Paul had no difficulty in holding the two together without feeling inconsistent, and it would be a mistake for us to try to apply a psychological or any other kind of explanation (Deissmann, Filson, H. J. Holtzmann, Joest, Lohmeyer, J. Müller, A. Schlatter, J. Weiss, Räisänen).

2. Paul had an unstable temperament. At one point he would write one way, and at another another, for he was not able to think consistently (Dove, Windisch, Wrede).

3. Judgment by works was a remnant of Jewish thinking which Paul fell back into, partly because his theological formulations were inadequate and possibly because judgment by works was a useful pedagogical support for his ethics (Bousset, H. Braun, Cohu, Feine, Goguel, H. J. Holtzmann, Pfleiderer, Pott, Weinel, Wetter, Wrede).

4. Paul progressed in his theology, either moving from the narrow Jewish doctrine of judgment by works to the broad view of justification by faith for all (Pott) or from a mechanical view of final retribution to a more spiritual understanding of religion (Wetter).

5. Paul's statements about judgment by works are purely hypothetical, particularly in the first part of his epistle to the Romans. He is arguing from a pre-Christian standpoint in order to show that the Jews face judgment even if there were no gospel and the law could be fulfilled (just as in Romans 7 the non-Christian world is looked at from a Christian point of view) (J. Knox, Lietzmann, Lüdemann, Sickenberger).

6. Judgment by works only has to do with degrees of blessedness in heaven (Holsten, Kabisch, Kühl), or, there are three kinds of judgment, one which determines who is truly Christian, one which annihilates the non-Christian, and one by works which determines how Christian the Christian has been (Mattern).

7. Judgment by works is to be added to justification by faith. Faith is the first work, but other works must follow, or, first there is justification which is forensic and later justification which is moral. Justification is therefore not a legal fiction, for through his emphasis on judgment by works Paul indicates that faith must be active (F. C. Baur, Donfried, Ernesti, Haufe, Jacoby, Jeremias, Lipsius, Lütgert, Lyonnet, Sanday-Headlam, Sanders, Titius, Weinel, B. Weiss, A. Zahn).

8. The ideal is justification by faith, but in fact Christians still sin. It is thus necessary to drill into Christians the importance of living as Christians by bringing in judgment according to works (A. Ritschl, Teichmann, Wernle, Windisch).

9. Justification by faith and judgment by works belong together, just as indicative and imperative (*Gabe* and *Aufgabe*) belong together. Justification by faith must not be made subordinate to judgment according to works; instead, everything must be seen in light of justification by faith, for the one who gives the gift (*Gabe*) is also the one who carries out the task (*Aufgabe*) and who then judges at every moment whether the individual has lived according to God's will or not. Yet judgment is the presupposition for justification, for the justifying God carries out his own judgment by doing himself what he demands of the individual (Bultmann, G. Bornkamm, H. Braun, Calvin, H. Cremer, Jüngel, Käsemann, Luther, Oltmanns, A. Schlatter, Synofzik).

10. Form criticism and tradition criticism make it possible to understand what Paul meant by using traditional materials pointing to rewards and punishments at the last judgment. It is not the simple fact that Paul used such materials which is decisive, but rather how Paul interpreted these materials. What additions did Paul make to traditional formulations? What function did these formulations have in their immediate context and, more importantly and finally, in the larger context of Paul's

theology? This investigation demonstrates that by means of his theology of justification by faith Paul radically reinterprets traditional materials which describe a last judgment according to works.

First of all, judgment by works never becomes an independent theme in Paul's theology the way, for example, the resurrection becomes an independent theme. Second, judgment materials are used in a very disparate fashion. God, Christ, angels, and even Christians become the judge at the last judgment. The standard by which people are finally judged can be their works, correct worship, keeping God's commands, and their attitude toward the gospel. The cause of final damnation is Satan and of final salvation is God and Christ, even though each individual is responsible for his or her own actions. Christians seem to escape the final judgment, yet some passages expressly state that all will come before the final judgment. Such disparity in using these materials shows that Paul is using them for his own purposes; he has reinterpreted his materials.

For example, in 2 Cor. 5:10 Paul has added "in the body" to traditional judgment material in order to combat the fact that the Corinthians were disparaging present existence in the body. In the traditional table of vices there is a double pattern of recompense, but Paul has modified the pattern so that the wages of sin is, as is usual, death, but the free gift of God (not: the wages of good works) is eternal life (Rom. 6:23). The "farmer's axiom" that what one sows produces what one reaps (Gal. 6:7) is not used to prove that one's deeds will produce corresponding results but is reinterpreted by means of Paul's well-known "flesh-spirit" antithesis in order to admonish the Galatians to keep the eschatological *kairos* in mind. The Christological statement of the Hellenistic church, "Jesus the one delivering us from the wrath to come" (1 Thess. 1:10), is reinterpreted in Rom. 5:9-10 so that the basis for future salvation is the justification which took place through Christ's death and resurrection (cf. Rom. 8:31-9).

No doubt Paul often does use traditional "judgment" material to support ethical admonitions, but this is only one of several methods he uses to support ethical admonitions, such as the Christ event itself, baptism, the body of Christ, missionary concerns, the imminent end, the Old Testament law, commandments of Christ, and pragmatic grounds. It cannot be denied that he does use traditional "judgment" materials, yet he uses them within the larger context of justification by faith. Such justification and such faith, however, presuppose responsible lives and continuous judgment of these lives by the one who justifies (Synofzik, Luz).[11]

One may quarrel with such typologies, claiming they do not cover all the options or they omit certain theologians. Nor are all of the options as acceptable today as several decades ago. The fact is that responsible theologians doing responsible work differ on how to understand Paul even though they may agree on many exegetical details. A striking parallel is the work done by a team of Lutheran and Roman Catholic exegetes on Peter in the New Testament and then on Mary in the New Testament. In spite of the fact they could agree and even agree to disagree on much of the material, finally they could not agree on the theological implications of their work together and had to admit that later developments influence how the New Testament is read.[12]

Lutherans hold, to be sure, that they base their understanding of "rewards" on Scripture, particularly on Paul. This does not mean that all Lutherans interpret Paul in exactly the same way or that this Lutheran claims to speak for all Lutherans. But there is a Lutheran stance, summed up in the slogan "justification by faith," and most Lutherans therefore, even while disputing certain points, will take the general approach described in the following pages.

Through baptism Christians have received the Holy Spirit (Rom. 8:9-10,14-16; 2 Cor. 1:22; 5:5), yet Christians continue to sin. How is such a contradiction possible? What sort of sin is this? Do sins committed after baptism have a causal relationship to one's lot after death? Can the Christian do good which merits reward?

Paul writes of sin in the singular except for places where he probably is using citations or liturgical material (cf. Rom. 4:25; 11:27; 1 Cor. 15:3,17; Gal. 1:4).[13] Sin in the singular is an arena in which we are caught, a power to which we are enslaved (Rom. 6:6,16,20; Gal. 3:22), the "flesh" (Rom. 8:7).[14] The "flesh" is made up of "passions and desires" (Gal. 5:24; cf. Eph. 2:3) and is equated by Paul with "desires" (Rom. 7:7). The root of sin is "boasting," self-assertion, self-exaltation; this must not, of course, be confused with a psychological understanding of sin, for the issues are theological: "What have you that you did not receive? If then you received it, why do you boast as if it were not a gift?" (1 Cor. 4:7). Thus no human being can "boast in the presence of God" (1 Cor. 1:29; cf. Rom. 3:27; Gal. 6:14). At times Paul can use "boasting" in a positive sense: "Let him who boasts, boast of the Lord" (2 Cor. 10:17; cf. 1 Cor. 1:31; Rom. 5:3,11), and even in a paradoxical sense: "If I must boast, I will boast of the things that show my weakness" (2 Cor. 11:30; cf. 12:9; Rom. 5:2). But basically "boasting" is the sin of self-reliance, synonymous with "putting one's confidence in the flesh" and the opposite of "boasting in Christ Jesus" (Phil. 3:3).

Yet after baptism we are free from sin (Rom. 6:22), although we sin nevertheless. Christians "sin daily and deserve nothing but punishment" according to Luther's Small Catechism.[15] Is sin after baptism something less or other than sin before baptism? Or, once baptized, has sin been conquered so that a person can never really fall away from Christ? Lutherans hold that sin is truly present, but if the Holy Spirit and faith are present, sin does not rule; when, however, holy people fall into open sin, faith and the Holy Spirit have departed. But at the same time: "If we say we have no sin, we deceive ourselves" (1 John 1:8).[16] Luther used the famous slogan, "sinner and justified at the same time" (*simul peccator et iustus*), to describe the status of the Christian before the parousia.[17]

Paul does not, of course, use the formula, *simul iustus et peccator*, but the cumulative effect of what he understands by sin in the Christian life points to an understanding of sin as real, active, dangerous, and ultimately deadly, and therefore to a situation properly described by *simul iustus et peccator*.

1. Paul admonishes Christians not to sin. Just as he admonishes Christians to imitate Christ and Paul, he also specifically admonishes Christians not to sin (e.g., Rom. 6:12-13; Gal. 5:21).

2. The "desires" which continue after baptism are still desires which are sin and of the flesh. This can be said without recourse to Rom. 7:7-25, which is widely conceded, especially since Kümmel's monograph on the subject,[18] to refer to life before becoming a Christian. Writing to Christians, Paul admonishes: "Walk by the Spirit and do not fulfill the desire of the flesh. For the flesh lusts [or: desires] against the Spirit, and the Spirit against the flesh, for these are opposed to each other, so that you do not do those things you would" (Gal. 5:16-17; cf. 5:24-25). Roman Catholics, to be sure, understand that sins after baptism are the consequence of concupiscence, which is not real sin, although it comes from sin and inclines toward sin (DS 1515).

3. Christians can and do sin. Immorality is present in Corinth such as is not found among the pagans; this person is to be delivered "to Satan for the destruction of the flesh, that his spirit may be saved in the day of the Lord Jesus" (1 Cor. 5:5). Just as the elect in the Old Testament could be rejected in spite of their divine election, so too Christians can fall if they sin, Paul warns (1 Cor. 10:1-12; cf. Rom. 11:20-1; 13:12; 14:15; Phil. 3:18-19, if Christians are meant). In a similar fashion Luther commented on Gal. 2:16: "In addition, we are sometimes forsaken by the Holy Spirit, and we fall into sins, as did Peter, David, and other saints."[19]

4. Paul uses both the indicative and the imperative, which is simply another way of expressing the paradox of living in two aeons at the same time. There is a dialectic of death and life, faith and sight (2 Cor. 4:8-11,16-18; 6:4-10; Rom. 8:10; 1 Cor. 13:12). And yet more is involved,[20] for Rom. 8:18-27 stands in a dialectical relationship to Gal. 6:15 and 2 Cor. 5:17: precisely in our helplessness and weakness can the glory of God be found, precisely in the cross is grace and strength (cf. 2 Cor. 4:7; 12:7-9). But this dialectic is also at the same time the dialectic between flesh and Spirit (Gal. 5:16-17).[21] Paul has a dialectical eschatology.

5. Christians die. This means that not only is there a tension between flesh and Spirit, but they are mutually exclusive (*totus iustus/totus peccator*). "Sin carries death within it. Death is present as that wherein it 'lives' and therefore as that wherein its 'life' is known (R. 5:21). Death is its power. . . . In death sin achieves its being in a very real sense."[22] Death is sin's intention, its hidden entelechy. "At the same time it is the form of sin's rule and the proof of the sinfulness of sin"[23] (cf. Rom. 5:14,17; 6:16,23; 8:2; 1 Cor. 15:26,56).   .

What does this discussion about sin have to do with eternal rewards and punishments? In 1521 Luther, admittedly in a polemic stance because the Roman Catholic Church had excommunicated him, wrote: "No one should doubt that all our good works are mortal sins, and so they will be judged by God's judgment and severity and will not be accepted as good solely by grace."[24] Because Luther took sin seriously, eternal rewards for good works could only be rewards in a very different sense. But Luther's view of sin was no more radical than Paul's, as has been indicated above. What Luther did was to restate Paul for the sixteenth century.[25] In fact, it might be said that Luther brought to full clarity what Paul meant.[26]

Yet someone may object that Paul uses language implying eternal rewards. "The decisive thing is that the doctrine of judgment according to works not be ranked above justification but conversely be understood in light of it."[27] Justification by faith does not, of course, exclude works, but such works have to be seen in the perspective of justification. What does this mean? As sinners we are condemned, and God judges us. But God also justifies us, and the gift and the giver are one; such justification actually takes place. At the same time (*simul*) God the judge cannot be separated from God who is grace; the righteousness of God which we receive as a gift through faith is a power active in the present calling us constantly to responsibility, and to that extent every day is the last judgment.[28] It is God who is active in our responsibility. As a result, the word "reward" takes on a very different connotation from the usual sense of recompense. "Reward" is the surprising, incalculable gift God makes, not the price one receives for one's work (Rom. 6:23).[29]

Paul describes the whole process in summary fashion: "Work out your own salvation with fear and trembling, for God is at work in you, both to will and to work for his good pleasure" (Phil. 2:12-13).[30] The basis is what God does. Because God does everything, therefore we have to do everything. And we shall receive everything. Does he not give us all good things, summed up in his love (Rom. 8:32, 35)?[31] Such love has no degrees. Nothing is lacking.

What does this mean for the question whether Paul's language implies eternal rewards?

1. Passages that mention "judgment by works" in a more general fashion are to be understood in terms of Paul's basic theology of justification. Here Paul is often adapting material from the tradition.[32]

2. Metaphors of "striving," "development," and "growth" do not refer to an independent process of growth and development or to a process which is continuous in the usual sense of a natural process. For there is no point where one has advanced beyond being wholly dependent on Christ or beyond the possibility of falling. There is no point where sin is no longer an enemy or at least not as great an enemy. We daily and continually begin anew in Christ.[33]

3. Metaphors concerning "reward" after death are usually in the singular: for example, commendation (1 Cor. 4:5); prize (1 Cor. 9:24; Phil. 3:14); wreath (1 Cor. 9:26); weight (2 Cor. 4:17); end (2 Cor. 11:15); fruit (Phil. 1:11); crown (Phil. 4:1).[34] For this reason it is inappropriate to press these metaphors in order to try to demonstrate that there are degrees of reward in heaven. The reward is simply salvation, being in Christ; a person cannot be partially in Christ or more than in Christ. The same is true for being separate from Christ; in spite of apocalyptic speculation it must be asked in what sense there can be degrees of hell.

4. The fantastic picture in 1 Cor. 3:11-15 must not be forced into realistic thought patterns, and it is not a description of purgatory. The passage is to be understood within the larger framework of Paul's doctrine of justification. Basically these verses assert that Christians are to be responsible (cf. 5:5; 11:32).[35]

5. Nor can 2 Cor. 3:18 be used to prove that there will be degrees of glory in heaven, for the verse is written in the present tense and

probably refers to the process of change described in 2 Cor. 4:7-16.[36] The very idea that there can be degrees of glory is hyperbolic. When Paul writes of star differing from star in glory (1 Cor. 15:41), he understands stars to be made up of varying quantities of light,[37] and stars do vary in intensity. But it is difficult to see how the fact that Paul uses the analogy of glory in the stars in order to prove a distinction between physical and spiritual bodies in 1 Cor. 15:35-50 shows there will be degrees of reward in glory.

After Paul, changes gradually began to take place. In Eph. 6:8 it states: "Whatever good any one does, he will receive the same again from the Lord, whether he is a slave or free" (probably reflecting Col. 3:23-25). Is this once again an instance in which imagery about rewards must not be pressed in a direction which conflicts with the thrust of Paul's theology? The question is whether it has been possible to translate Paul's theology of justification from its confines within an apocalyptic world view into another world view (whether timeless or not is a matter of debate) of ecclesiological universalism. Has something been lost in the translation? In Ephesians the apocalyptic dimension has been subordinated to another dimension which has the same thrust: predestination. Grace is the central concept, corresponding in large degree to Paul's righteousness of God; grace is that which God has (1:6-7; 2:7) and which God gives to human beings (3:7-8; 4:7, 29). Thus Ephesians has "grace alone" and "all is grace." But even though "grace alone" is maintained, its polemic function of criticizing every human claim to be absolute has been diminished. Justification has been reduced to an expression of the fact that Christians base their salvation on their baptism. The law becomes subordinate. For Paul the law is not simply a Jewish issue but plays a decisive role in evaluating who one really is before God; the law is a key to the polemic function of justification. In Ephesians baptism is no longer dying and being buried with Christ, for the one who has been baptized moves from death into life (2:1-7). Sin does not have the power it had before; there is a confidence in dealing with sin in the present (4:26; 6:10-11). Growth can occur, and rewards both in this life and the next are possible (4:15; 6:2-3, 8). A shift from Paul has clearly taken place.[38]

A similar shift has taken place in the Pastorals. To be sure, Paul's doctrine of justification is cited in formulaic fashion (Titus 3:3-7; 2 Tim. 1:9-11), but the question is: What function does justification have? It seems to be more decorative than constitutive, or, to put it another way, it is present verbally but does not function as it does in Paul. Justification (the gospel) becomes an absolute, an authority that in actual fact confirms the church; as a consequence, its critical function is suppressed. The law is mentioned only in 1 Tim. 1:8-11 and then in a way that misunderstands Rom. 7:12 and 16. As in Ephesians, the decisive role is played by baptism, and justification is seen as part of baptism (Titus 3:3-7). Justification and sanctification become two separate events; the indicative is separated from the imperative. Eschatology has been separated from justification, for it is that which comes only at the end, when the "crown of righteousness" is given to the one who has reached the goal (2 Tim. 4:8; cf. Titus 2:13). Since justification has lost its eschatological dimension, it becomes a message of salvation to the individual for the start of a new life. Good works are taken for granted, and the motivation for suffering is, in addition to the authority of the gospel itself, the reward which corresponds to what one has done.[39]

It may be that James misunderstands the real Paul. If that be the case, the best that one can say for James is that his answer to Paul is confused and confusing. The key to James is his understanding of the law, for by following the law one is able to produce works (2:1-15); James has a positive view of being able to keep the law (2:8), although a radical view of its requirements (2:10). But James does not have a radical view of sin; sin is not that serious (2:13; 4:17; 5:19-20). Faith has to prove itself by producing works (2:17-18). For Paul the law is not liberty (Jas. 1:25; 2:12) but slavery (Rom. 7:6), and faith does not have to prove itself because it is established by its object, Christ (Gal. 3:22). In James Christians are, to be sure, those who receive every good gift from God (1:17); they are God's elect (2:5). Yet except for 1:5 this is not made the basis of James' ethics. Abraham is the model, and his righteousness is "not established but acknowledged by God."[40] Good works can be accomplished, they produce rewards here in this life (5:16) and in the life to come (5:19-20), and finally they are rewarded with a crown for the one who has endured (1:12; cf. 5:7).[41]

What happened to justification by faith after Paul, or, to put it another way, what happened to judgment according to works in the post-Pauline period? A look at Ephesians, the Pastorals, and James has already produced some answers. Most of the time Paul was not forgotten, but the understanding of his theology was inadequate.[42] Sanders' assertion, "Paul's view could hardly be maintained, and it was not maintained. Christianity rapidly became a new nomism,"[43] fails to take into account the central place the doctrine of justification has in Christian theology. What Sanders in effect does is to make the way church history actually developed into the norm.[44] On the other hand, as Luz has pointed out, Paul's theology of justification did decline because it always requires two dimensions; first, the eschatological, the involvement of the person with new acts of God in history and the world, and second, the polemical, the continual, critical distinction between God and human thinking and acting.[45] The question that must be faced is whether Christian theology does not always require these two dimensions.

The Gospels

Space does not allow for a full-scale analysis of "reward" passages in the four Gospels, but interpretations of "reward" language in the synoptic Gospels fall into three categories:

1. Reward language is good pedagogy. It is an appeal to self-interest, but simple people need to be dealt with concretely (Wilder).[46]

2. The reward is the kingdom. Another way of expressing this is to say that the reward is having a relationship with God, salvation; how could anyone have anything more than that? "It is the will of God's love to give the kingdom to man, Luke 12:32; cf. Matt. 5:3" (Preisker, Berrouard, Bornkamm, Wagner, Wilder).[47] "What the servant receives in reward is nothing but communion with God," and this means being in God's service now and in the life to come (Reicke).[48] Everything is decided on the basis of one's relationship to Jesus.[49]

3. The reward is far beyond any calculations one can make. It is not commensurate. It is grace abounding. It is the divine surprise. It is beyond proportion (Matt. 25:21, 23; cf. Matt. 24:47 = Luke 12:44), a hundredfold (Mark 10:29-30 = Matt. 19:29 = Luke 18:28-30), overflowing (Luke 6:38; cf. Matt. 5:12 = Luke 6:23), undeserving (Luke 17:7-10; Matt. 20:1-16) (de Ru, Preisker, Wilder).[50] Nor is such abundant reward limited to the future, for it begins now (Mark 10:30; Luke 18:28-30). And before such a God no hypocrisy is possible. Since God alone is good (Mark 10:18 = Matt. 19:7 = Luke 18:18), who can claim the right to a reward?[51] The best illustration of what is meant by "undeserving" is the parable of the unworthy slaves in Luke 17:7-10. Strictly speaking, slaves are never paid, for they are themselves the property of their master. Although they cannot be paid, they can be rewarded, and, when they are, it is to be entrusted with more responsibility (Matt. 25:21, 23; Luke 19:17, 19)![52]

The *locus classicus* for the understanding of rewards and punishments in the Gospels is Matt. 20:1-16. De Ru has classified the five most important variant interpretations.[53]

1. The allegorical approach. With this method, of course, all sorts of ideas can be brought in; for example, the repeated summons is tied to the history of salvation and to the various ages when one can become a Christian (Irenaeus, Origin).

2. The key is verse 16: "So the last shall be first, and the first last." The point is that judgment is coming; do not oppose God's decision (de Reaucourt). But the verse is lacking even in some older Egyptian manuscripts and translations.

3. Again, the key is verse 16. In the age to come all earthly order will be reversed (Schlatter). But all receive exactly the same amount.

4. Each will receive an equal reward. But what surprised those who heard the parable was not the equal reward, but such a large reward for the latest workers (Pesch).

5. Verse 16 must be omitted from the interpretation. As often happened, a parable has been given a generalized ending which does not fit. The parable soars far above "reward" to describe God's overflowing goodness. The good news is being defended against its pious critics (Bonnard, de Ru, Dodd, Jeremias, Pesch, Preisker).

A key question is how any interpretation of Matt. 20:1-16 fits into the whole of Matthew's theology. Matthew's understanding of sin and anthropology is underdeveloped and comparatively naive. In his understanding of the law Matthew has described a congregation taking one step in Paul's direction, but he has not thought through the theological consequences of this step and remains in a certain sense "pre-Pauline."[54]

In the Gospel of John and 1 John "reward" language recedes into the background because the believer has received everything through Christ: "Apart from me you can do nothing" (John 15:5). To a large extent in the Gospel of John the idea of reward has been replaced by another concept: glory.[55] "The glory which thou hast given me I have given to them" (John 17:22, cf. vv. 10, 24). Passages such as John 5:25-29 that seem to imply judgment according to works must be understood in light of Johannine redaction and John's unique eschatology.

III. The Lutheran Confessions

The Lutheran Confessions, like Scripture, must be interpreted according to their historical contexts. At times medieval remnants linger, and at times a polemic stance leads to exaggeration just as an irenic stance leads to accommodation. In other words, the Lutheran Confessions cannot be cited in a wooden fashion. And surely if anywhere in the Lutheran Confessions the whole is to be understood in the light of justification by faith.

What the Confessions say about rewards and even "distinctions in the glory of the saints" is described at the beginning of this essay. Surprisingly, all of these statements are found within the long article on justification in the Apology! In the Apology how is it possible to reconcile justification by faith with rewards based on works?

First, the Apology itself makes it very clear. After reminding the reader that Christ is the end of the law (Rom. 10:4) and that Christ himself says: "Apart from me you can do nothing" (John 15:5), it concludes: "By this rule, as we have said earlier, all passages on works can be interpreted. . . . the fruits please God because of faith and the mediator Christ but in themselves are not worthy of grace and eternal life."[56] Second, speculations about conditions in heaven are not part of the gospel. We want to know more. But how the Lord has arranged things in heaven is not ours to know, nor do we need to know these things. As with the doctrine of predestination, we are not to "delight in concerning ourselves with matters which we cannot harmonize," for we must "carefully distinguish between what God has expressly revealed in his Word and what he has not revealed."[57] Third and most important, the issue is salvation itself. How does concern about rewards affect one's status before God? As the Apology points out, "The strong hear the mention of punishments and rewards in one way, and the weak in another; for the weak work for their own advantage." The strong may be helped "to escape despair amid afflictions" by knowing God wills to reward them.[58] But who is strong? In fact, the very thought that one is strong is already a sign of weakness. Who dares even think about rewards? Nothing can be allowed to detract from our sole comfort, which is justification by faith in Christ alone. Again, as with the doctrine of predestination, ". . .any interpretation of the Scriptures which weakens or even removes this comfort and hope is contrary to the Holy Spirit's will and intent."[59]

Conclusion

In light of the variety and complexity of biblical statements on recompense, how can one make sense of the whole? There are limits to the help that can be found in lexicography, for each word really has a meaning determined by its historical context. Historical context must be taken seriously when the Bible is taken seriously. What then is to be done with the fact that Proverbs and the book of Revelation support the law of recompense, whereas Ecclesiastes, Job, and Paul do not?

Everything depends on the biblical view of God. Is God like a certified public accountant? Or is God like a loving father who surprises his adopted children with gifts that are beyond all calculation? The God of the Bible is this loving father. Of course he gives us rewards, but in a very different sense, for his rewards do not depend on what one has done. They are God's incommensurable gift. Human beings have great difficulty at this point because of an inveterate tendency to turn every situation to their own advantage: rewards become merits, gifts become rights. It is not possible to avoid such abuse. But God continues to give us rewards.

4

SOME PATRISTIC VIEWS ON THE RELATIONSHIP OF FAITH AND WORKS IN JUSTIFICATION[1]

Robert B. Eno, s.s.

A perennial question for the heirs of the Reformation has been: If the Pauline theme of justification through faith is truly fundamental, why does it seem to fade away in most of the patristic literature? This unwelcome phenomenon has led some to view the post-Scriptural period as a time of sharp decline from the Pauline peak, although there were also, to be sure, occasional bright spots of Pauline revival, as in Augustine.

This essay intends to approach the question by looking at some patristic commentaries on Paul. In reading them, one must always keep in mind the spectrum of polemical issues which influenced their views and expressions of justification. For one thing, the Fathers were concerned about antinomianism. Thus, while they spoke of justification by faith, they were always quick to add: this must, of course, be a real faith, one that proves itself in works. They always supplemented Paul with James. Fighting against the Gnostics, they insisted that works were not to be looked down upon as merely unimportant externals. The Apologists, stung by pagan accusations of Christian libertinism, made a point of stressing Christian moral uprightness.

They were also concerned to combat Marcion and his sundering of the two testaments. In writing against him, theologians such as Origen sometimes went too far in assimilating the New Testament to the Old. Augustine was heavily influenced not only by his struggle against Pelagius but also by his earlier battle against the Donatists, which led him to emphasize love and the significance of common human sinfulness.

Christians soon became notorious for their belief that all sins were remitted in baptism, the great forgiveness of sins promised by Christ. Indeed, some pagan adversaries professed to be scandalized by the undifferentiated mercies of the Christian God. We are then surprised by the very different, stringent, and even hard attitude with which the serious sins of baptized Christians are viewed. Not that such postbaptismal sins were few and far between. On the contrary, Christian writings and sermons abound in exhortations to the baptized to repent and laments about the state of the church. The totally unmerited first forgiveness of sins through the boundless grace of God coexists in the Fathers with a far different and much harsher and more demanding attitude toward the sins of those already justified and baptized.

Origen

Origen of Alexandria (ca. 185-253) is not an easy author to interpret. Moreover, in relation to the later, and especially the Latin commentators, he is not representative. His commentary on Romans, though written ca. 243, exists now only in a loose Latin translation of Rufinus published ca. 405. In comparison to the other Pauline commentators studied here, Origen seems less orderly and consistent. This may be attributed to his technique in preaching and commenting on Scripture. The theological issues discussed depend very much on the words in front of him at any given moment. Bringing out one theological point here, he may stress another, even a seemingly contradictory point a few verses later. The polemical background of this commentary is also obviously not the same as that of the late fourth century.

One of Origen's prime targets is Marcion. Origen is at pains to demonstrate the compatibility and continuity of the two testaments. Thus he frequently tends to play down or even to obliterate the distinction between the two testaments, stressing rather the identity of the reality underlying law and gospel. He who believes in the law should also accept the gospel and vice versa. But the situation of the two testaments is not precisely the same either. There is to be progress from one to the other, from faith to faith. The old law then, correctly understood, will be interpreted in a spiritual rather than a literal sense.

Even given these precautions, it still must be said that Origen, while not denying salvation by faith, is less insistent on it than other commentators. This may be because he feels a greater independence from the text than do the others. The justice of God comes to all, Jew and

Gentile, through the faith of Christ, not from our own merits, but freely given. Faith itself is a grace from God. Yet he also states that the good pagan will not lose his reward for his good deeds.

Origen also makes the point that salvation by faith cleanses from *previous* sins. God gives the ability to avoid sin in the future, but Christians neglect the path of virtue. This forgiveness of sins by faith does not give a license to sin since the forgiveness in question is for past, not future, sins. Doers of the law, not mere hearers, will be justified. Faith and works go together like the two testaments. You must have both for perfection. He frequently stresses the need for virtues other than faith. These virtues, as he puts it, will also be reckoned as justice. Faith without works may be faith but not according to knowledge. Charity will cover a multitude of sins and the Christian doing good works confirms the law.

Despite his insistence on good works, he sees them as the fruits of justification.

> And this faith when justified, like a root taking in the rain, goes down into the soil of the soul, so that when cultivated by the law of God, there will rise up out of it shoots which will bear the fruits of works. Therefore, the root of justice is not from the works but the fruit of the works grows from the root of justice, that root of justice, indeed, by which God brings justice without works. . . .[2]

Origen is generally sparing of merit language, but at one point, using the same imagery, he speaks of the fruit of good works as our own. The one who is justified must now lead a good life. Few people are saved without (post-justification) good works, the good thief being one of the rare exceptions. He who does not love his neighbor does not love Christ. Faith is the foundation and beginning of salvation, but hope represents progress and growth, charity the perfecting and summit of the whole.

Marius Victorinus

The first Latin commentator on the Pauline writings was Marius Victorinus, who wrote after his conversion to Christianity in 362. He may have written on all the letters, but the only surviving commentaries are

those on Galatians, Ephesians, and Philippians. His role in the conversion of Augustine is well known (*Confessions* 8:2), and he is sometimes thought to have been an influence as well in the development of
Augustine's views on grace and justification.

It is quite clear that Marius Victorinus teaches salvation by grace
through faith. "We know that man is not justified by the works of the
law but through faith and the faith of Jesus Christ. . . . It is faith alone
that gives justification and sanctification."[3] The Spirit is received from
the hearing of the faith, not the works of the law. We are the children
of Abraham, and life will be accounted to us unto justice. We are not
saved by our own merits but by the grace of God.

But, as always, when one seeks to penetrate more deeply into these
themes, a more precise specification is difficult to pin down. When he
speaks of faith, does he emphasize the *fides quae*, the fact that it is
faith in Christ as opposed to Judaism and paganism? When speaking
of salvific faith, he sometimes clearly specifies content: faith in Christ
as the Son of God who suffered, died, and rose for us. Believing in
Christ is to gain immortality and merit eternal life.

When he stresses faith over works, do the scorned works really refer
to the Jewish law, especially the ceremonial law? On several occasions
he specifies the works of the law as Sabbath observance, circumcision,
and new moons. Christ has now emptied the law of meaning, the law
thus "carnally understood." Finally, one must ask the very general
question: Does he (and do the other commentators) simply repeat the
terms and phraseology of Paul without fully meaning or even understanding all that Paul understood and intended?

Victorinus makes it clear that love is necessary: it is the fulfillment
of the law. "If a person has faith, it necessarily follows that he will
have love and these two fulfill everything which the law of Christ
commands. . . . Faith frees and love builds."[4] All virtue in Christians
is love because it was God's love that freed us. " 'Walk in love.' A
great commandment, universally applicable, for love ends and perfects
everything. And in this is the whole law and the whole mystery of
Christianity, love and charity."[5]

Marius Victorinus makes it clear that we are freed from our sins by
believing in Christ. Yet it is clear as well that in life good works are
to follow this forgiveness of sins. Faith is the head of all the virtues,
so that we may be just. But there is a certain reciprocal effect as well.
Justice will benefit us if faith is there, but this faith will only be "full
faith" if we are just. Good works are necessary each day, yet they also

come from God and not from our merits. Thus all boasting on our part must be avoided. While we must do good works according to the rule and discipline of the commandments of Christ, we are to keep our minds on what is ahead, forgetting the past, including our good works, lest we think of our merits. We must live according to the rule of Christ, but we must do so as if we were starting anew each day. We do them all by the grace of Christ (but we are to do them!).

Ambrosiaster

The next witness chronologically is pseudo-Ambrose or Ambrosiaster, writing in the later fourth century, probably during the time of Pope Damasus (366-384). In his commentary on the Pauline letters, he too stresses salvation by faith. "They have been justified freely, because by God's gift they have been sanctified by faith alone, neither accomplishing anything nor rendering *quid pro quo*."[6] Grace and forgiveness of sins are gifts from God and not a reward for works. Sins are forgiven freely in baptism with a minimum of distress. Only a confession (of faith) from the heart is required. He who believes in Christ is saved without works; by faith alone he freely receives the forgiveness of sins.

With the coming of grace, the burdens of the law no longer exist for believers. We are now new creatures by regeneration. There is no need for the law when sinners are justified in God's sight by faith alone. The law makes sinners know their guilt, though it is not the cause of guilt. In times of difficulty we are made strong by faith in the promises by trusting in them. Not by human merits, but by the mercy of God, after baptism, we are justified and adopted as children of God. All this is the gift of God in Christ.

This is a very encouraging message, but there is more to be said. The question of works must also be looked into. He gives a good summary of the situation of the new Christian in his commentary on Titus. "God by his mercy has saved us through Christ. By his grace, we, born again, have received abundantly of his Holy Spirit, so that relying on good works, with him helping us in all things, we might be able thus to lay hold of the inheritance of the kingdom of heaven."[7]

Ambrosiaster frequently interprets the phrase "the justice of God" in the sense of God's fidelity to his promises. "It is called the justice of God which seems to be mercy because it has its origin in the promise. When that which has been promised by God is produced, it is called the justice of God. It is justice because what was promised has been carried out."[8]

He does not really envisage a law/gospel relationship as Luther would understand it. It seems that for him the law that does not bring salvation means those specific ceremonial or other aspects of the Mosaic law abolished by the Christian dispensation, i.e. the law of works concerning sabbaths, new moons, and circumcision. Circumcision is of absolutely no use. The old law of salvation by works, however, at least points to faith. "The work of the law is faith. . . ."[9]

Ambrosiaster is certainly not to be understood as hostile to law and works, however. There has always been a law of some sort given by God. First there was the law of nature and a natural justice. When the human race grew slack, the law of Moses tried to shock men into obedience through fear. Then men slipped into despair because they were not able to obey the law, and thus God in his mercy preached the gospel of salvation. Preaching faith in Christ, the apostles brought the mercy of God to bear upon the weakness of the human race. The gospel is just the old law minus the law of works (i.e., the Jewish ceremonial and dietary regulations). It was simply not fitting that the Mosaic law be maintained in the presence of the Lord. Christianity begins with the forgiveness of sins whereas the law is the condition for sin. Love is more spiritual. These are the works of the gospel, the Christian law, which replace the ceremonial law.

What does Ambrosiaster mean by faith? He mentions the necessity of love in connection with faith. "For justification, faith alone in love is necessary. For faith must be fortified with brotherly love for the perfection of the believer."[10] This faith must be, first of all, faith in Christ in the sense of an acceptance of the Christian religion. Even if Gentiles keep the natural law, they must in addition accept the one God. This is more important than abstention from other sins. He who believes in Christ keeps the law. This faith is the true and orthodox faith. It is precisely those who do not hold the full divinity of Christ, i.e., Judaizing Christians, who also hold out for the full observance of the Mosaic law.

Having been justified by the grace of Christ, the new Christian must follow the law of faith. Since we once were saved by God's mercy, we must be all the more vigilant for the rest of our lives—leading pure lives, calling down his love on us, and not rendering his grace useless. Christ calls us to the knowledge of faith and right living. After faith one must make progress in good works toward the proposed reward. The reformed sinner is to live under the law of God and not backslide lest grace be lost. The short formula for the Christian's postbaptismal success is: a good life and Catholic faith.

How can we continue to call God our Father if our lives do not conform to our words? Love is the foundation of all religion, so that without it nothing is of any use. In a way love is prior to faith and hope. Good works are required so that one's fiducial trust in God may grow; in fact, our works show how much we believe. Initial justification then is just the beginning of the race; we have to keep running. Even Paul had to exert himself to improve and gain the "merits" of justification and the reward because the justice of God despises the unworthy (!). Despite our initial justification by God's mercy, our subsequent life, our works, will determine whether we are justified or damned ultimately.

As can be seen, Ambrosiaster has no difficulty with merit language for the justified person. Having been washed, we must merit receiving the promise. Faith which is not forced is meritorious. He speaks of meriting mercy by faith, i.e., by believing in Christ. He even seems to speak of merit or reward gained by the good acts of a person who has not yet come to believe. The justice of God will not allow such acts to go unrewarded.

Resisting temptations daily, we further merit our future reward. All will be rewarded for their good works. Progress is made. The Pharisee seeks the rewards of justice now because he despairs of it in the next life. Leaders of the community who do well will be appropriately rewarded. The apostles themselves will get a "great reward." Once faith (understood as Christianity in general) is accepted and a moral life is achieved, reward will follow. "If anyone wishes to be justified before God so that it profits him as merit in the day of judgment, let him follow the faith of God."[11]

Pelagius

Ironically, Pelagius, the British monk whose name has gone down in the history of doctrine as "the enemy of the grace of God," is the one who in his commentaries on the Pauline letters, superficially at least, has the least objectionable interpretations. He is the one who puts the most emphasis not just on faith but on *fides sola*. Like the others, he begins by emphasizing that we are saved by the grace of God, not by our own merits. God justifies the convert by faith alone, not by his good works, which in fact he does not have. This is true for the Jews as well as for the Gentiles. The faith in question must, of course, be specifically Christian faith. Without it the other virtues are useless for justification. The law is also useless without faith in Christ. The law cannot justify for the simple reason that no one can keep it.

Another element peculiar to Pelagius is his emphasis on baptism in justification. "Without the works of the law, through baptism, he has freely forgiven the sins of all, however undeserving." [12] In connection with this it is important to note that Pelagius stresses that in the sacrament of baptism only a person's previous sins are forgiven. We are forgiven past, not future sins. We should no longer be concerned with past sins, but we should fear to go astray after we have been baptized. The faithful are baptized to wash away old sins and to help avoid future ones.

Herein lies the problem. Pelagius as well as the other commentators are perfectly orthodox in teaching that we are justified by Christ without any previous merits or works on our part. It is the situation of the Christian after baptism that demands works. The Christian must make progress. We must do good works for charity's sake but not boast about it. In this process he puts more than usual emphasis on imitating Christ, thus reminding us of his idea of the sinner's imitation of the first Adam.

The works of the old law will not save. No one can observe them all anyway. With Pelagius as with the other commentators, one has the well-founded suspicion that for him this nonsalvation by works means principally, if not exclusively, exemption from observing those aspects of the Mosaic law rejected by Christians, such as circumcision and sabbath observance. The Jews thought they could justify themselves by the law even though, adds Pelagius, they did not observe even the greatest commandments. Christians will not be saved by observing that law which must be reinterpreted spiritually in any event. They are saved by faith in Christ.

But once justified by faith, good works are to be done. He calls them variously the "works of justice" or the "works of faith." "To this end, our first faith is reckoned as justice so that the past is absolved; we are justified in the present and prepared for the future works of faith." [13] They are the "works of grace" to be done by the baptized-justified person. Baptism, he says, must make a difference in our lives, a difference that can be seen in our behavior.

Here the emphasis on James becomes heavy. The Christian who does not lead a good life has lost his faith. A faith which is on the lips but produces no fruit in practice is a false faith. Anyone who thinks that faith without works suffices is a false teacher. The reborn Christian walks in good works. Faith without works will not suffice to justify anyone already baptized. Faith is dead without the "works of faith." The faith that justified the new believer will suffice only if the person remains in that justification. To do that he must avoid occasions of sin. To lead such a life, asceticism, among other things, is necessary. Among the virtues charity is very important. "Peace and charity and faith make the Christian perfect; for just as charity without faith is sterile, so the same is true of faith without charity or peace."[14]

When it comes to merit language, once again Pelagius is preferable to Ambrosiaster. He speaks once of the merit of faith. He speaks of reward more often than merit, though even this is not very frequent. Everything we have done or suffered for the love of God will be rewarded, he says. We hope to receive a reward for our (moral) justice. But he reminds his readers that they have nothing of their own except the reward of their labors. The reward is given to the labors, not the person. Finally, faith is the recognition of the divine truth but not because of our merits.

Pelagius' commentaries on Paul then are superior in many ways to Ambrosiaster's. He speaks little of merit except to deny that we can receive God's grace because of any merits of our own. We are freely justified, but once we are justified, Pelagius, like the others, stresses the necessity of a faith that is active in love.

John Chrysostom

John Chrysostom (ca. 345-407) preached on the Letter to the Romans during his Antioch period (i.e., before 398). This work is cited several times by Augustine against Julian of Eclanum, thus raising the question of an early Latin translation. John, generally a moralist as a preacher, was also an enthusiastic admirer of Paul. He thus has a great deal to say about justification by faith as opposed to the works of the law. The "justice of God" means a quality of God but also that by which God makes sinners just, and this by faith, not by works. This salvation is easy and open to all. A great abundance of grace is revealed as well as ease in obtaining it; no works are necessary. The only human contribution is faith. The Jews, on the other hand, claiming justification through the law, asserted that they did not need grace. On the contrary, the law cannot free anyone. Abraham, a man rich in good works, was justified nevertheless by faith. But most people were not really able to keep the law. This is natural enough, and indeed it was intended to be that way so that, having been brought to the edge of despair, the average person would run to Christ for salvation by grace through faith. By the law Chrysostom seems to understand principally those parts of the Mosaic law rejected by Christians—"feasts, commandments, sacrifices." The justice of faith is much greater than all these. Jews, insisting on the law, make grace useless. We cannot save ourselves, but grace cannot save us either unless we are willing. All, especially Judaizing Christians who follow the law, are saying in effect that Christ is insufficient. Justice without Christ is no justice.

Once we believe, we are immediately justified. Through the cross justice is graciously bestowed on all, even though we were not previously just or doers of good works. The grace of God now given is greater than all sins committed since the beginning of the world; Christ did not just make up for the harm wrought by Adam, he brought about a far greater good. Once weak, we are now made powerful by grace. Christ did the fighting, but we enjoy the fruits of victory. For us the precise moment of this justification came in baptism. Christ is justice itself.

There is a delicate balance to be struck in this matter. One must avoid taking credit for justification because of good works done. We are saved by grace, and there is no place for boasting on our part. Yet we must be careful lest this emphasis on grace lead us to be overconfident. Trust in grace must not keep us from striving and working after our justification. "He [Paul] also mentions his own past so that you will not leave everything to God and just sit there sleeping and belching."[15] Grace talk should humble our pride, but it must not render us passive or lead to a false quietism.

After we have been justified, we must produce. Here faith without works is of no avail. Reward and punishment will ultimately depend on our works, not the works of the law, which is now a thing of the past. Although in one place he says of the grace received at baptism that it touches our very soul and plucks up the roots of sin, he does not seem so optimistic about the real state of the Christian people. In baptism we died and were buried with Christ, gaining justice and other blessings. We rise with Christ in baptism. This means that a real change has taken place in us and a corresponding change for the better should be visible in our daily lives. One cannot simply go on in one's former way of living. The passions are supposed to have been made subject to the will after baptism. One proof of the superiority of grace over the law is to be seen in the realities of virginity and contempt of death among Christians now. But in fact, on the everyday level of reality, after their baptism people seem to be changed for a sum total of about ten to twenty days.

Given the reality, Chrysostom felt the need as a pastor to exhort his people to lead better lives. Hell was real, he told them, yet Christians kept right on sinning. Against a common laziness and *laissez faire* attitude, he urged again and again the need for zeal, diligence, earnestness (*spoudē*). We need to show *spoudē* worthy of the gift. He speaks of two separate events in dying to sin: one happens in baptism and the other putting to death is done by ourselves after baptism. He is clearly recommending asceticism here. The burial of our old sins was Christ's gift. "But to remain dead to sin after baptism—this has to be the product of our own serious efforts (*spoudē*), however much God gives us a lot of help here as well."[16] God and baptismal grace continue to help, but, Chrysostom emphasizes, it is up to us to show a real change in our lives. There can be no sitting back and taking it easy. Even Paul strove to strengthen his resistance to temptation and sin. We are to be stricter, not less strict. The law is no longer in effect, in order that our standards may be higher, not lower. What is demanded of us may seem difficult and irksome. But this is the reaction of our sloth. We need to be prodded into greater diligence. Make a start, he urges his hearers, by helping the poor as you leave church. For the greatest virtue of all is charity, from which many blessings are produced and from which eternal rewards will be forthcoming for us.

Chrysostom does not hesitate to make explicit the motive of fear. Though we were initially justified by the pure grace of God, we thereafter must work out our salvation in fear and trembling. Only by living sober lives can we be saved from hell. "Our lot indeed is at present uncertainty to our last breath. . . ."[17] Security comes only with death. A little more on the bright side, he speaks in terms of rewards to come, though, it should be said, not inordinately. He reminds his hearers that the reward is greatest when one works without hope of reward. In particular, like some of the other Fathers, he makes a comparison that grates on the post-Reformation ear: If you, the wealthy, help the poor, you are simply transferring your wealth to heaven (i.e., by piling up a reward). There is a way of taking it with you! Above all, when he exhorts Christians to live a sober life, not to be presumptuous, or to work harder than ever, he reminds them of the rewards to come in the next life "after a little labor." He who has absolved from sins will crown the just.

Augustine

Augustine of Hippo, in general the most influential of the Western Fathers, holds a very special place of honor in this area of grace and justification. In fact, he does not seem to be that different from the other commentators we have studied except that he stresses the ongoing dependence of the Christian in the postbaptismal justification process on God's gracious initiative and help. But this emphasis does not lead him to downplay the activity of the Christian in life. Another specific emphasis of his is the role of love.

From the beginning Augustine taught the necessity of grace for salvation. As time went on, he strengthened and broadened his view of this dependence. We cannot live as we ought unless first justified by faith. We are powerless to help ourselves. We cannot observe the law without grace. Time and again he stresses that the law cannot save; rather it serves to point up sin. It tells us what we should do but does not give us the means to do it. "For the law gives its prescriptions to this end alone that when one has failed to fulfill these commandments, he will not be filled with pride; thus, by frightening him, the law fulfills its purpose of pedagogue, leading him to love Christ." [18] By its prohibitions the law actually renders concupiscence more acute. The law by itself is the letter that kills.

Augustine's attitude toward the law is not universally negative. The law does not just have a place in God's plan whereby it points to the need for a Savior. Without the Spirit and love the law is a dead letter. But once grace is given, the person is endowed with the faith and justice so that he can fulfill the law, spiritually understood. "Grace is shown through the law so that the law may be fulfilled by grace." [19] Here Augustine would cite one of his favorite verses: "Love is the fulfillment of the law" (Rom. 13:10).

The law cannot save; it drives us in turn to Christ who alone can save us. Our sins are forgiven by grace through faith. But Augustine, verbally at least, puts more emphasis on grace than on faith, i.e., he is interested in stressing as often as possible that the grace of God always comes before our works as meritorious. The law cannot heal what is wrong with us; only grace can do that. The law is good insofar as it tells us what ought to be done or avoided, but only the grace of Christ our liberator can enable us to do what ought to be done. Our sins are forgiven to start with, and we are enabled to live justly through faith, to do good works. Now under grace it is possible for us not only to want to do good but to be able to do it in fact. Again and again he reiterates that grace must come first and only then can good works follow. Salvation comes only from Christ. We are vessels of mercy who cannot justify ourselves. Any ability that we have to do good comes from God.

The terms "justice" and "justification" are widely used by Augustine. By ourselves, our "justice" is worthless. The Psalmist says with good reason to the Lord: "Hear me in *your* justice." God takes our sins on himself so that his justice might become our own. What is this "justice of God"? In several places Augustine defines it this way: "The justice of God is not that by which God himself is just but that which God gives to man so that he might be just through God."[20] It is God's own justice then that makes us just. We are justified by faith, not works; by the spirit, not the letter; by grace, not by any deeds of our own. The fact that our own salvation comes entirely from God leaves us no room for boasting.

Having been justified, what are we to do? We are now to fulfill the "spiritual works of the law." We are to become doers of the law but only after justification. We are called to do good works, and we can thus have what Augustine calls merits. But he constantly takes pains to recall that we can have no merits of our own. Without God's grace we can have only demerits of our own. Rather, only after having been justified are we enabled to do good works and to have any merits. While he does use merit language at times, he is careful to stress that anything we have that is good comes from God. Recall the oft-cited formula: "Thus God will crown not so much your merits as his own gifts."[21] Finally, Augustine especially views the functioning of the grace of God in the human subject in terms of love more than faith. The grace of faith works through love.

Now we must analyze more closely the life of the justified Christian. First of all, Augustine does not deny free will to the unjustified person. Yet, however much a person might wish and try, he cannot live a good life without grace. Free will without grace is capable of nothing but sin. Despite this state, the image of God in the human being has never been totally obliterated. Once restored by grace, the human will is not overridden by grace; on the contrary, it is now truly free for the first time.

One of the outstanding characteristics of Augustine's theology of grace and justification is his emphasis on the role of love. In one place he has a definition of *caritas dei* that is parallel to that of *iustitia dei*.

"The love of God that is poured forth in our hearts is not the love by which he loves us, but the love by which he makes us his lovers." [22] This also reminds us of one of his most frequently cited New Testament verses, Rom. 5:5: "The love of God has been poured forth in our hearts through the Holy Spirit who has been given to us." "For the fullness of the law is love, and, since faith calls for the Holy Spirit, through whom the love of God is poured forth in the hearts of those who do justice, in no way can anyone glory in his good works prior to the grace of faith." [23] We love only because we have been loved first. But love we must. He complains: "There are many who believe but do not love." [24] Faith without hope and love is just the faith of demons condemned in Jas. 2:19. Such a person may believe that Christ is, but he does not believe in Christ.

Love is the root out of which come all good fruits. Under grace the law is fulfilled in love. This love, as Rom. 5:5 states, is the Holy Spirit in us. This in turn should mean good works. Where faith-filled love is at work, there one will find a good life. Good deeds done out of fear rather than out of love might as well not have been done at all. Love does away with fear, and faith will give us hope in Christ. A life of faithful love should even help us reduce the power of concupiscence, the fleshly desires.

Good works are clearly to be part of the Christian life. He must warn people who say they believe but show little evidence of real faith in their lives. Real faith and good works go together. By this time someone may be ready to ask: Is not such Christianity in danger of becoming just another law of works? No, answers Augustine. Besides the fact that many Mosaic ceremonial laws have been left behind, what used to be enjoined with threats under the old law of works is now granted to belief under the law of faith.

At baptism all our sins are forgiven and in some places he specifies *past* sins. But we must continue to struggle with our faults; concupiscence remains. As indicated above, Augustine believed that the power of concupiscence could be reduced in the long run in this life. Carnal desires remain but they are not sins if they are not heeded and obeyed. One can speak of sin in the members, but it does not reign. There is no guilt if the sins forgiven are not revived (i.e., committed anew).

All our past sins are forgiven in baptism. It is a true renewal. Yet experience shows that we keep on sinning; otherwise we would not need to repeat daily: "Forgive us our sins." The Christian's postjustification state is still very much a process (*status viae*). "We have been justified; but justice itself grows as we progress." [25] Life is a daily fight against carnal desires. "Let us run with faith, hope, and desire; let us run chastising our body, giving alms to the deserving, pardoning the wicked with joy, wholeheartedly praying that the strength of those in the race holds up and that we ourselves remain docile to the precepts of perfection, lest we fall away in our pursuit of the fullness of love."[26] His program, then, includes prayer, asceticism, almsgiving, and faith, hope and love. This is *our* justice. We are daily helped by God's grace, but even granted that assistance, the works we do "begin to be also our merits." We must definitely be active. As he puts it in sermon 169.13: "He who created you without you does not justify you without you."[27]

Our progress should be a daily reality. He likes to cite or allude to 2 Cor. 4:16: " 'Our inner being is renewed from day to day' until perfect justice is attained as well as complete health."[28] In some sense we are *simul iusti et peccatores*, but it is a *partim-partim* sense for Augustine, not *totus-totus*.

And will any of us dare to say, "I am a just man"? I think to say "I am just" means "I am not a sinner." Yet if anyone dare say this, John will come to him: "If we say 'We are free of the guilt of sin,' we deceive ourselves and the truth is not in us" (1 John 1:8). What then? Do we have no justice at all? Or do we have it but not all of it? Let us look into it. For if we have some part of something, there is also a part we do not have; let that which we have increase and that which we do not have yet be filled in. For men are baptized and all things are forgiven them; they are justified, freed from sin; we cannot deny this. Yet there remains a struggle with the flesh, the world, and the devil. Of those that struggle, some overcome and others are overcome. . . . If we say we are not just at all, we slander the gifts of God. . . . But if we have faith, we already are somewhat just.[29]

Similarly, our justice is in proportion to our love.

A General Survey

It is not possible here to make anything like a complete survey of all the Fathers. The following is presented as a rapid overview of a number of relevant texts. The Apostolic Fathers have been seen as representing an almost total disappearance of the Pauline point of view. Their writings are all pieces written to confront some specific internal need of the church. They address those who are already Christians. It is not surprising then that so much space is devoted to exhorting Christians to lead better lives or attempting to regulate problems within the churches.

But even here due recognition is found of the primacy of God's grace. Clement of Rome says that we are not made just by ourselves or by our own works but by God's will through faith. As Abraham was saved by faith, so the blood of Christ sanctifies us. "What a great debt we owe Christ! Because it was his grace which saved us and not our works."[30]

Justin stresses faith in his *Dialogue with Trypho,* but it is clear that the burden of his message is that Jews must accept Christ and understand the Christological thrust of the Hebrew Scriptures. Thus it is difficult to decide whether when he speaks of faith in this context he means any more than acceptance of Christianity or that the old measures of salvation such as circumcision are now gone. There is a progression of requirements for salvation in Justin (as in the others): (1) repentance of sins; (2) recognition of Jesus as the Christ; and (3) observance of the commandments. After this comes the reward.

In Irenaeus as well it is difficult to specify what is meant by faith. He attacks the Gnostics for preaching salvation through their version of "faith" while they have only evil deeds to show as the fruits of their beliefs. He repeats, as do most of the others, that Abraham was justified by faith, but he means that Abraham had some explicit knowledge of Christ and future salvation history, thus stressing the unity of the two covenants over against Marcion. He seems here to be speaking more of the content of faith, the *fides quae.* The same inspiration seems to be behind Clement of Alexandria's extolling of faith when he states that the gospel is the fulfillment of the law. Tertullian in his longest work affirms that the faith of the just man is a faith in God as the author of both covenants, both Creator of the world and Father of Jesus. "Of old there was the law, but now the righteousness of God by the faith of Christ."[31]

Cyril of Jerusalem has a more dogmatic approach to faith—faith as assent to truth. When Gregory of Nazianzus compares his parents to Abraham and Sarah, he states that his father was justified by faith. In saying this he probably means only that his father, having been raised in an heretical sect, the Hypsistarii, later became a Catholic Christian. Leo the Great in particular seems to have a very dogmatic sense of faith. He urges the need for a faith in the real humanity of Jesus for justification. He cites Heb. 11:6, "Without faith it is impossible to please God," in connection with insisting on an integral doctrine and dogma.

Apart from this content-oriented view of faith, one can also find a view emphasizing the forgiveness of sins. Origen, against Celsus, comments on the miraculous ability of Christianity to reform sinners. "For without the Word . . . it is impossible for anyone to become sinless."[32] With a more touching degree of personal involvement and experience, yet still heavily tinged with the aspect of moral reform, Cyprian discusses his own conversion:

> For as I myself was held by the many errors of my previous life, of which I believed I could not rid myself, so I was disposed to give in to my clinging vices . . . in my despair. But afterwards when the stains of my past life had been washed away by the aid of the waters of regeneration, a light from above poured itself upon my chastened and pure heart; afterwards, when I had drunk of the Spirit, from heaven a second birth restored me as a new man. What seemed impossible could be accomplished. . . . An expression of gratitude . . . not ascribed to the virtues of man but proclaimed as of God's munificence. . . . Our power is of God; I say, all of it is from God.[33]

Basil, who stresses works a great deal, also confesses that we are justified by faith in Christ alone. However, the context, a homily on humility, points up the moralizing reference of the statement. Our glory is not in boasting about ourselves but in mortifying ourselves. Ambrose comes closer to a feeling for salvation by faith and the importance of grace. We see here no doubt one aspect of his influence on Augustine. For Ambrose, the law led us to recognize sin but could not grant forgiveness. We are all guilty; we cannot glory in any works of our own. We glory in Christ who has forgiven our sins. We rise again through God's grace. "Let no one glory in his own works since no one is justified by his deeds, but one who is just has received a gift, being justified by baptism. It is faith, therefore, which sets us free by the blood of Christ, for he is blessed whose sin is forgiven and to whom pardon is granted."[34]

While there is some emphasis on saving faith in some authors and very little in others, all urge the justified Christian on to greater efforts, to more zeal in leading a Christian life. "What shall we do then? Shall we be slothful in well-doing and cease from love? . . . Let us be zealous to accomplish every good deed with energy and readiness. . . . Let us do the work of justice with all our strength."[35] Follow the way of light and not of darkness. Be zealous in God's works. God will record the good works. A believer without good works is really not a believer.

As noted above, Justin states that the third condition for salvation after repentance and faith is observance of the commandments. Faith (orthodoxy?) is not enough; works must be present as well. All these authors stress the need for works. They speak first of the free forgiveness of sins by Christ. But the situation of the justified Christian is no longer the same as that of the preconversion pagan. We are saved by grace but not without good works, writes Clement of Alexandria. Origen resorts again to James to remind the reader in his commentary on John that faith without works is dead. When Celsus complains that good people are not wanted among Christians, only sinners, Origen replies that sinners are wanted, yes, but reformation as well as repentance is required.

Cyprian, whom we have seen praising God for the mercy shown in his own conversion, is also very strong on the need for Christians to lead good lives and on the correspondingly difficult path for the fallen Christian who seeks to return to communion in the church. The latter must make satisfaction to God by prayer and works. In his treatise on the Lord's Prayer, Cyprian writes that when we pray, "Hallowed be thy name," we pray that "we who have been sanctified in baptism may persevere in what we have begun . . . [For this] . . . we have need of daily sanctification."[36] Cyprian is one among several early authors who put great stress on almsgiving. This in particular irritates modern readers because of its close association with the idea of purchasing salvation, harkening back to Reformation controversies about indulgences. Cyprian cites Old Testament references such as Prov. 16:6 as authorities. But he makes it clear that he is talking about the problem of doing penance for postbaptismal sins, not about first justification.

> Surely not those sins which have been contracted before, for they are purged by the blood and sanctification of Christ. . . . Because the remission of sins is once granted in baptism, constant and continuous labor acting in the manner of baptism again bestows the indulgence of God. . . . The merciful one advises that mercy be shown, and because he seeks to save those whom he redeemed at a great price, he teaches that those who have been polluted after the grace of baptism can be cleansed again.[37]

Without going into greater detail, all the Fathers stress that after baptism good works are expected of the Christian. It is not either/or but both/and. "True religion consists of these two elements: pious doctrines and virtuous actions. Neither does God accept doctrines apart from good works, nor are works, when divorced from godly doctrine, accepted by God."[38] For some, love plays a more explicit role than for others. Gregory the Great, as a post-Augustinian, in saying, "It is not by faith that you will come to know God, but by love; not by mere conviction but by action,'' is not just reiterating the patristic emphasis on a balance between faith and works. ''None of these things is unknown to you if you possess perfect faith in Jesus Christ and love, which are the beginning and the end of life; for the beginning is faith and the end is love, and when the two are joined together in unity, it is God, and all other noble things follow after them.''[39]

The stress on good works may in itself be viewed more or less critically. But some of the potential pitfalls or aberrations quickly made an appearance in certain patristic authors. For Hermas, works of supererogation gain a greater reward. Tertullian, who, to be sure, frequently stretched logic and exegesis to gain a point, got around to proving by the notion of God's ''preferential will'' that failure to do the ''better thing'' was a sin. ''Even though you do not sin, you do fail to merit. And is not one's very unwillingness to merit itself a sin?''[40]

Despite these exaggerations or aberrations, the Fathers agreed on the gratuity of God's grace and mercy in forgiving human sins. The demand for works came to the Christian who was already justified. They were to show forth the gratitude of the undeserving wretch saved by God's love but were also the way one preserved the gift of salvation. Created a new person in Christ, the Christian who persevered would be rewarded.

> Therefore as a debtor to so great a benefit, do you not make repayment with your obedience? . . . . He has poured out on you the spirit of adoption. Count these blessings and associate them not so much with the bondage of debt as with the maintenance of the gift you have received. . . . See how he has forgiven you your earlier sins in order that the fact of your having sinned might not prove a hindrance to you. See how he exhorts you not to lose what you have received.[41]

Conclusion

This survey of the Fathers points in particular to one significant issue: the distinction between first and subsequent justification, or between justification and sanctification. Painting in broad strokes and making allowances for scattered exceptions, it seems that the Fathers taught that human beings initially were saved from their sins, were justified purely by God's mercy, by his grace with no merits or works of their own going before. The old law could not save of itself: it merely underlined the fact of human weakness and sin. Now with the coming of Christ the human race was to be saved by faith in Christ. After justification Christians were to lead lives of virtue, doing good to others.

Difficulty arises with the serious sins of those already baptized. Here in many cases the patristic view of the postbaptismal Christian life seems to place the Christian back into a law situation. He must obey commandments and do good works. If he does not do these things, punishment will follow sooner or later. A closer look at the patristic data shows that most of the Fathers looked upon the old law as still in effect except for the specific ceremonial, dietary, and other regulations rejected by Gentile Christians almost from the beginning. Gospel as faith meant simply accepting Christianity as opposed to Judaism or paganism. In some texts faith was even more clearly taken in a sense of what later theology would call the *fides quae*.

If the emphasis on gratuity of salvation and forgiveness of sins without our works is limited to first justification, if justification is identified with the moment of baptism, and if there comes a time when infant baptism is universal, then it is not hard to understand that the word of God's free forgiveness in justification would not impinge very forcefully on the conscience of the average Christian. If this same Christian then is exhorted to live a life of virtue and good works in order to be saved and rewarded in the next life and if in fact he does not live a very good life but is frequently exhorted to repent and threatened with divine judgments if he does not repent and, even if he repent, he is still menaced with long and painful purgatorial torments to make up for the penances he cannot do, it is not surprising that a law atmosphere will be generated. People will seek to cut corners, find shortcuts, cheap grace. Augustine, to be sure, among others, insists on the ongoing necessity of divine grace for all good actions subsequent to justification, but such theological fine points (in contrast to pastoral and devotional practice) are not prominent in the thoughts of the average Christian through the ages.

5

HOW THE EASTERN FATHERS UNDERSTOOD WHAT THE WESTERN CHURCH MEANT BY JUSTIFICATION

William G. Rusch

The sixteenth-century Reformation of the Western Church was largely prompted by anxiety over sin, expressed in Luther's searching question, "How do I find a gracious God?" It focused in all of its theological aspects on the relationship of God to an anxious humankind, seeking the meaning of existence and the assurance of salvation. For the Reformers the answer was found in what they believed was a rediscovery of the gospel: God saves ungodly men and women without condition of human merit. This was summed up in the phrase "justification by grace through faith." For the Roman Catholics the response was that God forgives only after first bestowing the grace that allows sinners to do those works which merit salvation. The Catholics claimed such teaching was in conformity with Augustine and Thomas Aquinas, although the Reformers made equal claim to the former. Both parties believed that human beings are totally hopeless in view of sin and thus dependent on God for salvation. Nevertheless, there are deep differences. The Reformers tended to accent faith or trust in opposition to despair, the Catholics humility and praise of God in opposition to pride. The question of the ultimate compatibility of these understandings has profound implications for the Lutheran-Roman Catholic relationships at this moment in the history of ecumenism.

The Reformation was thus a theological debate, occasioned by a deeply existential question, anxiety over sin, and therefore fundamentally a question of soteriology. The Reformers addressed this anxiety in terms of justification by grace through faith. They believed that it was precisely this justification that allowed men and women in their

131

despair to confront their basic meaninglessness and to proclaim that human existence can be justified and sinful at the same time. This same anxiety could have been raised for discussion in terms other than that of justification, e.g., in terms of hopelessness of humankind or the reality of God. The fact that "justification" became the language of debate was determined by some specific historical circumstances.

> That "justification" became the place of pain was determined by the tradition: by Pauline usage, by the Augustinian language of the medieval church in general and Luther's Augustinian order in particular, and probably also by the central place of "justification" in the feudal social and legal order.[1]

It must be noted that by and large all these components of the tradition are Western. Pauline usage involved reading Paul with Western eyes. Augustine never played the same kind of role in the Eastern Church as he did in the West. He never enjoyed the same influence. The implication of all this for an understanding of Greek patristic thought is considerable.

For the Greek Fathers, and indeed the entire Eastern Church, soteriology was equally as important as for the Western Church. In fact the claim could be made that it was the major motif of Eastern patristic thought. This was certainly true of the great fourth- and fifth-century controversies. The basic concern of Orthodox thought in these struggles was to maintain the conviction that only God himself is the source of salvation. In their teaching about soteriology, the Eastern Fathers were not oblivious to the terminology of justification. Even a quick glance at G. W. H. Lampe's *A Patristic Greek Lexicon*[2] under *dikaiosynē* and *dikaioō* reveals a number of patristic texts that speak of justification of Christians coming from God, or Christ, by grace through faith or by baptism. A fairly representative number of authors is given. An examination of the texts cited by Lampe would be instructive in terms of a word study of the use of *dikaioō* in its several forms. But it would not reveal the predominant teaching of the Eastern Fathers on soteriology. This is because of a different emphasis that was developing in the East as opposed to the West. The Western Church tended to be more pessimistic about humankind's plight than was the Eastern Church; it taught a doctrine of original sin that included the conception of humankind's physical solidarity with Adam and its participation in Adam's sinful act. This view was largely absent in Eastern thinking. The West also was more legalistic. As the penitential system of the Western Church developed, *justificare* played a role in soteriological thinking that *dikaioō* did not assume in the East. Also the influence of the Pelagian controversy marked the Western Church in ways unknown in the East.

Nevertheless, the conclusion should not be drawn that the Greek Fathers did not take the fall seriously. They drew a realistic picture of humankind's situation. They have an outline of a theory of original sin, but they never completed it. They saw the fall of the first parents as caused by the misuse of free will and insisted that our free will is the cause of our actual sinning. In terms of the need of divine grace, the position of the Greek Fathers is that grace and humankind's free will cooperate. But this should not be interpreted in the light of Augustinianism. The starting point and experience of the Eastern Church were different. Because this is the case, the vocabulary and concerns of the East or the West should not be read into each other. New Testament scholarship has taught us that it is not correct to assume that the same word carries the same meaning in every New Testament book. To do a word study of *dikaioō* in the Eastern Fathers and then compare it with *justificare* in the Latin Fathers would be highly misleading. The soteriological concerns of the Western Church that became focused around justification were discussed in the Eastern Church in a different framework. Since the Greek Fathers had not experienced the development of the penitential system of the medieval Western Church, they would not have understood the debates of the sixteenth-century church and should not be expected to provide answers to them.

This does not mean, however, that the Eastern Fathers should be judged deficient or unhelpful to Western theology because they did theology differently. Rather, they are to be seen as developers of a theology of salvation outside the framework of justification categories. The validity of this approach should not be tested by the presence or absence of justification terminology but by compatibility to what Eric Gritsch and Robert Jenson have called the "metalinguistic" stipulation,[3] and George Lindbeck has described as the "metatheological rule":[4] all church teaching and practices should function to promote reliance or trust in the God of Jesus Christ alone for salvation.[5] If Eastern patristic theology has done this, whether or not it has employed the vocabulary of justification, it is within the limits of legitimate diversity in the Christian Tradition.

The Eastern Fathers employed a variety of images to describe salvation made available through Christianity. These include healing (Justin Martyr, 2 *Apology* 13,4; Irenaeus, *Against Heresies* 5,17,3; Clement, *The Tutor* 1,2,6); the forgiveness of sins (Clement, *Carpets*

2,13,58); illumination (Justin Martyr, 1 *Apology* 12-19); and purification (Justin Martyr, 1 *Apology* 66,2). The Eastern Fathers did not have an interest in building these various images into a systematic treatment.[6] Indeed, had the controversy experienced in the Western Church made a similar impact in the East, these Fathers might well have spoken with greater sharpness in this area. But such was not the case. As a result, a variety of images and strands of thought on salvation existed side by side in ways that at least at first reading seem not to be compatible. For example, in the fourth century Gregory Nazianzus teaches in some passages in such a way as to rule out any doctrine of original sin and on other occasions he speaks of the involvement of all human beings in Adam's sin and fall (*Orations* 40,23; 33,9). He is not unique in this respect.

Nevertheless, while a number of ways are used to describe salvation in the East, one image soon assumes a preeminent place. This is the concept of *theosis* or *theousthai* and *theopoien*. Divinization and deification may be regarded as synonyms. Actually the words *theousthai* and *theopoien* occur in the literature earlier than *theosis*. The Eastern Fathers saw divinization as the goal of salvation. The terms described the process by which the blessings of salvation, immortality, or incorruption, seen as the result of Christ's saving work, may be progressively experienced by the believer in this life. *Theosis* meant a personal encounter between God and believer. Clearly deification spoke of the operation of saving grace enjoyed by believers who are indwelled with the Spirit and, by communion with the Father, are regarded as children of God. The complete realization of divinization occurs only at the final consummation. It was especially in its mystical forms that the Greek patristic tradition saw the final goal and result of forgiveness as deification. But the influence of divinization on all Eastern writers was significant. The first indications of divinization appear in the literature as early as Ignatius of Antioch (Eph. 4:21; 9:2; Pol. 6:1). Nevertheless, the full clarification of deification had to await the resolution of the conflicts over the deity of Christ. The church could hardly specify what it meant to promise that a believer would become divine until it specified what it meant to confess that Christ had always been divine. In spite of a lack of clarity at times, it was clear that the Eastern Fathers regarded salvation as more than simply a restoration of what had been lost in the first Adam. For whatever the final consummation brought, it had to incorporate what had been won in the second Adam.

In two places the Greek Fathers discovered materials that enabled them to work out their view of divinization. Although the Bible stresses the absolute transcendence of God, certain passages could encourage divinization as an understanding of salvation. These include Ps. 82:6, "I say, 'You are gods, sons of the Most High, all of you'"; 2 Pet. 1:4, " . . . and become partakers of the divine nature"; Pauline passages that speak of adoptive sonship like 1 Cor. 15:49; 2 Cor. 8:9; and Rom. 8:11; and John 10:34, where Jesus quotes Ps. 82:6. A reading of the Bible by the Eastern Fathers supported the view that there is a recreation of believers in the likeness of the Son of God. This transformation and renewal means that human mortality is replaced by incorruptibility and immortal life. For the Eastern Fathers divinization vocabulary could express the ultimate calling of men and women and the newness of a condition restored by the incarnation and redemption of the Son. Three main themes from Scripture aided their thinking: (1) the creation of human beings in the image of God (Gen. 2:26-27), (2) the adoption by the Son (Gal. 3:26), and (3) the imitation of God (Matt. 5:44-48).

The second source was the Platonic tradition. Plato saw the purpose of the soul to be free to escape this world and become, as far as possible, assimilated to God. Such views are developed in the *Phaedo* 82 a-c; the *Phaedrus* 248a, 253 AB (the myth of the charioteer); the *Theaetetus* 176 B; and the *Republic* 10,613a. These last two texts speak respectively about "assimilation to God" (*homoioois theooi*) and "by the practice of virtue to be likened to God as far as it is possible for a human being" (*kai epitedeyon areten eis hoson dynaton anthroopooi homoiousthai theooi*).

Such language was not overlooked by the Fathers. They found similar thoughts in Plotinus. A person's goal is not only to be free from sin, but to be a god, one of the gods who follow the just God. Indeed, it is to gods that a person should strive to become assimilated because gods are the original models of the good (*The Enneads* 1,2,6-7).

The Greek Fathers utilized both the biblical and Platonic traditions. Nevertheless, although they employed Platonic language, it must not be forgotten that they transformed that language to stand under Christian revelation. There is evidence in the Eastern Fathers of both a critical use of Platonism and even a reaction against it (see, for example, the description of Athanasius below). Divinization in all the Fathers is not seen as the accomplishment of the philosophical soul; it is rather God's work of grace. This theme is repeated constantly. For Plato the soul is divine. It is akin to the divine realm of the forms; indeed, it belongs there. Thus the soul's ascent was a process of becoming what it was, realizing its innate divinity. There are passages in the Fathers that sound strikingly similar to this. But a careful reading of the Fathers reveals that they did not uncritically accept the Platonic premise of the soul's kinship with the divine. Too much in the tradition of the church spoke against it.

Besides Ignatius of Antioch, hints of divinization are found in Justin (1 *Apology* 10,2; *Dialogue with Trypho* 124) and in Tatian (*Oration to the Greeks* 7). In Irenaeus' teaching of recapitulation, divinization is presented more fully. Irenaeus teaches that the believer is restored by Christ's recapitulation of Adam. Irenaeus wrote at one point: "Christ who by reason of his immeasurable love became what we are in order that he might make us what he himself is" (*Against Heresies* 5, proem), and: "The Lord redeems us by his own blood and gives his life for our flesh, and pours out the Spirit of the Father to unite and bring into communion with God" (*Against Heresies* 5,1,1; see also *Against Heresies* 4,38,3). Thus there are two images in Irenaeus: one of salvation by sharing in Christ's human conquest of sin, the other salvation by participation in the nature of the divine Logos. In this latter the union with the incarnate Logos and his Spirit is brought about during life by the operation of faith and love and through the sacraments. The influence of Ps. 82:6 in Irenaeus' thinking is clear (*Against Heresies* 3,6,1). Passages of importance in Irenaeus include *Against Heresies* 3,19,1; 4,20,4; 4,33,4; 5,6,1; and 5,8,2.

Theophilus of Antioch also taught divinization. He believed that if Adam had used the gift of freedom rightly, he could have achieved immortality and become a god. In his *To Autolycus* 2, 27 it is stated, ". . . so that if he should incline to the things of immortality, keeping the commandment of God, he should receive as reward from him immortality, and should become God. . ." (see also *To Autolycus* 2, 24).

Clement of Alexandria understood salvation as the attainment of likeness to God. It is a likeness that transcends the natural relationship given to man in creation, for it is participation in divine qualities bestowed by God's grace. Clement spoke of this likeness in connection with gnosis. His ideal gnostic, a son of God by adoption, is, Clement declared, a god even in this life (*Carpets* 7,16): "But he who has returned from this deception, on hearing the Scriptures, and has turned his life to the truths, is, as it were, from being a human being made a god." Clement maintained that a person is deified by illumination and the teaching of the Logos. The believer in baptism is illuminated and, illuminated, made a son, and a son is perfected and, perfected, is made immortal in fulfillment of Ps. 82:6. Thus the knowledge of God gives incorruptibility, which is to partake of divinity. The "gnostic" for Clement is able already to become a god (*The Tutor* 1, 5, 26; *Carpets* 5, 10, 63; 4,23,149; *Exhortation* 11, 114).

As would be expected, Origen followed in the same pattern. Like Clement, Origen can speak of salvation as the attainment of the gift of divinity (*Oration on Prayer* 27,13). Identification with Christ lifts a believer through the human nature of Christ to union with his divine nature, thus to God, and therefore to deification. For Origen there is a real kinship between the Logos and the soul because both are eternal. He spoke of a re-deification, a return to the beginning (*First Principles* 1, 6, 1-4; 3, 6, 1-3), although even in Origen this implies more than a restoration of the original creation. Origen also used Ps. 82:6 and Ps. 116:11 to support the Platonic notion of the flight of the soul into divine likeness (*Commentary on John* 29, 27, 29). A favorite expression of Origen's is "to know God." He was less reluctant to speak in this way than some Fathers. Origen realized that "to know God" is to "contemplate God" and involves more than intellectual recognition. He makes use of this in explaining "knowing God." For Origen, knowing God is to be known by God, and this means that God is united to those who know him and gives them a share in his divinity.

Therefore knowing God means ultimately divinization. Origen used both the verb *theopoieoō* and the noun *theopoiesis* to describe this. He can say that knowing God is having the image of God, which we are, and thus we are re-formed after his likeness. The image is perfected in that we become like God. Contemplation is the means for this, for contemplation is, for Origen, a transforming vision. He developed this idea in speaking of the transformation of Moses' face (*Commentary on John* 32,27). Origen also applies this transforming contemplation to the Logos, who would not remain divine unless he remained in unbroken contemplation of the Father's depths (*Commentary on John* 2, 2). This transformation of the image through contemplation is similar to the teaching of Plotinus. There is the Word who derives his divinity from the contemplation of the Father. Then there are the *logikoi*, who through contemplation of the Word, and through him, of God, are divinized. In Origen the soul's ascent is a process of becoming what it most truly is, of realizing its innate divinity. In the development of this scheme Origen was extremely influential. He provided a framework, but later Fathers would alter it to avoid what they believed to be the dangers of Platonism.

This is immediately apparent in the writings of Athanasius. It is true that in *Against the Pagans* Athanasius taught that by contemplation the soul can achieve a reunion with God, from whom it had fallen. Athanasius, unlike Origen, did not even mention the need of God's mercy for the return. But as early as *On the Incarnation* this teaching is changed. In *On the Incarnation* the soul is created out of nothing. It is frail; it depends on God's grace even for steadfastness after the fall. The fall has so damaged the soul's likeness to God that the incarnation of the image of God, the Logos, is necessary for salvation. Contemplation is no longer a means of divinization; it becomes one of the activities of the divinized soul. The soul does not become divine by what it contemplates, as Origen had taught. For Athanasius the Logos became human that we might become divine (*On the Incarnation* 54). This teaching, as expressed in *On the Incarnation*, becomes characteristic of Athanasius. Never again did Athanasius speak of divinizing contemplation, not even in the *Life of Anthony* where it might be expected. It seems in Athanasius there is a reaction against any notion that the soul is connatural with God. This reaction is the result of a doctrine of creation from nothing, which discloses the ontological gulf between God and the creature, and so between God and the soul. Therefore Athanasius broke with the Platonic teaching that the soul is connatural with the divine. Therefore contemplation is not the way by which the soul becomes divine. Divinization is the result of the incarnation. It is an act of God's grace. Divinization does not occur because of some direct relationship between the soul and God. According to Athanasius, soul (or human being) is divinized as it (human being) is restored to conformity with the image of God, i.e., the Logos. By the condescension of the Logos to the human fallen state in the incarnation human beings are restored. What is involved is an exchange of places between the Logos and humankind.

> He became man that we might be deified. He disclosed himself through a body that we might receive an idea of the invisible Father. He himself endured the insult from men that we might inherit incorruptibility. He assumed the created and human body in order that having as creator renewed it, he might deify it in himself and bring us into the kingdom of heaven according to God's likeness (*On the Incarnation* 54; cf. *Against the Arians* 2, 70).

Nevertheless, this does not mean for Athanasius that man became God or one with God in the sense in which he believed that the Son is one with the Father. If deification is the adoption into sonship (*Against the Arians* 1, 39), then it is adoption by grace. "We are sons, but not as the Son, and gods, but not as he is God" (*Against the Arians* 3, 20).

It appears that it is the insight of Nicene theology into the radical significance of creation from nothing that led Athanasius away from any understanding of *theosis* that involves a natural kinship between the soul and God, as taught by Platonism.

The fall was taken seriously by Athanasius, although not in Western terms. Adam and Eve allowed themselves to be distracted by the natural world. Thus they fell. They were deprived of the grace of the divine image. It was through the fault they committed by their free choice that the disintegrating forces latent in human nature were released. Thus the consequence of their trespass passed to all. While Athanasius never stated that it is impossible to live without sin, sinlessness is not the general human situation (*Against the Arians* 3, 33). If he acknowledged that a person must use free will to attain communication with God, there is no question but that the blessedness of which it consists is wholly a gift of God's grace. Athanasius became the spokesman of that tradition that God the Logos became man in order that humans might become partakers of his life (cf. *Against the Arians* 2, 69-70 and *On the Incarnation*, esp. 15-17).

All these ideas are continued in the Greek patristic tradition. They are found in the Cappadocians and in Cyril of Alexandria (Gregory Nazianzus, *Oration* 37, 13-15; 38, 8-10; Gregory of Nyssa, *Catechetical Oration* 37). It is in the works of Basil the Great that most clearly the problem of the relation of *theosis* as personal encounter and divine transcendence is worked out. Basil took up the distinction between God's essence and his powers, a distinction found in many Eastern Fathers. He stated carefully that the essence of God is absolutely inaccessible to a human being (*Against Eunomius* 1, 14). God is known only in his energies or actions (Letter 234, to Amphilochius). Yet for Basil and other Fathers (see, for example, John of Damascus, *On the Orthodox Faith* 1, 14) this is true knowledge, not just conjecture. In the Eastern tradition the understanding of *theosis* as personal encounter is maintained along with the paradox that God is absolutely incomprehensible and unknowable in his nature.

In Cyril there is a theology of divinization indebted to Athanasius and the Cappadocians and combined with a theology of the sacraments influenced by John Chrysostom (see *Commentary on John* 1, 3-4; 14, 160; *Commentary on Romans* 9, 3; and *On the Trinity* 4, 5 and 7). With Cyril of Alexandria the theology of divinization reached maturity. Later writers developed in their anthropologies a mystery of divinization which, it is possible to say, perfectly respected the trinitarian equilibrium, soteriology, and sacraments as taught by Cyril.

It is especially in the writer known as Dionysius the Areopagite that the mystical tradition of Origen—and with him of the Platonists—and the Eastern view of salvation as *theosis* come together. In fact, in Dionysius *theosis* replaces *theopoiesis*, no doubt under the influence of Proclus and late Neoplatonism. The Dionysian corpus reveals the scheme of "creation, deification, and restoration." For Dionysius the purpose of a hierarchy, celestial or ecclesiastical, was to achieve, to the degree possible, assimilation to God and union with him. Salvation cannot occur otherwise than by the deification of those who are saved. Deification is assimilation to God and union with him to the degree possible. The principle of deification was the beatitude of God himself, that by which he was God; his goodness conferred the gift of salvation and deification on all rational beings. It appears that in Dionysius' writings a change has taken place in the understanding of salvation as deification. It is now the goal awaiting the true mystic at the end of a process of purification, illumination, and union. It is true that in these texts John 1:12 is quoted to show that this deification, this likeness to God through union with him, has been made possible because God has given us the power to become his children. Deification can be understood as the imitation of God, his own gift, a gift of grace proceeding from the one who alone is God by nature and not by grace. Nevertheless, it is difficult not to conclude that under pressure from the mystical tradition of Neoplatonism the distinction between Creator and creature is in danger (see the *Celestial Hierarchy* 3,2; *Ecclesiastic Hierarchy* 1,2-4; 2,1).

Many of these ideas are repeated in the works of Maximus the Confessor, who commented on Dionysius' work about a century later. Maximus understood salvation, defined as deification, as the chief theme of the Christian faith and the biblical revelation. The two biblical texts, Ps. 82:6 and 2 Pet. 1:4, were extremely instrumental in his thinking. He understood the Psalter passage to indicate that righteous persons and angels become divine, and the Petrine text to describe the means of deification, i.e., union with Christ. As with Dionysius, in Maximus there is some ambiguity about the relative roles of grace and human free will in the process. Maximus spoke of deification as consisting in knowledge of God, love, and peace, which cannot be effected by any natural human power. It is available only through grace as a supernatural gift. Nothing created can deify. It rather belongs to the grace of God alone to grant deification on created beings. The ultimate source of deification is the interchange of deity and humanity which occurred in the incarnation. Human beings became God in so far as God became as human being. Maximus in a similar vein spoke of salvation, i.e., deification, as a reward granted by the Son as a gift to those who have believed in him. Here is another example of the antithesis between the grace of God and human freedom in the Eastern Fathers. It was simply present without the problematic character that it had in Western writers (*Ambiqua* 20, 42, 50, 64; *Questions to Thallasius* 9, 22, 40, 60, 61; *Scholia on Dionysius* 2).

In the writings of John of Damascus all the strands observable in the earlier Greek Fathers are present. Salvation is seen predominantly as deification; it is a gift from God, yet the place of human cooperation is acknowledged. If one is seeking one patristic text that summarizes the entire Eastern tradition on this matter, it may well be *The Exposition of the Orthodox Faith* 2, 13. Book 4, 9 is of note, but less helpful. Book 4, 3-13 connects divinizations with baptism, the Eucharist, and a virtuous life.

These themes continue to play a significant role in the thought of Gregory Palamas and Simeon of Thessalonica. But in these two teachers of Byzantine theology there is reflected a different age and theological agenda. The patristic era has long ended. Notwithstanding, in the Eastern theologians a striking continuity can be traced from the early Alexandrians to the fifteenth century.

Thus it seems possible to speak of a doctrine of divinization in the Eastern Fathers. Beyond vocabulary there are common conceptions of anthropology and a Greek tradition, visible from Irenaeus on, which is very different from that which prevailed in the later West, where a theology of grace was elaborated in place of a theology of divinization. The Eastern Fathers have in common a stress on the supernatural vocation of human nature. They consider that this vocation, from which human beings were detoured by sin, has found its radical accomplishment in the incarnation of Christ, who by the sacraments imparts to persons the privileges of his divine humanity.

As a final note, it should be mentioned that while deification never played the same role in the West as in the East, it was not entirely lacking in Western writers. Tertullian knows of it (*Against Praxeas* 13; *On the Resurrection of the Flesh* 49). Deification is present in Augustine (*Sermons* 47, 117, 166). In typical Western fashion Augustine links deification with justification. He states justification implies deification because by justifying human beings God makes them his children. If we have been made children of God, we have also been made gods, not through a natural begetting but through the grace of adoption (*Explanations on the Psalms* 49, 2; *Sermons* 121 and 259; *City of God* 14,

4, 2). In Augustine's thought, as in the East, Psalm 82:6 and Psalm 116:11 have their influence.[7] However, this Western thought lies outside the scope of this paper, but for some balance it should be acknowledged.

What conclusions are possible from this brief overview of Eastern patristic thought? The following stand out as those of value for the Lutheran-Roman Catholic dialogue:

1. The soteriological issues of the Reformation debate had not been addressed earlier by the Greek patristic tradition in terms of justification.
2. The Greek Fathers used several images to speak of the salvation granted to Christians. The preeminent image was *theosis* (or deification), although this word was not always employed.
3. The process of *theosis* cannot validly be translated into the categories that lie behind the sixteenth-century debate on justification. Nor should attempts be made to fit *theosis* into an Augustinian framework. (This is not to say that Augustine was unaware of *theosis*).
4. Although the Greek Fathers were indebted to the whole Platonic tradition, they ultimately transformed—or even rejected—this tradition at crucial points in light of their understanding of the biblical revelation. This means that in either case for them divinization is fundamentally the result of God's grace. While they maintained with firmness that the initial act of salvation is by God's grace, the Greek Fathers saw after this initial act a place for good works, works on the part of the believer that cooperate with this grace.

Is this latter view based on a misunderstanding of the nature of baptism, a confusion of law and gospel? The Greek Fathers taught that baptism embodied God's free gift of salvation which could not be earned by keeping the moral law. Yet they had the problem of the preservation of this gift, once received. *Theosis* as a gift and a process offered an answer. Keeping the law could not be required to win salvation; indeed, the law could not do it. But was the law required so that a person would not lose the salvation once given? If it was, then here is evidence of a legalism appearing in the Greek Fathers.

It seems that it is at this point that the Greek patristic tradition needs to be probed—not in its adoption of a theology of divinization, which recognizes that salvation is only from God through his grace, but in its teaching about the life of the Christian who has been thus saved by God. For example, how does the teaching of the Greek Fathers on this issue (see John Chrysostom on 2 Timothy, *Homily* 8, or Cyril of Alexandria, *Commentary* on John 9) compare with what is said about the Christian life in the Apology (4:346-365; BS 226-29; BC 160-63) and the Formula of Concord (FC SD 4:7-11; BS 940-41; BC 552-53; and FC SD 2:77-78; BS 903-4; BC 536)?

6

JUSTIFICATION LANGUAGE
IN THE MIDDLE AGES[1]

Karlfried Froehlich

The patristic and medieval tradition did not show interest in a separate treatise *De iustificatione*. Lutheran historians of the nineteenth century regarded this fact as supporting the impression of a "dark" Middle Ages and pointed with pride to the rediscovery of the doctrine by the Reformers. Catholic historians, on the other hand, used the marginal role of justification during the Middle Ages as an indication that it did not belong in the center of the church's doctrinal concerns until the sixteenth-century challenge by the Protestants made an official definition necessary. The absence of formal interest should not deceive us, however. Theologians today generally agree that justification language signals central Christian concerns which were discussed in countless ways from the very beginning. Justification touches on the fundamental structure of the relationship between God and human beings; it speaks of their role in this relationship and determines the very definition of salvation. Over the centuries these soteriological themes underwent considerable development, and the language of justification had an important place in this development, opening up ever new aspects of meaning and depth in the expression of Christian soteriology.[2]

Thanks to Augustine, the tradition of justification language in the West never lost its connection with the terminology of Paul, in whose epistles this tradition had its roots. The importance of the Pauline epistles for Augustine's own development is well attested. Under his influence a continuous flow of Pauline commentaries, produced to assist the *lectio divina* of the monasteries and the curricular requirements of the high medieval schools, kept the language of the apostle together with its Augustinian interpretation constantly before monks, priests, and theologians.

A glance at one segment of this exegetical literature, the medieval commentaries on the epistle to the Romans, allows one to appreciate the formative influence of the Pauline-Augustinian language on medieval justification theology. We will look at one representative commentary, Peter Lombard's so-called *Collectanea* of ca. 1140, which was the standard *glossa ordinaria* on the Pauline epistles, the so-called *magna glossatura* of the schoolmen.[3] In addition to quotations from the exegetical tradition, the Lombard included comments of his own and a number of thematic *quaestiones*. We will use his commentary paradigmatically to probe the general understanding of Paul's justification language in the twelfth century and thereafter and to find its connection with other themes such as original sin, concupiscence, grace, works, merit, and faith.

Original Sin and Concupiscence[4]

According to Paul justification is fundamentally the justification of the ungodly (*iustificatio impii*, cf. Rom. 4:5). In Peter Lombard's *Collectanea* the topic of original sin comes up in connection with Rom. 3:23 ("all have sinned"). The comment starts in an Augustinian vein, recalling Rom. 5:12 ("All have sinned, either by themselves or in Adam"), but it endorses a Pelagian formula as well: "They are not without sin either because they contracted sin from their origin or added to it by bad habits" (1361A). Obviously an underlying assumption is a universal, physically inherited sinfulness: "From one sinner, all are born sinners" (ibid.). While the Greek Fathers did not concur, Western exegetes after Augustine regularly read Rom. 5:12 in this way: "Through Adam's sin we as his posterity are shackled as if by hereditary evils" (1387C). Biblical texts like Eph. 2:3, Ps. 51(50):5, and Job 14:4 provided further proof. What we receive from Adam is not just death; it is both punishment and guilt: "From him we have received damnation and guilt together" (1361A). Both together form the essence of original sin. The distinction of two aspects—punishment (*poena*) and guilt (*culpa* or *reatus*)—comes from Augustine; he may have thought of a biblical text such as Ps. 31(30):5. This distinction remained central for the medieval theology of baptism and penance. Anselm of Canterbury inaugurated a new direction by applying Augustine's Neoplatonic view of evil to original sin also. He defined the latter primarily in the negative, as the absence of a required original righteousness. Concupiscence, misery, and death are but the penal consequences of this defect. Anselm's new emphasis became influential after the twelfth century, during which the experience of death and concupiscence was still related to the guilt and punishment of original sin in a variety of ways. The main compromise viewed the lack of righteousness as guilt, and concupiscence as punishment. During the later Middle Ages the continuing identification of original sin with concupiscence as both its *poena* and *culpa* indicated adherence to an old-fashioned Augustinian line for which Peter Lombard served as the example.

In Peter's *Collectanea* the term *concupiscence* draws an extensive comment at Rom. 4:7 ("Blessed are those whose iniquities are forgiven"): "Iniquities here refer to original sin, i.e., the tinder (*fomes*) of sin, also called concupiscence or concupiscibility, or the law of the members (cf. Rom. 7:23), or the indolence of nature, or other such names" (1369A-C). In Rom. 6:12 where Paul himself uses the term ("let not sin reign . . . to obey its *concupiscentiae*"), the Lombard's note interprets the plural in terms of three internal acts: the first impulse, delight, and consent. Paul, he says, does not forbid the first but the two others; they are the devil's weapons, active concupiscence. The comment, however, begins with the primary definition: concupiscence is the tinder of sin, innate vice (1407C-D). The term *fomes peccati* had a long patristic history, going back at least to Rufinus' translation of Origen's Homilies on Numbers; similar combinations such as *fomes peccandi* or *libidinis fomes* occur even earlier in Cyprian, Ambrose, and Ambrosiaster. Listening to Paul (Rom. 7:13-25), Augustine understood the reality of concupiscence, for him most strikingly evident in sexual desire, as the sickness of a disordered will which seriously affects both body and soul. The sickness concept dominated the early Middle Ages, but Anselm's new definition changed the picture.

In the late Middle Ages it was recognized that Anselm's new formula had led to the formation of schools of thought. When Gabriel Biel described three contemporary positions on original sin, he mentioned first the stricter Augustinianism of Peter Lombard and his followers who identified original sin, as a "morbid quality of the soul," with the "vice of concupiscence" (in II *Sent.* d. 30 q.2 a. 1, IA). His second school followed Anselm; it included Duns Scotus and Ockham. These theologians focused on the absence of original righteousness, the unfulfillable obligation of having this righteousness being the primary consequence (*debitum iustitiae originalis habendae*), concupiscence a distant second. The third school advocated a compromise; Alexander of Hales, Bonaventure, and Thomas Aquinas are classified here. As is well known, Thomas interpreted concupiscence as the matter, and the lack of original righteousness as the form of original sin. Biel saw himself somewhere in this camp and probably was closer to the great masters at this point than to the Anselmian wing. But other moderate Augustinians tried to avoid the compromise. They expanded the notion of concupiscence to mean all inordinate desire, identifying it with the Augustinian notion of self-love, *amor sui*. Yet the conclusion that this would automatically qualify all concupiscence as "sin" was rarely drawn. One obstacle was a theology of baptism which insisted that only the *fomes* aspect of concupiscence, not the *reatus*, remained in the baptized; another one was the widespread "Abelardian" tendency to make an act of the will, i.e., consent, the prerequisite of a full concept of sin; a third one was the "Anselmian" logic that concupiscence as a *habitus* was not a power but strictly a lack of supernatural assistance. In these ways the idea of a progressive overcoming of concupiscence as an evil inclination by a good one, i.e., the infused *habitus* of grace, seemed a natural alternative to the simple equation of concupiscence and original sin. Augustine, who took his clue from Paul's medicinal language, had already pointed in this direction: the more God's grace takes control, the more the remaining concupiscence must diminish.

Grace[5]

Peter Lombard's *Collectanea* praise Paul's language of grace time and again. Already the general preface to the Pauline epistles praises the apostle as the "advocate of grace" (1279C). The greeting of Rom. 1:7 ("Grace be to you") leads to the same topic. The Lombard explains: "This is the grace by which the ungodly is justified and sins are forgiven" (1316B). In this connection two Augustinian key phrases are quoted, both themselves derived from Paul: "By grace the one who was a sinner is made righteous" (*gratia fit iustus qui fuerat impius*, cf. Rom. 4:5); and "Grace would not be grace unless it be given gratuitously" (*nec ista esset gratia si non daretur gratuita*, cf. Rom. 11:6). The first became a medieval summary definition of justification; it was intended to safeguard God's absolute priority in initiating justification as the transformation of the sinner. The second represented a classical formulation of the anti-Pelagian argument in the Middle Ages; it stressed the free, totally undeserved nature of grace as a gift. This latter point appears again at Rom. 3:24 ("justified by his grace freely," *gratis per gratiam*): "Gratis, that is, without preceding merits; through his grace, that is, through gratuitous gifts; for the grace of God is God's gift, but the greatest gift is the Holy Spirit himself" (1361BC). The last phrase here introduces the Lombard's famous assertion, on the basis of Rom. 5:5 ("God's love has been poured into our hearts through the Holy Spirit which has been given to us"; cf. 1381C), that the gift of the infused love of God and neighbor is not only a virtue, but the Holy Spirit himself. The commentaries on Peter Lombard's *Sentences* reflect the excitement of the later debate over this point; it led to the rejection of his position by the great theologians of the thirteenth century but, on the other hand, encouraged the new distinction between created and uncreated grace at a time when all grace was understood in an Aristotelian vein as supernatural form, not just as a transforming power "operating" and "cooperating" as Augustine had said.

Drawing its terms from Phil. 2:13 and Rom. 8:28, Augustine's distinction was forcefully expressed during the later years of his Pelagian controversy, the beginning of what we call the "semi-Pelagian" phase. This very context suggests a main problem in the reading of Paul: the determination of the contribution of God and human beings to the process of salvation. Paul had posed it in terms of faith and grace against the works of the law; Augustine described it in terms of the complementarity of God's grace and a human nature endowed with free will. Yet in Paul's letters the indicative of God's saving act in Christ regularly leads to the imperative, the appeal to turn from the old ways and live out the new calling. This ethical appeal was of central significance for the Christian message to the nations. It was very much a part of the message of Augustine the preacher. Different from God's act of creating the world *ex nihilo*, his act of justifying the ungodly involved both sides: "He who created you without you does not justify you without you" (*Sermo* 169.11). With the patristic tradition, Augustine saw human participation primarily as a matter of the will. "God created him who did not know; he justifies him who wills; yet it is he who justifies" (*Sermo* 169.13). But how free is the human will after the fall? What can the ungodly contribute? Augustine's insistence on the impotence of the fallen will, and therefore on the absolute priority of God's helping grace (*auxilium gratiae*), did not fully answer the question. It established the indispensability of grace, but there was room for new thought about the extent to which human nature was left intact or "wounded" (Luke 19:30,34), capable of participating and starting the process or at least preparing itself for God's gracious intervention just as matter must be disposed to form. Medieval theologians discussed these problems in a new climate of growing confidence in the potential of the human intellect even after the fall, a fervent desire for perfection through ascetic and monastic lifestyles, and a sophisticated academic theology.

Nevertheless, a certain framework was provided by history. The official victory of Augustinianism and the rejection of "Pelagianism" as a heresy was a given. No medieval theologian could want to be a Pelagian; at least in this sense, everyone thought of himself as an Augustinian.

Modern research has shown, however, that, due to several factors, both designations had an extremely complicated history during the Middle Ages.[6] First of all, there was the problem of sources. Knowledge of the official decisions in the Pelagian controversy was incomplete. The canons of the North African synod of 418, e.g., remained accessible through their inclusion into standard collections of canon law; an important document like Pope Zosimus' *Epistola tractoria*, however, was unavailable. Most astonishing is the lack of awareness of the semi-Pelagian controversy which continued after Augustine's death in Gaul. Here the issues of predestination, the irresistibility of grace, and especially the *initium fidei*, the beginning of the justification process, were discussed and finally decided along moderately Augustinian lines; a presbyter Lucidus was forced to recant any teaching of double predestination; determinism was rejected, and in the matter of the *initium fidei* even the very desire to be saved was attributed to divine grace. The Middle Ages knew, but made little use of, the so-called *Indiculus Coelestini*, a collection of ten brief chapters opposing semi-Pelagianism drawn up by Prosper of Aquitaine and endorsed by Pope Coelestine. The crucial canons of the so-called Second Council of Orange (submitted in 529 to a regional gathering of bishops by Caesarius of Arles and endorsed by Pope Boniface II in 531) were, however, simply forgotten. They appeared in some Gallican manuscripts of the seventh and eighth centuries but, since they were not copied for any major collection, remained unknown until Peter Crabbe published them in his edition of councils in 1538, just in time for use at the Council of Trent. Thomas Aquinas was one of the exceptional minds who, on the basis of a close reading of the late Augustine and the *Indiculus*, became aware of the semi-Pelagian issues and their doctrinal consequences. Another source problem was posed by the circulation of numerous Pelagian and semi-Pelagian writings under orthodox names. Jerome's authority alone covered several major works of Pelagius, including the *Letter to Demetrias*,

De divina lege, and *Libellus Fidei,* as well as the Pauline commentary. Even Augustine was claimed as the author of Pelagian literature; a most interesting case is the influential *Hypomnesticon* or *Hypognosticon.*

Whether a particular position was indeed "Pelagian" or not can obviously not depend on the polemical fervor of its opponents. At any rate, the label and the fervor were clearly in evidence in the later Middle Ages. The name-calling indicates at least that the Pauline-Augustinian framework of justification language and its anti-Pelagian bias were very much alive throughout the period. Interest in *sola gratia* in the sense of "never without grace" remained a shared concern. On the other hand, under the dominance of the Aristotelian form/matter distinction, theologians in every camp had to pay more attention to the human contribution in the process of salvation. How far the shifts to new modes of expression actually led away from the traditional framework is a matter for debate.

Works and Merits[7]

As a counterterm Paul's language of grace envisioned "the works of the law." Rom. 3:20 and 3:28 offered the classical statement of justification by grace without the works of the law. The Lombard followed the traditional understanding of these works as the works of the old dispensation, the Jewish ceremonial laws, at the same time trying to protect the works of the new order; the old observances did not justify in the way the good works we now perform in charity justify (1358D). "Without the works of the law"—this means: without circumcision, new moons, or sabbaths. But Paul's parallel term, the "law of faith" (3:27), showed the Lombard that this exclusion concerns only the works preceding faith, not those which follow it; without the latter, faith is in vain. This conclusion is drawn from Jas. 2:17,20,26, but also from Paul himself (1 Cor. 13:2) and from Abraham's exemplary obedience (1364-65A); it is boosted by Augustinian texts (cf. 1432 on Rom. 8:2).

The insistence on "good works" for the Christian did not, however, entail the idea of merits which would obligate God in any sense. In fact, the word *merit* does not occur in Paul. Augustine took it over from the North African tradition. Rom. 4:3-4 does, however, speak of "reward" (*merces*): "Abraham believed God, and this was reckoned to him as righteousness. Now to one who does works, his reward is not imputed according to grace but according to his deserts." Paul meant the sentence as a defense of justification by grace. Following his lead,

Augustine's merit language had no room for human claims on God: ''If God wanted to return the reward owed before grace, he would hand down the punishment due to sinners'' (1367D). A famous Augustinian dictum expresses the situation concisely: ''When God crowns our merits, he crowns his own gifts'' (*Ep.* 194.5.19; *De gratia et lib. arb.* 6.15). Peter Lombard seems to have endorsed this argument. The idea of merit as changing something not owed into a legal or moral debt which is owed was a new development at the end of the twelfth century; it evolved into the standard definition in the thirteenth century. At about the same time a distinction began to be made between ''congruous'' or proportionate and ''condign'' or fully deserved merit. The latter term probably was suggested by Rom. 8:18 in a curious combination with Heb. 13:16 which appears already in the Lombard's *Collectanea* (1141f.). In this new context, the Augustinian denial of true human merit was retained either by declaring all merit dependent on God's prior grace or by regarding congruous merit as sufficient for human salvation through God's gracious acceptation. The emphasis on God's ''acceptation'' as the proper framework of justification language, and especially of the discussion of merit, was characteristic of most late medieval theologians after Duns Scotus. The term certainly had biblical and even Pauline roots in those passages that speak of God's impartiality defying human standards (e.g., Rom. 2:11; Gal. 2:6; Eph. 6:9; Col. 3:25).

Faith[8]

Paul's counterterm to righteousness by works of the law was righteousness by faith. The connection of faith and justification occurs time and again in Romans: 1:17; 3:21-31; in the discussion of Abraham's faith, 4:1-25; 5:1; and 10:6-11. It was in his translation of Rom. 3:28 that Luther inserted the *particula exclusiva*: ''For we hold that a person is justified by faith *alone* without the works of the law.'' Since patristic times the Latin tradition had known the formula *sola fide* as an expression of Paul's theological antithesis. It appeared in Marius Victorinus' Pauline commentary, in Ambrosiaster, and with astonishing frequency in Pelagius' commentary. But the exclusivity of justification by faith was always carefully hedged. Rom. 4:4-5 apparently provided the warrant for the caution. Peter Lombard refers to the *sola fide* in a typical paraphrase which is taken from Ambrosiaster: He who has time to work receives his reward not according to the order of grace but as his due; only to him who has no time but believes in Christ who freely forgives the sinner (like the good thief crucified with Jesus), his faith alone is reckoned as righteousness (1367B). If Abraham's faith alone was reckoned to him as righteousness, this meant no more than that his believing was "a sufficient cause of righteousness" for salvation (1367A). Faith alone is a possibility, but an exceptional one. In the ongoing life of the believer faith has to be active in love. Indeed, this was the point of Augustine's treatise, *De fide et operibus*: "The faith of Christ, the faith of Christian grace, is that faith which is active through love" (Gal. 5:6). Even in the interpretation of Rom. 3:28 the stress on necessary works of love remained prominent during the Middle Ages. In the *Collectanea* the preceding verse, Rom. 3:27, with its contrast between the law of faith and the law of works gave rise to a special *quaestio*: "Why is the law of faith not a law of works?" The answer is that it is not a law of Jewish ceremonial works, but if Paul calls it a *law* of faith, he means a faith active in love (1364-65A). We sense the basic Augustinian discomfort with the unmitigated alternative: faith, not works. With Augustine, the author concedes that no merits can precede faith, and even that all good works done outside the Christian faith are ultimately futile (1365A), but bare faith cannot "make righteous."

The comment on Rom. 4:4-5 quoted above also reveals difficulties with Paul's imputation language. For Paul the term *imputare* takes its meaning from the nonimputation of sin, as the reference to Ps. 32:2 in Rom. 4:8 shows: "Blessed is the man against whom the Lord does not reckon his sin" (cf. Rom. 5:13; 2 Cor. 5:19). Medieval theologians had no problem with this usage even though the Lombard wonders whether the phrase "sin was not imputed" (Rom. 5:13) means "it was not believed to be sin (*non putabatur*) by men; I do not talk about God. . ." (1389C). But a positive imputation of righteousness? Would it be "mere" imputation, less than the giving or bestowing of *iustitia*? According to the Vulgate the Pauline phrase echoed Gen. 15:6: *reputatum est illi in iustitiam*, the subject being Abraham's believing (Rom. 4:3, 5, 9, 11, 22; Gal. 3:6). In a comment on Rom. 4:23, the answer to the question is unambiguous: "Through his very believing [Abraham] received what was promised and was made righteous" (1377C). Imputation means no less than being made righteous.

Faith that makes righteous looks both backward and forward; it grasps the forgiveness of sins, and it prepares one for a new life in grace. Thus, Paul's justification *ex fide* was frequently read as a reference to Christian baptism. The Lombard's commentary explains the two aspects of baptism in a remark on Rom. 4:11: "in circumcision sins only were forgiven, but grace for doing good was not provided, nor were virtues given or augmented. In baptism, however, sins are forgiven, the grace of cooperation is conferred, and virtues are increased" (1372C). This double aspect was especially important when the relation of faith to infant baptism was considered. With Augustine, medieval theologians looked at faith in terms of the transformation process to which the justification language was pointing. "Through faith the sinner is justified. Thus, just as an adult is justified through the power of faith, a child is justified through the sacrament of faith, i.e., God turns the ungodly into a godly person, a faithless one into a faithful" (1379A). The "faith" of the infant must be seen as a gift for growth, as an "infused habit," the power to do good.

Other occurrences of *fides* suggested the same emphasis on a faith active in love. The wording of Rom. 4:5 ("to the one who believes in him"), e.g., was an occasion to mention the Augustinian hierarchy of believing. "To believe in him" is more perfect than "to believe that he is" or "to believe him." To believe *in* God is the highest form of faith; it qualifies faith as a gift of God and means "to love by believing." "Through this faith the sinner is justified, i.e., the ungodly is turned into a righteous person so that henceforth faith itself begins to work through love" (1367C). The initial stage of faith, simple intellectual assent to propositional truth, was regarded as important but not sufficient for justification. Again, Paul's difficult phrase, "from faith to faith" in Rom. 1:17, suggested the same notion of stages of believing. The simplest division would speak of different parts of the content of faith as it is confessed in the creed (1323C). According to Ambrosiaster the Pauline notion of faith envisaged the orthodox Christian beliefs in contrast to those of Jews and pagans (1323B). On a different level, however, the Lombard answers the question What is faith? by starting with the definition of Heb. 11:1 ("faith is the substance of things hoped for, the conviction of things not seen") and then bringing in the distinction between a superior *fides qua* which, formed by love, is a virtue, and an inferior *fides quae*, unformed, raw faith which even the demons may have (Jas. 2:19: "You believe that God is one: You do well, even the demons believe and shudder") (1324B). The distinction between faith as total attitude and faith as content appears in ever new forms in the Middle Ages. Hugh of Saint Victor speaks of cognition as the matter, affection as the substance of faith (*De sacr.* 1.10.3). Later Scholastic theologians continued Lombard's terminology of "unformed" and "formed" faith. With their Aristotelian conceptuality they read Gal.

5:6, "faith which works by love" (*fides quae in caritate operatur*), as saying "faith formed by love" (*fides caritate formata*); thus love could now be understood as the indispensable form of faith. At the same time they used the *habitus* theory to distinguish this infused virtue from a merely acquired faith. The point was that justification required a faith which went beyond mere intellectual assent. In the early thirteenth century a new distinction began to be made on the basis of Heb. 11:6-7 ("Without faith it is impossible to please God; for whoever would draw near to God must believe that he exists") between a minimal implicit faith and a full explicit faith in the revealed truths of Christian doctrine. Yet whatever was expected, however much explicit faith was regarded as necessary for full salvation, it was only a preliminary step. The faith by which one was justified, i.e., "made righteous," had to be more.

"More," however, did not mean more human effort. On the contrary, justifying faith itself was always regarded as a gift of God. Augustine had corrected himself at this point, against the semi-Pelagians: "I erred in a similar manner, believing that the faith by which we believe in God is not a gift of God but comes from us . . . for I did not think that God's grace preceded faith" (*De praedest. sanct.* 3.7). His insistence, based on Rom. 10:14, that faith is the answer to God's gracious calling and thus is itself part of God's moving of the will, was echoed in much of medieval theology. In Thomas Aquinas' description of justification, faith is the first conversion, the very fruit of God's converting action in the infusion of grace. Even where the complementary need for *fides acquisita* and *explicita* in terms of correct beliefs was emphasized in the later Middle Ages, the role of the *fides infusa* as a supernatural gift of God was never doubted.

Our survey of themes has not been extensive. Nevertheless, starting with Peter Lombard's *Collectanea*, it may have demonstrated the enormous influence of Paul's language in its Vulgate form on the substance and expression of justification in medieval terminology. Just as "theology" as a discipline grew out of the exegetical work of the early Middle Ages, so medieval thought on justification owed its primary verbalization to Paul. Moreover, the Augustinian interpretation of Paul was generally accepted as an integral part of the *doctrina* which theologians sought in the letters of this Apostle. New factors, such as the introduction of Aristotelian concepts into theology or shifts in the practical concerns of late medieval theologians, could open up new perspectives but could only reinterpret that language.

Iustitia

Before we trace some shifts in the use of the term *justification* itself, we shall take a look at its major component, *iustitia* (righteousness), in medieval thought. Following Paul, the central concern was with God's righteousness, *iustitia Dei*. The language of the Pauline epistles warned theologians that the understanding of the phrase as an attributive genitive designating a quality in God was not sufficient. In commenting on key passages in Romans (1:17; 3:24-25; 10:3-4) Augustine regularly took *iustitia Dei* to refer to a righteousness given to the unrighteous by God. His treatise *De spiritu et littera* contains many instances which make this point: God's righteousness is "not that by which God is righteous, but wherewith he clothes man when he justifies the sinner" (9.15); "it is called the righteousness of God because by imparting it, God makes people righteous" (9.18). It seems likely that Augustine understood the idea of such a communicated *iustitia* to be a parallel to the Pauline notion of the infusion of love (Rom. 5:5). It explained *iustitia Dei* from the act of justification, not vice versa, and thus retained an important element of Paul's language. The Augustinian definition found a strong echo throughout the Middle Ages. Denifle's collection of exegetical texts was meant to demonstrate its dominance among exegetes. Holl has shown, however, that in Denifle's texts three traditions are intertwined. One, based on Pelagius' commentary, interpreted the righteousness of God as retributive justice; another, indebted to Ambrosiaster, saw it as God's commitment to his promise; only the third was Augustinian.

Indeed, the problem of God's righteousness in itself could not be totally neglected. In the relationship between God and human beings, where commutative justice or mutual fairness are inappropriate terms, *iustitia* had to be distributive justice or impartial retribution, as Aristotle had made clear. But does a God who justifies sinners act in accordance with this *iustitia*? Obviously, God's distributive justice needed to be distinguished from his mercy; the relationship between God's *iustitia* and *misericordia* remained a central problem for medieval soteriology. If God's action was called justification, then the *iustitia* involved here was a figurative term for his mercy, not justice in the proper sense.

A decisive contribution to this problem was Anselm's fresh definition: *Iustitia* is a rightness of the will kept for its own sake. Landgraf has masterfully described its background, implications, and effects. By distinguishing *iustitia* from an immutable value of "rightness" (*rectitudo*) and locating it in the will, Anselm was able to define his main concern, sin or "injustice," as the lack of the rightness owed by the will. Abelard, one of the first users of the new definition, drew the conclusion that sin in the proper sense must always involve an act of the will; this raised the issue of baptized infants, who should not then be called "righteous" but only "quasi-righteous," as Anselm remarked. Anselm himself already applied his definition to the relationship between God's justice and mercy: "When you punish the wicked it is just, since it accords with their merits; and yet when you spare the wicked it is just, because it befits your goodness (*condecens est*) though not their merits" (*Prosl.* 10). Justice and mercy have to be held together as appropriate expressions of the same divine will. From this oft-repeated statement the subsequent tradition derived the double concept of God's distributive justice (*retributio meritorum*) and fitting goodness (*condecentia divinae bonitatis*) as the full description of what *iustitia Dei* means. In Anselm's words: "Not that you reward us as we deserve, but you do what befits you, the highest good" (*Prosl.* 10).

The Lombard still worked without this double concept, but the *Sentences* commentaries discussed it regularly at the point where he had raised the issue, namely, in the doctrine of the last judgment (*IV Sent. d.46*). Under Anselm's influence *iustitia Dei* was broadened to include God's mercy. Thomas Aquinas could express the relationship in terms parallel to nature and grace: "Mercy does not abolish justice but is a certain fullness of justice" (*S.T.* Ia q.21 a.3 ad 2). Thus he continued the figurative use of *iustitia* when applied to God's merciful dealing with the sinner. The Franciscan tradition appropriated the Anselmian definition by locating God's *iustitia* resolutely in his will. Whatever God wills is just. In thinking of the justification of the ungodly, Bonaventure made the distinction between true justice and *condecentia divina* a matter of God's ordained power in which divine clemency regularly "intercedes" against the strict demands of distributive justice. Duns Scotus completed this line by claiming not only the unity of God's justice in his inscrutable will but attributing the justification of the sinner to another subcategory, God's *liberalitas* or bounty. It was a subcategory, to be sure. But, Scotus argued, God is true to himself only when he exercises his *iustitia* in this particular fashion. He owes it to himself to be gracious.

The contradictory concerns of late medieval theology make it difficult to generalize about the fate of a particular notion. Like many others,

Gabriel Biel did not reach *IV Sent. d. 46* in his *Sentences* commentary. The available syntheses of his thought point to a clear understanding of the unity of justice in God's will: God's will alone is the true rule of all justice. Again, however, it is a unity of separate virtues which, while being unfailingly exercised in God's promised world order, are only exceptional forms of his true, immutable demand of righteousness. Here the concept of justification is derived from a general notion of *iustitia*, not vice versa, as had been the case in Augustine. The same shift applies even to such an "Augustinian" notion as the "double justice" connected with Catholic reform theologians of the sixteenth century like Gropper, Pflug, Contarini, and Seripando: Internal righteousness acquired by the infusion of grace and the cooperation of the free will still does not suffice before "God who is truly just" (*Deus vere iustus*); the external righteousness of Christ's infinite merits must be applied or imputed in order to allow God's mercy to complete the process of salvation when we face the last judgment. On the other hand, here was a movement taking seriously Augustine's hesitation in speaking of the communicated righteousness as "our own." Even when it is given, it remains God's or Christ's righteousness. But the tradition had cut through the ambiguity of the Augustinian language. In grace, *iustitia* as rightness of the human will *is* possible and can be real in the life of the Christian. Righteousness *is* a human virtue truly available even in this world. There were righteous people, particularly in the Old Testament, men and women who had God's testimony that their righteousness met the standards even of his distributive justice. Medieval theologians agreed that the process of justification does make *iustitia* in some sense the property of the recipient. "The righteousness by which the sinner is justified begins with God and ends in human beings" (Hugh of St. Cher, *Comm. Rom.* 1:17). It is interesting to note that the mystical tradition tended to emphasize this point. Bernard of Clairvaux already asked: "I should call myself righteous, albeit by his righteousness. . . What has been made righteousness for me (1 Cor. 1:30) should not be mine? If my guilt has been passed on, why not my graciously given righteousness also?" (*C. err. Abael.* 6:16). Late medieval mystics added a strong sense of paradox: mine, yet not mine; it understood the righteousness of God reaching human beings as an utterly divine reality, superior to anything the human virtue of justice may mean. Here the two dimensions of "outside of us" (*extra nos*) and "in us" (*in nobis*) become fused. As Bengt Hägglund has said: "The terminology of justification in mysticism is interchanged with the terminology of union with God."[9]

Justification[10]

When we turn, finally, to the term *justification* itself, we are facing a rather astonishing history. From relative obscurity as one technical term among many others, *justification* rose to central prominence in some of the major theological disputes of the late Middle Ages. The etymological understanding of the word was summarized in a frequently quoted saying from Augustine: "What else are the justified but those who have been made righteous (*iusti facti*), namely, by him who justifies the ungodly so that the ungodly becomes a righteous person?" (*De spir. et. litt.* 26.45). This simple explanation reveals the fundamental view of justification as a divinely initiated transformation. Justification in this tradition meant a person's amazing conversion, being turned both toward God and away from sin. Medieval theologians retained the notion of justification as an inner change and as a process, but they did not always keep the Augustinian priorities. Augustine's formula was generally quoted in a slightly different form: "the ungodly becomes a godly person (*ex impio fit pius*)." For the early Middle Ages with their interest in penance, moral progress, and perfection, the remission of sin remained in the foreground until the qualitative change could be explained with greater precision with the help of Aristotle or a mystically enriched Augustinianism.

Early medieval occurrences of the term *justification* apart from the exegesis of Paul seem to interpret it in reference to the beginning of the Christian life, i.e., baptism. The Ambrosiaster's interest in baptismal references may have been a factor. We find the mention of justification as an effect of baptism from Carolingian times right through the twelfth century. Hugh of St. Victor still contrasted circumcision as a "dark" sign with the water-bath of baptism as the "sacrament of justification" (*De sacr.* 2.6.3). In this connection the remission of original sin was the focus of attention because of the predominance of infant baptism. Anselm's new definition of *iustitia* did not change this focus but enhanced the forensic aspect of the term. Parallel to a strong use of Augustinian transformation language, Bernard of Clairvaux reflected this forensic tendency. Protestants have often noted Bernardine texts which seemed to emphasize imputative justification.

In the early theological systems of the twelfth century the term was still without a home. Peter Lombard, who saw it mainly as equivalent to "cleansing from sin," had several contexts for it. One was the discussion of grace and free will (*II Sent. d.26 c.4* and *27 c.5f.*) where he defined both God's prevenient grace and the human free will as the "cause" of justification in the motions of faith formed by love. But there was also the echo of Abelard's atonement theory in the section on Christ's work (*III Sent. d.19 c.1*): "Christ's death justifies when through it love is kindled in our hearts." Most important, consonant with contemporary developments in sacramental theology, the Lombard used the term in his section on the "sacrament" of penance (*IV Sent. d.14 c.1* and *17 c.1*); most commentaries would discuss it in this context in the later Middle Ages.

Landgraf has shown that it was a question raised in the first context that led to further clarification: "Can one rise from sin to new life in God by oneself?" The clarification took the form of a systematic *processus iustificationis* laid out in four parts, a schema which was to dominate all later systems. The standard form goes back to Peter of Poitiers, who developed it in his *Sentences* commentary: "Four things concur in the justification of the sinner: the infusion of grace, the movement arising from grace and free will, contrition, forgiveness of sins" (*Sent.* III.2; PL 211:1044). None of these elements is chronologically prior to the others; the order is one of "nature." Every element by itself is called justification, but none can be within a person without the others. Peter's list as well as his sequence reflect the tradition of the centrality of grace and the remission of sin; they also reveal a new psychological interest in the inner effects of grace (contrition) and the meritorious cooperation of the free will. The scheme became very popular in the schools of the twelfth and thirteenth centuries, particularly among the commentators on *II Sent. d.26* or *IV Sent. d.17*; Albert the Great introduced his discussion by flatly stating: "Everyone says. . . ." It proved to be a flexible formula, able to accommodate a variety of interests. Differences among the lists such as changes in the order often reflect such peculiar emphases. Thus the Porretan school placed the remission of sins first, as a caution against the Pelagian danger of allowing a mortal sinner to participate in meriting forgiveness. William of Auxerre placed the infusion of grace first, followed by the remission of sins and their eternal punishment; he wanted a clean basis for the habit of grace as the context of the Christian life, which would then also include the remission of temporal punishment.

The syntheses of the thirteenth century saw no need to abandon the scheme. Bonaventure used it in the traditional sequence but displayed special interest in the sinner's disposition (points two and three). Grace transforms the will; the psychology of justification is basically a moral one. One must speak of justification in the double sense of "infusion" and "exercise" of righteousness, the latter being related to a faith active in love. But Bonaventure's pastoral concern already led him to single out the church's sacraments as the locus of this justification; while he regarded the actual confession to a priest as not absolutely indispensable in penance, he insisted that the intention to confess was implicit in any perfect contrition. The same concern encouraged a reinterpretation of required contrition as mere "attrition" or even minimal regret (Duns Scotus' *parum attritus* or *non ponens obicem*). The idea was that this relaxation of the requirement of perfect contrition would enhance the assurance of sacramental justification *ex opere operato* for the troubled sinner who might be unsure of his or her own sufficient remorse.

Aquinas' explanation was dependent on the fourfold scheme as well. In his *Summa theologiae* the topic of justification appears in the section on grace. IaIIae qq. 109-112 deal with the nature of grace; they are dominated by a strong Augustinian emphasis on God as sole cause and author. Q. 113 describes justification as grace's first effect (*gratia operans*); q. 114 deals separately with merits as its concomitant effect (*gratia cooperans*). The Augustinian emphasis on transformation remains central, but it is expressed in the Aristotelian language of motion. "Justification is a motion by which the soul is moved by God from a state of guilt to a state of righteousness" (q. 113 a.5c). This definition clearly reflects the fourfold scheme; the sequence of articles in q. 113 confirms this impression: article one defines justification as "remission of sins," focusing on the goal of the process; article two establishes the priority of grace: "Justification of the sinner in its entirety consists in the infusion of grace as its origin" (cf. q. 113 a.7c); articles three and four discuss the motion of free will toward God; article five, the motion of free will away from sin; article six finally describes the remission of guilt, which remains the main aspect of forgiveness, while the punishment for sin and its mitigation now belong in a developed doctrine of penance. In the course of article six, all four elements are summarized once more. The traditional emphasis on the remission of sin lacks forensic flavor, despite the separation of *culpa* from *poena*. Capturing the other aspect of the Augustinian spirit, however, the article speaks of the imparting of a new quality, a transformation of human existence at its core. Speaking of grace, it stresses the infusion of a "virtue" (*habitus*) of grace; speaking of faith, a faith "formed by love."

In justification the dynamic ordering of human existence to God is restored; sin as guilt is remitted though the tinder of sin remains. But for Thomas the transposition into a state of grace means much more than the restoration of what had been lost. It means elevation, the raising of human nature toward its supernatural destination, God himself.

The great systems of the thirteenth century assured the ongoing influence of the "four-elements" schema on later medieval theology. But the modern distinction between a Thomistic, a Franciscan, and an Augustinian school, or recent classifications of various forms of nominalism give us no help in analyzing the late medieval uses of the term justification. Detailed studies of justification in particular theologians show all kinds of combinations between Augustinian, Thomist, Scotist, and nominalist elements which do not allow us to establish convincing interdependence or clear lines of development. The diffusion of terminology may have been the consequence of a widening horizon within which the old Pauline term now was functioning. Late medieval theology accepted the basic understanding of justification as the initial process of the Christian life, its first beginning in baptism and its renewed beginning in penance. The requirements for adult baptism were easily shifted to justification in the sacrament of penance. But the focus on the total life process with its chances of an ever new beginning through the sacraments integrated justification into the even wider process of God's final plan for all creation. The tradition had argued for justification occurring "in an instant," not in a time sequence. The new horizon did require attention to the temporal factor in its widest sense: looking forward, the link of justification with final salvation had to be addressed: the continuing role of grace, perseverance, the conditions for surviving the last judgment; looking backward, the link with creation had to be faced, with human nature as such, with the abiding goodness of God's handiwork, and, in a voluntarist tradition, with predestination.

Thus theologians were led back to the traditional problems with the anti-Pelagian stance. Is one who is outside of grace really incapable of performing any works that are inherently good or meritorious? The traditional answer was Yes on both counts because of the Augustinian understanding of radically fallen nature. The thirteenth century had opened up avenues for possible reconsideration by distinguishing the natural state, however much affected by sinfulness, from the supernatural state of grace. For Thomas Aquinas the "virtue" (*habitus*) of infused grace does produce merits precisely because its works are God's

own works, and human nature is ready for the reception of grace precisely because nature itself is God's good creation and therefore by
definition under God's general grace.

Within the fourfold schema of justification this perspective directed
attention to the role of free will and contrition, the motion toward God
and away from sin. Duns Scotus with his voluntarist emphasis inherited
from the earlier Franciscan school saw the warrant for any form of merit
not in the state of grace itself but in God's gracious acceptation as an
act of his free will, which deliberately limits the infinite options available
to him under his "absolute power." As we have seen, this acceptation
theory became very important for late medieval theologians, Scotists
or not, when they addressed the conditions for final salvation within
the "ordained power" of God or discussed the possibility of inherently
good works "by purely natural powers" (*e puris naturalibus*). Very
few followed Scotus in his strong emphasis on predestination as the
necessary safeguard of God's sovereignty over the ordained order of
salvation. Those who did were immediately drawn into a consideration
of the place of Christ in this contingent plan and thus in the justification
process—another important legacy of the earlier Franciscan tradition.
Others rejected Scotus' predestinarianism but used his theory of acceptation in order to make room for human efforts and for God's accommodation to their imperfect goodness. For all these conflicting concerns,
justification language took on an ever greater significance. As the traditional term for the basic transformation in the relationship between
human beings and God, justification remained the touchstone of soteriological speculation. But the context for its use had become too broad.
In the long run the bewildering possibility of using the term as the
description of that transformation under any angle of the expanded theological agenda led to renewed interest in the roots from which justification language in the Western tradition had emerged: Paul's epistles.
It seems no mere coincidence that Martin Luther claimed his discovery
of the true meaning of justification as the fruit of his exegetical endeavors. He was not alone in turning to the Pauline source again. But
now the linguistic form of the Latin Vulgate, which was such an integral
part of the fabric of medieval theology, no longer determined the options
of the exegete. There was exciting freedom to encounter in a fresh way
the "original" Paul—in Greek.

7

THE ORIGINS OF THE LUTHERAN TEACHING ON JUSTIFICATION

Eric W. Gritsch

An Enduring Problem

The question of "origins" is a complex one because the genetic history (*Entstehungsgeschichte*) of Luther's teaching on justification is intimately connected with the history of its impact (*Wirkungsgeschichte*) on Luther's reform movement. The influences on Luther as well as the historical impact of his teaching are difficult to determine. Luther research has been plagued by inconclusive debates regarding Luther's change from a medieval "Catholic" to an "evangelical" view of justification, for Luther himself left very few clues on the precise circumstances of what has been dubbed the "tower experience" (*Turmerlebnis*): some psycho-historical evidence emerging from "table talks" about a kind of conversion in the tower room of the Augustinian monastery in Wittenberg; the influence of the late medieval tradition, especially nominalism (as represented by William Ockham and Gabriel Biel) and German mysticism (especially the *Theologia Germanica*, which he attributed to John Tauler); and the autobiographical fragment of 1545 in which Luther recalled his discovery of the Pauline doctrine of justification, expressed in the phrase "the righteousness of God" (*iustitia Dei*) in Rom. 1:17.[1]

The problem of "origins" is further compounded by the insistence on the part of Luther and the sixteenth-century Lutheran Confessions that the doctrine on justification was not new; it was rather the rediscovered treasure which would once again reform the church catholic. "We have introduced nothing, either in doctrine or ceremonies, that is contrary to Holy Scripture or the universal Christian church.''[2] At the same time Luther and his followers regarded the doctrine of justification as not just one doctrine among others, but as ''the article on which the church stands and falls'' (*articulus stantis et cadentis ecclesiae*) and as the sine qua non of Christian unity.[3] This article of faith has been acknowledged as the driving force of Lutheranism, and yet its specific *Lutheran* as well as its *ecumenical* meaning have been quite controversial ever since the sixteenth century. In short: the Lutheran teaching on justification has become a neuralgic theme, and any ''objective'' appraisal of it is a difficult task indeed.[4]

This paper traces the Lutheran teaching on justification from Luther to the formulation of a normative Lutheran position in the Augsburg Confession of 1530. What is offered is a distillation of research, leading to some conclusions concerning the ecumenical significance of the Lutheran teaching on justification.

Luther

Luther developed his initial ideas on justification in the context of his academic assignment at the University of Wittenberg: biblical exegesis, with special concentration on the Old Testament.[5] He began with a series of lectures on Psalms (August 1513–Easter 1515) and continued with an extensive exegesis of Paul (on Romans, Easter 1515–September 1516; on Galatians, October 1516–March 1517; and on Hebrews, April 1517–March 1518). Sometime before 1518 Luther had a kind of ''conversion experience'' which, combined with his exegetical work, led to his proposals for reform resulting in the ''reformation.'' Research on the exact date of the ''tower experience,'' as well as an investigation of Luther's early writings, especially his exegetical works, has remained inconclusive, and scholars have argued for both early (1514) and late (1518) dates.[6]

Luther was influenced by Ockhamism and German mysticism, but Paul and Augustine played the decisive role in the formulation of Luther's theology.[7] Having learned from Nicholas of Lyra (ca. 1270-1349) to stress the literal sense of Scripture, Luther found the combination of the literal and tropological (moral) sense a powerful tool to relate biblical texts to questions raised by individual believers like himself. Neither the sacrament of penance, centered in the monastic demand to mortify the flesh, nor Scholastic theology, as presented especially by Peter Lombard (d. 1160), had helped Luther find the gracious God he sought.[8]

John Staupitz, the vicar-general of the Augustinian Hermits and Luther's father confessor, forced Luther to come to terms with himself by requiring him to study Scripture in order to teach it.[9]

It was Scripture that taught Luther "penance" (*poenitentia*) meant total concentration on Christ crucified. In 1545 the sixty-two-year-old Luther recalled how he had wrestled with Scripture in order to find the proper meaning of Paul's phrase in Rom. 1:17, "the righteousness of God" (*iustitia Dei* in the Latin Vulgate).

> I hated that word "righteousness of God," which, according to the use and custom of all teachers, I had been taught to understand philosophically regarding the formal or active righteousness, as they called it, with which God is righteous and punishes the unrighteous sinner. . . . At last, by the mercy of God, meditating day and night, I gave heed to the context of the words, namely, "In it the righteousness of God is revealed, as it is written, 'He who through faith is righteous shall live.' " There I began to understand that the righteousness of God is that by which the righteous lives by a gift of God, namely by faith. *And this is the meaning: the righteousness of God is revealed by the gospel, namely, the passive righteousness with which merciful God justifies us by faith . . . Here I felt that I was altogether born again and had entered paradise itself through open gates.*[10]

The genitive "of God" (*Dei*) suggested to Luther that righteousness belongs to God alone and that no human righteousness can appease him through "good works."

Thus Luther had rediscovered the ancient prophetic insight into the covenant between God and Israel: one is righteous "by faith alone" (*sola fide*), that is, by complete trusting in God who alone is able to sustain a never-ending relationship between himself and his people. "The righteous shall live by faith" (Hab. 2:4). That is the only way to discover the *gracious* God, since human righteousness finds only the God of wrath. In Christ God judges sin and promises salvation. In Christ he discloses his contrariness as both the creator who exacts punishment through the law and as the redeemer who promises mercy through the gospel, the story of Christ. God cannot be appeased by even the greatest humility. Instead, God offers us the righteousness of Christ, who atoned for sinful creatures. There are, then, two kinds of righteousness: an alien righteousness, which is the righteousness of Christ given to those who live by faith in Christ alone; and another righteousness, which issues from faith and is embodied in love of neighbor, by which the self is crucified.[11] Luther felt "born again" because he had discovered what Christ did, rather than what he, Luther, could do to please God.

Luther had arrived at his understanding of "justification *by faith alone*" (his translation of Rom. 3:28)[12] through a combination of personal struggles (which he labeled *Anfechtung, tentatio*) and vocational commitment to academic theological reflection. As a consequence, he criticized the "Pelagian" nature of medieval Scholastic theology, with its doctrine of "cooperation" (*cooperatio*) between human will and divine grace.[13] There is a fundamental difference, according to Luther, between the medieval Scholastic "theology of glory" which speculated about the invisible God and his works, and a "theology of the cross" which focuses on Christ crucified. Theses nineteen and twenty of *The Heidelberg Disputation* (1518) clearly reveal Luther's new theological stance based upon his study of Psalms, Paul, and Augustine:

> 19. That person does not deserve to be called a theologian who perceives and understands the invisible nature of God through God's own works (Rom. 1:20).
> 20. But he deserves to be called a theologian who comprehends what is visible and world-oriented in God through suffering and the cross.[14]

In short: "True theology and recognition of God are in the crucified Christ."[15] Luther argued that a proper renewal of the church could be achieved by a reform of theology to stress the proper distinction between the old life of Adam in sin, which is exemplified by works-righteousness, and a new life in God through grace. In this sense Luther's teaching on justification was the centerpiece of a theology which was totally Christocentric and, as such, crucifies all pride in any theological ego. As Luther put it in his lectures on Galatians in 1535:

> This is the reason why our theology is certain: it snatches us away from ourselves, so that we do not depend on our own strength, conscience, experience, person, or works, but depend on that which is outside ourselves, that is, on the promise and truth of God, which cannot deceive.[16]

Luther shifted the discussion from the Scholastic question of the relationship between nature and grace to the problem of the relationship between grace and faith. His conclusion was that faith apprehends divine grace by trusting completely in the work of Christ, which is communicated through word and sacrament. To live "by faith alone" therefore means to distinguish between the gospel as God's unmerited promise of salvation, and the law, as the constant reminder that sinners can never satisfy God's demands. The proper distinction between law and gospel, therefore, is Christian existence under eschatological conditions: to let

God be God (to hold on to his promise disclosed in Jesus Christ) and to acknowledge the power of sin (to let the law reveal the human desire to be like God, as in Gen. 3:5).

Luther called the proper distinction between law and gospel "the greatest skill in Christendom"[17] and the most difficult task of theology. For to him it meant living "simultaneously as sinful and righteous" (*simul iustus et peccator*). This was no longer an ontological statement about "two realms" (physical-metaphysical, form-matter, spiritual-material, etc.); rather, it was a recognition of creaturely existence "before God" (*coram Deo*) and "before the world" (*coram mundo*). Before God one is "justified" because of Christ's "alien righteousness" experienced in faith, while before the world one remains a "sinner" because of the temptation to be like God, experienced as "original sin." Epistemologically speaking, Luther shifted from an *analysis of being* to an *analysis of relationship*,[18] thus opposing what he understood to be the medieval Pelagian tradition of confusing law and gospel. Luther's teaching on justification rests on the fundamental recognition that God has disclosed his "real work" in the gospel: that he wants to be known as the redeemer rather than as the creator. As creator he may be known in part through reason and philosophy, but he can only be "known" as redeemer in what Luther regarded as the most sensitive organ to detect relationships, "conscience" (*Gewissen*). Conscience experiences the constant conflict between God's dual righteousness: an "imputed perfect righteousness" (which is God's promise that his creatures will be saved, the gospel) and a "natural imperfect righteousness" (which is the internal creaturely drive to please God).[19] Luther insisted that the gospel is powerful enough to transform the righteousness of *faith* into a righteousness of *love*, but only as a *consequence* of "justification" and not as a *condition*. "Love" (*caritas*), therefore, is no longer to be understood as "grace in nature" or as a "superadded" gift working for one's salvation through "good works" (leading to a good conscience before God). Love is instead the "power of God in the gospel" (Rom. 1:16) moving the sinful creature from egocentric self-righteousness to unselfish love of the neighbor in need. "Faith makes the person, the person does good works; good works neither make the faith nor the person."[20] "Justification" occurs in the "cheerful exchange" (*fröhlicher Wechsel*) of Christ's righteousness and human sin.[21]

Luther's exegesis of Romans, which led him to a totally Christocentric view of justification, was intimately related to his appreciation of the ancient trinitarian tradition whose centerpiece was the second article of

the Apostles' Creed. Luther's explanation of this article in the Small
Catechism of 1529 is a splendid example of how one can speak of being
justified by faith in Christ without even mentioning the word "justification."

> I believe that Jesus Christ, true God, begotten of the Father from eternity,
> and also true man, born of the Virgin Mary, is my Lord, who has redeemed
> me, a lost and condemned creature, delivered me and freed me from all
> sins, from death, and from the power of the devil, not with silver and gold
> but with his holy and precious blood and with his innocent sufferings and
> death, in order that I may be his, live under him in his kingdom, and serve
> him in everlasting righteousness, innocence, and blessedness, even as he
> is risen from the dead and lives and reigns to all eternity.[22]

By rethinking the dogma of the trinity in Christocentric and soteriological terms, especially in the light of the Pauline and Johannine
corpus,[23] Luther was led to attack abuses in doctrine and piety, like the
sale of indulgences, while at the same time affirming ecumenical Christian dogmas, especially the canon of Scripture and the dogma of the
trinity. Luther therefore considered himself to be closer to the authority
of Scripture and the tradition of the Fathers in the first five centuries
than to the medieval Scholastic tradition.

The origins of Luther's teaching on justification are grounded as much
in Luther's personal struggle (*Anfechtung*) over his quest for a gracious
God as they are in his intellectual wrestling with the question of the
meaning of "incarnation" in relation to soteriology.[24] His conflict with
the left wing "enthusiasts" (*Schwärmer*) clearly discloses the link he
made between justification and the trinitarian dogma, since his key
arguments against the "sacramentarians" are Christological.[25]

There is a close relationship between Luther's *experience* of justification and the *structure* of his thought. Luther contended that a theology
which is grounded in the article of justification must safeguard the
mystery of God's incarnation in Christ against metaphysical speculation
and ecclesiastical idolatry. But such a theology must also lead the faithful
to adoration of God's majesty by making the proper distinction between
human pride and true worship. That is why Luther could say that the
article of justification is both a "rhapsody" and a "concept."[26] As
such, "the locus *de justificatione* contains all articles of faith."[27] "Nothing in this article can be given up or compromised."[28]

The Augsburg Confession of 1530

Luther's "hot" formulations of justification appeared in a "cool" fashion in the Augsburg Confession. The Confession, the carefully drafted work of Philip Melanchthon, was a response to Emperor Charles V's request. Luther was satisfied with it, even though he commented that he could not step as softly or as quietly as Melanchthon.[29]

The Confession itself was meant to correct not only abuses of "tradition," such as the private Mass and others listed in Part 2 (articles 22-28), but also the abuse of the gospel. The Lutherans summarized the correction with the slogan "justification by grace through faith alone."[30] Melanchthon deliberately chose a scheme and a language which he thought would appeal to the opposition. First, he restated the trinitarian dogma in accordance with the Nicene Creed, with a heavy emphasis on its soteriological function. Accordingly, the articles on God, Christ and the Holy Spirit (1 and 3) focus on original sin (2) which must be combatted "through baptism and the Holy Spirit."[31] Melanchthon then demonstrated how Christ rules believers through the Holy Spirit until his return on the day of the final judgment (4-17). Thus the dogmatic section of the Confession is a rigorously Christological interpretation of the work of the Holy Spirit.[32]

Christian life begins with justification, without the merit of works, and with the imputation of faith in and on account of Christ (4: "justification"). Justifying faith is transmitted through the divinely instituted office of the ministry of word and sacraments, the means by which the Holy Spirit "produces faith, where and when it pleases God, in those who hear the Gospel" (5: "ministry").[33] Wherever there are believers leading a new life (6: "new obedience"), there is the gathering of the church, the earthly body of Christ (7-8: "church"). Baptism, Eucharist, confession, and penance constitute the sacramental and moral dimensions of the church, which must be properly governed and must be distinguished from "temporal government" (9-16) until Christ returns (17).

The first section's last four articles clarify the Lutheran position on free will, sin, good works, and the cult of the saints, who are to be viewed as examples of faith rather than mediators of salvation (18-21). Part 2 of the Confession lists "matters of dispute, in which an account is given of the abuses which have been corrected."[34] Melanchthon showed that such matters as public worship, priestly celibacy, fasting, monastic vows, and episcopal authority are *adiaphora* intended to serve the well-being of the church but are not necessary for salvation (22-28).

Melanchthon and the signers of the Augsburg Confession claimed they were defending ecumenical tradition when they defined the gospel in terms of "justification by grace through faith alone." Moreover, they were convinced they had taught nothing which was contrary even to the Roman church "in so far as the latter's teaching is reflected in the writings of the Fathers"; and thus they thought their opponents could not disagree with the dogmatic articles of the Confession.[35] Even Luther later commented: "We will never again get as close together as we did at Augsburg."[36]

Melanchthon's confessional statement on justification (article 4) is formulated in such a way as not to offend Catholic theologians ("It is also taught among us. . ."). Traditional terminology was used in the Latin version (*"satisfactio,"* *"imputatio"*), although the emphasis was on faith and on Christ (*"homines iustificentur propter Christum per fidem"*).[37] The decisive statement on the relationship between "justification" and "sanctification" is made in article 6 (*"de nova obedientia"*):

> . . . it is necessary to do good works commanded by God. We must do so because it is God's will and not because we rely on such works to merit justification before God, for forgiveness of sins and justification are *apprehended by faith.* . . . The same is also taught by the Fathers of the ancient church, for Ambrose says, "It is ordained by God that whoever believes in Christ shall be saved, not through works but *through faith alone (sola fide)*; and he shall receive forgiveness of sins by grace (*gratis*)."[38]

However, the Catholic opposition did not agree, and the *Confutatio* of August 3, 1530, described the Lutheran doctrine of justification as "diametrically opposed to the evangelical truth, which does not exclude works."[39] Defending the Confession's assertion of "justification by grace through faith alone," Melanchthon produced the first Lutheran theological monograph on justification, in which, on the basis of Scripture and with the support of the ancient tradition (mainly from Augustine), he argued the orthodoxy of the Lutheran stance (Apology of the Augsburg Confession 4).[40]

Conclusions

What a Catholic scholar said about Luther describes very well the ecumenical intention of the Lutheran doctrine of justification: "Roman Catholic theology will have to ask itself whether it can afford to leave

Luther in the hands of Lutheran theology.''[41] Catholic theologians have begun to rehabilitate Luther, and Cardinal Jan Willebrands was moved to comment that Luther may be a "common teacher" because of his teaching on justification.[42] In light of the increasing cooperation between Lutherans and Catholics in the investigation of the Lutheran teaching on justification, some conclusions can be drawn concerning Lutheran-Catholic relations.

1. Luther rediscovered the centrality of the doctrine of justification through a critical encounter with both Scripture and tradition (mainly Paul and Augustine). His teaching on justification therefore is quite "catholic" in the sense that his personal quest for a gracious God led him to a creative expression of the soteriological implications of the trinitarian dogma. The origins of the Lutheran doctrine of justification are thus more intimately connected to the dogmatic development of the ancient church than to a late medieval Catholicism which was no longer "catholic" and had succumbed to "subjectivism."[43]

2. Luther's radical insight that sin is the desire "to be like God" (Gen. 3:5) led him to the conviction, which he found verified especially in the Hebrew Psalter, the prophets, and Paul, that justification is possible only through faith in Christ crucified. Consequently, any doctrine of justification can only serve as a bridge to a totally Christocentric theology in the life of the church. Thus it can be said that the Lutheran *sola fide* is "the test for the authenticity of faith in Jesus Christ."[44] For Luther there are no more "natural assurances" in the sense of self-justification before God. Instead, humanity is directed to Christ who alone justifies.[45] Thus it can be said that the Lutheran doctrine of justification communicates both real death through the law and real life through the gospel (2 Cor. 3:6). "It is not that one must live merely to avoid dying, but that unless we die we shall not live."[46]

3. The Lutheran perspective on justification, centered in the radical notion of *sola fide*, confused and annoyed theologians trained in the Scholastic tradition, with its Pelagian tendencies which advocated co-operation between nature and grace. Mistrusting new theological formulations, Catholic theologians attacked Luther for teaching a doctrine of justification without good works.[47] But Lutheran theologians have also had difficulties living with this article as the article on which the church stands and falls. Thus the judgment can be made that the church, in both its Catholic and Lutheran representatives, has stumbled over the stone on which the church stands and falls.[48] It may be that the article of justification always humbles the church because of its tendency to

be institutionally triumphant. Luther did not succeed in persuading his church to reform itself by the article of justification. But his call to let God be God should not be forgotten.

All we aim for is that the glory of God be preserved and that the righteousness of faith remain pure and sound. Once this has been established, namely that God alone justifies us solely by His grace through Christ, we are willing not only to bear the pope aloft on our hands but also to kiss his feet.[49]

8

"FAITH ALONE JUSTIFIES": LUTHER ON *IUSTITIA FIDEI*

Robert W. Bertram

THESES

Introduction

Thesis One. The one theme in the Augsburg Confession that aroused both the strongest opposition from papal critics and simultaneously, from Melanchthon and Luther, the strongest claim, namely, the claim to be "the main doctrine of Christianity," is this: in Christ God graciously justifies sinners altogether through their faith, independently of the work which their faith of course does. The issue, in short, was *sola fide*.

Thesis Two. Even though some Roman Catholic admirers of Luther prefer him to Melanchthon and use that as a reason for not acknowledging the Augsburg Confession, and though some Lutherans may share that preference, it is the Augsburg Confession and the other Lutheran Confessions, not Luther, which in fact are normative for Lutherans in interconfessional dialogue.

Thesis Three. On the other hand, the Lutheran Confessions themselves occasionally invoke this or that writing by Luther not only as suggestions for further reading but as landmark insights into the word of God which the Confessions honor as precedent and with which they identify ecclesially.

Thesis Four. Specifically with reference to the topic at hand, justification by faith, the Formula of Concord (1577) concludes its article

172

on that subject by reaffirming Melanchthon's "Augsburg Confession and its subsequent Apology" but then, for a more "detailed explanation," recommends also "Dr. Luther's beautiful and splendid exposition of Saint Paul's Epistle to the Galatians" (FC SD 3:66-67).

Thesis Five. That recommendation is worth heeding not only because Luther had been preparing those lectures on Galatians (1531) almost simultaneously with Melanchthon's writing and rewriting of the Apology (promoting interesting speculations nowadays about mutual influence) but simply for the reason which the Formula of Concord cites, "by way of a detailed explanation" of justification by faith. Luther's classroom lectures, even as edited from students' notes, do in fact reveal a depth not immediately evident in Melanchthon's more public, churchly Augsburg Confession and Apology.

Thesis Six. The hope is, by recourse here to Luther's "detailed explanation" in his lectures on Galatians, we might help make the Augsburg Confession's knotty issue of *sola fide* a bit clearer, perhaps even winsome, and not only to our Roman Catholic partners but also to Lutherans.

Thesis Seven. What Luther's lectures might contribute to the *sola fide* of the Augsburg Confession (and of the Apology) is, in particular, his clarifying of faith's *iustitia*: what is it about faith which is justifying; how is it "righteous"? For therein lies faith's *sola*, namely, in its surpassing value.

Thesis Eight. What Luther's lectures say about *iustitia fidei* (a) magnifies the value of faith as much as any fideist might, but precisely as a way of redirecting believers to their value in Christ (theses 9-16, below) and (b) magnifies as much as any imputationist might how Christians' value is something "reckoned" to them, but to them as believers, because of how valuable their faith is (theses 17-21, below).

Part I: Faith's Deficient Righteousness

Thesis Nine. There is no concealing the fact that Luther makes a major point of insisting, more boldly and explicitly even than Melanchthon does, that "faith alone justifies," faith "makes a man God," and "if you believe, you are righteous."

Thesis Ten. Nor can Luther's extolling of faith be explained away as an unbiblical departure which, in the heat of polemics, had lost touch with Scripture, or with everything in Scripture except Paul.

Thesis Eleven.   Nor can the unique value of faith be explained by the fact that faith after all is the doing of the Holy Spirit or of Christ in us. That much, as Luther points out, must be said of all the other godly things as well which Christians do: love, obey, serve, pray, and the like. Of course there is a sense in which love, not faith, is "the greatest of these," yet still not great enough—as faith is—to save or to justify.

Thesis Twelve.   Those statements by Luther which sound most suspiciously like fideism (a faith in faith itself) are those which mete out Christians' righteousness according to the measure of faith they happen to have. For instance: "As much as I grasp, that much I have" (*Quantum comprehendo tantum habeo*).

Thesis Thirteen.   The trouble with such a quantifying, relativizing statement of the sinners' justification is not that it gives them credit for doing something righteous, namely, for believing God and to that extent "having" him. On the contrary, precisely by limiting their justification to whatever measure of faith they happen to have, the statement seems to deny the gospel's claim that in Christ they are righteous altogether. The statement, *Quantum comprehendo tantum habeo*, turns out to be not reassuring but accusing.

Thesis Fourteen.   The first step toward a solution (the second and third steps follow in theses 15 and 16) comes in the form of a distinction: not the distinction between Christ's total victory and our insufficient one but the distinction rather between our *own* total victory, which we find only in Christ, offered us in the promise, and our *own* insufficient victory, which is all we find in ourselves. Everything depends on where we look at *ourselves*. At ourselves as Christ's? Or at ourselves alone?

Thesis Fifteen.   A second step in the solution is that, as believers locate their own vindication in the victory of Christ, they assert a new mastery also over the law, yet not by complying with the law but by surmounting it.

Thesis Sixteen.   A third stage in the solution is that, as the law exposes believers in the littleness of their faith, they in turn respond by utilizing that very criticism as a reminder of their need of Christ. Thus the rule, *Quantum comprehendo tantum habeo*, which begins by humbling, functions in the polar dialectic of Christian subjectivity to redirect believers' attention away from their believing and back to the one they believe in.

Part II: Faith's Surplus Righteousness

Thesis Seventeen.   Also the opposite misinterpretation of Luther, objectivism, seems at first glance (as fideism did) to be well attested by Luther's own statements, particularly on the matter of divine imputation. This is the case especially if we make the initial mistake of assuming that the value that Christians enjoy "objectively," that is, in God's regard for them, and the value of their believing that, are separable.

Thesis Eighteen.   Once more, therefore, it is necessary to recall that for Luther what makes faith righteous is not that God somehow pretends it is righteous when in fact it is not. Granted, faith is righteous at all only if what it believes, Jesus' gospel, is itself righteous. But then, conversely, the gospel's own righteousness does characterize as well the believing, the sacrificial and doxological believing of that gospel. Believing is as right, or righteous, as what it believes.

Thesis Nineteen.   In the passage from Galatians that Luther is expounding ("Thus Abraham believed God and it was reckoned to him as righteousness") what is the unrighteous reality which God reckons as righteous? Not Abraham's *faith*—faith is already righteous—but *Abraham!* God reckons his righteous faith to "him" as righteousness—to the whole unrighteous Abraham, who is far more unbeliever than believer. There is something surpassingly righteous about his faith, however feebly he believes, which makes it accruable, gives it surplus value for him even in his unrighteousness.

Thesis Twenty.   But that does bring us to a radical opposition, not within ourselves but within God, not between the righteousness of our faith and the righteousness (that same righteousness) which is reckoned to us, but rather between the God who "hates sin and sinners" and God—the same God—who nevertheless loves those sinners. To believe, in face of his holy indignation, that he does love them would be wrong unless he himself reconciles that fearsome "opposition" (*contraria*). In Christ he does, thus vindicating the faith of those who depend upon this Christ to be right in order for themselves to be.

Thesis Twenty-one.   The way faith shares in that very righteousness which it believes is analogous to the way faith shares in the *truth* which it believes. Faith *is* the truth trusted.

Part III: An Ecumenical Reflection

Even though the Lutheran confessors and their papal critics, in their theologies of justification, disagreed vehemently over the *sola fide* (as opposed to "faith formed by love" [*fides caritate formata*]), still their very disagreement on that point presupposes a common commitment between them which they not only agreed upon but which they agreed was decisively important. And this common presupposition of theirs distinguishes both of them from many subsequent theologies which have been mightily influential but much less radical.

The determinative assumption which Luther shared, as Melanchthon did, with the pontifical Confutators is this: for Christians to have that sort of ultimate value which assures their viability with God, it is not enough merely that he values them whether or not they themselves acknowledge that; rather, what is essential to his valuing them is that they in turn receive that as subjects, autobiographically, and that the very way they respond is itself part of what makes them so valuable to him. The divine rescue depends that fully upon human history, both Jesus' history and also the history of his followers.

True, this common catholic insistence upon the decisiveness of Christians' "having" the divine mercy autobiographically and having it righteously in order to have it all only intensified that other question to which both sides also subscribed: How, then, in face of such historical contingency, can Christian teaching do justice also to the unconditionality of the divine grace in Jesus Christ? For the Lutheran Confessors the only biblical and catholic way to be faithful to both concerns was to insist upon not only the *SOLA fide* but the *IUSTITIA fidei*.

COMMENTARY

Comment on Thesis One.   What was it about the Augsburg Confession especially that had drawn the fire of the Pontifical Confutation and thus confirmed Melanchthon's— even more, Luther's—apprehensions that "in this controversy the main doctrine of Christianity is involved?"[1] What possible "chief topic of Christian doctrine" (*praecipuus locus doctrinae christianae*) could here have been so in jeopardy that Melanchthon was now driven to devote at least a third of his whole long Apology to this one embattled doctrinal center, as Luther meanwhile was straining to do the same, so consumed were they by this single issue? Was not the issue only too obviously the issue of "justification?"

Yes and no. For merely to name the "article on justification" with no further specification is to leave out of account that one feature *about* justification which was for the Lutheran confessors especially crucial and for their Roman critics especially objectionable, namely, that justification is always and only *by faith*. Indeed, for these Confessors the *sola fide* characterizes not only the forensic theme of justification but every other soteriological theme as well. If anything, justification simply serves to expose how basic the *sola fide* is to Christian doctrine throughout. *Sola fide* is a dimension, as the Roman *Confutatio* and the Lutheran *Apologia* lavishly document, which implicates the widest imaginable range and variety of biblical texts, many of which have no conspicuous connection with justification.

It is this confessional preoccupation with *sola fide* which has appealed—baselessly, no doubt—to later Lutheran fideists and, by reaction, has embarrassed later Lutheran objectivists. The latter, eager to prevent a subjectivist reading of the Augsburg Confession, have effectively subordinated its *sola fide* and have emphasized instead that justification is *propter Christum* and *sola gratia*—which of course it is. But those elements were not at issue at Augsburg, at least not frontally. What was at issue frontally, as the *praecipuus locus doctrinae christianae*, was the Confessors' insistence that sinners are justified (or forgiven or reborn or vivified or saved or whatever) entirely by their faith. Only because that dimension of Christian soteriology was at stake were its other features, its Christological and gratuitous features, thought to be endangered.

Therefore simply to declare without qualification that the principal concern of the Apology or the Augsburg Confession is its concern with justification is at best a half-truth. And this half-truth in turn—also in its generalized version, namely, that justification is the main issue of the Reformation itself—begets other, worse half-truths. It begets the inference, for example, that if in later ages justification does not happen to be particularly at issue, the Reformation must then be correspondingly irrelevant. Or it begets the understandable criticism from biblical scholars that a reading of all Scripture through the single grid of justification is, though perhaps confessionally flattering, indefensible exegetically. In any case, to mistake the discussions at Augsburg as a vague, unspecified controversy about justification in general is to render those discussions practically irretrievable for Lutheran-Roman Catholic negotiations today.

On the other hand, though it is a mistake to suppose that by "the main doctrine of Christianity" Melanchthon meant the doctrine of justification as loosely as all that, the mistake is understandable. For the title that is editorially inserted above article 4 of his Apology does read, simply, "*De Iustificatione.*" And later on in the Apology (18:3) Melanchthon himself refers back to article 4 simply as "the article on justification." Likewise the corresponding fourth article in the Augsburg Confession, the original to which Apology 4 is the sequel and the "substantiation," was similarly entitled "*Von der Rechtfertigung.*" That same shorthand was common with Luther.

Nonetheless, already in his opening sentence of Apology 4 Melanchthon explicitly broadens his defense to include all of what the papal critics had condemned not only in the Augsburg Confession's fourth article but "in the fourth, fifth, and sixth articles, and later in the twentieth."[2] The Augsburg Confession's fifth article had dealt with "The Office of the Ministry," the sixth article with "The Ministry of the Church," and the twentieth article with "Faith and Good Works." Apology 4 now grapples with what the Confutation had condemned in all four of those articles. But Melanchthon sharpens all that it condemned into a single issue, an issue which admittedly comes to its climax in the article on justification but is by no means unique to that article: *sola fide*. "They condemn us," he says, "for affirming that men receive the forgiveness of sins by faith and by faith in Christ are justified."[3]

Melanchthon was right. The Confutators had condemned the Lutheran Confessors at Augsburg precisely on the point of *sola fide*. At one place, for example, the Confutation reads:

> Their ascription of justification to faith alone is diametrically opposed to the truth of the Gospel, by which works are not excluded. . . . Their frequent ascription of justification to faith is not admitted since it [viz., justification] pertains to grace and love.[4]

At another place the Confutation explains that "their [the Lutheran princes'] reference here to faith is approved in so far as *not faith alone* (as some incorrectly teach) but faith which works by love is understood."[5]

The clash, at least directly, was not over the question of Christ or of grace. As for grace, says Melanchthon, already the old Scholastics were "boasting in the schools that good works please God because of grace and that therefore we must place our confidence in God's grace."[6] What those Scholastics had meant by grace, of course, may have raised a further problem. But even if they had understood it as they ought, as "God's grace and mercy toward us," still, "whenever this is mentioned, faith should be added, since we take hold of God's mercy . . . only by faith."[7] And as for the *propter Christum*, "in the schools they also boast that our good works are valid by virtue of Christ's suffering. Well said! But why not say something about faith?" "For," as Melanchthon concludes, "if the doctrine of faith is omitted, it is vain to say that our works are valid by virtue of the suffering of Christ."[8] As Melanchthon reminds his readers later on in article 12, "Our opponents expressly condemn our statement that men obtain the forgiveness of sins by faith. . . . This is the chief issue on which we clash with our opponents and which we believe all Christians must understand."[9]

That "the chief issue" at Augsburg was not justification in general but, more pointedly, justification *sola fide* is easily documented by the immediate sequel to the Augsburg Confession, especially by Melanchthon's Apology and most especially the Apology's fourth article. The entire inner progression of that article argues for *sola fide*, both in its first main section on "promise" as well as in its second section on "law." By what, and by what alone, is the promise of divine mercy grasped? Only-faith-not-works. And which works, and only which works, qualify as "good"? Only-works of-faith. Either way, the contention throughout is for *sola fide*.

But even without analyzing the logic of Apology 4's lengthy and tedious argument, something so superficial as a word count within that article will already signal the same conclusion. As often as *iustificatio* and its cognates (*iustificare, iustus, iustitia,* and the like) occur in their approved sense (as opposed to the sense which the Confutators are said to ascribe to them), the term *fides* and its cognates (*fiducia, credere, apprehendere,* and the like) occur more often. For that matter, in the more than 230 occurrences of the "justification" terms, more of these than not appear in association with "faith" terms. In addition, again as many "faith" terms appear in connection with other soteriological words, like *remissio peccatorum, reconciliatio, accessum habere, misericordia,* and the like. If any term outnumbers the "faith" terms, it is *Christus* (ca. 330 times)—and even that may not.[10] But word counts aside, there is more substantial evidence from the documentary account of the negotiations at Augsburg to demonstrate what priority the controversy had to give, and gave more and more, to the issue of *sola fide*.

As new research on the subject accumulates,[11] the suggestion becomes more and more plausible that these years from 1530 on, during and after the imperial diet at Augsburg sharply intensified the problem of *iustificatio sola fide* as a problem of unfinished business not only for Melanchthon but for Luther as well. At first, during the early days of the diet, this doctrinal issue seems to have been relatively little in evidence. But as it loomed larger in the ensuing discussions, the "gospel" which Luther's letters from the Coburg urged Melanchthon not to compromise is the gospel "that we live by faith and by faith alone" (*ex fide vivere et sola fide*).[12] Next, in view of the direction which the proceedings at Augsburg took during the month of August, Luther contemplated writing on the subject of justification in a book of his own.[13] It is presumably in this connection that he outlined his *Rhapsodia seu conceptus in Librum de loco iustificationis.*[14] A mere snippet—but on the subject of *sola fide!*—did show up that autumn in his open letter *On Translating*, where he expressed the hope, "If God gives me grace, I shall have more to say about it in the tract *On Justification.*"[15]

Luther reproached himself for having let the enthusiasts (*Schwärmer*) distract him from the work he ought properly have been doing all along, on justification.[16] It may be that what he now hoped to accomplish in his projected book was in fact accomplished by his Galatians lectures of 1531 or in his later disputations *De iustificatione*, or, for that matter, already accomplished for him and to his satisfaction by his younger colleague's Apology, article 4. Perhaps. Yet the fact remains, as Robert Stupperich observes, "Unfortunately Luther never wrote his book after all, *De Iustificatione*," the book which was intended to demonstrate "that justification occurs independently of works altogether by faith" (*iustificationem contingere sine operibus et sola fide*).[17] As for Melanchthon, though he was less than satisfied with his product in the Apology and attempted in repeated efforts to bring the matter of justification to better clarity, he records his left-handed thanks to the Confutators for having compelled him at Augsburg to face anew that central issue in justification when other questions on the agenda had come close to crowding it out.[18]

Comment on Thesis Twenty.   It is not faith that needs to be covered by God's imputation. But sin does. Faith is not sin. However—and this is the rub—sin "really is sin." Sin is the real *contrarium.*[19] God reckons "sin as not sin, even though it really is sin."[20] If what faith believes about God is to be at all warranted, then it is for God to warrant such faith by overcoming this opposition (*contraria*) in his relations with sinners. ". . . God overlooks all sins and wants them to be covered *as though* they were not sins."[21] But a merely supposititious "as though" is not good enough.

That this is a real and not a trumped-up paradox, Luther will not let his students forget.

> These two things are diametrically opposed: that a Christian is righteous and beloved by God, and yet that he is a sinner at the same time. For God cannot deny His own nature. That is, He cannot avoid hating sin and sinners; and He does so by necessity, for otherwise He would be unjust and would love sin. Then how can these two contradictory things both be true at the same time, that I am a sinner and deserve divine wrath and hate, and that the Father loves me?[22]

"Who will reconcile those utterly conflicting statements?"[23]

Who will? Surely not believers by somehow joining these opposites through the sheer passionateness of their own subjectivity. Yet it is the righteous mark of their faith that they know who does reconcile them: "Only the Mediator between God and man, Jesus Christ" (1 Tim. 2:5). To this quotation Luther immediately adds another: "There is no condemnation for those who are in Christ Jesus" (Rom. 8:1).[24]

With that Luther brings his lecture on Gal. 3:6 to a climax and a close. Only at the last moment has he disclosed where the one real conflict emerges when God reckons the righteousness of faith as the righteousness of sinners. It is not a conflict between the subjective righteousness of their faith and the objective righteousness which God graciously imputes. For these are one and the same righteousness, namely the righteousness of their faith simply credited to them in their entirety as sinners. No, the conflict rather is between their being righteous at all (whether "in the heart" or imputed), on the one hand, and their being sinners on the other hand. How can they be the one and still be the other, if God is truly righteous? Only at the very end does Luther identify the one in whom alone, and in biographical fact, *that* conflict, that great conflict (*magna pugnantia*), was fought out and reconciled: "Jesus Christ, the one and only mediator between God and human beings" (*unicus Mediator Dei et hominum Iesus Christus*). If because of him it is right for God to forgive sinners, then it is right for sinners to trust God's forgiveness and for exactly that same reason: in Christ the *contraria* within God's own attitude are overcome. That reconciliation within the deity, yet also within human history in Jesus, is what grounds faith as right and for that reason alone makes faith in this God righteous enough to accrue to sinners in their entirety.

Comment on Thesis Twenty-one. It might be helpful, by way of conclusion, to listen in on Luther's comments upon faith as "truth," according to which "the truth about God" becomes, in faith, "the truth of the heart."[25] Thus the object of faith, without ceasing to be that, determinatively characterizes and belongs to the believing subject as well. In the second period of that same two-session lecture that we have been analyzing, namely, on August 29, Luther takes pains to prove that "truth is faith itself."[26] Some of Luther's critics (possibly Johannes Cochlaeus) had argued "that the Hebrew term [in Genesis 15] means 'truth,' not 'faith,' " and, moreover, "that the vocable 'faith' means 'truth' in Hebrew and that therefore it is being misapplied" when Luther translates it as "faith."[27] Luther denies that the two terms pose any real difference. On the contrary, "truth is faith itself" (*Veritas est ipsa fides*).[28] "Faith is nothing else but the truth of the heart."[29]

This quotation could mislead us into supposing that by "truth of the heart" Luther intends some brand of "truth as subjectivity" in the superficial sense that faith is true when it is subjectively heartfelt, when it corresponds to its object by an appropriately matching pathos. To be sure, faith is a decisive change of the self (or it is not faith at all) beginning with the crucifixion of the believers' *ratio*. But that death of their flesh and its replacement are necessarily brought about by what they believe, the cruciform intervention by God in Christ. At any rate, the quality of their believing subjectivity, though of course there is that, is clearly not what Luther here means by faith as "truth" (*veritas*).

That "faith is . . . the truth of the heart" Luther immediately explains: "that is, the right knowledge of the heart *about God.*"[30] Faith is right, or true, only when it is right about its object. Similarly, when Luther speaks, as he did the week before, of faith as "obeying the truth," he does not mean that faith is true when it conforms psychologically or ethically to some norm for obedient behavior. No, people "disobey" the truth when they falsify the object ("Christ Jesus . . . portrayed before their eyes"), when they are "bewitched, deceived . . . by erroneous opinions," when they are "concerned how to resist the truth and how to evade the arguments and passages of Scripture. . . ."[31] For a person to have faith is to "think correctly *about God,* . . . [to] have the truth *about God,* . . . [to] think or judge correctly *about him,* . . . [to] have a true idea *about God.*"[32]

Notice in the following quotation the determinative force of the object.

> Thus truth is faith itself, which judges correctly about God, namely, that
> God does not look at our works and our righteousness, since we are unclean,
> but that He wants to be merciful to us, to look at us, to accept us, to justify
> us, and to save us if we believe in His Son, whom He has sent to be the
> expiation for the sins of the whole world (1 John 2:2). This is the true idea
> about God, and it is really nothing other than faith itself.[33]

A moment before, Luther had been making the same point with a paraphrase of John 16:27. Christ says to the disciples about himself—about
"this object, this 'I' sent from the Father into the world": "Because
you have taken hold of this object, the Father loves you, and you please
him."[34]

Faith is right when it is right about its object. What is right about
faith is not that it is from the heart. That much can also be said of
unbelief, "the inner diseases *of the heart*, such as unbelief, doubt,
contempt and hate for God."[35] The "heart" can just as easily be the
throne of the beast "reason" (*ratio*). Faith is in the heart, of course; it
is *fides in corde*. Where else could it displace the hostile *ratio*? But the
way faith does that, the way it performs its righteous sacrifice, is by
believing what and whom it does, "the Gospel of Christ the crucified."[36] The opposition here between faith and reason is not that the
one is from the heart and the other is from the head. No, what is wrong
about *ratio* is that it is wrong about its object, God. It "cannot think
or judge correctly about Him. Thus when a monk supposes that [his
works] . . . make him acceptable, . . . he does not have a true idea
about God; he has an idea that is wicked and a lie."[37] Therefore, if
faith is only as right as its object, namely, the God whom it believes,
then the righteousness of faith hinges altogether on whether that God,
so believed, is righteous indeed. That much we have said before.

However, the purpose that prompts this concluding postscript about
Luther's equation of faith with "truth" is to avoid that opposite danger,
the sort of preoccupation with the object, the truth-about, which neglects
the subject, the truth-in. Much as Luther's faith depends for its truth
on the object it believes, nevertheless the "truth" in this case—that is,
the Hebrew "truth" which Luther equates with faith—characterizes not
only the object but the subject as well, and the two inseparably. Truth
in this context is not just about an objective, separate reality. Truth is
that reality believed—believed and realized. Truth is the real situation
in the form of its being believed. Granted, as we did, Luther speaks

also of "truth" in a more objective sense, "the truth about God" (*veritas de deo*), but he does so with reference to the *unbeliever*, who "does not *have* the truth about God."[38] Faith, on the other hand, is not only truth-*about*. But simultaneously, exactly because it is the believer's "*true idea* about God" (*vera cogitatio*), his "right *knowledge of the heart* about God," therefore faith is also a truth-in or a truth-of: "truth of the heart."[39] "Having" the truth is itself truth.

Elsewhere Luther even intimates that there is a difference between merely *having* "the gospel," which is not enough, and having "the *truth* of the gospel," which is what faith is. Unfortunately, "many have the Gospel but not the *truth* of the Gospel."[40] For example, the inconstant Peter before the Judaizers at Antioch, though he certainly had the gospel and had been preaching it and "knew the doctrine of justification better than we do,"[41] nevertheless had to be accused by Paul of failing and of swerving from "the truth of the Gospel."[42] To have the truth of the gospel is not only to have its words but so clearly to have it in head and heart that it can be distinguished from the law in face of even the direst personal temptations to the contrary.[43] "Truth is faith itself," the truth about the object as well as the truth *of* the believing subject.

9

JUSTIFICATION ACCORDING TO THE
APOLOGY OF THE AUGSBURG CONFESSION
AND THE FORMULA OF CONCORD

John F. Johnson

In the Epitome of the Formula of Concord theologians of the Augsburg Confession declare that in accord with the divine word and the Augsburg Confession sinners are justified before God solely by faith in Jesus Christ. Thus Christ alone is our righteousness.[1] The Solid Declaration of the Formula names justification by faith the chief article of the entire Christian doctrine "without which no poor conscience can have any abiding comfort or rightly understand the riches of the grace of Christ." In support of this thesis the German version of the Apology is invoked. In addition, the writings of Luther are cited: "Where this single article remains pure, Christendom will remain pure, in beautiful harmony, and without any schisms."[2]

Clearly the article regarding justification by faith as expounded by those willing to answer for their doctrine, faith, and confession at the last day before the Lord Jesus Christ[3] purports to be in complete accord with both the Augsburg Confession and its Apology. Moreover, the Formula's exposition of this chief article was thought to be in agreement with the pure doctrine of the divine word as the sainted Dr. Luther explained it.[4] Indeed, the reader is referred to Luther's beautiful and splendid exposition of Paul's Epistle to the Galatians.[5]

There are some obvious differences between the Apology and the Formula with regard to justification. Article 4 of both the Augsburg Confession and the Apology bear the title "Justification." In the Formula justification by faith is treated under the wider theme "The Righteousness of Faith Before God." In the Apology the teaching on justification is intimately linked to the work of Christ and to the gospel which is defined as the promise of forgiveness of sins. In the Formula the specific question in controversy among theologians of the Augsburg Confession is whether Christ is our righteousness according to his divine nature or according to his human nature alone. But there are other more subtle differences, sharpened nuances, even contrasting emphases.

I. The Historical Perspective

A discussion of the Apology of the Augsburg Confession necessitates some prior knowledge of the historical, theological, and ecclesiastical milieu out of which the Augsburg Confession emerged as the chief confession of the Evangelical Lutheran Church. Luther's bold stand at the Diet of Worms in 1521 not only occasioned the imperial ban, it gave impetus to a number of ecclesiastical reforms which led to significant differences in faith, customs, and ceremonies. On January 21, 1530, Charles V, alarmed by the spread of evangelical teaching among the churches of Germany (and fearful of the power of the Turkish armies amassed at the borders of the empire), summoned a Diet to convene April 8 in the historic imperial city of Augsburg. The express purpose of the Diet was to resolve divisions in the churches so that all opinions might be reduced to one single Christian truth. To the mind of the emperor this would allow the Christians of Germany to live once again in unity in one church.

A. The Augsburg Confession

In response to this call for unity the Elector of Saxony commissioned a number of theologians to prepare a document to treat those articles of faith regarding which there was dissension. That document, composed by Philip Melanchthon on the basis of previously drafted articles, was read June 25 in the bishop's palace before the emperor and assembled princes, bishops, electors, and representatives of free cities of the empire. Written in both Latin and German, the Confession of Augsburg (known as the *Augustana*) claims to teach nothing at variance with the Scriptures or the church catholic or even the church of Rome as known from its writers.[6]

Article 4 answers the question as to how sinners are justified before God. The shorter Latin text reads:

> Also they [our churches] teach that men are not able to be justified before God by their own strength, merits, or works, but are freely (*gratis*) justified

for the sake of Christ (*propter Christum*) through faith (*per fidem*) when they believe they are received into favor and that their sins are forgiven for the sake of Christ who by his death made satisfaction for our sins. This faith God imputes for righteousness before himself, Rom. 3 and 4.[7]

Reaction to the content and conciliatory tone of the *Augustana* was varied. Upon hearing it (some claim he slept throughout the reading), Charles V, hopeful that doctrinal consensus might be achieved, selected some twenty Confutators to prepare a response to the "Saxon" Confession. Under the theological supervision of Johann Eck, who had ably demonstrated his theological prowess in the Leipzig Debate (1519), the Confutators produced a document which they presented to the emperor on August 3. It was the *Augustanae Confessionis Responsio*, more familiarly known as the *Confutatio Pontificia*. It rejected article 4 of the *Augustana*.[8]

B. The Apology

Charles V endorsed the *Confutatio*. True to character, he imperiously demanded that the Lutherans forthwith subscribe to it. His invitation, not surprisingly, was refused. At the September 22 meeting of the Diet a refutation of the *Responsio* and defense of the Augustana, written by Melanchthon,[9] was submitted to the emperor. He summarily rejected it. Melanchthon commended his cause to Christ with the prayer that the afflicted and scattered churches be restored to godly and abiding harmony.[10] The Apology affirms that in the controversy over justification the main doctrine (*praecipuus locus*) of Christianity is involved.[11]

Membership in the Smalcald League was conditioned on acceptance of both the Augsburg Confession and the Apology. Both were recognized as valid confessional statements by the Wittenberg Concord of 1536. The Formula of Concord regards the Apology as explicating the true and proper sense of the Augsburg Confession.[12]

C. The Formula of Concord

The period between the framing of the Apology in 1530 and the adoption of the Formula in 1577 was marked by theological strife, ecclesiastical confusion, and political turmoil. After Luther's death in 1546 the emperor sought to crush the evangelical cause, not by superior theological debate, but by superior military arms. In 1548 he forced the agreement known as the Augsburg Interim upon the churches of the

Augsburg Confession. Its object was to regulate ecclesiastical affairs in Germany until all controversial issues were settled by the Council of Trent (1545-63). The Interim taught that in justification God absolves the sinner from guilt, but also makes him better. Renewed by the Holy Spirit, an unjust person becomes just. The Interim also declared that faith obtains the gift of the Holy Spirit by which the love of God is infused. After this has been added to faith and hope, the sinner is justified.[13]

In the same year Melanchthon, supported by theologians of the Wittenberg and Leipzig faculties, prepared the so-called Leipzig Interim. Its article on justification was almost a replay of the Augsburg Interim. Not only was "by faith alone" (*sola fide*) omitted; faith was coordinated with other virtues, and good works were declared necessary for salvation. Righteousness was understood as infused (*iustitia infusa*).[14]

The political power of the emperor was broken when in 1552 he concluded the Peace of Passau, which granted religious toleration. In 1555 the Peace of Augsburg recognized the legal right of the churches of the Augsburg Confession to exist within the empire.[15]

The Peace of Augsburg was the political answer to dissent between Lutherans and Roman Catholics. The Formula of Concord, the only Lutheran Confession written after the death of Luther, was the theological answer to discord and disunity among Lutherans.[16] Some theologians followed the leadership of Melanchthon and Bugenhagen who championed the cause of reform at Wittenberg.[17] Theologians such as Flacius and Amsdorf held that they were more loyal to Luther's own theology. Others, represented principally by Martin Chemnitz, took the lead in seeking concord by resolving the controversies in light of the prophetic and apostolic witness of the Old and New Testaments.

Work on the Formula was begun in 1567 by Jacob Andreae, chancellor of the University of Tübingen, who in 1548 had been deposed as pastor in Stuttgart because he refused to consent to the Augsburg Interim. He was later assisted in the work by Chemnitz, Nicholas Selnecker, and others who pledged in 1577 that the Formula was their faith, doctrine, and confession, in which by God's grace they were willing to appear before the judgment seat of Christ to give account of it.[18]

D. *The Osiandrian Controversy*

Andrew Osiander resigned as pastor of St. Lorenz in Nürnberg when the Augsburg Interim was introduced. In 1549 he became professor of theology at Königsberg. He rejected the forensic character of justification (*actus forensis*) in favor of a justification before God based on the infused essential righteousness of the divine nature of Christ. Already in 1525, influenced by mysticism, he had taught that the only righteousness which avails before God (*die Gerechtigkeit, die vor Gott gilt*) is God himself.[19]

In 1551 Melanchthon advised Osiander that, while the essential righteousness of Christ effects renewal in believers, they have forgiveness of sins and are reputed to be righteous before God on account of the merits of Christ.[20]

II. The Theological Perspective

The Apology contends that those who confessed their faith at Augsburg hold the gospel correctly. Furthermore, they cannot surrender or abandon the truth that is necessary to the church.[21] That truth was succinctly confessed in article 4: (1) We are not justified before God by our own strength, merits, or works; (2) we are freely justified for Christ's sake through faith which believes that sins are forgiven; (3) this faith God imputes for righteousness before himself. Romans 3 and 4 are cited as texts supporting this thesis.

Article 4 was condemned by the Confutators. In rebutting the condemnation Melanchthon provides a Christological interpretation of what he names "the chief article of Christian doctrine" (*praecipuus locus doctrinae Christianae*).[22] The *Augustana's* confession of justification amplifies the honor of Christ; it furthermore brings consolation to pious consciences.[23] According to the German text, it serves the clear understanding of the entire Scripture and right knowledge of Christ. Melanchthon suggests that the Confutators understood neither grace, faith, forgiveness of sins, nor righteousness before God.

A. The Apology

In addition to its rejection of article 4 the Roman party rejected articles 5, 6, and 20. One is not surprised, since there is an organic connection between them. Article 4 answers the question as to how the sinner is justified. Article 5 answers the question as to how the sinner obtains the faith which God imputes for righteousness (*fides iustificans*). Article 6 treats good works as unfailing consequences of such faith. Good works are commanded by God, but are never to be trusted to merit justification before God. Article 20 is a larger commentary on good works, which the Lutherans were falsely accused of forbidding.[24]

In defense of the Augsburg Confession Melanchthon clarifies the central issues of articles 4, 5, 6, and 20. Justifying faith (*fides iustificans*) is not mere knowledge (*notitia historica*); it is assent to the promise of God in which remission of sins is freely offered. Assent is certain trust, "faith of the heart" (*fiducia cordis*), the wish (*velle*) to receive the offered promise of justification.[25] This is elaborated in Apology 4:48-60.

The question as to how faith is obtained (CA 5) is treated in Apology 4:61-74. Melanchthon insists that while the claim of merit must be excluded, the word and sacraments must not be excluded. He further argues in Apology 4:75-86 that to be justified is to possess remission of sins and that faith is our righteousness before God. In Apology 4:87-106 he appends testimonies of support from Scripture and the Fathers.

The response of the Confutators to articles 6 and 20 of the *Augustana* prompts Melanchthon in Apology 4:107-400 to a detailed discussion of the believer's obedience to the law of God, the necessity of good works, the impossibility of pleasing God apart from justifying faith, and a proper understanding of the biblical concept of reward. Far from disowning good works, the Apology compellingly argues that believers receive the Holy Spirit in order to obey the demands of God's law. Later the Formula supports this position of the Apology by approvingly quoting Luther's preface to his translation of Romans:[26]

> Faith is a divine work in us that transforms us and begets us anew from God, kills the Old Adam, makes us entirely different people in heart, spirit, mind, and all our powers, and brings the Holy Spirit with it. Oh, faith is a living, busy, active, mighty thing, so that it is impossible for it not to be constantly doing what is good.

Melanchthon's response to the rejection by the *Confutatio* of articles 4, 5, 6, and 20 of the Augsburg Confession is prefaced by his now famous distinction between law and promise which constitute, he claims, the two chief doctrines of Scripture. After defining promise in terms of forgiveness and justification, Melanchthon charges: "Of these two doctrines our opponents select the law and by it seek forgiveness of sins and justification."[27]

In the Formula of Concord Melanchthon's (and Luther's) distinction between law and promise (gospel) is called an especially brilliant light in which one must read the writings of both the prophets and apostles. The gospel is defined: "Christ our Lord himself assumed and bore the curse of the law and expiated and paid for all our sins that through him alone we . . . obtain remission of sins through faith.''[28]

B. The Formula of Concord

The Formula was composed in two major parts. Part 1 serves as an Epitome of articles in controversy among theologians of the Augsburg Confession. Part 2, the Solid Declaration, is a comprehensive and definitive exposition of those articles. Both the Epitome and the Solid Declaration affirm that theological controversy must ultimately be settled in conformity with the Holy Scriptures, which serve as the only norm according to which both doctrines and teachers are to be judged.

In addition to the Osiandrian controversy, theological conflicts emerged with regard to the relationship of the law of God to the regenerate (antinomian controversy), the reintroduction of certain Roman ceremonies in public worship (adiaphoristic controversy), the necessity of good works on the part of the believer (Majoristic controversy), and the condition of man's will in the experience of conversion (synergistic controversy).

Articles 5 and 6 of the Formula define law and gospel in their strictest senses. Law is the revelation of God's will and wrath over sin and unbelief; gospel is the revelation of grace and forgiveness. Everything that condemns is law; everything that comforts is gospel. Nevertheless, since Christians are as yet imperfectly renewed, they need the law also for instruction in Christian life.

Article 10 states that rites and ceremonies which are contrary to the word of God must not be regarded as ''matters of indifference'' (*adiaphora*).

Article 4 of the Formula answers the contention of George Major, a follower of Melanchthon, that good works are necessary to salvation. While good works are necessary, they must never be introduced into the article of justification as though the believer could trust in works for salvation.

Articles 1 and 2 severely define the role of the will of the unregenerate in conversion and the role of the will after conversion by the Holy Spirit.

Article 3 treats ''The Righteousness of Faith Before God.'' Affirmative theses state the ''pure doctrine'' of the Christian church over against two false and mutually contradictory teachings: (1) Christ is our righteousness only according to his Godhead; and (2) Christ is our righteousness before God only according to his human nature.[29] However, the question of our righteousness before God involves the nature of faith, the proper understanding of the word "justify," the reason why faith justifies, and the role of good works on the part of the justified.[30]

Subscribers to article 3 confess their intent to remain steadfast in the doctrine of justification by faith as explicated in the Augsburg Confession and the Apology.[31]

III. Particular Theological Emphases

A. Faith and Promise

All Scripture, states the Apology, should be divided into two chief doctrines. For in some places the Scripture teaches law, understood as the Decalogue; in others, the promise of Christ which is to be understood as forgiveness, justification, and eternal life. This promise is not conditional upon any merits of ours; it offers justification freely; it is the gospel of reconciliation. In summary, the gospel is the promise of forgiveness of sins and justification.[32]

Faith is human response to this promise, but a response created by the promise itself. Faith which justifies before God (*fides iustificans*) accepts this promise. Oppressed by sin and death because of the law which always accuses the sinner before God, the sinner cannot trust in anything other than the promise of mercy in Christ. "When a man believes that his sins are forgiven because of Christ . . . this personal faith (*fides personalis*) obtains the forgiveness of sins and justifies us."[33]

Such faith must never be conceived as mere historical knowledge of events connected with Christ, such as his birth, life, or even his death. Neither can such faith ever coexist with mortal sin. Faith trusts God's promise of forgiveness. Melanchthon is not guilty of broad generalization here. He forcefully argues the point in showing how such faith radically differs from the righteousness of the law, invoking not only the authority of Scripture but even the Fathers (such as Augustine in *Grace and Free Will* 9:2).

To avoid any misunderstanding, Melanchthon presses the correlative relationship of faith and promise. Only faith can accept the promise. Three elements always belong together: (1) the promise itself; (2) the fact that the promise is free; and (3) the merits of Christ. This is accepted by faith. Furthermore, faith does not justify by itself. Faith justifies only because it clings to promised mercy.[34] That is surely the genius of Melanchthon's exposition.

The Formula sounds the theme of justification as effecting two realities: (1) absolution from sin; and (2) adoption as a child of God by sheer grace through the obedience, death, and resurrection of Jesus Christ. The Formula testifies that these are true spiritual treasures which are offered by the Holy Spirit in the promise (gospel) and that faith is the only means whereby sinners can apprehend them and make them their own.[35] The Formula also emphasizes the correlative relationship of faith and promise when it confesses that faith is solely instrumental. Grace and forgiveness of sins are realities offered by God in the promise. Faith does not constitute a cause (*causa*) of grace or forgiveness. The sinner is not justified on account of faith (*propter fidem*) but through faith (*per fidem*).[36]

Clearly, both the Apology and the Formula stress that the object of saving faith is God's gracious promise of forgiveness. In sharp contrast, the law always accuses the sinner (*lex semper accusat*). Only the promise calls for that faith by which the sinner is accounted as righteous before God.

B. Faith and Justification

Faith which clings to the promise of forgiveness in Christ justifies. Arguing against the notion that love is the greatest virtue and that therefore love should justify, Melanchthon exclaims: "That virtue justifies which takes hold of Christ . . . this virtue is faith."[37] But Melanchthon eloquently argues that faith justifies because we receive remission of sins and the Holy Spirit by faith alone.[38] Moreover, justification takes place only through the word, and the word is received only by faith. Therefore it follows that faith justifies. The Apology permits no doubt on this vital point. We obtain remission of sins only by faith in Christ; remission of sins is the same as justification; faith in Jesus Christ justifies. But faith justifies not because it believes, but because of its object, Christ.

Exactly what does it mean to be justified before God? The Apology recognizes that justification has a double sense. To be justified, writes Melanchthon, means to make unrighteous persons righteous or to regenerate them. But justification also means to be pronounced or accounted righteous. Scripture, says Melanchthon, speaks both ways.[39]

But Melanchthon apparently understands the making of a righteous person out of an unrighteous one in terms of receiving forgiveness from God. He equates justification and remission of sins. He explicitly adds that this effects the sinner's regeneration or renewal. Commenting on the command of Christ, recorded in Luke 24:47, to preach penitence and remission of sins, he says: "Faith receives the forgiveness of sins, justifies and quickens us."[40] Indeed, as Melanchthon summarizes his argument, which was to make clear that by faith alone we receive forgiveness of sins, he writes: "By faith alone we are justified, i.e., out of unrighteous men we are made righteous and regenerated men."[41]

However, when the Apology addresses the Confutators' use of Jas. 2:24, "A man is justified by works and not by faith alone," it unambiguously states that to be justified here does not mean that a wicked person is made righteous but that he is pronounced righteous in a forensic sense, as even in the passage, "The doers of the law will be justified" (Rom. 2:13), where the word "justified" is used in a forensic sense. Melanchthon provides this commentary on Jas. 2:24: " . . . men who have faith and good works are certainly pronounced righteous. . . . God pronounces righteous those who believe in him from their heart and then have good fruits, which please him because of faith."[42]

Melanchthon also understands justification in a purely forensic sense in Rom. 5:1: "Since we are justified by faith, we have peace with God." He claims that the word "justify" means to absolve a guilty person and pronounce him righteous on the basis of the righteousness of Christ which is communicated to the sinner through faith.[43]

The Formula quotes the Apology as teaching that the article of justification by faith is the chief article of Christian doctrine. But it defines the article in terms of the sinner being absolved and declared utterly free from all sins and from the verdict of damnation.[44] This forensic justification is offered in the gospel. And faith apprehends it. Faith justifies precisely because it lays hold on the merit of Christ in the promise of the holy gospel. In this context the word "justify" is to be understood as declaring righteous and free from sins.[45]

What has happened to the other meaning of justification? After asserting that the word "justify" means in this article to pronounce free from sin, the Formula grants that in the Apology "regeneration" is sometimes used in place of "justification." When this occurs, says the Formula, the terms mean the same thing. Otherwise the term refers to renovation and must be cleanly distinguished from justification by faith.[46] The Formula insists that renewal follows justification; it must not be confused with justification.

The Formula employs such linguistic precision in order that the article of justification remain pure. That which precedes faith and that which follows faith must never be inserted into the article. Good works are the unfailing consequence of justifying faith. True faith cannot coexist with mortal sin; neither is it ever without the fruit of good works. Luther is cited: "Faith alone apprehends the blessing without works; and yet faith is at no time ever alone."[47] The Formula also rejects out of hand the notion that believers are justified before God both through the imputed righteousness of Christ (which is by faith) and through their own inchoate new obedience. Rejected as well is the notion that believers are justified in part by the righteousness of Christ and in part by their own obedience, imperfect though it be.[48] Once again it must be remembered that the Formula does not attempt to present a dogmatic system.[49]

C. Faith and Righteousness

Sinners obtain forgiveness of sins only by faith in Christ. From this thesis the Apology concludes that God declares faith to be righteousness. Rom. 4:4-5, 9 is cited as support. Melanchthon argues:[50]

> Forgiveness of sins and justification are identical;
> Faith alone receives forgiveness of sins;
> Ergo, faith alone justifies.

After adducing various testimonies from Scripture to prove the minor premise, Melanchthon restates the argument: Faith alone justifies because we receive remission of sins and the Holy Spirit by faith alone. We are accounted righteous by faith. Therefore faith is the very righteousness by which we are accounted righteous before God.[51] Faith is righteousness in us by imputation.[52] The gospel proclaims this righteousness of faith in Christ.[53]

The Formula attributes to the Augsburg Confession the teaching that the righteousness of faith is the remission of sins. But the Formula links the righteousness of faith to the obedience of Christ. Through faith this obedience is reckoned by pure grace to all believers as righteousness.[54] By obedience, moreover, the Formula clearly means the sufferings, death, and resurrection of Christ by which he satisfied the demands of the law of God and paid for our sins.[55] This is what the Holy Spirit offers through the Gospel and sacraments, to be appropriated by faith.[56] In stressing the total obedience of Christ (from his holy birth to his death) the Formula wants to insist that our righteousness before God rests neither upon the divine nor the human nature of Christ, but upon the entire Christ as he gave himself to the Father for sinners.[57]

As to the relationship between the essential righteousness of God and imputed righteousness (*iustitia imputata*), the Formula concedes that the Triune God dwells by faith in those who have been justified. But this indwelling of the righteous God follows the righteousness of faith, which is the gracious acceptance of sinners on account of the obedience and merits of Christ.[58]

D. Faith and Works

Faith that brings to God a trust in the promise of mercy justifies. This faith God imputes to the sinner for righteousness. This faith also brings the Holy Spirit so that believers can, in response to the forgiveness of sins, obey the law of God, love God, and truly fear God.[59] Thus justifying faith produces good works. But faith never receives forgiveness of sins on account of love or works. The Apology insists that the believer cannot love at all unless the heart is confident of forgiveness through Christ. Once that confidence is in the heart, love follows. As support the Apology cites Gal. 5:6, in which the apostle speaks of faith working through love.[60]

So there is an inseparable connection between faith and the good works which necessarily follow faith.[61] Faith which brings the Holy Spirit produces new spiritual impulses in believers as God puts his law upon their hearts (Jer. 31:33).[62]

This empowers the Christian to love God and neighbor. However, one must not naively imagine that perfect obedience to the law of God is the unfailing consequence of justifying faith. While it is impossible to separate faith from love for God, it is clear that the law of God requires works that can never be fully satisfied by the believer's performance. Moreover, even the complete keeping of the law, if possible, would not please God for its own sake but only for the sake of faith in Christ.[63]

> We must conclude, therefore, that being reconciled by faith we are accounted righteous because of Christ, not because of the law or our works. The incipient keeping of the law pleases God because of faith; because of faith our failure to keep it is not imputed to us.[64]

Because justifying faith regenerates, Melanchthon understandably urges good works. As confessed in Augsburg Confession 6, good works are not optional; they must necessarily be done as an exercise of faith and as a means to give thanks to God.[65] In them Christ sanctifies hearts and shows his victory over Satan.

The value of good works in the life of the justified is further emphasized by Melanchthon's understanding of merit. Good works are meritorious. Obviously, in light of all that Melanchthon has said about faith and promise, good works do not merit justification. But they do bring spiritual rewards both in this life and in that which is to come.[66]

Melanchthon even grants that Christ connects the promise of forgiveness with good works.[67] However, he interprets such passages to teach that when eternal life is granted to works, it is granted to the justified only. They alone are motivated by the Spirit of Christ.[68]

In supporting the Augsburg Confession and the Apology, the Formula stresses the absolute necessity of good works on the part of the justified Christian. Faith is itself a good work. But the Formula insists that in our justification before God all human works and merits must be excluded as in any sense constituting a meritorious cause of justification. Even faith does not justify as a good work but only because faith lays hold on the merits of Christ in the promise of the gospel.[69] The Formula quotes Luther: Faith which alone apprehends the blessing without works is at no time ever alone; but the Formula hastens to reject the notion that faith cannot justify without works or that faith justifies insofar as it is associated with love. Faith justifies solely as instrument and means to embrace God's forgiving grace.[70]

The Formula provides a more detailed relationship between faith and works in article 4: "Good Works." Some theologians had taught that good works are necessary for salvation; others, that good works are necessary, but not for eternal salvation. Some had even imagined that good works are somehow detrimental to salvation by grace alone. The argument centered on the word "necessary."

In response to this confusion, the Formula asserts that it is the will of God that the justified do those good works which are clearly prescribed by God in his word. Such "truly good" works are true fruits of faith to which God attaches both temporal and eternal rewards.[71] But while it is impossible to separate works from faith,[72] such good works and merits are completely excluded from the article of justification.[73]

When believers do good works, the Holy Spirit works in them, and God is pleased with them for the sake of Christ. Good works may be regarded as harmful to salvation if, and only if, they somehow become the basis for the believer's assurance of righteousness before God. If this happens, the good works are not to be faulted; the fault rather lies with the believer who has misplaced confidence in them. But when good works are done with the proper intent, they do serve as an indication of the believer's salvation.[74]

In concluding article 4 of the Apology, Melanchthon expresses the hope that "good men will find it useful for strengthening their faith and for teaching and comforting their conscience."[75] Who does not see, he asks, that "this doctrine—that by faith we obtain the forgiveness of sin— is most true and certain and indispensable for all Christians?"[76] Melanchthon also expresses the deep conviction, already confessed in the Augsburg Confession, that what has been written in the Apology agrees not only with the prophetic and apostolic Scriptures, but with the holy Fathers Ambrose, Augustine, and many others, and with the entire church which confesses with certainty that Christ is the justifier.[77]

The following may serve as summary theses supported by the Augsburg Confession, the Apology, and the Formula of Concord.

A. Faith in Christ Justifies

1. Faith in Jesus Christ justifies the sinner before God.
2. Faith is in itself a work, an act of the believing sinner.
3. Since faith is wrought by the Holy Spirit, faith is a good work.
4. But faith does not justify because it is itself a good work or virtue.
5. Faith justifies the sinner before God because and only because it clings to its object of trust: the grace of God, Christ, the promise of forgiveness.

B. Faith in Christ Regenerates

6. Justifying faith regenerates and renews the sinner.
7. Therefore faith produces works of love and other virtues required by the law of God.
8. But faith does not justify because it renews the sinner or produces love or other virtues.
9. Justifying faith is never without works, but it justifies solely because it clings to God's promise in Christ.

C. Faith in Christ Is Imputed for Righteousness

10. God imputes the sinner's faith to the sinner for righteousness.

11. This righteousness is not the essential righteousness of God in the believer.

12. Neither is it the infused essential righteousness of either the divine nature of Christ, or his human nature, or both natures.

13. The righteousness of faith is the obedience of Christ, i.e., his life, death, and resurrection.

14. The righteousness God imputes to faith is real righteousness before God.

15. Faith is the only means by which the sinner accepts Christ and in Christ obtains the righteousness which counts before God, since for the sake of Christ alone faith is reckoned for righteousness.

10

FROM AUGSBURG TO TRENT

Jill Raitt

When the *Confessio Augustana* was read before Emperor Charles V and the assembled Diet in Augsburg on June 25, it elicited a surprised and favorable response from most of the "Old Believer" participants. On June 26, they told Charles that the CA was learned, mild in tone, and filled with the gospel and God's word. There were, however, some points that required an answer equally based on Scripture and sound learning.[1] Philip Melanchthon's failure to address certain areas of dispute was also noted, and the Protestants should be asked whether the CA contained all the issues or would it be necessary to discuss others.

This peaceful approach was reinforced on July 4 when Melanchthon wrote to the papal legate, Campeggio, that:

> We have no doctrine different from the Roman Church. . . . We are ready to obey the Roman Church if she can overlook or let pass certain matters that we cannot now change, even though we would wish to. . . . We honor the Roman Pope and the whole ecclesiastical organization, if only the Pope does not cast us off. Then we could easily come to union. . . .[2]

On the canon of the Mass, Melanchthon was sure some mode of accommodation could be found, while the liturgy itself would not appear so different. Melanchthon also said that private Masses and Masses for the dead were no longer a possibility in Lutheran lands. Lastly, Melanchthon agreed that bishops must retain their jurisdiction over spiritual matters.

Such unexpected willingness to remain part of Roman Christendom raised hopes on the part of the Old Believers. But the "matters" Melanchthon asked the church to overlook were those which made the most impact on the people, namely, communion under both kinds, a married priesthood, monasteries converted to day schools and hospitals or even given over outright to secular lords who dismantled them, and the abrogation of set days of abstinence and fasting.

Given the other concessions, Campeggio thought that communion under both species and a married clergy might be tolerated following the precedents in the Prague Pact of 1439 concerning communion under both kinds for the Hussites and the Decree of Union pronounced at Florence in 1439 concerning married clergy for the Greek churches. The Roman Curia rejected Campeggio's compromise and held firm to the 1520-21 papal denunciations of Luther and his followers.[3]

Up to this point not the doctrine of the CA but matters of church polity and liturgy were the subject of dispute. But theologians had been working on their response to the CA. When it was read on July 12, it was rejected as too long and far too harsh. Indeed, the Emperor found it ". . . scandalous, . . . more of an insult than a reply or Christian admonition. . . ."[4] After more rejected attempts, the sixteen Confutators finally addressed themselves to the CA, accepting some parts and rejecting others. The finished Confutation was read on August 3. Satisfied at last, the emperor declared the Protestants refuted and urged them to accept the Confutation.[5] They were to accept it, however, on the basis of hearing it only. No copy was given them. During the reading, Camerarius kept careful notes which provided the Protestants with a basis for their Apology. Here we shall deal only with the *rejected* points pertinent to justification.

The Confutation denies "that men are born without fear of God, without trust in God." Such language, it argues, applies to adults, not infants, and refers to an actual sin. The Confutators also declared that concupiscence is not a sin; the pope had already condemned Luther on this point. Concupiscence does remain after baptism, and it may be called "sin," as Augustine does, in the sense that all are born children of wrath.

With regard to justification, the Confutation asserts that it is a Pelagian error to say that one can merit grace by one's own powers alone. On the other hand, it is a Manichaean error to deny that one can merit with the help of grace. This statement is followed by a plethora of scriptural texts. Under the article on ecclesiastical ministry, the Confutation agrees that the Holy Spirit is given through word and sacraments as instruments, but it denies that these instruments work through *faith alone*. Rather, faith works through love (*dilectionem*); e.g., in baptism, not only faith, but hope and love are infused. *Sola fide* is attacked again in article 6 on the new obedience. While the CA's affirmation of the necessity of good works is praised, the Confutation asserts that justification is not to be attributed to faith alone since it is due more to God's grace and to love. Here again, scripture passages are cited followed by patristic texts. In article 18 on free choice, the Confutation again asks for a *media via* between Pelagians and Manichaeans. The CA, article 20, on faith and good works is rejected, and the Confutation affirms that one merits only in virtue of Christ's merits. As James McCue has noted, the Confutators, working out their first global attack on Luther's theology, could see that theology only in the light of earlier heresies and so tried to steer a traditional course between Pelagianism and Manichaeanism.[6]

When the Protestants rejected the Confutation, war seemed imminent. Negotiations continued, however, and resulted in intensive efforts to find a resolution of theological differences through discussions which took place August 16-30, 1530.[7] During the first week a committee of fourteen met daily. Protestants and Catholics were each represented by two princes, two jurists, and three theologians.[8] The committee moved rapidly through the first three articles, making the same distinctions on each side that would be made at Regensburg in 1541. On article 2, Roman Catholics preferred to speak of the results of original sin as a "lack of original justice," while the Protestants preferred to speak of a lack of faith and trust. The collocutors agreed that grace is absolutely necessary to rise from sin and that concupiscence remains even after justification. Concupiscence, the Roman Catholics conceded, is *materially* sin since it comes from sin and leads to sin, but sin exists *formally* only when the will yields to the promptings of concupiscence. Both sides agreed that their differences on this point were verbal rather than real.

The discussion of CA 4-6 was more extensive and left important points unresolved. Eck conceded that merit is God's grace, while Wimpina affirmed that nothing proceeding from human will alone is meritorious. But the Roman Catholics could not allow the word *sola*, arguing that justification by faith *alone* is not scriptural. From a pastoral point of view it leads the people to consider works and love superfluous. Eck contended that of the two, faith and love, love is more necessary than faith for justification.[9] Melanchthon insisted that the word *caritas* (love) turns one's thoughts to human ability rather than to God's work in us, while Eck meant by *caritas* or *Liebe* the infused virtue which *is God's work* in us.[10] This lack of understanding was not resolved.

Eck and Melanchthon argued at some length about the scriptural basis of the *solus*, citing Pauline texts but without either convincing the other.

Finally, the Roman Catholics agreed to accept CA 4 with the understanding "that forgiveness of sins is through grace which makes one pleasing to God (*gratia gratum faciens*) and faith formally and through word and sacrament instrumentally." Here again, both sides read their own interpretations into the formula. For Melanchthon the "grace which makes one pleasing to God" meant the gift of faith while Eck took it to be the infused virtue of charity.[11] Melanchthon continued to identify "love" with human ability and therefore to deny it a place in justification. Nevertheless, the fourteen agreed upon CA 4 with the Roman Catholics claiming that the Protestants had yielded on the *solus*, which the Protestants then vehemently denied. The Protestants claimed victory in the omission of the word *caritas*. The agreement was therefore, from a negative point of view, based upon an unresolved misunderstanding. From a positive point of view, the fourteen agreed not to engage in merely verbal battles.

CA 7-10 caused no problems, while CA 11 was reserved for the discussion of the CA, Part II. There was agreement about the first paragraph of CA 12, but considerable discussion over the parts of repentance, especially with regard to *satisfaction*. All agreed that satisfaction had no part in the forgiveness of sins, but the Protestants denied that God required satisfaction at all. Both guilt and punishment are completely remitted, they argued. This issue remained unresolved since the Roman Catholics maintained that satisfaction was necessary for the remission of temporal penalties. On the other hand, the Roman Catholics had moved beyond the Confutation by conceding that satisfaction was not required for the remission of guilt.[12]

CA 13 and 16-19 were easily agreed upon. CA 14-15 were set aside for later discussion.

Good works, the subject of CA 20, provoked considerable discussion. While all agreed that good works must be done, their reward or meritorious quality was disputed. Once again, the collocutors agreed that the discussion turned more on verbal than real difficulties. They agreed further that God promised to reward works done out of faith and grace, but the issue of their meritorious nature and the trust one could put in good works remained unresolved.[13]

CA 21, regarding the invocation of saints, resulted in an impasse, with the Roman Catholics affirming and the Protestants denying the validity of calling upon the saints for help. It remained, the Protestants argued, a source of superstition and abuse.

The results of the work of the Committee of Fourteen were summarized by the recorder Spalatin. The discussants agreed on fifteen out of the twenty-one articles in the CA. Of the remaining six, there was partial agreement on 12, 20, and 21, while 11, 14, and 15 were put off for the Committee of Six to consider in the context of CA Part II. At the conclusion of the Reichstag, including the work of the Committee of Six, the Roman Catholics reported that the Lutherans refused to yield on five points:

1) It is not necessary to confess each and every sin.
2) Satisfaction is superfluous with regard to the punishment due sins.
3) The choice of foods and days is an imposition both unnecessary and contrary to the gospel.
4) No human work, no matter how good, can be called meritorious.
5) To invoke the saints is dangerous because it leads to idolatry and superstition.

The hardening of the Protestant attitude in the second week may be due to instructions given to Melanchthon to compromise no more.[14]

In spite of these five points, both Eck and Melanchthon felt that there had been substantial agreement. Only the problems of merit and satisfaction remained thorny. Thus Melanchthon denounced both merit and satisfaction as doctrines detracting from God's free justification of the sinner, while Eck had already conceded that satisfaction did not enter into the forgiveness of a penitent and that all merit was, in reality, grace. Melanchthon continued to consider "love" as a result of the exercise of human natural powers, while Eck consistently argued that *caritas* was God's greatest gift of grace. On August 24 the Committee of Six found its work put under constraint by instructions given to Melanchthon not to make further concessions.[15] By August 29 the discussions ended with the Protestants saying *non possumus* and appealing to a council.[16]

Adding to the difficulty of resolving theological disagreements were the problems arising from the political and social changes which had occurred throughout the past decade. Church lands had changed hands, edifices were torn down or basically altered, new liturgical practices were introduced, and ecclesiastical discipline was radically overturned. The Protestants listed as matters on which they could not yield:

1) They must be able to preach their doctrine of faith, good works, and Christian freedom.
2) They must be able to give communion under both species.
3) Private Masses and Masses as sacrifices for the living and the dead were to be abolished.
4) Married priests were to be tolerated.

5) Monasteries were to be abolished or at least their inmates to be allowed to leave without penalty.[17]

On the matter of episcopal jurisdiction there was long debate, and the Protestants were willing to accept bishops as necessary for good order and, at one point, all but Chancellor Brück agreed to accept papal primacy. They added, however, that they would then be like the Jews living under Pharaoh.[18] Their solution to these unresolved points as well as to the disposition of church lands was to allow everything to remain as it was until a council should decide. In the interim Charles would oversee ecclesiastical revenues in Protestant territories to assure that monks and nuns turned out of monasteries were provided for and that remaining lands and revenues were used only for charitable purposes, e.g., schools and hospitals.

Adding to the pressure to find answers was the threat of war within the empire and on its borders. Melanchthon wrote to Luther on September 4 that they were at an impasse with the emperor:

> We answered that nothing more could be conceded—so it stands. Today we are deliberating about conditions of peace which the adversaries urge. It may be sent on to you. I counsel peace. Our allies judge we shouldn't lose a chance for peace if it can be honestly obtained. War would be catastrophic. I learned today from a prince and friend of the Emperor that the Swiss are thinking of perturbing the public peace and the Turks are definitely preparing a horrible expedition.[19]

By September 7 Charles V was considering the alternatives of war or council. On their side, the Protestants refused Truchsess' and Vehus' *Provisorum* which demanded, in essence, no further Protestant expansion. The Protestants also argued that the CA was not a complete statement of their doctrine and so discussion of the CA would not resolve all their differences.[20]

On September 22 Chancellor Brück offered the emperor the Protestant Apology or refutation of the Confutation. Charles refused to look at it, handing it back immediately. Melanchthon, its principal author, left Augsburg the next day. He rode to Coburg and then went on, with Luther, to Wittenberg. Even while on his return journey Melanchthon worked on the Apology, which appeared in its final form in April 1531 and became, with the CA, a fundamental document of the Lutheran church. Disenchanted with his abortive efforts to prevent a definitive split in the church, Melanchthon attacked abuses and answered the

Confutation thoroughly, charging the Roman Catholics with responsibility for dividing the church.

On September 23 Charles imposed a recess that carried with it a threat of war if the Protestants refused to accept it. Since the recess demanded, in effect, a return to Roman Catholic doctrine and practice, the Protestant princes rejected it and began to leave Augsburg.

Charles, however, did not have sufficient support from the Roman Catholic Estates to begin a war against the Protestants. He therefore urged Clement VII to call a council. Clement agreed, but in reality had no intention of doing so. Conciliarism was still a papal fear, as were the political consequences of a strengthened Hapsburg Empire. But the main deterrent to a council was Francis I, who conspired with the newly formed Smalcald League against Charles V.

The Smalcald League was founded February 27, 1531, to strengthen the Protestant princes against the emperor. Faced with a coalition of dissidents, both Charles V and Clement VII sought means to control the spread of Protestantism. Charles suggested an interim which would maintain the *status quo* until a general council could decide the doctrinal and ecclesiastical issues. The pope, to avoid such a council, relaxed ecclesiastical discipline in Germany, hoping to defuse the protests against Roman abuses. Clement would not, however, go as far as Cardinal Cajetan, who suggested that while maintaining the sacrifice of the Mass, communion could be distributed in both kinds, married priests could be tolerated, and the observance of discipline regarding feast days and fasting and the reception of the sacraments would no longer bind under mortal sin. Cajetan's most extraordinary suggestion, however, was that only a general confession of faith be required, namely, that one believe what the universal church believes without further specificity.[21]

While Clement delayed the council by insisting that both France and England consent to it (and Henry VIII was hardly disposed to please Clement, who had not annulled his marriage to Catherine), the Roman Catholic Estates in Germany urged Charles V to convene the council as had Constantine. Charles, loyal to the papacy, refused. Even the protesting princes agreed to a council, but when John Frederick of Saxony consulted the Smalcald League, the answer was firm: council—yes, but *iuxta morem ecclesiae consuetum*—no. That is, the League demanded that such a council should be in Germany, open and free, i.e., not under the control of the pope, and based solely on Scripture.

On Clement's death, September 25, 1534, Alessandro Farnese was elected pope and as Paul III began to reign on October 13, 1534. Paul

III put the council among his first three priorities and sent as Nuncio Pier Paolo Vergerio to obtain the consent of Christian rulers. Difficulties were first suggested by Chancellor Leonhard Eck of Bavaria, who set his political hatred for the Hapsburgs above Christian unity. Difficulties then multiplied, and the choice of Mantua as a location for the council was used as an excuse to disapprove. Vergerio even met with Martin Luther on November 13. Luther agreed to go anywhere to defend his doctrine, but the Smalcald League, distrustful of Paul after Clement's vacillations, objected to both Mantua and the presidency of the pope.

Francis I ended discussion of a council by invading Savoy in February, 1536. Then Francis tried to bypass both emperor and pope and achieve unity himself through discussions with Melanchthon and Bucer. This effort failed because the League, and Luther himself, distrusted both of the theologians' demonstrated willingness to compromise.

Meanwhile, both Francis I and Henry VIII used the Smalcald League against the emperor and the pope. Henry flirted with the League, and Luther wrote out articles to which Henry was asked to subscribe should he wish to join the League. But Henry's advantage lay in manipulation of, rather than union with, any continental power. Against Henry Paul III tried to organize continental embargoes to back up the excommunication already drawn up but not yet delivered. A council would present Henry with a united European Christendom already shocked by the execution of Bishop Fisher and Thomas More.

On June 2, 1536, with Francis I's "approval," the pope published the Bull of Convocation setting May 23, 1537, as the date for the opening of the council and Mantua as the location. All bishops, abbots, prelates, the emperor, and princes were asked to attend. But neither the Smalcald League nor Francis I agreed. The League rejected the council on the same grounds as before and on February 24, 1537, published its hostile reply. Francis did not allow his bishops to leave France. Sadly, on May 21, 1539, Paul III issued a bull suspending the council: *suspensio ad beneplacitum.*[22]

But the bull convoking the council at Mantua galvanized the Protestant forces. Out of the articles prepared for Henry VIII, Luther drew up the Smalcald Articles, which set out theological points on which Protestants should refuse to yield. The League's representatives did not sign the articles, and Melanchthon opposed their adoption on the grounds that they would cause division rather than unity within the League. Nevertheless, the clergy at Smalcald signed the articles, which subsequently were incorporated into the *Book of Concord* (1580).

Part I of the articles consists of noncontroversial statements about God. Part II speaks of (1) Christ and redemption offered to faith alone, and (2) the "abomination" of the Mass, which leads to the doctrine of purgatory and to the observance of holy days and Masses for the dead, indulgences, prayers to saints, pilgrimages, relics, and other abuses which encourage an attitude of works-righteousness, idolatry, and superstition. Part II ends with an assertion that under Christ, our unique head, all bishops are equal; the pope is called "anti-Christ."

Part III consists of the "Christian articles" on sin, law, repentance, the gospel, the sacraments, and excommunication as a *civil* penalty first and a Christian penalty secondarily. It continues with ordination, the marriage of priests, the church—which consists of Christ and his people, and lastly the doctrine of justification, which reaffirms Luther's teaching in a combination of "forensic" and regenerative justification. The article on justification asserts that: (1) one is given a new and clean heart; (2) God accounts one holy and righteous although (3) sin remains in the flesh and is not completely removed; and (4) good works follow faith and are a result of renewal and God's forgiveness.[23]

On the Catholic side, and in order to retain control of those elements that might otherwise develop conciliarist tendencies, Pope Paul III appointed a blue-ribbon commission of young, reform-minded prelates, some of whom he had recently made cardinals: Contarini, Carafa, Pole, Sadoleto, *et al.* In March 1537 the commission produced the reform document *Consilium de emendanda ecclesia.* It called for an end of the most flagrant abuses, especially the notion that popes were exempt from every law and could sell spiritual benefits, i.e., indulge in simony. *De emendanda* addressed also church administration generally and demanded that the curia and all the curial offices be reviewed and cleaned up or eliminated.

To prepare for the council when it should finally succeed in meeting, if not to make its work with regard to the Protestants unnecessary, Charles himself called Roman Catholic and Protestant theologians to a diet which was originally convoked to meet at Speyer, but an epidemic there caused it to be moved to Hagenau in June 1540. With very little accomplished, the theological colloquy was moved once more to Worms on October 28 and actually opened on November 25. During the last months of 1540, under the direction of Nicolas Granvelle, Charles V's chancellor, the Roman Catholic John Gropper and Martin Bucer met secretly at Worms.[24] Gropper was assisted by Gerhard Veltwyck, and Wolfgang Capito from Strassburg joined Bucer. The four of them drew up the "Regensburg Book,"[25] which formed the basis for debate when the colloquy, moved yet again (this time to Regensburg), was formally opened on April 5 by the emperor himself.[26] The reform-minded Cardinal Contarini had arrived in March as papal legate and raised the hopes of all that this colloquy might succeed. Indeed, Contarini proved so excellent an influence that the Roman Catholic collocutors met with him before and after each session.[27] Contarini had especially to try to manage John Eck, the most unyielding of the three Roman Catholic participants,[28] Eck, John Gropper, and Julius Pflug. For the Protestants there were Philip Melanchthon, Martin Bucer, and John Pistorius.[29] Luther was still under the ban of the edict of Worms and so could not attend, and Melanchthon was charged by his prince, the Elector John Frederick of Saxony, to remain faithful, not to Luther's writings, but to the Augsburg Confession and its Apology. Besides the six collocutors, the papal legate, and the emperor, others attended the colloquy, including John Calvin en route to Geneva from Strassburg. Five imperial electors were present as were two French ambassadors, one representing Roman Catholics and the other, Protestants.[30] The papal nuncio, Cardinal Morone, though skeptical of the usefulness of a colloquy, also attended. The Bavarian Catholic dukes, jealous of Hapsburg power, opposed the imperially organized colloquy but sent as their spokesman the tireless John Eck.[31]

The colloquy followed a set program. Rather than basing their discussion on the CA or other clearly Protestant material, the emperor's chancellor, Granvelle, proposed the Regensburg Book, which he had kept secret and which he introduced at this point as the work of Flemish theologians![32] At each session Granvelle read the passage to be considered. What was truly astonishing was the progress made each day and the agreement reached on the fall, free will, the cause of sin, and original sin. All of this was accomplished by April 28. They turned now to article 5 on justification. Melanchthon and Eck both rebelled against the text in what would better be named Granvelle's book, and it was set aside.[33] Each side then prepared drafts. A stalemate seemed to occur until, through the influence of Gropper and Pflug, backed by Contarini, the Protestants were allowed "to amend the Catholic draft so radically that nothing remained in it which they found incompatible with the Augsburg Confession."[34] On May 2 the jubilant announcement was made that the collocutors had agreed upon the crucial doctrine of justification.

The final form of the formula on justification is found in the fourth volume of the *Corpus Reformatorum*.[35] The most familiar aspect of

Regensburg article 5, *De iustificatione hominis*, is the so-called double justification. It builds upon the first four articles, also agreed upon, which deal with the "condition of mankind and the integrity of nature before the fall," "free choice" (*De libero arbitrio*), "the cause of sin," and "original sin." In the first article, the state of integrity is more than a just balance among human faculties, for in making man to his image and likeness, God adorned him magnificently in body and in mind with intelligence, liberty, virtue, and an innocent beauty. In article 2, we learn that the first couple could, if they had wished, through the accepting and assisting grace and power of the Holy Spirit, have kept the commandment given them and so preserved the image of God in which they were created. Once lost, this free choice exists differently in each of three stages: (1) after the fall but before the reparation; (2) after the reparation but before glorification; (3) after glorification. After the fall the only liberty that remains is *freedom from coercion* whether to do good or evil. But the *ability to do good* is gone. After Christ's reparation, however, the children of God are once more free. They are helped by the Holy Spirit, freed from bondage to sin, and enabled to serve justice. In Christ it is possible both to avoid sin and to obey the commandments. The article continues to interpret the Pauline passages in terms of being truly virtuous since sin no longer dominates. This is not the "acceptance" language of Luther, but rather reflects an expectation of radical change enabling good works.

The cause of sin is simply the evil will of the devil and of persons turned away from God. This evil will is not in any way from God but wholly from the devil and from human beings. Notable in this article is the phrase that by his disobedience, Adam lost *living faith* and the *love of God*. In the state of integrity, therefore, faith was a necessary virtue.

Original sin is defined as the lack or defect of original justice that ought to be there. Original justice is then described as the grace of God and to consist in having God's image and likeness, for which everyone is created. It is to be crowned by the knowledge and love of God and the gift of the Holy Spirit. When these were lost, nothing was left but incredulity and disobedience. Concupiscence is described as the corruption and inordinate disposition of the human powers, or the vicious inclination to evil. In short, original sin is both the lack of original justice which ought to be there and the presence of concupiscence, a vicious habit. These two together make it impossible for the unregenerated not to fall into every kind of actual sin, for in them the devil is efficacious. Original sin is therefore distinct from, but the root of, all actual sins, including those of thought and omission. Lastly, Regensburg affirms that original sin is passed on only by physical propagation. With regard to its psychological effects, although the light of nature (the *lumen naturae*) remains, it is completely inefficacious to restore God's image. Only the laver of regeneration in the word of life, through the merit of Christ, is able to renew that image. Baptism removes the guilt of sin through the merit of Christ and restores the grace of God. It represses the power of concupiscence through the gift of the Spirit of Christ, who excites new and holy movements in an individual, as the apostle says in Romans 5. After baptism the material of sin remains, i.e., concupiscence, but not its guilt or its formality, which is completely removed. But on account of the merit of the passion of Christ and through the indwelling of Christ himself, what remains of sin [concupiscence] is not computed [imputed] as sin. There is no sin where there is no guilt. The article then quotes Augustine against Julian where Augustine says that concupiscence is sin, but the authors explain that it is only because concupiscence *leads into* actual sin. When this happens there must be a new remission, or nonimputation. Concupiscence in the unregenerated, however, means eternal death because to it is still attached guilt. The article closes with an exhortation to vigilance, to prayer, and to mortification of the flesh with its vices and concupiscences.

Article 5 on justification opens with an underscoring of the four previous articles: after the fall, no one can be reconciled to God and freed from sin except by the unique mediator Christ, the God-man. By Christ, individuals are not only freed from sin and reconciled with God but made sharers (*consortes*) of the divine nature and children of God. In adults these benefits of Christ are not available except by a prevenient motion of the Holy Spirit, moving one to detest sin. This motion is through faith, by which the mind, surely believing everything revealed (*tradita*) by God, also most certainly and without doubt assents to the promises given by God. By this faith one is directed to God by the Holy Spirit, and therefore faith receives the Holy Spirit, the remission of sins, the imputation of justice, and innumerable other gifts. The article then declares: "Therefore this doctrine is firm and sane that the sinner is justified through a living and efficacious faith."

Efficacious faith, living faith, is then described in both Protestant and Catholic terms. It grasps the promise, leads to God, receives mercy promised in Christ, receives the free goodness of God, namely, the remission of sins and reconciliation on account of the merits of Christ, and cries to God, "Abba, Father." It could do none of these things, however, unless also simultaneously charity is poured in, healing the will. The healed will then begins to fulfill the law. Faith is therefore efficacious through charity. But meanwhile this also is true, that by this faith one is justified, that is, accepted and reconciled to God insofar as faith apprehends mercy and justice which are imputed on account of Christ and his merits, not on account of the dignity or perfection of the justice communicated to the faithful in Christ.

And there at long last is the double justification of the Regensburg Colloquy. There is a communicated justice and a justification which is given not on account of that communicated justice, but solely on the merits of Christ. The inherent justice that is given can in no way be depended upon. Security lies only in the justice of Christ by which one is reputed just, that is, accepted by God as righteous. The doubtful, however, are not to be discouraged or excluded since perfect certitude is impossible to an individual due to remaining psychological weakness (*imbecillitas*). Those lacking strong faith are rather to be exhorted and told of the promises of Christ, while they should pray: "O Lord, increase our faith."

Lastly, good works merit a reward in this life and in the life to come. Good works cannot earn justification, but they can earn growth and blessing. Here also there is a double justification operating, for the reward is not given "according to the substance of the works as *human* works, but insofar as they are done in faith and are from the Holy Spirit who dwells in the faithful concurrently with free choice, as a partial agent."

With this agreement, everyone at Regensburg felt victorious and happy. If there could be agreement on justification, what possibly could bar the way to complete reconciliation?

Contarini thought he knew what would cause dissension and so postponed the next agenda items, the nature of the church and papal primacy. The colloquy moved to sacramental doctrine, but here it was Contarini as much as Eck who caused the end of friendly discussion. Contarini affirmed that since the doctrine of transubstantiation had been used at the Fourth Lateran Council, there could be no yielding on this point.[36] The Protestants could not affirm it since they regarded transubstantiation as a doctrine that involved many "abuses" like the adoration of the reserved sacrament and the processions of Corpus Christi. The collocutors went ahead with the remaining points, working in separate groups. On May 27 the papal consistory disapproved of the formula on justification, disheartening news which reached Regensburg on June 8.[37] On June 12 Luther wrote to Melanchthon enclosing a copy of his letter to Johann and Georg von Anhalt rejecting the justification formula. Luther found "free will," "efficacious charity," and other objectionable matters in it.[38] But the colloquy had already broken down effectively on May 14 when the Protestants agreed only that confession was useful, but refused to admit that it was necessary. On June 15 the pope directed Contarini to inform Charles V that the pope would at last convoke the long-awaited council.[39]

With the failure of Regensburg, even the anticonciliar curia feared the spread of Protestantism and began to call for a council. On June 29, 1542, Paul III published the bull of convocation. The date was set for November 1, 1542, and the place, Trent, technically in the empire and so "in German lands" but an Italian-speaking city on the southern side of the Alps. Two weeks later Francis I declared war on Charles V. Should a council succeed in uniting the powerful princes of the empire against the Turks, what was to prevent them from turning west toward France once the Turks had been driven back? Francis also once again boycotted the council, commanding that the bull of convocation not be promulgated in France. On November 1, 1542, only two bishops, both Italian, were in Trent. Once again, therefore, on September 29, 1543, Paul III issued a bull of suspension. Charles' troops were marching through Italy to do battle with the Duke of Cleves, and, when Charles and the pope met, their mutual distrust had not abated. Charles, of course, wanted Protestant help against Francis I and at the Diet of Speyer in 1544 conceded several points that angered the pope. But with the signing of the Peace of Crépy in late 1544, on November 30, 1544, the Council was once again convoked for March 13, 1545. It was not formally opened, however, until December 13, 1545.

But the Council of Trent, to which the Protestants decided not to come because they considered that it was not free, nor Christian, nor properly on German land, did nothing to heal the breach between Roman Catholics and Protestants. It was not free, the Protestants argued, because it was called by and dominated by the pope; it was not Christian because it would not rest on the principle of *sola scriptura*, and it was hardly honest to call Trent a German city. When the Tridentine decree on justification with its anathemas was published in 1547, there was little hope any more of any kind of agreement on doctrine. Political events were no more auspicious. During the council itself the Smalcald League formally challenged the emperor to battle. They could do little else, for Charles, strengthened by his rapid victory over the Duke of Cleves, decided that the League was weak enough to chastise with force. Reinforced by papal revenues and troops, Charles responded to the League's refusal to attend the Diet of Regensburg in June 1546 and war began.

In the increasingly bitter years prior to the Smalcald War, the rhetoric defending taking arms against the emperor had steadily increased. Two justifications were given by Protestant lawyers: (1) that the emperor, by supporting the pope, had broken faith with the princes and was therefore reduced to a private citizen against whom defense was legitimate; (2) that the emperor ruled as *primus inter pares* and so could not override the just demands of the Estates. Luther himself moved from counseling patience under tyranny to an apocalyptic argument in which he denounced the emperor as the servant of the pope who is the anti-Christ, the beast or *Beerwolfe*, against whom it was one's Christian duty to do battle. In early 1546 Melanchthon and Bugenhagen gathered and published whatever they could find of Luther's that justified taking arms against one's sovereign.[40]

But the war was badly managed by the League and during its course Maurice of Saxony signed an agreement with Charles. When John Frederick of Saxony lost the battle of Mühlberg, Charles passed the electoral dignity of Saxony from John Frederick to Maurice. Philip of Hesse and John Frederick were both imprisoned, but both were dealt with lightly. Indeed, Charles could not afford to make permanent enemies in Germany for Paul III was trying to use Francis I to balance Charles' increasing power.

At the end of the Smalcald War Charles was in firm control and made one last effort to restore order weighted in favor of the Roman Catholics. Efforts failed to find a compromise acceptable to the more moderate Lutherans and in August, 1547, the Diet assembled at Augsburg appointed a committee made up of Julius von Pflug, Michael Helding, suffragan bishop of Mainz, and John Agricola, Protestant court preacher and General Superintendent of Joachim II of Brandenburg. (Bucer had been invited but refused.) The resultant *Book of the Augsburg Interim*, published as an imperial edict on May 15, 1548, is known as the Augsburg Interim because its conditions were to apply only in Germany in the "interim" until the council enacted necessary reforms. The section on justification followed the Council of Trent and in other ways adhered to Roman doctrine and practice except in the matters of communion in both kinds and clerical marriage. Nor did Charles demand the return of church properties, although no further secularization of church goods was to be allowed. Only Joachim of Brandenburg and the Elector of the Palatine signed the Interim. All other Protestant princes and the southern German cities opposed it. Maurice of Saxony excused himself on the grounds that he had to consult his Estates and theologians.

While many Protestant theologians fled, among them Bucer, Musculus, Blaurer, Brenz, and Flacius Illyricus, Melanchthon remained to assist Maurice of Saxony with a series of theological consultations regarding the Interim. Throughout 1548 discussions and letters of advice resulted finally in the so-called Leipzig Interim, completed on December 24, 1548. The debate concerning *adiaphora*, "indifferent" matters, is well known. What is of particular interest here are the attitudes exhibited by both Roman Catholics and Lutherans and the section of the Leipzig Interim on justification and good works.

Between Regensburg and the declaration of the Interim had come Trent on justification and the Smalcald War. The voices of the victorious Roman Catholics grew harsher, while those of the Lutherans indicate both their awareness of their weakened situation and their determination not to yield on their central doctrine of justification.

During the months of consultation in Saxony, Melanchthon had occasion to set down a lengthy explanation of justification and its relation to good works. This document, written at Pegau on July 8, 1548,[41] was appended to the Celle Interim of November 19.[42] The two documents then became the statement of the Leipzig Interim.

Melanchthon's explanation is a development of the many theological declarations produced in Saxony, but it goes further in trying to mediate the Lutheran and Roman Catholic positions. Most noteworthy in this regard is the section "On Good Works":

> . . . and it is true that everlasting life is given according to the will of the Lord Christ by grace and that at the same time the heirs of everlasting happiness are all those who turn to God and through faith receive forgiveness of sins and the Holy Spirit.[43]

Melanchthon had made clear earlier[44] that justification is the work of God's mercy without our merits so that all glory is God's. He then qualifies this by saying that God's mercy works with a person, not as with a block of wood, but rather God's mercy brings it about that one's will cooperates (*mitwerket*) if one has reached the age of reason.[45] Such cooperation is the result of God's prevenient grace (*vorgehende Gnade*) which moves the heart and will to fear God's wrath and grieve for one's sins.

Melanchthon also stresses points made in his four judgments on the Augsburg Interim and by other theologians consulted by Maurice.[46] As one would expect, Melanchthon stresses the work of Christ which alone merits the forgiveness of sins. The role of the sinner, moved by grace according to Christ's will, is first to shrink before God's wrath. Grief for one's sins follows as one recognizes that sin makes one God's enemy. Only after fear and grief is the sinner prepared to come before the throne of mercy and grace.

One of the points in the *Book of the Augsburg Interim* that most angered the Lutheran theologians was the belittling of faith as only one among other virtues, and indeed only a "preparation" for justification. Against this position Melanchthon describes true living faith by which, according to Paul in Romans 4, we are justified. True faith through the Holy Spirit brings with it all the other virtues, especially love. To make of faith a mere belief in credal articles is to reduce it to that dead faith possessed even by devils. This is not justifying faith. Indeed John is right when he says that without love one remains in death because true faith and love are inseparable. Virtues may be called justification in a certain sense, i.e., as its result, never as its cause.

Melanchthon also attacks the Roman Catholic doctrine that in this life one can never be certain of one's salvation. Doubt, writes Melanchthon, is a result of original sin, indeed a punishment for sin. To counter doubt, God has promised salvation in Christ, and that promise is as firm as God's own unchangeable nature. The worst sin is to doubt God's promise. Faith grasps the promise and believes that God wills the conversion of the sinner, even the sinner who falls from grace, for after justification one still experiences the war of the flesh and the spirit and realizes that no one is just in God's sight. This realization should prevent one from ever trusting in one's own righteousness and make clear the need for constant justification.

In the short section on good works Melanchthon insists that the Lutherans have taught from Scripture and according to the mind of the church in all times. Good works are both good and necessary, indeed they are commanded by God in the ten commandments and in the New Testament. The commandments are, in fact, the basis of a good or bad conscience. This statement leads Melanchthon to consider what can happen to one who has been justified. Such a one may go against God's commands and conscience and so grieve the Holy Spirit. Unless such a one turns back to God, he will receive eternal punishment. Indeed, we learn from David's adultery that such a sinner will drag many others into punishments even in this life.

In this section Melanchthon also speaks of conversion and says that those who turn to God, by Christ's will and grace, will find eternal life: " . . . who *turn* to God and by faith receive forgiveness of sins and the Holy Spirit."[47] Melanchthon is here trying to yield to Roman Catholic insistence on scriptural conversion texts and at the same time make it clear that to "turn to God" is the work of Christ, the Holy Spirit, and faith, a point on which there should have been agreement had not the Roman Catholics reduced faith to preparation for justification.

After insisting upon the need for good works, Melanchthon mentions two "monkish errors": (1) that we can *earn* blessedness through the worthiness of our works; and (2) that we can share our merits with others. Although rewards for good works are indeed promised in Scripture, works are never the cause of justification or even of eternal life. Melanchthon does not elaborate further on this point here, but moves on to mention very briefly the "works" made into commandments by monks and bishops regarding worship. He says we must have a right understanding about what is necessary for God's service and what should be kept or rejected, but he says no more about it in the Pegau document, which ends here. The Leipzig statement continues with articles on church authority and ministry, marriage, the Mass, images, canonical hours, feasts, and abstinence from meat. For these articles it incorporates much of the Celle Interim,[48] and it is these last articles that raised the *adiaphoristic* controversy. The effort at Leipzig to be reconciled with Roman Catholic doctrine and practice multiplied *adiaphora* or those issues which were not specifically scriptural and therefore "indifferent." Melanchthon even consented to a return to Roman Catholic liturgy in Wittenberg. But Flacius Illyricus, a professor at Wittenberg, departed to Magdeburg. From then on the differences between the "Philippists" (followers of Philip Melanchthon) and the "Gnesio-Lutherans" (genuine Lutherans) grew increasingly acrimonious.

In 1549 Paul III died and Julius III called for the second session of Trent. But by 1552 the Peace of Passau worked out between Maurice of Saxony and the Emperor's brother Ferdinand indicated that the division between Protestants and Roman Catholics was permanent. The terms at Passau were essentially those of the Peace of Augsburg of 1555. Western Christendom was permanently divided.

11

THE DECREE ON JUSTIFICATION IN THE COUNCIL OF TRENT

Carl J. Peter

On September 17, 1983, the members of the Lutheran-Roman Catholic Dialogue in the USA unanimously approved a consensus statement which asked whether the doctrine of justification by faith need any longer separate their churches.[1] The path that led to this agreement had taken the participants back in time. That should come as no surprise. Each group has a confessional tradition contributing to its identity. Neither could responsibly disregard the public expressions of Christian faith made by its religious ancestors in the sixteenth century.

For the Roman Catholics this was especially true with regard to the Council of Trent. There was no way they could get away with ignoring it even if they had been inclined to do so. They had to take a stand and did so without embarrassment. Far from repudiating the Tridentine teaching on justification, they introduced it repeatedly to illustrate their own concerns and convictions with regard to the gospel message of divine forgiveness.[2] Their Lutheran counterparts did not regard such a stance as an insurmountable obstacle to agreement.

What was this teaching which the Roman Catholics would not consign to oblivion and to which the Lutherans reacted with theological restraint and apprehension rather than outright and straightforward rejection? An answer must be given to this question for the sake of readers who may wish to judge for themselves how much of a consensus has in fact been reached.

Given that a summary of Trent's teaching on justification appears in the consensus statement itself, another does not seem to be called for here. Something else will be offered, namely, a presentation of the Tridentine position on four issues that have been a source of dispute between Lutherans and Roman Catholics. These are: (*a*) the need for justification; (*b*) human cooperation in its reception; (*c*) its nature and effects; and (*d*) merit.

Before going any further, however, it will not be amiss to recall a number of ground rules that governed the proceedings of the council and that should be kept in mind while interpreting its teaching. First of all, both doctrine and discipline were of concern to those who gathered at Trent in 1545, but there was no ready agreement as to which should be given priority. As a result of a compromise, it was decided to give equal attention to both; decrees on doctrinal issues as well as others mandating reform of church life and practice would be formulated, debated, and approved simultaneously. As a prime example of the first, the decree on justification was intended to set forth Roman Catholic teaching at the midpoint of a century marked by bitter religious controversy.[3] As is true of most of the other doctrinal decrees, its format consists of chapters (sixteen in this case) and canons (thirty-three in number). The former embody an effort to state doctrine positively and at some length; in the latter, positions are expressed succinctly only to be opposed and rejected with an anathema.[4] Far more care and debate were devoted to the formulation of the canons, a good number of which resulted from a consideration and repudiation of propositions taken to represent the thought of the Reformers.[5]

The Importance of Context

Both the Augsburg Confession of 1530 and the Council of Trent in 1546 dealt with justification only after treating the need that human beings have of Jesus Christ and his saving action in their lives. It is of course in the doctrine of original sin that the Christian churches have confessed how great that need really is.[6] The Council of Trent did this both by stressing how desperate the plight of human beings is when left to their own resources and then by insisting on the efficacy of the measures God has provided in Jesus Christ by way of remedy.[7] Its hope was to win over those who held contrary views and to encourage those who already shared its faith on these matters.[8]

To be specific, in the third canon of its fifth session the council denied that the damage done to human beings by original sin could be repaired by any efforts of human nature or through any other remedy than the merit of Jesus Christ.[9] At the same time it highlighted baptism as mediating that merit and as conferring a grace which brings about forgiveness and removal of *all that is truly sinful* in its recipient.[10]

Trent thus laid the groundwork for its teaching on justification when it took two strong and clear positions with regard to original sin. They can be summarized in the following fashion. Relying solely on their own native powers, human beings are religiously and morally in a hopeless condition even before they make their first choice between right and wrong. Nevertheless God has come effectively to their rescue through Jesus Christ in the sacrament of baptism.[11] The importance of both points for a proper interpretation of the decree on justification can scarcely be exaggerated.

Trent on the Need for Justification

The human condition that was described by Trent in its decree on original sin is referred to again at the beginning of the decree on justification. The Gentiles, it is noted, have a human nature endowed with certain powers; the Jews have as well the law of Moses; both have free choice. All of this is true, says the council, even though the common human lot is original sin. What then is the need for Jesus Christ? Would not at least adults be able somehow to help themselves stand as they should in the eyes of God? Would not their works, either in the observance of the law or at least in following their conscience with the powers nature gives them, enable them to seek for righteousness? Perhaps, as a result of original sin, they cannot do all that they should do to be forgiven, but can they not at least avoid the conduct that condemns and thus merit God's compassion and grace? It was with the intention of answering questions such as these that the council began to treat of justification.

The stance it took could not be clearer. Human assets do not suffice—not the works of nature, nor those of the Mosaic law, nor those in general which are still possible for a free choice that is not destroyed, however weakened it may be. Human works of whatever kind are not of themselves enough; God's grace given through Jesus Christ is needed.[12] This is the unmistakable meaning of the first canon of Session 6.

But the issues are not thereby all resolved. One could hold that fallen human beings need such grace merely to *facilitate* their living as God wishes and meriting life everlasting. The unspoken assumption would be that free choice could accomplish both but just barely and only with the greatest difficulty. Trent would have none of this. To live righteously one needs to be *enabled* and *empowered* by God's grace. That grace is an inspiration and aid that comes from the Holy Spirit. It is given prior to the passage of human beings from sin to forgiveness. Without it no one can believe, hope, love, or repent in such a way that the grace of justification is bestowed.[13]

When one consults the chapters corresponding to these canons, their tenor is much the same. There may in fact be even more stress placed on the human inability to merit the grace of forgiveness. The beginning of justification in the adult is said to be found in the grace of God which prepares and precedes any human work involved in that process. That prevenient grace comes from a call made by God to human beings who are in such a condition that they have no merits.[14] They are rather turned away from and against God because of sins. Justification is a wholly undeserved gift of God because nothing at all that precedes it, whether faith or works, truly merits the grace which justifies.[15] It is to this last text that Heiko Oberman has called attention. Trent may not, he maintains, be saying as much as might at first sight appear.

He notes that the Latin term chosen to express merit is a form of the verb *promereri*. He then goes on to argue that by recourse to this verb (instead of *mereri*) the council excluded merit in the strict sense (*meritum de condigno*) but not necessarily all forms of merit (*meritum de congruo*). The failure on the part of Trent to make a blanket exclusion of merit is significant. It may be good grounds for those of the Reformation tradition to wonder whether justification for Trent is not partly effected by God's grace and partly merited by the sinful human being.[16]

The members of the dialogue noted possible Lutheran fears and Roman Catholic reactions to the issue raised by Oberman. That was in a rather long footnote at the end of the consensus statement.[17] In addition to what the reader will find there, the following observations may have some relevance.

1. For Trent, because of the divine promise in Christ, eternal salvation (heaven) is both a grace and a reward for the justified adult who hopes in God and perseveres to the end in good works.[18] But justification is only a grace for the sinner, who has no merits; nowhere is it proposed as a reward for works of nature, free choice, or some combination of these with divine grace.

2. What is more, in the Oberman hypothesis congruous merit of justification is not excluded by Trent (though it is not asserted either). Whatever that nonexclusion may mean, there are no grounds for saying it makes the resources of fallen human nature a remedy for original sin. This would imply a clear contradiction with the teaching of Session 5, as has been seen earlier.[19]

3. A blanket exclusion of any and all congruous merit would have required a very time-consuming discussion of the various meanings attached to that term. Trent clearly wished to say that the acts posited with divine grace prior to justification are not sinful and that they are the preparation for justification. To deny any kind of congruous merit might imply that God does not fittingly (*modo congruo*) complete with justification what God has begun in the sinner with grace showing itself in acts leading to conversion. At the same time the use of *promereri* would show that the merit of reward for the good done by those justified cannot be applied to the grace-assisted works of sinners on the way to justification.

4. Does it seem likely that one and the same decree: (*a*) would urge those already justified to work out their salvation with fear and trembling;[20] and (*b*) by silence allow sinners to trust rather in themselves and their own abilities to *merit* the first grace leading to God's forgiveness? The text and background of the decree on justification give no grounds for alleging such an inconsistency.

Justification: Process and Human Cooperation

What happens to the sinner and what, if anything, does the sinner do when justification occurs? Answering this question, Trent says it finds a "clue" (*insinuatur*) for its response in Col. 1:12-13. There God's activity is highlighted.[21]

Justification, then, is a journey, a passage, a movement that takes place without being initiated by the one involved. The Latin noun Trent chooses to describe it is *translatio* (a transferral, here a term in which a human being is brought from one state to another). The biblical text is at work stretching human understanding; God is snatching sinners out of the clutches of sin and bringing them into the kingdom of his son. A human being born as a descendant of Adam is brought to a state of friendship with God and is adopted into the divine family. If one asks how this happens, the reply is that it is through the second Adam, Jesus Christ.[22]

A number of points have thus been made. It is a human being who is justified. One who starts out as a sinner ends up as a friend and intimate of God because of and through Jesus Christ. Relying on biblical images, the council attempts to give to the eyes of faith a faint glimpse of the reality of divine forgiveness.

But this fact is simply undeniable. The justification of an adult is proposed as involving a preparatory process. It is not that one moves (continuously or by fits and starts) from being unjust before God to being less and less so because one is more and more healed by Christ's grace that gradually expels sin. It is rather that justification follows a conversion process. Trent proceeds to describe the proces. that leads up to the moment when the unjust become just.

The preparation for justification is said to begin with God's grace and with faith on the part of the sinner. This faith comes *ex auditu* ("from hearing," namely, the word of God). In it the sinner *freely* acknowledges and reckons with the truth of a message manifesting God's promise to be merciful to human beings who desperately need and yet in no way deserve such treatment. The process does not begin with fear or with repentance. It begins with faith. That faith comes from God's grace enabling the sinner to accept freely God's revelation of human sinfulness and promise of forgiveness. In more contemporary terms this faith, which accepts that revelation and promise as *true*, is incipiently self-involving for the sinner. It is not a detached and impersonal awareness of the truth of just any proposition; it is an appreciation of the truth of a general situation that involves the believer and calls for a reaction. In this faith the general need of forgiveness comes home personally to the sinner, who is struck with a fear resulting from a keen awareness of the distance between God and self. Such fear is beneficial in directing the sinner to the divine mercy promised in Jesus to all the unworthy, and therefore to himself or herself as well. Devastated by the prospect of divine justice, the sinner is brought by grace to hope when confronted with the prospect of divine compassion. In context, hope means confidence that the forgiveness God has promised to all in Jesus will be given to the one who has come to believe, fear, and hope here and now. This hope leads to a beginning of love of God as the source of all justice and therefore to a hatred and detestation of sin, that is, to the repentance necessary before baptism (Acts 2:38). Finally comes the desire to receive baptism, to begin a new life, and to observe the commandments of God.[23]

For Trent the God who originally created human beings without their active involvement does not justify them without their free engagement. To be justified is to be turned freely by God's grace from sin to divine friendship. This process of being turned involves a human turning and thus cooperation.

Does this mean that the work of justification is partly that of the human being and partly that of God? Furthermore, does this make the human being rather than God the decisive agent because he or she can stop the whole process leading to justification by refusing to cooperate? The criticism expressed in these questions calls for some sort of a response.[24]

First of all, does Trent's description mean that God accomplishes only part of the work leading to justification? Based on the conciliar text, the following at least is undeniable. Trent attributes the initiation of the conversion process to grace; there is no other remedy for original sin. That grace is undeserved. It operates by way of a divine call and invitation. The need for an active agency of grace is stressed. Still, the sinner moved by grace ". . . does not do altogether nothing . . ." in the process.[25] This "not-doing-altogether-nothing" is then described as acceptance of the inspiration coming from grace although the sinner could opt for rejection instead.[26]

Receiving the grace one could reject is the believing, fearing, hoping, beginning of love, repenting, and desire of baptism that were described above. That receiving, one recalls, is a choice against rejection. Not to reject the grace one is well able to reject is freely and as a result of God's grace to refrain from doing what a sinful creature could do on his or her own resources, namely, sinning yet more.

As a whole that preparation is God's work; his grace precedes, accompanies, and completes it; to that grace all that is positive in the process relates entirely and not just partially. As a whole it is also the work of the unjustified human being who does not do altogether nothing when all he or she does as a result of grace is not to sin further at any stage of the process. Two senses of wholeness applicable in radically different ways to two infinitely distinct sources!

The second criticism asks whether it is the divine or human agency that is decisive in the conversion process. In reply it may be said that decisiveness has much in common with wholeness. For all that is positive in the process leading to justification, God is decisive; for the fact that more sin does not occur by rejecting the grace leading to justification, the sinful human being is decisive. In the second case decisiveness has reference to what does not happen although it could. Called by grace to be justified, the human being does not respond: "I prefer to remain the way I am, God!" That restraint, that refraining from uttering a sinful refusal to the invitation of God's grace, does not suffice to start, maintain, or complete the process leading to forgiveness and new life; there God is decisive just as the human would be in further sin and possible damnation. Again two senses of decisiveness applicable in radically different ways to two infinitely distinct sources!

Trent spoke guardedly but did endorse human cooperation with God's grace in the process leading to justification. It did not thereby intend to exalt the sinful creature at the expense of the God of mercy or to give sinners unwarranted confidence to the detriment of Christ's grace.

Justification: Its Nature and Effects

What follows the conversion process in the adult is justification itself.[27] The latter is said to involve ". . . not merely the forgiveness of sins but also sanctification of the inner human person through a voluntary reception (on his or her part) of grace and gifts. . . ."[28] One who was God's enemy becomes a friend and an heir in hope of life everlasting (Titus 3:7).[29]

Trent then proceeds to an analysis of justification in terms of its "causes." The agent at work is the merciful God, whose *efficient causality* is expressed in terms that deserve special attention. Under no obligation to do so (*gratuito*), God not only washes clean and sanctifies (1 Cor. 6:11) but also signs and anoints the sinner with the Holy Spirit of promise, the pledge of our inheritance (Eph. 1:13ff.).[30] Aristotelian terminology has to be stretched to refer to this divinely-effected conversion; biblical symbols are introduced to point to God's dealing with the sinner in a way Aristotle never even imagined in his metaphysics. God the Father vivifies the sinner with nothing less than God the Holy Spirit.[31]

In terms of merit the cause is Jesus Christ, who out of love (Eph. 2:4) for us while we were yet sinners (Rom. 5:10) won justification for us by his suffering and cross.[32] The role of faith is stressed when baptism is introduced as the *instrumental cause* and then called the sacrament of the faith without which no one is ever justified.[33]

The sole *formal cause* is the justice of God, not that by which he is himself just but that by which he makes us just.[34] This is the justice, the text goes on to say, by which we are renewed and by which we are not only reckoned just but are so in fact. Each of us receives his or her own justice according to the measure meted out by the Holy Spirit, who distributes to each as he wishes and according to the proper disposition and cooperation of each recipient.[35] When the merits of Jesus Christ are communicated to sinners, something happens. Through the Holy Spirit the charity of God is poured forth into the hearts (Rom. 5:5) of those who are justified. The latter are engrafted into Christ and united with him; they receive not only the forgiveness of sins but also faith, hope, and charity.[36] What is it that is within a justified person and that makes him or her just in his or her own distinctive way? This is, in the council's terms, to ask about formal causality; to this question Trent answered: "A created justice distinct from that of God and Christ!" What is more, this created justice, received in baptism, will suffice, if preserved without mortal sin, for one to enter into eternal life. But the sufficiency in question presupposes that the justified are anointed with the Holy Spirit and engrafted into Christ. Because the merciful God gives himself to the sinner, the latter becomes just; this involves an internal renewal or change that is dependent on the presence of the Holy Spirit and on vital union with Jesus Christ. God's promises of forgiveness and new life are kept; concupiscence by its very presence in the justified is not sin in the proper sense of the term; the justice received in baptism is real and transformative despite the weakness and inclination to sin that remain in the baptized.

Up to this point little has been said about faith. It did figure prominently as the beginning of the process leading to justification.[37] It was later invoked to single out a salient feature of the sacrament of baptism.[38] It was also said to be infused (bestowed rather than won as a result of achievement) together with hope and charity when sins are forgiven in justification.[39] But does this bring out the importance the Scriptures attribute to faith? Almost as if to answer such a question, Trent turns to faith after the causal treatment of justification.[40] It states that ". . . faith is the beginning of human salvation, the foundation and root of all justification. . . ."[41] The word *all* (*omnis*) does not appear as an accident. Its selection by the council may be significant even today. Scholastic disputes had again divided Scotists and Thomists at Trent. What kind of cause is faith in justification? Dispositive? Instrumental? Or even partially formal? Such subtlety may seem extravagant today; it did not then. According to the *Acta*, in this context Cardinal Cervini intervened. This was in a special group set up to deal with unresolved issues. He suggested that such disputes might be avoided. Faith might be described as the root and foundation of *all* justification, the *all* referring to the disposition leading to justification, the actual realization or conferal of justification, and the growth of justification.[42] His was the formula the council finally endorsed in explaining what St. Paul meant by saying the sinner is justified by faith and *gratis* (Rom. 3:22, 24). How this solution is to be judged in relation to Melanchthon's concern that the importance of faith not be restricted to the beginning of justification[43] readers will have to judge. Trent clearly intended to stress the *permanence* of the foundational role of faith in justification.

The Fruit of Justification: Merit and Good Works

Toward the end the decree faces the neuralgic point of merit.[44] The treatment is remarkable for what is missing. No distinction is made, for example, between merit which is condign and that which is merely congruous. There is as a result an absence of the Scholastic subtlety that may have been useful in some contexts but that was deemed un-called-for in this formulation of doctrine. What is more, no effort is made to determine whether the relation between works performed by the just (under the influence of divine grace) and life everlasting rests on the intrinsic nature of the graced works or on a simple divine fiat that could have been otherwise. The Thomists and the Scotists could and would continue to dispute the matter while affirming in the decree that God's recognition of the value of the works of the just derives from a promise that God made and keeps. But the absence of such *theologoumena* is no more striking than the presence of so many appeals to Scripture. The following texts are cited in whole or part and constitute the greater part of the chapter dealing with merit: 1 Cor. 15:58; Heb. 6:10; 10:35; Matt. 10:22; 2 Tim. 4:7ff.; Eph. 4:15; John 15:5; Rev. 14:13; John 4:14; Rom. 10:3; Matt. 10:42; 2 Cor. 4:17; 1 Cor. 10:31; 2 Cor. 10:17; Jas. 3:2; 1 Cor. 4:4; Rom. 2:6. It is on these texts that Trent's doctrine of merit is intended to rest and that advice is given to prevent people from being misguided in their own spiritual life as a result of assumptions about merit.

A further word is now in order with regard to the content; perhaps the text can best be grasped if it is allowed to speak for itself. For those who persevere in good to the end and who hope in God, life everlasting is to be proposed both as a *grace* mercifully promised to God's children through Jesus Christ and as a *reward* to be rendered or bestowed faithfully for good works and merits as a result of God's promise.[45] One notes the importance attributed to the biblical category of *promise* in the description of life everlasting as grace and reward.

What accounts for the possibility and actuality of merit in the just is not an optimistic anthropology but rather a biblically based Christology. Jesus Christ exerts a continuous influence on the just as the head on its members and the vine on its branches.[46] That influence always precedes, accompanies, and follows every good work performed by his followers; without this there is no way that such works could be pleasing to God and meritorious. But given that influence, something is said to follow.

Nothing is lacking that would keep the just from satisfying fully God's commands in this life and from *truly meriting* (*vere promeruisse*) life everlasting if they die in grace.[47] To find fault with all the conduct and achievements of the just is seen as derogatory to Christ's power, which is truly at work in them.

To avoid self-confidence, the just are reminded that justice is theirs because it inheres in them but that the same justice is God's because he infuses it in them through Christ's merit.[48] To be sure, it has been promised that not even a drink of cold water given to one of the Lord's little ones will go without reward. What is more, the troubles of the present are slight and short-lived, whereas their outcome is an eternal glory which far outweighs them. Still no Christian should dare to trust or glory in self rather than the Lord, whose goodness to humans is so great that he wishes his gifts to be their merits.[49] Because in many things we all sin, it is important to remember that we shall be judged by God and not by ourselves. He it is who will bring to light what is hidden in darkness; he is the one who will give praise to each of us. The just must remember this especially if they examine their conscience and are tempted to be satisfied with what they find!

The decree concludes with a canon to the effect that the doctrine which has been formulated about justification does not derogate from the glory of God and the merits of Jesus Christ.[50]

Conclusion

Lutherans and Catholics may wish to focus their attention on a number of issues that stand out as a result of this interpretation of the Tridentine decree on justification. The following are especially worthy of consideration. Even if Luther and Lutherans were misunderstood at Trent, can Lutherans today see in the doctrine articulated by Trent on justification a truly Christian understanding of the gospel? Does the element of human cooperation in justification and its growth still imply for Lutherans a *partim-partim* view of human salvation? Trent clearly meant to maximize the role of faith in all justification; do Lutherans today regard the results as sufficient or at least as not deficient to the point of being necessarily church-divisive? Is all *merit talk* anathema to Lutherans or could they see a truly Christian church having careful recourse to such discourse to bring out aspects of the gospel in need of affirmation? Are there truths and values that both the Augsburg Confession and Trent affirm regarding justification in a time-conditioned language that might be rearticulated today by joint efforts of Lutherans and Catholics in a way that may let God's word be heard more effectively? The author, while thinking Trent gave important and true answers to rather precise questions, answers this final question with a decided affirmative.

12

A QUESTION OF COMPATIBILITY:
A LUTHERAN REFLECTS ON TRENT[1]

George Lindbeck

The theme of this essay is the possible compatibility of Tridentine and Lutheran confessional teachings on justification, with special attention to those points at which the incompatibility seems greatest. Since the essay in its unrevised form was prepared for a group familiar with earlier Lutheran attempts by Peter Brunner and Wilfrid Joest to give comprehensive descriptions and evaluations of Trent,[2] it was possible to concentrate on selected issues. The choice of these issues is to some extent influenced by Catholic difficulties with the Reformation position, such as those raised in essays by Carl Peter for this dialogue, but the main focus is on Lutheran problems with the Roman Catholic position.

The specific issues that receive the most attention are those of sin and inherent righteousness. These are dealt with in part 2. Part 1 takes up certain preliminary questions.

1. Preliminaries

A. The suggestion that Tridentine and Lutheran confessional teachings on justification may be compatible is a modest one. To say that two positions are possibly compatible means no more than that they have not been proved contradictory. Contradictions, however, are notoriously difficult to establish. One must show that "x" is denied on the one side in precisely the same sense that it is affirmed on the other, but this can rarely be done in any rigorous way outside of mathematics and the exact sciences. In other areas, including theology, irreconcilability is often undemonstrable.

To be sure, reconcilability is also hard to demonstrate. Ultimately, as Rahner has noted in his essay on Küng's book on justification in Barth,[3] the only proof of the compatibility of diverse doctrines is the establishment of communion between the churches that adhere to them. The irresolvability of the debates over the compatibility of the diverse New Testament theologies points in the same direction. It is apparently impossible to reach generally convincing conclusions regarding the actual compatibility of the irreducibly different affirmations about justification that we find in Paul, James, John, and the Synoptics apart from acceptance of the unity of the canon and of the faith it attests. In the absence of this starting point, the most that can be shown is possible compatibility.

In the light of these considerations, we must limit ourselves in this essay to the possible reconcilability of Trent and the Lutheran Confessions; the question of actual reconcilability can be settled only by the development of ecclesial communion. Further, the problem is not whether the two doctrines agree with each other in the sense of saying the same things, of making the same doctrinal affirmations despite their varied theological conceptualities. On the contrary, they may well be ineradicably and unsystematizably different. The modest aim of the present exercise, in short, is simply to dispel the polemically nurtured supposition that the two positions necessarily contradict each other. It is at least as plausible to argue the opposite: whatever the intention of their authors, they fail to be mutually exclusive.

More concretely stated, the question is whether Trent and the Lutheran Confessions anathematize each other. Some of the Tridentine canons were intended to condemn the Reformers, but do they caricature rather than rightly characterized the Reformation teachings they reject?[4] Conversely, can Trent's understanding of justification be interpreted in such a way as to avoid Lutheran suspicions of heresy? If the answer in both cases is "yes," the two descriptions of justification may be regarded as noncontradictory despite their ineradicable diversity.

This conclusion, it must be stressed, can be combined with continuing debates over which position is superior. Thus Lutherans who agree that Trent restated a soundly Augustinian view of the primacy of grace which was appropriate against Pelagian pride in the fifth century may yet regard it as pastorally and biblically deficient on the grounds that it did not address the sixteenth-century issue of the terrified conscience. It thereby failed to combat, even if it did not directly affirm, fundamental errors.

Similarly, Catholics may hold that the fatalistic, Manichaean, and antinomian consequences drawn by many from Luther's teachings[5] warranted Trent's rejection of the language and conceptuality of *sola fides*. Yet they might add that this rejection does not imply the denial of the reality to which *sola fides* points nor preclude the use of the language in other and more favorable settings.

If something like this is the case, however, then a doctrinal reconciliation which was practically impossible in the sixteenth century may be possible today. If Catholics no longer fear that the Lutheran understanding of justification implies fatalism, Manichaeanism, and antinomianism, then they no longer have their sixteenth-century reasons for rejecting it. Similarly, if Trent is explained in the scriptural, patristic, and contemporary idioms employed by many contemporary Catholic theologians, then Lutheran objections, at least as traditionally formulated, become obsolete. Theologies and doctrines which were once in ineluctable conflict may now be doctrinally compatible.

B. A second preliminary point is that this paper deals with Trent chiefly from the perspective of the Lutheran Confessions rather than from that of Luther. Luther's theology, to be sure, is for most purposes more important than the official Lutheranism of the *Book of Concord*, just as Augustine's thought is more important than the official Augustinianism of the Synod of Orange. Ecclesiastically authoritative doctrine does at times need to be considered, however, and this dialogue is one of those occasions.

As it happens, this simplifies our task. Catholic questions about potential fatalism, Manichaeanism, and antinomianism are less pressing than they might otherwise be. Rightly or wrongly, Luther can be read as affirming the irresistibility of grace and double predestination in a treatise such as *Bondage of the Will*,[6] but there is no trace of these doctrines in the Augsburg Confession, and they are explicitly repudiated in articles 2 and 11, respectively, of the Formula of Concord. Article 1, furthermore, repudiates the Manichaean-sounding language of Flacius, and article 6, the antinomianism of Agricola (which, to be sure, was expressly attacked by Luther and had already been excluded, it would seem, by what the Augsburg Confession says about the new obedience). It can thus be argued from a Catholic perspective that on predestination, freedom, and *sola gratia*, the Lutheran Confessions, despite differences in theological conceptuality, affirm the same doctrinal positions as Orange, Thomas Aquinas, and Trent itself (although Trent, because of its use of *promerere*, is not as unequivocal in its affirmation of *sola gratia* as Orange or Aquinas).[7]

C. A third preliminary concerns the relation between the Tridentine "intellectualist" and the Reformation "fiducial" understanding of faith, together with the related issue of the certainty of salvation. For the purposes of this essay it is assumed that Roman Catholics are right when they argue (1) that Trent could have combined *assensus* and *fiducia* in its concept of faith and (2) that this would have made it possible to affirm that justification is in one sense *sola fide*. Carl Peter supports the first point by holding that a *pro me* or self-involving element is implicit in the Tridentine concept, and the second when he discusses the permanence of the foundational role of faith.[8] In this essay it is also assumed that those are right who argue (3) that Luther's certitude of faith and the certitude of hope affirmed in the Roman Catholic tradition do not exclude each other.[9] These three points do not constitute agreement (as is apparent when we consider, for example, the primarily future reference of the certainty of hope in contrast to that of faith), but taken in conjunction, they make it difficult to think of Trent and the Reformation, in spite of their different conceptualities, as making mutually exclusive affirmations about the nature and role of faith. Specifically, Trent's concept of faith considered by itself permits, even though it does not assert, the central Reformation affirmation that believers ultimately trust God alone for salvation and not themselves or even what God works within them.[10]

Yet there are other aspects of Trent's teaching which seem to make this impossible. It rejects the Reformers' denial of inherent righteousness and their way of insisting that the justified remain sinful, but both these theses are, from the Reformation perspective, essential to the *sola fides*.

2. Sin and Inherent Righteousness

In reference to sin it is relatively easy to argue for doctrinal compatibility (not, be it noted, agreement) between Trent and the Reformation on the status in the justified of the concupiscence which afflicts all those born in original sin, but more difficult to argue for doctrinal compatibility when one takes *simul iustus et peccator* into consideration.

A. On the first point, as Pfnür and others have shown,[11] verbal reconciliation between the two sides seemed possible even in the sixteenth century. Both parties were willing to say that the concupiscence which remains in the justified after baptism (1) is from sin, inclines to sin, and must be constantly and stoutly resisted even though (2) it no longer dominates or alienates from God as it does in the unjustified, and (3)

it is forgiven. The first two points in conjunction with other considerations led the Roman Catholic participants in discussions at Augsburg
(1530) and at Worms (1541)[12] to grant the admissibility of saying, as
the Reformers did, that concupiscence even when forgiven is sin. Trent,
however, while agreeing with the first two points,[13] declares that it is
not properly called sin. Thus if the status of being unforgiven is part
of the definition of sin, Trent's usage (original sin is not sin in the
justified) is appropriate, whereas if this status is not part of the definition,
the Reformers' way of speaking is correct.

When one goes beyond this verbal level, however, and asks why
definitional preferences differed, the answer becomes complicated. The
variety of ways in which Augustine and the medieval tradition understood concupiscence and original sin contributed to a great diversity of
positions in the Reformation debates. There was no clear-cut confrontation between two well-defined opposing views.[14] Sharp controversies
developed at Trent,[15] and the council, in accordance with its usual
policy, adopted the definition that embraced the widest possible range
of Roman Catholic teachings (including such nominalist ones as those
of Gabriel Biel, which had been the original and main obejct of the
Reformers' attacks). Thus some of the understandings of concupiscence
and original sin represented at Trent may have been compatible with
those of the Reformers, while others were not.

New ways of looking at the problem have developed since the sixteenth century, and one of these, suggested by the work of such authors
as the Lutheran, Edmund Schlink, and the Roman Catholic, Otto
Pesch,[16] may be mentioned by way of example. The Reformation way
of speaking, one can argue, is appropriate in a penitential context, while
the Tridentine recommendation fits a doxological one. It is necessary
when confessing one's sins before God (*coram deo*) to ask forgiveness
for all that contradicts God's perfect holiness, including evil impulses
which are not consented to and are thus not sins before human beings
(*coram hominibus*). On the other hand, it is equally necessary on occasion to praise God for freeing his saints from the guilt of these impulses
and for conquering them so they do not issue in actual sins. From one
perspective, original sin remains; from the other, it has been removed.
On the ordinary language level there would seem to be no problem. It
is only when one tries to impose a single univocal meaning of "sin"
in all contexts that difficulties arise. On this view Melanchthon was
basically correct in suggesting that whether concupiscence is properly
called sin depends on the "place" of speaking.[17]

B. This accord becomes problematic, however, when one turns to *simul iustus et peccator* and, more specifically, to the condemnation in canon 25 of the decree on justification of the view that "in every good work the just man sins at least venially."[18] These words are not *ipsissima verba* to be found in the Lutheran Confessions, but there is no doubt that what is here condemned is so deeply embedded in Luther and Lutheran theology that it has the force of official doctrine. Unlike the disagreement over what to call concupiscence after baptism, this cannot easily be analyzed as a verbal difference. It does not have to do with whether involuntary evil impulses are to be called sinful but with whether all voluntary acts of even the most saintly persons are in reality sins. The Reformers claim that all human actions need forgiveness, while Trent denies this.

Yet when one looks closely, it becomes apparent that the difference in perspectives which we have already noted once again applies. Luther himself makes this clear. In his fullest *ex professo* treatment of the thesis that even the best acts of the justified are sin,[19] he clinches his argument with what he calls a "dramatic representation." Latomus had cited Paul as a saint who performed at least some acts "without sin," but Luther replies:

Let us take St. Paul or Peter as they pray, preach, or do some other good work. If it is a good work without sin and entirely faultless, they could stand with proper humility before God and pray in this fashion: "Lord God, behold this good work which I have done through the help of your grace. There is in it neither fault nor any sin, nor does it need thy forgiving mercy. I do not ask for this, as I want Thee to judge it with thy strictest and truest judgments. In this work of mine I can glory before Thee, because Thou canst not condemn it, for Thou art just and true. Indeed, I am certain that Thou canst not condemn it without denying Thyself. The need for mercy . . . is cancelled, for there is here only the goodness which thy justice crowns." Latomus, doesn't this make you shudder and sweat? And yet it is certain that all this could, indeed should, be said by so righteous a man, for it is especially before God that truth ought to be spoken, nor ought one to lie because of God. The truth is that a work without sin deserves praise, needs no mercy, and fears not the judgment of God. Indeed, it is proper to trust and hope in it . . . for we have something with which to encounter God himself, and his judgment and truth, so that we ought no longer fear him nor rely on his mercy.[20]

In short, *coram deo*, standing before the judgment seat of God where the final truth about what we are and do is ultimately exposed, it is absurd to think that even the best deed of the best person is without sin, is not in need of mercy.

For Luther this was not speculative theology but scriptural teaching. His favorite (though not only) proof text was Isa. 64:6: "All our righteousness is as filthy rags" (or, in the more vivid Vulgate version, which was also a favorite of Seripando's: "*quasi pannus menstruatae universae iustitae nostrae*"). He also appealed to Augustine:

> For instance, he says in a letter to Jerome that no man has so much love in this life that it need not be increased. He asserts that, "In so far as it is less than it ought to be, it is a fault," and then continues: "Because of this fault . . . if we say we have no sin, we deceive ourselves, and the truth is not in us. Because of this fault there is not a righteous man upon earth that does good and sins not." This is what Augustine says.[21]

Yet after insisting this strongly on the sinfulness of all the acts even of the justified, Luther notes that there are situations in which it is misleading to say that "all our righteousness is as filthy rags":

> I can excuse the fathers who were tempted, or driven by necessity, vigorously to deny that sin remains after baptism, for they fought against those who absolutely denied grace. It was therefore in order to commend grace that they asserted that all sin is taken away. What they say fits the subject matter beautifully and well, for their opponents disputed regarding the reign of sin, denying that it is removed; but this is a godless view, for the whole of sin is truly annulled so that it definitely no longer reigns.[22]

The conclusion that follows from this is that for Luther a Tridentine emphasis on the removal of sin from the justified is legitimate when directed against those who minimize the transforming power of grace, the genuineness of the renewal wrought in the redeemed. He, however, did not regard himself as one of these minimizers. His views are not at all similar to later theories of a purely external or extrinsic imputation of righteousness that developed in some Lutheran circles after the Osiandrian controversy. The meaning such theories give to "the just man sins in every good work" is not Luther's meaning. If it is an external, imputation understanding of the statement which canon 25 condemns, then it does not strike at Luther.[23] Or, to put the same point a bit more cautiously, if canon 25 does not reject Augustine's position that the imperfection of love in even the best works has something sinful about it, then it is at least an open question whether it excludes Luther's *simul iustus et peccator.*[24]

C. Noncontradiction on the subject of sin, however, could be combined with disagreement on inherent righteousness. For Lutherans, however, the central problem is not where Catholics generally see it. It does not lie in Trent's insistence that "justification itself . . . is not only the remission of sins but also the sanctification and renewal of the inward man."[25] Lutherans fully agree that justification is, as Joest puts it, "something more than the nonimputation of sin, namely, a creative renewal of life as well."[26] They can make their own Trent's concern as characterized by the Roman Catholic, Michael Schmaus: "When God declares man righteous for Christ's sake, this is not an empty word, but a word endowed with spirit and power, a word of divine *dynamis*, which penetrates the innermost fibre of man and transforms and re-creates him there."[27] This point could be extensively documented from Luther, from the Lutheran Confessions, from contemporary Lutheran theologians of many persuasions, and, indeed, from essays presented by Lutherans in this dialogue.

Yet Lutherans affirm this authentic renewal of the justified while avoiding the language of inherent righteousness. They do not talk of the transformation of the old self by the infusion of grace, but are more likely to speak in terms of the gift, birth, or creation of a new self. The redeemed self is discontinuous with the old. It is constituted by the new relation to God in which it stands, not by an alteration of its prior and continuously existing identity. Instead of using the imagery (or metaphysics) of the change of an enduring substantial self, Luther often speaks of believers as living outside themselves in Christ. The true self of the justified, one might say, is "excentrically" rather than "inwardly" located.[28] Given this anthropology, this way of picturing human beings under grace, talk of inherent righteousness is both an unnecessary and unusable way of expressing the reality of the renewal of the justified.[29]

From this Lutheran perspective, therefore, the problem is not that Trent affirms and the Reformation denies genuine renewal, but rather that Trent conceives of renewal in terms of inherent righteousness. The difficulties that Lutherans see in this are familiar. Justifying and sanctifying grace, so it is argued, becomes a property or *qualitas* of the human subject. A major focus of sixteenth-century polemics, it will be recalled, was the Scholastic notion of grace as a habit or disposition of the soul. Here more than anywhere else, Luther claimed, Aristotelian philosophy corrupted theology.

One must, to be sure, distinguish between those medieval theologians who denied the ability of sinful human beings to contribute to salvation apart from grace and those who were "New Pelagians," or as Melanchthon puts it in the Apology, between the more and less "sensible" Scholastics.[30] For the first, the infusion of righteousness is wholly the work of God; for the second, it partly depends on the independent contribution of human freedom. Yet even the first, "*sola gratia*" position does not answer the Lutheran objection.[31] To conceive of the new righteousness in Aristotelian terms as a qualitative property inhering in a substantial self is to give support, even if unwittingly, to the constant human temptation to rely on something within the self, something other than God. This is subversive of justification by faith. To trust God's gift rather than God himself is to have no defense against the twin pitfalls of anxiety ("Have I received the gift?") and complacency or pride ("I have received the gift").

One way of meeting this Reformation difficulty is to follow contemporary Roman Catholic theologians (from de la Taille and Mersch to Rahner and Schillebeeckx) who employ in varying degrees patristic and Eastern notions of divinization or participation in the divine life in order to make the point that the created grace of inherent righteousness is totally and continuously dependent on uncreated grace, on God himself.[32] Inherent righteousness is simply the effect in human beings of incorporation into Christ and of the indwelling of the Holy Spirit. It is not a quasi-independent external product of God's efficient causality. There are texts in Trent which lend themselves to this interpretation, as Carl Peter points out,[33] and when this reading is followed, Reformation *desiderata* are to some extent met. It is primarily Christ living within the justified who is their inherent righteousness (a thoroughly Lutheran thought) and Trent's insistence on infused created grace becomes a way of saying that union with Christ is genuinely transformative of the human person. Thus it can be argued that when Aristotelian categories are given a participationist interpretation, they can no longer be as easily misused as they were in the sixteenth century. They no longer need promote a way of thinking and speaking which subverts justifying faith by encouraging reliance on the gift rather than the Giver.

This is an appealing way of making an Aristotelian *gratia infusa* compatible with Reformation insights. Otto Pesch relies heavily upon it in his interpretation of Aquinas (who was, so the argument goes, much more participationist than his followers later became as a result of the isolating and individualizing modes of thought characteristic of nominalism).[34] Trent, however, cannot be as easily interpreted in this way as Thomas.

The additional difficulty is that in Trent the inherent righteousness which is a created effect is said to be the *causa formalis* of justification in the specific sense that the justified "may bear it before the tribunal of our Lord Jesus Christ and may have life eternal."[35] The righteousness which is given to the justified as their own is sufficient for declaring them just at the last judgment. At this point no second, alien righteousness is needed (such as the mercy of God because of the merits of Christ). Eternal life is merited because of the goodness of good works.[36] Even when this goodness is regarded as wholly the gift of grace, the picture that emerges seems to be the exact opposite of the one sketched in *Contra Latomus*. There the God-wrought renewal, however wonderful it may be, is imperfect in such a way that it requires forgiveness before the tribunal of Christ, whereas here it does not. If so, all the dangers which the Reformation saw in "virtue" (*habitus*) language reenter with a vengeance.

I am aware of only one attempt to deal directly with this problem, although there may be others. Reinhard Koesters argues that one should not think of Trent as affirming a double judgment (viz., first, a declaration of righteousness which affects sinners "on the way" [*in via*] and makes them inherently just, and, second, a final eschatological judgment at the end of life or history). Rather, the initial transforming declaration of righteousness has eschatological validity: when God accepts sinners, he does so definitively (which, for Koesters, does not deny that human beings can turn against God's forgiveness and lose justifying grace). Thus it is one and the same judgment which is pronounced at the beginning and end of the justified life. In both pronouncements it is a word of mercy and forgiveness in Christ which simultaneously creates inherent righteousness and accepts it as worthy of eternal life.[37] If this is accepted, then Trent's teaching on inherent righteousness as the formal cause of justification, like its apparent denial of the *totus peccator* in canon 25, is compatible with Luther's *contra Latomus* parable of the last judgment. Inherent righteousness is the effect rather than the cause of God's pronouncement that this human being is just. Thus, real though it is, the justified cannot appeal to it or rely upon it *coram deo*.

Luther presumably would be satisfied with this. He would ask for nothing more than that Trent allow the gospel of justification to be proclaimed in the radical terms mandated by his *Contra Latomus* minidrama. He would no doubt have difficulties with the particular way in which Trent deploys a particular theological conceptuality in describing justification (just as he had difficulties with Augustine's formulations), but what he asked for was freedom for the *sola fides*, freedom to proclaim trust for salvation solely in the Giver, not the gift (much less the self). Only if this were denied would there be doctrinal incompatibility on justification.

3. Conclusion

Other problems could also be discussed, most notably the bearing of the doctrine of justification on issues such as sacraments, doctrinal authority, and church order, but these questions have been an integral part of the agenda of this dialogue group since its commencement in 1965.

Whatever the omissions, however, we have said enough to reach conclusions. The most important is that the more one examines the question, the more improbably it seems that the positions of Trent and the Reformation on justification are incapable of being made compatible. Both allow for the affirmation that salvation is *sola gratia*, i.e., unconditionally free in the mode of "efficient" causality, and this makes it difficult for them clearly to anathematize each other on whether salvation is also *sola fide*, i.e., unconditionally free in the performative mode of promise.[38] Like all statements, the Tridentine and Reformation formulations are susceptible of a wide range of interpretation (although there is also a range of affirmation which they definitely and permanently exclude). It is scarcely surprising if some of the interpretations overlap, not in the sense of positively agreeing but in the sense that they fail to contradict each other. The crucial question, therefore, is not whether it is possible to construe these two very different doctrines of justification as compatible or incompatible (the answer in both cases is almost self-evidently "yes"), but how Lutherans and Catholics can together proclaim the justification of the godless in the present situation. It is their ability or inability to do this which will reveal whether the ways they now understand and employ their historic doctrines are contradictory or noncontradictory, church-dividing or capable of coexisting in a single community of faith.

13

RECENT LUTHERAN THEOLOGIES ON JUSTIFICATION BY FAITH: A SAMPLING

Robert W. Bertram

Thesis One

When recent Lutheran theologies have confronted the Reformation claim that justification by faith is the "article by which the church stands or falls," their reactions, though mixed and reflecting a variety of readings of what the Reformers meant, do tend to reaffirm the confessional tradition of justification by faith as the "chief article."

Is the gospel of justification by faith still, if it ever was, the *articulus stantis et cadentis ecclesiae*? Recent Lutheran answers range from no to yes, mostly toward yes, and even the no's are too dialectical to be quoted as flatly as that and without qualification. This predominantly affirmative chorus is all the more remarkable in a time when, at least until recently, the entire conceptuality of justification was deemed to be no longer meaningful for moderns. That sense of anachronism is shared not only by Ernst Troeltsch and Paul Tillich but by some of the same Lutheran theologians who in this present sampling insist that justification by faith is the key to the gospel nevertheless.

At the negative end of the spectrum, one of the most persuasive Lutheran demoters of justification by faith has been Krister Stendahl. He has argued "that the doctrine of justification is not *the* pervasive, organizing doctrinal principle or insight of Paul, but rather that it has a very specific function in his thought," namely, to deal with the *ad hoc* problem of relating Jews and Gentiles and not with the generic

241

"problem of how *man* is to be saved." Paul is not to be translated "into a biblical proof-text for Reformation doctrines." However, in view of what Stendahl understands by "Reformation doctrine" as "the introspective conscience of the West," in view also of what alternative doctrine he reflects in his own emphasis on salvation history, the question arises whether his own doctrinal center, complete with juridical ("critical") overtones, is all that far from justification by faith.[1]

In the writings of Wolfhart Pannenberg, especially those in English, justification by faith has received little mention, except in references to the theological past, and relatively scant affirmation. A monograph by Pannenberg in German and two recent lectures of his in the United States[2] reflect an understanding of justification by faith (and inevitably therefore a criticism of it) not unlike Stendahl's; though it is Lutheran Pietism that bears the chief blame for the morose Protestant preoccupation with "guilt consciousness," still the historic seeds of that preoccupation inhere in the Reformation's doctrine of justification by faith, given its background in medieval penitentialism and authoritarianism. On the other hand, there are also counterindications in these same writings that, while Pannenberg does not accord justification by faith priority, he does value at least its "extrinsicism" in the way Luther's concept of faith places us "beyond ourselves in Christ" (*extra nos in Christo*).

Even Paul Tillich, whose identification with Lutheranism was at best ambivalent and who doubted that the Reformation doctrine of justification by faith could still be made intelligible for this age, labored to "discover anew the reality which was apprehended in that earlier day," "the thing itself," "the boundary situation," "the Protestant principle," having himself been shaped by that "so-called 'material' principle of the Protestant churches."[3]

On the other hand, some of the most explicitly Lutheran theologians may seem at first glance to have displaced justification *sola fide* with some new theological center: Anders Nygren, with *agape* or "theocentricity"; Werner Elert, with law and gospel or reconciliation; Regin Prenter and Gustav Wingren, with creation; Gerhard Ebeling, with the happening of the word of God. Yet each of these theologians not only asserts but is at pains to explicate how his apparently different theme really amounts to the same thing as justification by faith and indeed necessitates it.

Not only in his later *Commentary on Romans*, where Nygren left little doubt that justification by faith is quintessential gospel,[4] but also in his *Agape and Eros*, a historical-scientific effort at "motif-research," the theology of Luther culminates the distinctively Christian theocentric tradition of love, and precisely in his gospel of justification *sola fide*.[5]

The fact that Elert's mature systematics, *The Christian Faith*, is organized around the theme of reconciliation rather than around justification sustains a decision he announced three decades earlier in his little *Outline of Christian Doctrine*. "It is possible, of course, to develop the whole Christian doctrine of salvation out of the conception of justification, but . . . under the influence of philosophical idealism, justification became a mere change of man's disposition, and the boundaries between God and man were obliterated."[6] But when instead Elert moves the "reconciliation of God and man into the focal position," he more than ever has to demonstrate that this is not "arbitrary exoneration" which evades "the Creator's original demands on his creatures, namely, to justify themselves before him."[7]

Prenter, a Dane, and his Swedish colleague, Wingren, have labored (also co-labored) to restore primacy to a Christian theology of creation in contrast to a tradition, in part Kierkegaardian, which had set creation and redemption at odds dualistically. But for neither of these theologians does the interest in creation preempt justification *sola fide*. For them the two emphases come to nearly the same thing. Prenter's systematics, *Creation and Redemption*, cites not only Lutheran but ecumenical reasons for following the general progression of topics in the Augsburg Confession, though he admits that that is not the only or even the best plan. Apart from formal considerations of progression, however, he reaffirms confessionally the Augsburg Confession's "structural principle," namely, "a message of salvation at the center of which is justification by faith in Christ alone—the center toward which everything else points."[8]

In Wingren's most recent book in English, his semi-autobiographical *Creation and Gospel*, he notes how reviewers have observed that in his writings "the voice of Irenaeus can be heard with increasing clarity whereas the voice of Luther has become weaker and weaker." To this Wingren adds: "I hope these reviewers are right," but soon explains why: "People in the twentieth century stand psychologically closer to the heathen of the classical period than to the slave under the law of the sixteenth century, who was burdened with guilt. . . . " Still, if in the sixteenth century "the important contrast was between forgiveness and guilt, not between resurrection and death, as in the second century," the truth remains, "fundamentally the two are the same," with perhaps one notable exception. "Unique to Luther, as opposed to Irenaeus, is his intensive concentration on 'justification by faith alone' and therefore the subsequent sharp contrast of the Law to the Gospel.'' On that Lutheran issue Wingren, not contra Irenaeus but contra Barth, has been front and center.[9]

Ebeling has stressed the need to balance Reformation studies with "modern thought," and he himself, having begun as a church historian, has moved into systematic theology, especially hermeneutics, with a strong advocacy for "proclamation" to people when and where they live.[10] All of this might lead us to imagine that in his theological writings, surely the more proclamatory ones, such an old chestnut as justification by faith would have dropped from use. But even when, for purposes of proclamation, he translates that phrase into "the reality of faith," he openly admits, "I intend to present simply the so-called doctrine of justification." For "this is the point on which simply everything depends: the reality of faith is the justification of man." Moreover, this is "the *so-called* doctrine of justification" because "justification by faith alone . . . is not one doctrine besides many others, but constitutes the whole of Christian faith."[11]

Theologians like Nygren, Elert, Prenter, Wingren, and Ebeling, who at first appear reluctant in their prioritizing of justification *sola fide* but soon allay that misimpression, may remind us of the second son in our Lord's parable, the one who began by declining to work in the vineyard but then did so after all. There is now a new generation of Lutheran theologians who are less oblique in seizing upon the thematic of justification, also its terminology, as basic to the gospel. Historian Gerhard Müller, while he grants Barth's contention that the centrality of justification does not speak for Protestantism in general, nevertheless reports that at present this doctrine is again receiving more attention than it has previously in this century.[12] The mere fact that Müller can now acknowledge Elert as one of the three recent agenda-setters (along with Ritschl and Barth) for any new theologizing about justification, after Elert had long received silent treatment, may be one straw in the wind.

Carl Braaten is another member of this new generation. Seldom since the days of Francis Pieper, the former court dogmatician of the Lutheran Church–Missouri Synod, whom Braaten criticizes on other grounds, has an authoritative theologian in American Lutheranism so elaborately endorsed (though with some of Pieper's same reservations) the centrality of justification the way Braaten has. Confident that the vocabulary of "righteousness" at least might be revived (for instance, through the current interest in "rights"), Braaten maintains: "The article of justification which Luther rediscovered . . . belongs to the foundation of the whole Christian church.'' Lately he has gone that assertion one better: ''it is more than that, for if it lies at the gospel's center, it has to do fundamentally with the standing and falling of not only the church but of the whole of humanity.''[13]

What looks to be a formative factor for a whole new generation of Lutheran clergy in America is the book by Eric Gritsch and Robert Jenson, *Lutheranism, the Theological Movement and Its Confessional Writings*, a manual whose every chapter radiates from the Reformation's distinctive ''proposal of dogma,'' namely, ''justification by faith alone, without the works of the law.'' What ''makes that a doctrine by which the church stands or falls,'' Jenson explains, is its ''metalinguistic character,'' stipulating not this or that telltale vocabulary but a certain ''*kind* of talking.'' ''It does not say: Talk about justification and faith. . . .'' Unpacking the words 'justification' and 'faith,' the proposed dogma says:

> Make the subject of your discourse those points in your and your hearers' life where its value is challenged, and interpret the challenge by the story about Christ, remembering that when this is rightly done your words will be an unconditional promise of value.

The Lutheran Reformation, Jenson adds, had its own formula for this kind of ''language analysis'': ''rightly divide law and gospel.''[14]

With theologians like Braaten and Jenson, does not justification by faith acquire an imperialism, at least an aloofness, which the Lutheran Confessors themselves would not have recognized? To say that is to misrepresent Braaten and Jenson. True, it is not the Confessors' habit to call justification by faith a ''dogma,'' as Jenson proposed, or even a ''doctrine,'' as Braaten sometimes does, a term which the Confessors usually reserve for the ''gospel'' (*doctrina evangelii*). For them justification by faith is one of several ''articles'' (*articuli*) articulating the one gospel, as the article on original sin also does, or the article on the church, that is, ever so linguistically, in so many earthly words. But then Jenson should not be misunderstood to be saying that ''metalinguistic'' means independent of any and all language or even of a quite finite range of language. Justification by faith, in *addition* to being itself one languaging of the gospel, is at the same time a normative language *about* all other gospel languagings—in that sense, *meta*. We might say, after the manner of language philosophers, that justification by faith is L_2 as well as L_1.

Müller, similarly, says justification by faith is "not so much 'doctrine' as it is a criterion (*Massstab*) of proclamation."[15] Luther, in the Smalcald Articles, referred to it as one *Artikel*, all right, but as *der Hauptartikel, der erste Artikel*. The Apology of the Augsburg Confession speaks of "our rule" (*regula*), and the Formula of Concord locates the doctrinal norm not in the Scriptures as such but in that scriptural "shape of doctrine" (*forma doctrinae*) which gives all Scripture its doctrinal identity.[16] Thus, with latter-day Lutheran theologians the confessional tradition of a *Hauptartikel*, and now (meta)-linguistically, continues.

Thesis Two

On the other hand, some Lutheran theologians object that to ascribe primacy to justification is to subvert what alone is absolute, God's grace in Jesus Christ, who after all must be revealed through the whole array of biblical and ecumenical "pictures" and not only in one relative picture like justification, lest that one become absolutized.

One spokesman for this criticism is Horst Georg Pöhlmann, in his book entitled *Rechtfertigung*. Although the book has not been widely read in the United States, it does explicate a point of view which until recently has been held by many Lutherans also in this country. What is Pöhlmann's objection to making justification by faith the "article by which the church stands or falls" (*articulus stantis et cadentis ecclesiae*)? Is it that that competes with Jesus Christ, who alone deserves such priority? That does seem to be Pöhlmann's ultimate objection, and the one on which this review will concentrate.

In, with, and under his Christocentric argument, however, Pöhlmann, without clearly distinguishing, raises another objection, and does so over and over, namely, that exalting the Pauline "picture" of justification by faith suppresses other, equally valid "soteriological pictures" (for example, the Synoptics' "kingdom of God"). The implication seems to be that elevating one soteriological picture (*Heilsbild*) over other *Heilsbilder* impoverishes not only biblical and ecumenical diversity but also, and *thereby*, Jesus the Christ. Pöhlmann seems to be saying, though not always outright, that the *Heilsbilder*, on one hand, and God's deed in Christ, on the other, like "pictures" and "pictured" (*Ektyp und Archtyp*), are related as finite to infinite, as part to whole, as relative to absolute, so that the absolute, the person of Christ, though he does need to be pictured or revealed, is sinned against by our "absolutizing" any one of his relative "pictures."[17] If that idealist-revelationist logic does reflect Pöhlmann, it may or may not reflect other Lutherans who nevertheless might still agree with his general antithesis: where justification dominates, its sheer dominance diminishes Christ.

For his Christocentric polemic against a rival centricity of justification, Pöhlmann takes his cue, as other Lutherans have, from Karl Bartn's criticism of Luther or, more recently, from Hans Küng's reiterating of Barth's criticism. Pöhlmann's discussion of "the theological ranking of justification" begins with this quote from Küng's book, *Justification: The Doctrine of Karl Barth and a Catholic Reflection:* "The doctrine of justification is *not* the central dogma of Christendom. . . . The *central dogma of Christendom* is the *Christ*-mystery." But Küng was here reaffirming Barth, whom Pöhlmann also quotes: "The *articulus stantis et cadentis ecclesiae* is not the doctrine of justification as such but is rather that which grounds and climaxes that doctrine, the confessing of *Jesus Christ*, . . . the knowledge of *his* being, *his* doing for us, to us and with us." Barth added: "It could probably be shown that *that* was also what Luther meant."[18]

For his contention that the preeminence of Christ necessitates the subordination of justification, Pöhlmann finds some encouragement in the Helsinki assembly of the Lutheran World Federation, though not encouragement enough. In this assembly the question of the *articulus stantis et cadentis ecclesiae* was addressed head-on and, as Pöhlmann is glad to report, that pride of place was often conceded to Christ, yet not unambiguously so. For instance, the assembly's final "Document 75," for all its admitted Christ-centeredness, Pöhlmann still finds misleading as it stands. Why, he asks, should "Christ's act itself" still depend in some privileged way on just *this* "image," justification by faith? "Does that not at least arouse the impression that one New Testament half-truth is being overextended into the whole truth . . . ? Is it not rather Christ who is the 'one subject' [*'eine Sache'*] of all the New Testament's soteriological concepts, including justification?"[19]

It is this Christocentric challenge, effectively mounted by the Barthians (and Pöhlmann is by no means the only Lutheran to have been aroused by it) that has helped to evoke some of the Lutheran counterassertions which we sampled earlier. Witness, as another sample, Ernst Käsemann's arguing that Christology and justification, far from being separable, are mutually interpretive. Justification, he says, "is and remains applied Christology."[20] It is my impression that the Christocentric disjunction which Barth's critique of the Lutheran "chief article" presupposed, namely, that justification cannot be that central without compromising Christ, is no longer as persuasive as it once was, especially among Lutherans, and hence that a position like Pöhlmann's is less and less representative.

Thesis Three

Significant is what the above complaint (Thesis Two) leaves out, namely, that the Lutheran Reformers centered attention not only on the forensic picture of *justification* by faith but at least as much on justification by *faith*, and that for them *sola fide* was the constant amidst diverse soteriological metaphors, and that precisely because Christ is central (through whatever metaphor) so also must *sola fide* be.

Although this essay is not directly about the Lutheran Reformation but about Lutheran theologies now, what must be recognized is that these current theologies, especially on the matter of the *articulus stantis et cadentis ecclesiae,* try explicitly to come to terms with the Reformation tradition. And what Peter says about Paul says as much about Peter as it does about Paul, also in what is omitted.

Before we come to the point, however, a preliminary observation is needed. We noticed above in the complaint that justification-centeredness militates against Christ-centeredness, the following corollary argument: the concept of justification is only one among many soteriological metaphors or "pictures" and therefore ought not be absolutized at the others' expense. In a moment we shall suggest that the Reformers likewise used the metaphor of justification almost interchangeably (almost!) with other metaphors. However, we ought to be mindful that, when the Reformers compared the article of justification with other *articles*, they were not just comparing it with other *soteriological metaphors.* No, the articles with which justification by faith was compared and found to be superior for articulating the gospel were such articles as those on original sin or repentance or the ministry, none of which is strictly a picture of *salvation* the way justification is. But that exactly was the Reformers' point. That was one reason, at least, why justification was better for conveying the gospel.

What is more to the point, however, is that the whole antithesis between Christocentric and justification-centric is, from the standpoint of the Reformers, gratuitous and probably wrong. For them, what makes that article of justification preeminent is its own very different antithesis: not between justification and Christ but between faith in Christ and works of the law. True, that accent upon *sola fide* in opposition to "the works of the law" (*operibus legis*) the Reformers found in other soteriological pictures as well, like redemption or liberation. Hence we have not yet explained what the forensic picture brings to the task which the nonforensic or less forensic ones do not. Our point now is that, with the Reformers, the thing about the article of justification (or any equivalent metaphor) which needs to be kept "first," "principal," is the premium it places upon our faith in contrast to our merits. For without that priority Christ himself does not retain priority. The centrality of *faith* (whether "justifying" or "saving" or "victorious" faith) and the centrality of Christ are not mutually exclusive but, on the contrary, mutually implicative.

That confessional point is largely muted, perhaps overlooked, in Lutheran theologies like Pöhlmann's which reflect the Barth/Küng critique. Pöhlmann does find some comfort in the fact that for the Luther of the Smalcald Articles, at least, the *Hauptartikel* is Christological. So it is. "The first and chief article," the one which at the upcoming council can never "be given up or compromised" is, as Luther says repeatedly, the article which deals with "the office and work of Jesus Christ, or . . . our redemption [*Erlösung*]."[21] But the way Pöhlmann reads the texts, the chief article is "actually Christ and *not the doctrine of justification*."[22] His importing that alien either/or suddenly reverses the intention of Luther, for whom Christ's redeeming work is indeed first only so long as justification *sola fide* is first. As Luther pointedly explains,

inasmuch as this must be believed and cannot be obtained or apprehended by any work, law, or merit, it is clear and certain that such faith alone justifies us, as St. Paul says in Romans 3, "For we hold that a man is justified by faith apart from works of law" (Rom. 3:38), and again, "that he [God] himself is righteous and that he justifies him who has faith in Jesus" (Rom. 3:26).[23]

All of this, very definitely including the indispensable *sola fide*, is what Luther intended by the *Hauptartikel* on the "office and work of Jesus Christ, or our redemption."

As we shall see, the allergy which some Lutheran theologians have had against the Reformation's *sola fide* has not been unprovoked. But the fact remains that the secret of justification—that it is only by faith—

is then lost in the process. With that loss it is no wonder that justification may no longer be seen as "first" without seeming to compete with Christ. For it is precisely justification's dependence on faith which insures its dependence on Christ.

Thesis Four

On the other hand, the Reformation accent upon faith has by no means been forgotten, least of all by those theologians in the Bultmann tradition who have been preoccupied with faith as a radically new form of subjectivity. But that preoccupation only heightens their critics' suspicion, namely, that *sola fide* then threatens to compromise the "object" of faith, *sola gratia propter Christum.*

A pivotal place in recent Lutheran discussions of faith belongs to Bultmann's treatment, in his *Theology of the New Testament*, of Paul's understanding of faith. The more Bultmann labored to show that faith is not faith in faith, or else it is not faith at all, the more preoccupied he needed to be with faith itself. For Bultmann, Paul's " 'faith' is the condition for the receipt of 'righteousness,' taking the place of 'works,' which in the Jewish view constitute that condition." However, that does not mean that faith, just because it is not an "accomplishment," is therefore not a "deed." On the contrary, faith is the deed *par excellence*, through its character as "decision," "obedience," "surrender," and "renunciation" of the self.[24]

May not this very concentration upon faith overshadow the object to whom faith submits? On the contrary, says Bultmann: "The attention of the believer does not turn reflectively inward upon himself, but is turned toward the object of his faith," "Jesus Christ," "God's prevenient deed of grace which preceded faith."[25] But might this not still suggest that what characterizes God's "grace" as gracious is simply that it encourages human faith, that that is all that is saying about it, and that it converts unbelievers into believers—and very unfinished believers at that—as if God's deed in Christ were but a means to altering people's subjectivity?

Bultmann does at times speak as though "the message which demands acknowledgement of the crucified Jesus as Lord" is valuable for just such instrumental reasons, namely, that it "demands of man the surrender of his previous understanding of himself." Usually, though, Bultmann's statements are more two-edged than that. True, he does say that it is not "at all that *God* needed to be reconciled; it is *men* who receive the reconciliation which God has conferred." On the other hand, God has conferred that reconciliation "not by removing their subjective resentment toward Him but by removing the objective state of enmity which, in consequence of sins, existed between Him and men."[26]

A representative Lutheran critic of Bultmann, in some ways resembling Bultmann's Barthian critics, is Helmut Thielicke, who charged that according to Bultmann the significant change achieved by Christ is "in the human consciousness," in our new and true understanding of ourselves.[27] Thielicke's position has enjoyed wide reception among Lutherans in America, especially pastors. Similarly, the bishops of the United Evangelical Lutheran Churches of Germany at their 1952 assembly issued a pastoral letter condemning the theology of demythologizing (without mentioning Bultmann by name) as "false doctrine." The bishops drew support from an officially sponsored volume of essays, *Ein Wort Lutherischer Theologie zur Entmythologisierung*, edited by Ernst Kinder.[28] Some of these essays reached American readers through the English translation by Carl Braaten and Roy Harrisville, *Kerygma and History*.[29] A basic charge which the essays levelled against Bultmann's theology of justification by faith is that it denies the "objective factualness" of redemption history.[30]

It is one thing to protest that the Bultmannians, by overemphasizing what Jesus does to us (evokes new existential decisions), thereby underemphasize what God does to Jesus (raises him from the dead) or what Jesus does for God (enacts God's being reconciled). It is not necessarily the same objection when critics like Wingren or Stendahl or Pannenberg protest that whatever God has done in Jesus must at least affect a wider range of beneficiaries than the believers in their subjectivity—for example, the whole history of salvation, universal history, or all creation. The latter criticism, taken by itself, need not be opposed to Bultmann's view of the basic relation between God and Christ.

In fact, Bultmann's alleged fideism or individualism, as well as his neglect of creation, are charges which apparently can be taken seriously and accommodated by a leading disciple of Bultmann, Ernst Käsemann, though admittedly with small thanks from his fellow Bultmannians. On a lecture tour of the U.S., at that time Stendahl's own context, Käsemann granted that salvation history "forms the historical depth and cosmic breadth of the event of justification." But "the doctrine of justification" is still "the key to salvation history," and faith still the key to justification. Moreover, what continues to make faith so valuable, for Käsemann as for Bultmann, is that by God's word we are being "called out of ourselves." The need is: "We do not transcend ourselves." The solution is: "God comes to us in his promise and makes us righteous—righteous in that we, as the receivers, allow him to come to us." Accordingly, "to talk about the 'object' and 'content' of faith is completely inadequate and highly confusing. . . ." ". . . [W]hat belongs to the world cannot become the content and foundation of our faith, even in the form of salvation history."[31]

In retrospect, it seems to be a special burden for current Lutheran theologies of justification to manage two apparently incompatible accents simultaneously. How to do justice to the Reformers' most embattled *sola* of all, *sola fide*, and at the same time do justice—not only not compromise but maximize—*sola gratia propter Christum*? Indeed, how to accomplish the latter expressly by means of the former? How to emphasize the "wholly by faith" in such a way that God's gracious deed in Christ is not only not demoted thereby but is, as the Reformers would say, "necessitated" thereby? Probably none of the parties to the present Lutheran theological scene would want to evade this confessional challenge by somehow combining a little *sola fide* with a little *solus Christus*, or even by holding subjectivity and objectivity in "creative tension." It seems that some such question as this continues to haunt Lutheran theology: What is it about Christ that commends to God those who believe in him? Conversely: What is it about faith in Christ that it alone, of all the things Christians do, should commend them to God?

Francis Pieper flourished before the time of Bultmann, but his influence in some sectors of American Lutheranism has survived into recent times. Pieper, too, as some of Bultmann's critics, found a major threat to the gospel in the current fideism (*Ich–Theologie*) that threatened to debase faith into self-trust. Thus he responded with an elaborate counteremphasis upon the "objectivity" of justification, and he emphasized that faith is "merely" the "hand that receives" grace. His treatment of *sola fide* and the "righteousness of faith" was largely defensive, disclaiming what these confessional themes dare *not* mean rather than extolling faith as that which God counts positively as righteousness.[32]

Not unlike Pieper in this one respect is Braaten in his recent essay on "The Christian Doctrine of Salvation." He too grants, though almost in passing, that "justification by grace alone [is] *received* through faith alone." But his more urgent concern by far is to reverse the present, post-Enlightenment "soteriological shift," "an earthward shift from superhuman to human power," and to recover "the significance of the atoning death of Jesus and his resurrection." The impression arises that, in order to recover that classical Christian transcendence, there must somehow be a corresponding reticence about faith. Otherwise the human subject might be tempted to take over. Braaten's references to faith tend to be cautionary. "Faith does not produce the meaning of the salvation event; it can only receive it in radical gratitude." Or: "The Protestant type of exclusivism has stated that apart from faith there is no salvation";[33] here again the nervousness about faith is that it might restrict grace. The fideist distortions seem to have traumatized and immobilized Lutheran reactions to the point where the Confessors' once bold *sola fide* has become virtually irretrievable.

Thesis Five

Though it is true that the Reformers' gospel of justification highlighted *sola fide*, it is also true that they paid special attention to the forensic idiom, that is, to the divine law. There has been a major effort in recent Lutheran theology not only to reappreciate the gospel's intrinsic seriousness about the law but also to see in that very criticalness of the law why sinners can be justified "only by faith."

There may be disagreement as to just where on the spectrum Dietrich Bonhoeffer belongs in the controversy between the Barthians' "gospel-law" and the Lutherans' "law-gospel." But there is little doubt that he has been enormously influential (also in America) in reviving Lutheran seriousness about the Christian disciple's accountability to the divine law, under whatever terminology. Reviving Luther's notion of "cheap grace"—which has since become a household word (and not only in parsonages), Bonhoeffer made it popularly clear how that Lutheran malady necessitates recovering Luther's original, "costly" understanding of justification and, only because of that, faith.

What Bonhoeffer meant by cheap grace is "the grace which amounts to the justification of sin without the justification of the repentant sinner who departs from sin and from whom sin departs." Costly grace, by contrast, "is costly because it condemns sin, and grace because it justifies the sinner." "In both cases we have the identical formula—'justification by faith alone.' Yet the misuse of the formula leads to the complete destruction of its very essence." But Bonhoeffer asks: "Did not Luther himself come perilously near to this perversion . . . " with his shocking advice, "Sin boldly, but believe and rejoice in Christ more boldly still"? No, unlike "cheap grace" Lutheranism, which has taken Luther's formula as a premise rather than as a conclusion, Luther saw it only as "his very last refuge." "Take courage and confess your sin, says Luther, do not try to run away from it, but believe more boldly still." The experience which taught Luther that this grace "had cost him his very life, and must continue to cost him the same price day by day," was which experience? "In the depth of his misery, he had grasped by faith the free and unconditioned forgiveness of all his sins." [34]

What Elert identified as "the problem of justification" is posed by "the total testimony of Christ," also in the Synoptics and the Johannine corpus but most explicitly in Paul's "relationship of Gospel and Law." "The Law demands that man justify himself before God. But then the question immediately arises whether the Gospel frees him from this obligation to his Creator." Yet that, says Elert, "is entirely impossible, since it would strip God's Law of all serious intent." The challenge to a theology of justification is to show that the gospel does in truth meet "the basic demand God makes of His creatures."

It is true, says Elert, that God's justifying of sinners includes his declaring them righteous, but saying only that much could easily be misconstrued as an arbitrary, even fictitious exoneration of sinners who in fact are still sinners. Rather, the justified sinner is one who stands before God, bereft of every last excuse and thus reduced to silence, awaiting the verdict which he can only trust will be just and, in that trust, listens. However, "silence and hearing alone are not yet faith," not even when what is heard is "the Word of God." For the law, too, is God's word. "Faith springs solely from the Gospel, and it consists only in the conviction that the Gospel's content, that is, the person and work of Christ, apply to the believer." Only that way can "*Christ* our righteousness" and the "righteousness of faith" be harmonized as one and the same. But then "Christ's righteousness is not, as it were, credited to us externally." On the contrary, " 'we have been united with Him in a death like His;' and only thereby 'shall we be united with Him in a resurrection like His.' " [35]

Similarly, Prenter, in his argument for "law and gospel" (as opposed to "gospel and law"), wishes to make room for a universally human "immediate acknowledgement of guilt [as] the sinner's veiled response to the demand of God's law." But then,

> when God's answer is heard, the immediate acknowledgement of guilt takes on the character of a Christian acknowledgement of sin. And this is the object of the theological use of the law.

However, Prenter explains, "the theological use of the law is not . . . a use of the law alone." "The judgment, when it is God's radical judgment, is never without the grace of the promise." "It is the law, not the gospel, which reveals sin. . . . But the law cannot reveal sin if it is divorced from the gospel."[36]

Applying this concept of law and gospel to his theology of justification, Prenter addresses the question of the righteousness of Christ and of faith. "The righteousness of Christ, his atonement, which is imputed to man through forgiveness is, however, not to be understood as an external, juridical righteousness which in a purely legal manner is transferred from Christ to the sinner. . . . When the sinner receives the promise of forgiveness and in faith relies upon that promise, he is not only in an external sense counted righteous, but he *is* righteous in the full sense of the word. He can never become more righteous and holy than he is in the moment when he believes that his sins are forgiven." Prenter goes on to explain that last sentence. "Progress . . . does not mean that faith is followed by another and more perfect righteousness (for example, in terms of works or love. . .). Progress can mean only that everything which is contrary to faith, all forms of self-righteousness, all the aspirations and strivings of the old man are more and more overcome, so that only faith remains."[37]

It is significant that in these last three samples— Bonhoeffer, Elert, Prenter—such an uninhibited use of forensic-legal categories should appear, at all places, in a manual of Christian discipleship (Bonhoeffer), in a chapter on the effect of the Holy Spirit (Elert), and in a discussion of Christian "renewal" (Prenter) and still, in all three cases, as the righteousness which is "only by faith."

14

JUSTIFICATION IN CONTEMPORARY CATHOLIC THEOLOGY

Avery Dulles, S.J.

The theology of justification in Roman Catholic teaching has undergone no dramatic changes since the Council of Trent, which gave the classic response to the problems raised by the Reformation. The general thrust of Trent was to reduce justification to an element or aspect of grace. Catholic theologians have felt more at home with the theology of grace, viewed in its transforming impact on the recipient (rather than simply as God's graciousness), and have generally given only passing attention to justification as God's forensic deed on behalf of sinners. Justification is rarely discussed at length except in polemics against, or dialogue with, Protestants.[1]

Even in twentieth-century Catholicism there remains a fear that the category of justification, with its forensic overtones, can too easily lead to a vapid nominalism or an empty eschatologism, in which the present efficacy of God's love is overlooked and justification is understood in a purely extrinsicist fashion. Further, some fear that justification language, being primarily taken up with the religious anxieties of the individual, tends to bypass the social dimension of sin and redemption, which are better brought out by other New Testament terms. Beyond this, some point out that the category of justification, being correlative with sin, looks on grace too exclusively as a remedy for sin, as though its only effect were to restore nature to its pristine integrity without also drawing its recipients into the sphere of properly divine life. In this connection allusions are made to the patristic and Orthodox notion of *theōsis*.

Although, for reasons such as these, justification is not a central category in contemporary Catholic dogmatics, every major theological system has to address itself to the question how the sinner is brought into a state of friendship with God. In this sense justification remains a continuing theme. From the time of Trent until the early twentieth century, justification was studied primarily with the conceptual tools of late Scholasticism. It was accordingly understood as an efficacious divine intervention whereby a supernatural accident was infused into the human soul as a kind of ornament rendering it pleasing in God's sight. This accident ("sanctifying grace") made its possessor inherently righteous and able to perform meritorious actions, thus earning a strict title to eternal rewards. The justified person possessed a variety of infused virtues that reduplicated on the supernatural plane the qualities of the naturally virtuous soul as understood in Aristotelian philosophy.

In the twentieth century there has been a strong movement away from Scholasticism, especially in its modern forms. In part the new tendency was supported by the Thomistic revival, which led to fresh interpretations of the Angelic Doctor. Even more powerfully, it has been supported by other trends such as the biblical revival, the patristic revival, and personalistic phenomenology. As a result of these movements, the leading Catholic theologians of the past generation have considerably modified the theology of grace found in early twentieth-century Scholastic manuals. In the following pages an attempt will be made to summarize recent Catholic theories of justification with the help of Karl Rahner and other prominent systematic theologians.

1. Imputed and/or Inherent

In reaction against some Protestant statements that stress the alien or extrinsic character of justification, Catholics have tended to emphasize that righteousness is really communicated to the recipient, who becomes inherently just. God's justifying sentence is regarded as effective and thus as producing what it declares. Not untypically Karl Rahner, while admitting that the objective event of God's act in Christ is causally prior to any change in the redeemed, holds that the subjective justification of the individual is really identical with that individual's sanctification. He criticizes Hans Küng for leaving it unclear whether justification and sanctification are two aspects of a single process or two successive phases.[2] Piet Fransen, like Rahner, holds that justification and sanctification are "simply different approaches, through different symbolisms, to one identical reality: that through grace we share in the divine life."[3] Catholic theologians often list other terms such as redemption, regeneration, new creation, adoption, reconciliation, and divine in-dwelling as virtual synonyms.

Even while admitting that these terms might refer to identical realities, many Catholic theologians regard justification language as indispensable. Hermann Volk, for example, holds that imputation is an essential aspect of the event of justification, for according to Paul righteousness is given by grace through the merits of Christ, which are reckoned to the believer.[4] Ricardo Franco takes the term justification in the active sense as signifying primarily God's judgment which creates a new bond between the human person and God.[5] In this sense, he insists, justification is not a mere synonym for the infusion of grace. It signifies not simply that we are made just but that we are acknowledged as such by God, whose eschatological judgment determines both our present condition and our ultimate destiny. Because of the centrality of the forensic element, it would be wrong to imagine that we are pronounced righteous because we are inherently such. Rather the reverse: any inherent righteousness of ours is consequent upon God's gracious, creative sentence of pardon, involving nonimputation of the sins we have committed. Understood in this way, the term justification brings out the free, interpersonal, and forensic character of God's saving action on our behalf—properties not equally well signified by other biblical and theological categories.

In speaking of inherent righteousness or sanctification, Catholic authors today try to bring out more clearly than did some post-Tridentine authors that the righteousness of the creature always remains a gift; it is a participation in the righteousness of God, given in Christ. Rahner, in particular, insists that ''created grace'' is an essentially relative entity, having no absolute existence of its own.[6] The Aristotelian categories of substance, nature, virtue, and the like do not sufficiently indicate the relational and interpersonal character of the gift. Our righteousness is, so to speak, the imprint upon us of the righteousness of Another. In that sense the Reformation categories of *iustitia aliena* and ''imputed righteousness'' convey an important truth that Catholics do not wish to ignore.

2. Created and/or Uncreated?

Luther is said to have repudiated the category of *gratia creata*.[7] Trent, without using this technical term, did speak of ''inherent'' righteousness (DS 1530; 1661). Some modern Catholic authors write as though justification were reducible to the production of the physical accident of "sanctifying grace." More recent Catholic theology has tried to profit more from the insights of the Greek patristic tradition, which has persisted in some strains of Western Catholicism thanks to the studies of Lessius, Cornelius a Lapide, Petavius, Möhler, Newman, Scheeben, and others.[8]

In a highly influential essay Rahner argued that even on Scholastic principles created grace must be seen as a secondary element in justification.[9] Since grace is the inception of the life of glory, he contended, it should be analyzed in categories derived from the theology of the beatific vision, in which the saints know God immediately as he is in himself. The so-called light of glory, although it inheres immediately in the souls of the blessed, is not an intermediary (*species impressa*) through which they see God but rather a disposition qualifying them to see God immediately. In beatitude God, as form (or, more precisely, quasi-form, since God does not enter into composition with the creature), is immediately present to the human intellect. By his interior presence God disposes the soul to receive him and thus produces the light of glory. The light of glory is therefore an effect rather than a cause of God's beatifying presence.

Applying this analysis to grace, Rahner maintains that sanctifying grace, as a created entity, is not what effectively relates us to God. The principal element in justification or sanctification is the "uncreated grace," that is to say, the triune God who communicates himself. The union with God effected by uncreated grace produces in the soul a disposition for this union, called created or sanctifying grace. Sanctifying grace, as a finite reality, would not be capable of effecting the mysterious union with God which is designated in the New Testament as the gift of the Holy Spirit, newness of life, and the like.

Following up on the earlier articles of Maurice de la Taille on "created actuation through uncreated act,"[10] Rahner's essay helped to focus the attention of Catholic theologians on the uncreated gift, which must be understood in personal rather than physical categories. Piet Fransen, who has developed his theology of grace in the language of indwelling and encounter, points out that Luther was at home with such personalist language thanks to his study of the German mystical tradition.[11] By rehabilitating the category of uncreated grace, therefore, Catholics may find a path toward rapprochement not only with Orthodox but also with Protestant Christians.

The questions here under discussion, subtle and abstract as they may seem, have important implications for one's religious attitudes. If justification were primarily the reception of an accident into the soul, we would have to be grateful for this created gift, but we could not praise and thank God as we do if he bestows himself. Paul and John testify that in grace God communicates himself and personally dwells within us.

3. The Trinitarian Character of Grace

Expressing in Scholastic categories the causes of our inherent righteousness, Trent referred to Christ as meritorious cause (DS 1529). This text, taken alone, could convey the impression that Christ is our redeemer only because he paid the penalty of human guilt and vicariously merited graces for Adam's progeny. Later, however, Trent's decree goes on to speak of charity as perfectly uniting us to Christ and making us living members of his body (DS 1531). This text suggests a present, mystical union between Christ and those who are justified by his grace.

In contemporary Catholic systematic theology the categories of meritorious or satisfactory causality are applied to Christ with great reserve since they easily lend themselves to falsifying the relationship between the Father and the Son. Faith and piety are not helped by the concept of the Father punishing his innocent Son for the sins of others, or by the idea that Jesus' expiatory death appeased the Father's anger and made the Father propitious toward us. The current tendency is rather to speak of Jesus as the efficacious symbol in whom the Father's redemptive love triumphs over all that could resist it. Through his death and resurrection, as the culmination of his career, Jesus becomes "the expressive presence of what—or rather, who— God wished to be, in free grace, to the world, in such a way that this divine attitude, once so expressed, can never be reversed, but is and remains final and unsurpassable."[12] The salvific will of God, insofar as it is not merely nominal but real, necessarily includes this self-expression in objective, historical form.

The "uncreated grace" whereby we are justified, because it consists primarily in God's personal self-communication, relates us to each of the divine persons. As Son, Christ communicates to his members the filial and servant character of his own existence. Because we are mystically identified with the second person of the Holy Trinity we become, in the memorable phrase of Emile Mersch, "sons in the Son" (*filii in Filio*).[13] In relation to the Father we become adopted sons and daughters. The Holy Spirit, as the subsistent love uniting the Father and the Son, inwardly attunes us so that we are able to accept in loving freedom the self-communication of the Father in his incarnate Son. Building on a long tradition of trinitarian mysticism going back to Bonaventure and Ruysbroeck, contemporary theologians such as Rahner and Fransen hold that the justified believer has distinct, proper (nonappropriated) relations to each of the three divine persons. God's presence in history is the extension into time and space of his eternal, triune existence.

4. The Ecclesial Character of Grace

In Aristotelian categories the church, with its preaching and sacramental ministry, is frequently described as the instrumental cause of justification (cf. DS 1529). While this manner of speaking can be instructive, contemporary Catholic theologians tend to envisage the church in its social and visible aspects as prolonging and participating in Christ's symbolic or sacramental mode of causality, a mode of causality that combines certain aspects of final and exemplary causality but which cannot be fully reduced to Aristotelian categories. As the supreme realization and manifestation of all grace and holiness, Christ is first in the order of the divine intention and in the order of exemplary causality. As a real symbol, the humanity of Christ, in its visible aspects, is the unsurpassable manifestation of grace. All redemptive grace, according to this theory, both tends toward, and lives off, the full self-expression of God's redemptive designs in Christ. The church, in a manner analogous to Christ, may be called necessary for salvation. In Rahner's words,

. . . the Church is the sacrament of salvation for the world because she points to and renders present that grace in the world as eschatologically victorious which will never more disappear from the world, and which is insuperable in impelling this world towards the consummation of the kingdom of God, whatever the pitfalls which may lie in its path. This sacramental sign of grace is an effective sign not inasmuch as it would call forth a resolve of God to bestow grace which would not exist without it, but inasmuch as through it precisely this will of God to bestow grace manifests itself at the historical level, and thereby at the same time also renders itself historically irreversible.[14]

In the framework of this theory Rahner nuances somewhat the traditional understanding of the way in which the church and the sacraments confer grace. They do not transmit grace as something which they formally precontain, like water in a pitcher (although the language of

Trent's fifth canon on the sacraments, DS 1605, might seem to suggest this). Rather, they transmit grace by bringing it to symbolic realization. They are real symbols of the grace of those who participate in the sacramental action, and beyond this, of God's gracious presence in the whole world. As Rahner puts it: "What is brought to effective manifestation in the dimension of the Church in the sacraments is precisely *that* grace which, in virtue of God's universal will to save, is effective everywhere in the world where man does not react to it with an absolute denial."[15]

The ecclesial character of all grace and salvation, if understood in the categories of instrumental causality, might seem to rule out the bestowal of justification on the unevangelized. But if Christ and the church are understood rather in terms of symbolic causality, final and exemplary, it can be argued that the secret presence of grace among all peoples is precisely what is brought to symbolic visibility in Christ and the church. Rahner, holding that all grace is in a hidden way related to Christ and the church, speaks of "anonymous Christians," meaning those who live by the grace of Christ without awareness that they are so doing.[16] Rahner's thesis has been an object of much debate. Rahner himself attaches no importance to the term "anonymous Christian," but he does insist that it is possible for non-Christians and even atheists in good faith, even though they lack explicit faith in Christ, to be justified, to live in the grace of Christ, to have the gift of faith, and to attain eternal salvation. In so holding Rahner seems to be supported by a number of important texts from Vatican Council II (e.g., *Lumen gentium* 16, *Gaudium et spes* 22, *Ad gentes* 7).

5. Word and Sacrament

In the type of theology we have been expounding, grounds are given for affirming a profound relationship between the word of Christian proclamation and the acceptance which that word wins for itself in the faithful hearer. Rahner distinguishes between the inner word of God's spiritual self-communication and the outer word of Christian proclamation. These two forms of the word, he affirms, are essentially interconnected and mutually complementary. Without the inner grace the external word could not be received as the word of God, and without the outer word the human person would not be challenged to take a definite decision, nor would faith and salvation be present in a bodily, social, and historical form adapted to human nature. The word of God,

Rahner goes on to say, brings with it the reality it signifies. Proclamation is therefore a salvific event in which God graciously communicates himself. Rahner is conscious here of ascribing to the word of God qualities commonly ascribed to the sacraments. For him sacrament is not opposed to word but is on the contrary the supremely efficacious realization of the word of God.[17]

In this aspect of his theology Rahner exemplifies a major trend in contemporary Catholicism to stress the inner unity between word and sacrament and to rehabilitate the importance of both Scripture and preaching. His work stands in solidarity with that of Otto Semmelroth, Hermann Volk, and many others.[18] This Catholic word-theology received official support from Vatican II in its Constitution on the Liturgy (*Sacrosanctum concilium* 56), its constitution on divine revelation (*Dei verbum* 1 and 21), and its decree on the ministry and life of priests (*Presbyterorum ordinis* 4).

Drawing on certain elements of Rahner's sacramental theology and of Paul Ricoeur's doctrine of symbol, Regis Duffy, an American sacramental theologian, maintains that theology would do better not to take its departure from biblical or dogmatic concepts, which are derivative from, and inadequate to, the experienced mystery.[19] Categories such as "imputed" and "imparted" justification are static, dichotomized terms expressing limited aspects of a dynamic event more concretely symbolized by worship. Sacramental symbolism suggests the inexhaustible richness of a mystery which is at once objective and subjective, forensic and moral, communal and individual. The manner in which we worship shapes and manifests our real definitions of justification, no matter what definitions we may verbally profess.

A correct theology of worship, according to Duffy, brings out the ecclesial and eschatological aspects too often neglected in the theology of justification. God in Christ shows forth his saving purposes for the many who are to be incorporated into the eschatological community. Our grateful response must retain this orientation and must not be allowed to degenerate into a self-serving individualism or an empty sacramentalism "which rejoices in God's future only because it makes no demands on our present."[20] Baptism and the Lord's Supper symbolize the commitment to participate communally in the actualization of the kingdom. Justifying faith, therefore, cannot be merely cognitive or fiducial; it must include the "new obedience" of love. Inasmuch as the eschatological fulfillment is both already and not yet, the individual believer and the church itself may be correctly called both justified and sinful. *Simul iustus et peccator* will never be better understood than when we symbolize and respond to a presence we cannot control.''[21]

6. Acts Prior to Justification

In the Pelagian and semi-Pelagian controversies, it was debated whether the sinner, without the help of grace, could by prayer or good works move toward justification. In the Second Council of Orange, the church accepted the negative answer of Augustine, an answer reaffirmed by many leading theologians of the Middle Ages and by the Council of Trent. Since Trent it has been axiomatic in Catholic theology that one cannot take a single step toward justification by one's unaided natural powers.[22]

The question whether one can perform naturally good acts without the help of grace, much discussed in the later Middle Ages, is of interest only on the assumption that there are situations in which the grace of God is not given. In view of their position regarding the universal efficacy of Christ's redemptive mediation, Rahner and many other contemporary theologians argue that grace is omnipresent, at least as offer, and that therefore every free moral act, considered in the concrete, is either an acceptance or a rejection of the proffered grace. In that case "every morally good act of man is, in the actual order of salvation, also in fact a supernaturally salutary act."[23] Correspondingly, any act not sustained by grace is, in its concrete actuality, a sin.

Granted that every salutary act depends on grace and that no act prior to justification can strictly merit justification, it must still be asked whether one can, with the help of grace, be disposed or dispose oneself for justification. On the basis of his studies in the history of the doctrine of *gratia operans*, especially in Thomas Aquinas,[24] Bernard Lonergan defends the Tridentine answer to this question. To avoid the disruption of violent change, God brings it about that justification is preceded by a series of preparatory steps involving operative and cooperative grace.[25] Operative grace is that which God effects within us without our free cooperation (*in nobis sine nobis*). Such grace is necessary for our hearts to be turned to God in love, for unless God were to convert our hearts, our love would remain confined to the limited horizons of self-interest. Operative grace, in Lonergan's phrase, replaces the "heart of stone" with a "heart of flesh." Once this initial conversion has been effected, the sinner can begin to cooperate in a subordinate and dispositive way in the process of justification. The grace of conversion, besides being operative, is also cooperative insofar as it is the principle of free acts of love, faith, hope, and repentance (cf. DS 1525-26). "Operative grace is religious conversion. Cooperative grace is the effectiveness of conversion, the gradual movement towards a full and complete transformation of the whole of one's living and feeling, one's thoughts, words, deeds, and omissions."[26]

Lonergan's thought on the process of conversion harmonizes with that of Rahner, who in various writings emphasizes that human freedom, although not destroyed by original sin, has been so wounded that it needs to be liberated by God's prevenient grace in order to be capable of accepting the help offered to it in Christ and the church.[27] "Wherever a person attains his salvation in freedom, he will attribute to God both the capacity for and the act of his freedom, in praise and in thanks, for it is an act which God has given him in a grace for which there are no reasons."[28] Not only the possibility of acceptance but the very act of acceptance, Rahner insists, is a pure grace.[29] Thus the Catholics can accept the Reformation principle of *sola gratia*.

7. *Sola Fide*?

More problematical, perhaps, for Catholics is the Reformation formula, *sola fide*. Hans Küng, among others, has made a strong case for the acceptability of this formula.[30] For him it makes good sense when it is used to express the fact that in justification the sinner stands with empty hands, receiving everything as a sheer gift from God. Faith, in this formula, includes trust in the Lord from whom one expects everything. In the Pauline sense faith is the radical surrender of boasting or self-glorification.[31]

Granted that hope is included in the Reformers' concept of fiducial faith, one must still ask whether the *sola* in the formula does not seem to exclude love, which, according to Trent, is essential for justification (DS 1530-31, 1561). Although faith without love has always been regarded as truncated (*informis*), certain statements in Trent and in the Catholic theological tradition could give the impression that faith and love are extrinsic to each other and that the former could be complete without the latter. Charity or love might seem to be something that we decide to do on the basis of faith, so that in the last analysis we would be justified not by faith but by works.

Contemporary Catholic theology responds to this objection by pointing out, in the first place, that love is no less a grace than faith. Love is not our achievement but God's gift; indeed, it is the outpouring of the Holy Spirit in our hearts (cf. Rom. 5:5). In love, as in faith, we surrender ourselves unconditionally to God so that "theologically speaking, love is no more a work than faith."[32] As for the distinction between faith and love, it is not merely Scholastic, but has a biblical basis in texts such as 1 Cor. 13:13 and Gal. 5:6. Yet, as developed by Scholastic authors, the distinction of the three theological virtues sometimes tended to "obscure the totality of the single and basic act of justification which God's grace bestows on man freely and as freedom. . . ."[33] A faith not animated by love would not be a proper response to the gospel; even as faith it would be defective.

As Louis Bouyer points out, Luther himself understood faith as a loving response to the God who bestows his gifts upon us.[34] Comparing the doctrines of Aquinas and Luther, Otto Pesch contends that the latter, in rejecting *fides caritate formata*, misunderstood the Thomistic formula as though it meant that charity were something extrinsically added to faith. In reality, Pesch maintains, charity is an inner moment of living faith, and thus the Thomistic thesis that justifying faith must be enlivened by charity does not really contradict the Lutheran thesis of justification by faith alone.[35]

8. The State of Grace

The initial attraction by which God draws the human heart to himself is seen in Catholic theology as preparatory for the decisive moment when a person ceases to be the slave of sin and stands in the grace of Christ (cf. Rom. 5:1-2; 6:1-23; 2 Cor. 1:24; Phil. 4:1; 1 Pet. 5:12).[36] The traditional concept of a "state of grace" is often called by other names in contemporary theology. Lonergan, for example, speaks rather of "the dynamic state of being in love with God."[37] The terms "sanctifying grace" and "state of grace" are in his opinion too "ontic"; they correspond to a stage of theological development at which meanings had not yet been sufficiently grounded in the world of interiority and experience.

For Rahner justifying or sanctifying grace is simply the free acceptance of that self-communication of God which is permanently present as offer and which, when accepted, effects its own acceptance. Fransen and others, further exploring the nature of the acceptance, develop the concept of the "fundamental option."[38] The human person, they maintain, is constituted by a basic existential choice, which in turn becomes the foundation for many particular decisions. This basic choice is called an ''option'' to distinguish it from the casual and superficial choices that do not affect the inner self or personal center. It is called a ''fundamental'' option because it sets the direction for a multitude of other decisions.

The call of grace, according to this theory, comes to a person at the center of the ''I,'' in which one is present to oneself in a transcendental, unreflexive awareness and at the point where one disposes of oneself.[39] At the core of our person we are confronted by an either/or. Either we accept God's gracious invitation to acknowledge him as our God or we do not.[40] The passage from sin to grace, or from grace to sin, must therefore be instantaneous. Once made, the good option perdures until by serious sin we retract our fundamental option and make an option that centers us on some other object, such as the self or a created idol.

The theory of the fundamental option calls for a reconsideration of the manner in which baptism and penance can be said to justify their recipients. These sacraments are seen as symbolic realizations of the grace of conversion in its historical tangibility. The causality at work in these sacraments is two-directional. On the one hand, the basic attitude of the participant contributes to the positing of the sign or sacrament. On the other hand, the sign sustains and intensifies the inner attitude. ''Thus this concrete process of self-fulfillment is itself all along and in all cases a 'real symbol' under which the individual brings to fruition this basic attitude of his, his *option fondamentale*.''[41] In various essays Rahner has reinterpreted the sacrament of penance, arguing that the sacramental action itself transforms the sinner's imperfect sorrow for sin into a wholehearted turning to God, who bestows forgiveness.[42] Since the rite of reconciliation is essentially connected with a change of attitude on the part of the recipient, the personal and sacramental dimensions are inseparable.[43]

A similar reinterpretation could no doubt be given to the sacrament of baptism. Adult baptism, in which the baptized individual asks for the sacrament, is considered the normal, though not necessarily the most frequent, case. The doctrine of the fundamental option would have to be applied somewhat differently to infant baptism, in which the free response to the grace of the sacrament could not take place until later in the life of the recipient.

9. Consciousness of Grace

Neo-Scholasticism was profoundly influenced by the Molinist thesis that sanctifying grace is a ''physical accident'' of a purely entitative (or ontic) nature, in no way accessible to consciousness. This view was difficult to reconcile with the New Testament and with patristic theology, both of which characterize the life of grace as life, light, consolation, and the like. Under Rahner's leadership many contemporary Catholic theologians have returned to the Thomistic theory (later defended by John of St. Thomas and Suárez) to the effect that grace as a spiritual reality brings with it a supernatural formal object, or, in more modern terminology, a new perspective and a new horizon of consciousness.[44] We have already seen how in Lonergan's theory conversion implies a shift of intentional consciousness arising out of the love of God poured forth by the Holy Spirit in our hearts (cf. Rom. 5:5).

Rahner likewise explains how God's personal self-communication in grace gives a new specification to the transcendence of the human spirit. This does not, however, mean that we can clearly discern by introspection whether we are motivated by grace, still less whether we are in a "state of grace." As Rahner points out, our capacity for self-reflection is too feeble to permit us to distinguish clearly between a general orientation toward being in its transcendence (which is the connatural formal object of the human spirit as such) and a grace-given orientation toward union with the God of eternal life.[45] Thus any judgment whether we are actuated by supernatural motives must rely, in part, upon a difficult process of discernment, in which criteria such as the fruits of the Holy Spirit (cf. Gal. 5:22-23) will play a part.[46] Rahner's doctrine of the consciousness of grace, therefore, does not lead to an "enthusiastic" self-reliance such as was condemned by the Council of Trent (DS 1533). The empirical aspects of our faith, hope, and love are not infallible indices that we have actually received the grace of justification.

Notwithstanding these cautions, both Rahner and Fransen have thought it possible to sketch a certain phenomenology of grace. Rahner speaks of various key moments in which the presence of God makes itself felt as the source of pure joy, even in the midst of suffering, or as empowerment to forgive, love, or obey with one's whole heart, or as making it possible for a dying person to submit peacefully to the approach of death.[47]

Fransen over a period of several decades developed a similar psychology of grace. Following the fourteenth-century Flemish mystic, Blessed John Ruysbroeck, he asserts that God's gracious action begins in the mysterious depths of the human spirit and only gradually irradiates the peripheral regions of which we are more clearly conscious, including our physical well-being. Since grace directs the heart to God, it brings with it, even in situations of pain and sorrow, a peace and joy not of this world.[48]

10. *Simul Iustus et Peccator*

Trent unequivocally taught the reality of the transition from unrighteousness to righteousness that occurs in justification. It denied that grace consists merely in God's favor or in the nonimputation of sins (DS 1528, 1561). For this reason Catholics remain to this day somewhat nervous about the formula, *simul iustus et peccator*, which might suggest that we are justified only in hope or in a purely nominalistic way that leaves us internally untouched. Von Balthasar and Rahner, in particular, have insisted that at the moment of justification the sinner undergoes a real, internal transformation and thus in a true sense ceases to be a sinner.[49]

With the reservation just stated, however, Catholics can give qualified approval to the formula. The grounds for such approval have been set forth by authors such as those just mentioned, as well as by Hans Küng and Otto Pesch.[50] They would include considerations such as the following:

a) Any goodness that is ours is a gift from God, so that all we have truly from ourselves is prevarication and sin (cf. Orange II, DS 392).

b) The justification given to us in this life remains from start to finish a gift of grace. It is a participation in the righteousness of Christ, whom Paul calls our righteousness (1 Cor. 1:30).

c) Concupiscence remains in the baptized. Although according to Trent, concupiscence is not sin in the true and proper sense of the word, concupiscence is in the concrete tinged with sin inasmuch as it arises from sin and is conducive to sin (DS 1515).

d) Even after justification we retain sinful attitudes, habits, and other after-effects of our past sins, called by Augustine "*reliquiae peccatorum.*"

e) We live in a sinful world in which the atmosphere is contaminated by the cumulative effects of sin.

f) Like Christ himself, who was "made sin" for our sakes (2 Cor. 5:21), we are mysteriously in solidarity with a sinful race.

g) We are constantly subject to temptations, into which we would fall were it not for the grace of God that enables us to resist.

h) Without an altogether special privilege of grace, even the just fall frequently into venial sins, which cannot easily be distinguished from those which are mortal.

i) Even the church is in some sense sinful, since it does penance and in its public liturgy prays for forgiveness.

j) Even the saints—or rather, they especially—pray like the publican in the Gospel, "God, be merciful to me a sinner" (Luke 18:13).

k) Our definitive redemption is something to which we look forward as an eschatological gift.

These observations on the sinfulness of the justified do not negate the reality of interior righteousness, but help us not to misunderstand this doctrine. As von Balthasar observes, the Catholic who speaks of being "justified and sinner at the same time" must go even further than Luther and Barth in stressing the paradox, for the affirmation of sinfulness must be combined "with another perspective that is presented just as clearly in Scripture: in this present age the Christian, now freed from sin, participates in the divine life through grace and is under no compulsion to sin further."[51] The formula need not, in fact, imply that after justification our unrighteousness is identical with that of the unjustified, for, as Otto Pesch points out, even Luther recognized a clear distinction between sin which rules in the hearts of the unjustified (*peccatum regnans*) and the sin which is held in check by righteousness (*peccatum regnatum*).[52] If some such distinction as this is admitted, there is no reason why the formula should be objectionable from the Catholic point of view.

11. Satisfaction

In the preceding section mention has been made of the remnants of sin which perdure even after forgiveness. This consideration sets a favorable context for the question of satisfaction, which has been treated with particular depth and clarity by Karl Rahner, whose thought we shall here summarize.[53]

As sometimes presented, satisfaction seems to suggest that God, when he forgives, is not quite willing to forget the past and still insists that the sinner make amends for the evil done. Understood in this way, the requirement of satisfaction seems out of keeping with the loving mercy of God who justifies sinners by pure grace in view of the superabundant satisfaction already rendered by Christ.

In recent Catholic theology satisfaction is understood not as limiting God's forgiveness but rather as clarifying the stages in which that forgiveness comes to, and is appropriated by, those in need of it. This can best be explained by a prior consideration of sin and its effects.

Sin in its essence is a free decision to evil, rendering a person guilty before God. The sinful decision arises out of the inmost kernel of the spiritual person, but, as the deed of an embodied spirit, it objectifies itself in various ways. It modifies the sinner's own psychic and bodily organism, engendering evil attitudes, inclinations, and habits. The sins of persons in community result in a distorted social situation, which leaves its mark on all involved. An inner act of repentance, inspired by faith, provides assurance that the guilt of sin is forgiven in Christ, but it does not instantaneously or automatically heal all the effects of sin. Even after the guilt has been remitted, the person and the environment remain impaired by the results of sin, making it difficult for individuals and groups to persevere in good. The secret roots and impulses of sin are not eradicated.

For the evil of sin to be completely rectified, repentance and love must penetrate all those dimensions of reality that were affected by the sinful decision. This rectification, insofar as it opposes itself to the inclinations and habits set up by sin, may be experienced as painful. The penalty here in question, however, is not arbitrarily decreed by God but is a necessary aspect of the corrective process. Because these penalties are part of a moral order willed and sustained by God, they may be called divine punishment, but without any implication that God creates punitive instruments in order to exact compensation.

Concretely, satisfaction takes the form either of laborious performance of good deeds or of patient endurance of adversity. When pursued with discretion, penances freely undertaken by a forgiven sinner, or imposed as a sign of repentance by a confessor or spiritual guide, can be salutary. In the same perspective, the kind of suffering that comes to individuals and groups through illness, bereavement, and other misfortunes can take on positive Christian meaning. Penance does not, of course, take the place of sincere and trustful repentance, but, presupposing such repentance, it enables love and contrition to penetrate the multiple levels of one's existence and relationships so that the Christian grows in the likeness of Christ.

The traditional Catholic teaching on purgatory and indulgences, in spite of certain theoretical vacillations and practical abuses, may be viewed as an effort to apply the doctrine of forgiveness and satisfaction to the life of the Christian in the church and in the passage from time to eternity. As Rahner points out, Paul VI's Apostolic Constitution on Indulgences (1967) makes considerable advances over earlier Catholic statements on the subject and incorporates certain ideas, such as that of Christ as the true "treasury of the church" (*thesaurus Ecclesiae*), which correspond to those of the young Luther.[54] Thus the thorny issue of indulgences may be amenable to ecumenical dialogue.

12. Good Works

In continuity with the Council of Trent, Catholic theologians of our day insist that good works are both possible and necessary for continued life in the grace of God (DS 1539, 1575). Good works are held to proceed from the human person, but only because and insofar as that person is liberated and animated by the grace of God which includes and enhances human initiative. Far from being semi-Pelagian, therefore, the Catholic affirmation of human responsibility is compatible with the Augustinian idea of "grace alone."

Paradoxically, it may be held that the more God sustains us with his loving assistance, the more freely and autonomously we act. In the words of Karl Rahner:

> The radical dependence and the genuine reality of the existent coming from God vary in direct and not in inverse proportion. . . . Not until one experiences himself as a free subject responsible before God and accepts this responsibility does he understand what autonomy is, and understand that it does not decrease but increases in the same proportion as dependence on God.[55]

A number of twentieth-century Catholics are concerned to rebut the objection of Feuerbach and Marx that Christianity lulls its faithful into an attitude of passive waiting on God, who alone can save people from their ills. A Uruguayan liberation theologian, Juan Luis Segundo, complains that the Lutheran doctrine of justification by faith alone, with its accompanying *soli Deo gloria*, "turns faith into a confident but essentially passive acceptance of God's fixed plan for human destiny and the construction of his eschatological kingdom."[56] Liberation theology, according to Segundo, respects the role of human freedom and initiative in the realization of the kingdom of God.

It is frequently asked whether the Council of Trent, by succumbing to a static, individualistic concept of righteousness, tended to discourage commitment to social action on behalf of the gospel. An American Jesuit, Richard Roach, while admitting that Trent is open to an individualistic interpretation, argues that since human righteousness is a participation of the righteousness of God, as Trent taught (DS 1529), and that since God's righteousness is always identical with itself, justification draws people together into community. God evidently intends that his justice be reflected not only in individuals but also in the social order. Once the justice of God is seen as requiring transformation in human society, Trent's requirement of good works can be interpreted as implying a mandate to promote justice in society.[57]

Unlike Roach, a Brazilian Franciscan, Leonardo Boff, concedes that Trent's text on justification was elaborated from a totally individualistic standpoint and portrayed justification as a static condition. He believes, however, that the original sense of the texts can be "prolonged" so as to bring out the social and dynamic character of God's justifying action. Boff himself would prefer to substitute the term "liberation" for "justification." Liberation, he maintains, has its origin in God's free and gracious initiative, transforms its recipients, involves them in a process of renovating praxis, and thereby serves to revolutionize social structures. "Since a person is never a person in isolation but is essentially social, we can conclude that a structural revolution of the world is necessary if the conversion of the nuclear person is to be real and effective. . . . God and human beings collaborate to bring about the birth and growth of the kingdom of God in history until it attains its final fulfillment."[58]

13. Merit

The Council of Trent affirmed the doctrine of merit in a carefully circumscribed manner. It emphasized that we can merit neither justification itself (DS 1525) nor our final perseverance in grace (DS 1572). But the council also said that the righteous merit eternal life and that good works which proceed from grace merit an increase of grace and of heavenly glory (DS 1582).

As Fransen points out, the term *merit* and its derivatives in Latin and other languages have a more juridical ring than most of the equivalent terms in Greek.[59] Even the Latin term *meritum* in the Fathers and the Roman liturgy had a wider meaning. But when used in the context of law, merit talk encourages a juridical mode of thinking, in which certain acts are regarded as founding a claim in justice to a proportionate reward. On reflection, the legal or commercial analogy proves misleading, for there is no strict proportion between good works and the heavenly reward. Besides, it is impossible for a creature to have a claim in justice against the Creator.[60]

As Fransen goes on to say, it is regrettable that some Catholic authors, in their polemical enthusiasm, failed to guard against the dangers of merit language. "Many superfluous controversies could have been avoided if a better expression had been found to convey the biblical message that promises us eternal life and entrance into the kingdom of God if we live according to the commands of God and Christ."[61]

When we do talk of merit, we would do well, Fransen reminds us, to recall that it exists only within God's covenant and on the basis of his free covenant promises.[62] Its ground is not the works done, taken in the abstract, but rather the personal dignity of those in whom the triune God graciously takes up his dwelling.[63] Whatever merit our deeds may have depends upon their being preceded, accompanied, and followed by God's free grace (DS 1546). Thus it is correct to say, as did Trent, paraphrasing Augustine, that in rewarding our merits God crowns his own gifts (DS 1548).

Rahner, in a comment on Küng, seeks to escape the juridical overtones of merit language by stressing that our works performed in grace are the beginning, and in that sense the cause, of what we shall enjoy in heaven. The connection is objective, like that between sowing and harvesting.[64] In the same context Rahner points out that the doctrine of merit gives no ground for the supposition that the prospect of reward "may be made the first and last *motive* of the Christian life." Every Catholic schoolboy, he says, should know that this supposition is unambiguously false. "Man's merit (in the objective sense) is precisely in the act of love, which seeks for no reward. But such 'merit,' bestowed on him by God's grace, is objectively and truly valuable in heaven."[65]

As Küng rightly observes, ecclesiastically approved prayers can often give the best answer to theological objections against the Catholic doctrine of merit.[66] He quotes several prayers from the Roman liturgy and from the writings of the saints. In one of these prayers, Theresa of Lisieux confesses that, having no confidence in her own good works, she is content to wrap herself in the righteousness of the Lord. Perhaps one may add that such a loving act of confidence is a splendid example of what Catholic theologians might reckon as a meritorious work!

The prayers quoted by Küng illuminate the fiducial aspect of justification. They make it clear that faith comes to flower in an assured hope and that this hope is founded not on our own powers and merits but on the mercy and love of God as known to faith. Blessed Claude de la Colombière, for instance, prays:

O Lord, in hope alone hast Thou established me. Men can take away both wealth and honor. Sickness may take away the strength and the means to serve Thee. I can even lose Thy grace through sin; but I shall never lose my hope; I shall keep it to the last moment of my life. Others may support themselves on the innocence of their lives, on the strictness of their penitence, in the number of their charities, or on the fervor of their prayers. Thou, O Lord, in hope alone hast established me. For me, Lord, this is all my confidence, it is my confidence itself.[67]

Certainly this prayer does not savor of the "presumptuous trust of the heretics" condemned by the Council of Trent (DS 1533). Rather, it may be thought to embody what Trent referred to as the confidence of those approaching justification "that God will be propitious to them for Christ's sake" (DS 1526). In the judgment of Otto Pesch, the certainty attributed to Christian hope by Thomas Aquinas closely resembles the assurance of salvation advocated by Luther.[68] In accordance with his general thesis regarding the different thought forms of Lutheran and Thomistic theology, Pesch holds that Luther, speaking existentially from within the commitment of faith, escapes the doctrinal difficulties that would arise if he were claiming a sapiential certitude of his own election to eternal glory. So too, we may suggest, Blessed Claude's assurance that he would not lose his hope, while it could not be defended as a theoretical certitude, is unexceptionable in the mode of discourse proper to prayer.

14. Law and Gospel

As several Catholic commentators have observed, the doctrine of law and gospel, as the twofold form of the word of God, stands at the heart of Luther's entire system and provides the structural framework for his doctrine of justification.[69] A review of contemporary Catholic responses to this doctrine, without adding anything essentially new, may serve to recapitulate much of what has been discussed above under headings such as imputed righteousness, *sola fide*, and *simul iustus et peccator*.

The duality of law and grace has a good biblical foundation, especially in Paul. The law-gospel dialectic, proposed in an unacceptable form by Marcion, is detectable in certain passages of Origen and Augustine. Medieval scholastics such as Robert of Melun and Thomas Aquinas, in their treatises on the relationship of the old law to the new, foreshadowed some of Luther's insights. Thus the law-gospel contrast, as Gottlieb Söhngen observed, has a Catholic past.[70] Nevertheless it was not thematically taken up by Trent, nor has it been in modern Catholic systematics. Walter Kasper regards it as regrettable that law and gospel never became a major theme in Catholic theology.[71]

Both Roman Catholicism and Lutheranism have sought to steer a middle course between antinomianism and legalism. According to each tradition, the law of God imposes a genuine obligation, but it must not be allowed to preclude the word of pardon and grace that comes to us in Christ without our deserving it and hence, in a certain sense, in spite of the law which condemns us.

A theology of law and gospel, therefore, can be, by Catholic standards, fully orthodox. In this perspective law might be understood not simply as a written code, but as anything that makes known to us our obligations before God and our guilt in violating his will. Gospel, on the other hand, would be the free word of pardon and grace that comes to us, finally and decisively, in Jesus Christ, the source of all salvation. The Malta Report of 1971 showed how fruitfully Lutherans and Catholics can today collaborate in a joint statement on this theme.[72]

The preceding pages, however, make it clear that there are certain ways of stating the law-gospel distinction that are unlikely to win acceptance from the Catholic side. Law is not to be dismissed as a mere foil permitting God's mercy to stand out more clearly. Neither in Tridentine nor in contemporary Catholicism is it admitted that God commands the impossible (cf. DS 1536, 1568). Nor is law understood as if it turned those involuntary impulses called ''concupiscence'' into formal sins. Gospel, on the other hand, is not understood as a mere judgment of forgiveness that leaves us as helpless as before. It comes as God's saving power to all who believe. While liberating us from the power of sin and death, it binds us to God in Christ. On the last day the Lord Jesus will reward the good works of those who have obeyed and will inflict ''vengeance upon those who do not know God and upon those who do not obey the gospel of our Lord Jesus'' (2 Thess. 1:8). As Joseph Fitzmyer points out, much of the recent discussion of law and gospel and of canon and gospel rests upon an excessively narrow concept of gospel, seen only as *iustificatio impii*, rather than upon "the rich, varied, and multifaceted reality that Paul describes."[73]

Emphasizing the positive relationship between law and gospel, Catholic authors quote the aphorism of Augustine, "The law was given so that grace might be sought; grace was given so that the law might be fulfilled."[74] To accept the gospel, they point out, is not simply to be excused from the requirements of the law (unless one means only the old ceremonial law of Judaism) but to be drawn into a new obedience and to be empowered to share in the work of the kingdom. Christ, who transcendently fulfills the law in his own person, embodies all that is positive and salutary in law. "A man's salvation," Kasper remarks, "does not depend on his attitude towards the law but on his attitude towards the person and word of Christ." Faith, then, is not a mere acceptance of forgiveness but "an unconditional surrender of self to the dominion of God in Christ."[75]

Ever since the Reformation Catholic theology has been striving to correct what it regards as Luther's imbalances without falling into imbalances of its own. Trent, while it did not canonize the categories of Scholasticism, was powerfully influenced by the theology of the schools, against which Luther had himself reacted. Trent therefore gave strong emphasis to human responsibility and to the created gifts of grace, and this emphasis became excessive in post-Tridentine Scholasticism. Contemporary Catholicism, in search of a more theocentric outlook, has borrowed heavily from the mystical tradition and from post-Kantian transcendental philosophy. Dissatisfied with the anthropology of Aristotle, this theology draws on modern personalist phenomenology. Distrustful of the objectifying categories of the Scholastic tradition, the new Catholicism is strongly oriented toward mystery and symbol. A theology that approaches justification in terms of uncreated grace and symbolic actuation may perhaps succeed in transcending the impasses of the sixteenth century and inaugurating a fruitful dialogue with Lutheranism.

15

FORENSIC JUSTIFICATION AND LAW IN LUTHERAN THEOLOGY

Gerhard O. Forde

Almost from the beginning forensic justification has been both the blessing and the bane of Lutheran theology. Confessional and Orthodox Lutherans have of course insisted on it as *the* true sign of genuine Reformation teaching and the standard by which all teaching is to be judged. Roman Catholics, however, have seen it as pure "extrinsicism"; since justification is totally extrinsic to the believer, it effects no real change or transformation and is therefore something of a legal fiction. Justification, if it is purely forensic, is not effective. This has been the basic charge through the years. Even within the Reformation camp forensic justification has not always been accepted with unqualified approval. As early as the controversies over the views of Andreas Osiander, who wanted to understand righteousness in terms of the indwelling of the divine nature in the soul, voices were raised against it. Those early confessional struggles served, however, only to reinforce the insistence on a purely forensic understanding of justification in Lutheranism. Whenever questions or threats arise, the characteristic Lutheran move in this regard has been to insist all the more on justification as a purely forensic act.

The Kantian revival of the latter half of the nineteenth century brought renewed concern for the doctrine of justification in Protestant theological circles, especially those influenced by the work of Albrecht Ritschl. With that came also renewed questioning of a purely forensic justification, often in connection with increasing admiration for the erstwhile "heretic" Osiander.[1] The Ritschlians, following the lead of their master, launched something of a polemic against forensic justification, claiming that justification, particularly for Luther, was to be understood as an analytic judgment rather than a synthetic one. An analytic judgment was understood to be one based on a view of the outcome of the process of justification, while a synthetic judgment is forensic in the sense that it declares the truth. Karl Holl, the virtual father of modern Luther scholarship, brought the argument about forensic justification into contemporary Lutheranism in this form.[2]

Therefore the question arises for this essay: Is justification for Lutheranism to be understood in a purely forensic sense? If so, how can that be related to Roman Catholic fears of extrinsicism, a justification that is not effective? If not, how can the traditional Lutheran concerns that found expression in the doctrine of forensic justification be safeguarded and expressed today? I shall pursue this question in the light of historical investigation and subsequent reflection. My thesis will be that the traditional insistence on forensic justification (a synthetic, not an analytic judgment) was essentially right and proper but that the persistent difficulty over the question arises because of certain presuppositions about the place of law in the theological "systems" involved. The problem, that is, is not with forensic justification per se but with the understanding of law, i.e., the system of justice presupposed but usually left unexamined.

1. Definitions

Forensic justification is here taken to mean that justification comes to the sinner from without by the judgment of God, by his *imputation*, his *reckoning*. It issues from the divine *forum*, or *tribunal*. As *actus forensis* (a purely legal judgment made solely on the part of God and his reckoning in the light of Christ) it is to be distinguished from an *actus physicus* (a judgment made on the basis of or entailing some physical, moral, psychological, or otherwise empirically verifiable change or endowment in the creature). To my knowledge, Luther himself never used the term *forensic* as such, but of course repeatedly speaks of *imputation* as the divine act through which righteousness comes to the sinner and does on occasion speak of the divine "tribunal."[3] It was Melanchthon who first gave the term official currency when he spoke of "forensic usage" in the Apology: "In this passage [Rom. 5:1] 'justify' is used in a judicial way [Lat. *forensi consuetudine*] to mean 'to absolve a guilty man and pronounce him righteous,' and to do so on account of someone else's righteousness, namely, Christ's, which is communicated to us through faith."[4] For the purposes of this essay we can treat "imputed" and "forensic" righteousness as virtually the same.

From these beginnings in Luther and Melanchthon, the concept developed into the *actus forensis* of the later dogmaticians. Heinrich Schmid sums up the view of the Orthodox fathers thus:

> The effect of faith is justification; by which is to be understood that act of God by which He removes the sentence of condemnation, to which man is exposed in consequence of his sins, releases him from his guilt, and ascribes to him the merit of Christ. . . . "Justification denotes that act by which the sinner, who is responsible for guilt and liable to punishment (reus culpae et poenae), but who believes in Christ, is pronounced just by God the judge." This act occurs at the instant in which the merit of Christ is appropriated by faith, and can properly be designated a *forensic* or *judicial act*, since God in it, as if in a civil court, pronounces a judgment upon man, which assigns to him an entirely different position, and entirely different rights. By justification we are, therefore, by no means to understand a moral condition existing in man, or a moral change which he has experienced, but only a judgment pronounced upon man, by which his relation to God is reversed, and indeed in such a manner, that a man can now consider himself one whose sins are blotted out, who is no longer responsible for them before God, who, on the other hand, appears before God as accepted and righteous, in whom God finds nothing more to punish, with whom He has no longer any occasion to be displeased.[5]

One can sense from this summation both something of the grandeur and precision of the Orthodox view but perhaps also something of the anxiety in attempting to hold to it. It is stated boldly, but pains must be taken to guard against contamination from moral conditioning or change in the one so justified. But then the counterquestion immediately arises: Does anything at all happen in justification? If not, in what sense is such justification effective at all?

2. The Systematic Problem

The difficulty in the understanding of justification arises, no doubt, because the very term implies a legal or moral process. It presupposes a standard, a law, according to which the justice in question is to be measured. Given such presuppositions, the term justification could only mean to "make just" according to the scheme. Justification would then have to mean some sort of movement from the state of being unjust to the state of being just, a movement from the state of sin or guilt to the state of righteousness. The sin could not coexist with the righteousness.

Thus the medieval tradition described justification as a movement from a *terminus a quo* to a *terminus ad quem* comprising (*a*) the infusion of grace, (*b*) a movement of the free will toward God in faith, (*c*) a movement of the free will in recoil from sin, and (*d*) the remission of guilt. Such movement was to be called justification because every movement takes its species from its end, the *terminus ad quem*. Even though the movement may be instantaneous temporally, it can be understood only as a movement, a change in the moral subject from sin to righteousness effected by grace.[6]

The result of such thinking in terms of movement, however, has meant that the dogmatic tradition has been plagued with a problem, especially when justification is equated with remission of sins. In its simplest form it may be put thus: If justification comes at the beginning of the process, the process is unnecessary; if, however, it comes at the end of the process, justification is unnecessary. It is difficult to see, that is, how both justification and the process can coexist in the same scheme. If justification is real, the process tends to become fictional; if the process is real, justification tends to become a fiction.

3. Luther on Justification

The significance of Luther's view on justification in this regard is that it can be understood only as a complete break with the attempt to view it as a movement according to a continuous scheme of law or progress. For Luther the divine imputation of righteousness for Christ's sake meant shattering of all such schemes. Justification therefore does not come either at the beginning or the end of a movement; rather, it establishes an entirely new situation. Since righteousness comes by imputation only, it is not at all a movement on our part. We can be candidates for such righteousness only if we are completely sinners. That means of necessity for Luther that in place of all schemes of movement from sin to righteousness we must put the *simultaneity* of sin and righteousness; imputed righteousness brings with it the *simul iustus et peccator*, where the *iustus* and the *peccator* are total states.

This understanding of the matter is quite clear already in Luther's commentary on Romans.[7] Luther leaves no doubt throughout the entire commentary that the most vital enemy of the righteousness of God is not so much the godless sinner as the "righteous" who think in terms of law and intrinsic moral progress. Aristotle in his Ethics, Luther says, bases sinfulness and righteousness only on what a person does.[8] The gaining of righteousness could then be real only to the extent that sin is expelled. Imputed righteousness could then only be a legal fiction or a manner of speaking due to the incompleteness of the process or in view of its end. Against such thinking (*ad modum Aristotelis*) Luther sets thinking *ad modum scripturae*, in which the divine judgment or imputation is the true and creative reality which unmasks the reality and totality of sin at the same time. It would make no sense for God to impute righteousness if we were already even partially righteous. It would make no sense for God to forgive sin if we were not actually sinners. Thus in order that "God may be justified when he speaks and true when he judges" (cf. Rom. 3:4), the human way of speaking and judging *ad modum Aristotelis* must be rejected. Before the divine tribunal no saints, but only sinners can stand.[9] Imputed righteousness for Luther means a complete break with thinking in terms of schemes of law and process—and necessarily so because the divine imputation is fully as opposed to human righteousness as it is to human unrighteousness.

The divine imputation thus exposes us as sinners at the same time as it imparts righteousness. And Luther was insistent that these be understood as total states. If one does not so understand the matter and persists in thinking in terms of a continuous scheme or process, the *simul iustus et peccator* will simply turn to poison, a false comfort for lazy sinners. It becomes the platitude that no matter how hard we try, we have to settle for the fact that we will probably never make it because we are, after all, *simul iustus et peccator*. In the way it has too often been understood, it merely rescues the legal scheme in the face of failure.

Luther's insistence that the *simul* means two totalities is designed precisely to combat such thinking. The imputation of righteousness by God for the sake of Christ as a totality exposes its opposite in all its forms: the schemes and pretentions of human righteousness as well as the perfidy of unrighteousness. Sin as a totality is exposed and in that very fact it is likewise attacked. Sin as a total state can be fought only by faith in the total imputed righteousness. Anything other than that would lead only to hypocrisy or despair.

The *simul* is not the equilibrium of two mutually limiting partial aspects but the battleground of two mutually exclusive totalities. It is not the case that a no-longer-entirely sinner and a not-yet-completely-righteous one can be pasted together in a psychologically conceivable mixture; it is rather that real and complete righteousness stands over against real and total sin. . . . The Christian is not half free and half bound, but slave and free at once, not half saint, but sinner and saint at once, not half alive, but dead and alive at once, not a mixture but a gaping opposition of antitheses. . . . Luther goes even further: that kingdom of judgment in which the situation of our being as sinner is so totally depotentiated is nothing other than the kingdom of the last things. In the final analysis it is this and the coming aeon that stand opposed to each other in the *simul iustus et peccator*. The person in Christ is the person of the new age. The judgment of God which proclaims this person as established over against the opposing earthly situation is likewise the anticipatory proclamation of the new world. The faith which receives and grasps that new status in Christ is an eschatological event; it is ever and anew the step out of this world of the visible, tangible, given reality, the world in which the *totus peccator* is the reality, into the eschaton.[10]

Only the divine imputation as total reality reveals the totality of sin and only through the faith which accepts both is the true battle of the Christian life joined. For the battle is not merely against sin as moral fault, but also against sin as spiritual fault, as "intrinsic" righteousness and hypocrisy.

4. Luther and the Question of Progress in Sanctification

What then of progress? Is the imputed righteousness "effective" in the progress of the Christian life? The *simul iustus et peccator* as total states would seem to militate against any such understanding. And there are indeed many utterances of Luther that would seem to substantiate just that.[11] Sanctification is simply included in justification since it is a total state. A total state admits of no increase or decrease. Sanctification in that light is simply to believe the divine imputation and with it the *totus peccator*. There can be no more sanctification than where the judgment of God is revered and believed. But God is revered only when the sinner stands still where God enters the scene. That place is one where sinners must realize that their way is an end, that Christ is for them, and that glory is to be given to God alone. Only those who thus "repent" are sanctified.

Thus the way of the believer, if it is a movement at all, is a *transitus* from nothing to all, from what one has and is of oneself to what one ha' and is in Christ. Such a *transitus* can never, of course, be a completed fact this side of the grave. Nor is it a continuous line which admits of degrees of approximation of its goal. Rather, each moment could only be at once beginning and end, start and finish. The Christian

can never presume to have reached a certain stage which then is supposedly surpassed or left behind or forms the basis for the next stage.
The Christian who believes the divine imputation is always surprised,
always overtaken again by a new beginning. "To achieve," says Luther,
"is always to begin again anew."[12]

Yet this is not the full picture. In many instances Luther does speak
of a kind of progress, indeed, even of the Christian as one who is *partim
iustus, partim peccator*.[13] In this vein he speaks of faith as a beginning
but not yet the whole; not a perfect fulfillment of the law, but only the
beginning of it. Indeed, what is still lacking will not be imputed for
Christ's sake. Here faith in the imputed righteousness is understood as
only the first fruits of the Spirit, but not the whole. Such faith is only
a beginning because it is the beginning of the actual *hatred* of sin and
thus the beginning of its expulsion and consequent doing of good works.
In faith the law is fulfilled by imputation (*imputative*) but thereafter is
to be fulfilled in reality (*expurgative*) because when the Spirit is given,
one begins from the heart (*ex animo*) to hate all those things which
offend the Spirit. Indeed, one begins to hate not only the things but to
hate one's very self (*odium sui*) as sinner and to hope and long for the
day when such will no longer be the case. We are to do good works in
order finally to *become* externally righteous, and it is not enough just
to have sins remitted by grace but they are totally to be abolished
eventually.[14]

Has Luther simply contradicted himself in this kind of utterance? Has
he just gone back on everything he said about the imputed righteousness
as necessarily bringing with it the *simul* as total states? Some would
say that this kind of formulation represents early failure to escape from
medieval formulations. Others might say that in later battles with antinomianism or moral laxity in the reform movement, Luther, like Melanchthon, changed his emphasis somewhat. But one cannot have it
both ways. Since such material can be found both early and late in
Luther, it no doubt belongs to the permanent substance of his thought.

But how is it to be interpreted? Does it mean that a notion of progress
just displaces all that has been said about forensic or imputed righteousness, the *simul*, and the "beginning again"? The remarkable fact,
however, is that talk of this sort often occurs precisely in the same
context as talk of the *simul*. An outstanding example is in the Romans
commentary alluded to above where the *simul* was set forth. After
speaking of the *simul* as the only way to understand Paul in Rom. 4:1-
7, Luther moves immediately to a discussion of concupiscence. He

scolds Scholastic theologians for thinking *ad modum Aristotelis* that sin is actually removed by what they call grace. He says that he was entirely led astray by this "because I did not know that though forgiveness is indeed real, sin is not taken away except in hope, i.e., that it is in the process of being taken away by the gift of grace which starts this removal, so that it is only not reckoned as sin." Then he goes on to say:

> But this concupiscence is always in us, and therefore the love of God is never in us, unless it is begun by grace, and until the concupiscence which still remains and which keeps us from "loving God with all our heart" (Luke 10:27) is healed and by mercy not imputed to us as sin, and until it is completely removed and the perfect love for God is given to the believers and to those who persistently agitate for it to the end.[15]

What Luther seems to be saying is that thinking *ad modum Aristotelis* led him to an entirely false notion of human sanctification and progress. The basic scheme of law always remains intact. The only question is then one of what is accomplished according to such a scheme either with or without what was called grace. In order to maintain the reality of grace one has consequently to *assert* the removal of sin. But this in turn can only direct one's attention to oneself to ascertain if such removal of sin has actually taken place. If it has not, one could only then be driven to question whether grace had in fact been given—or received. The either/or again comes into play: either the progress tends to make the grace fictitious or the grace makes the progress unnecessary. Here attention comes to be focused on the scheme and the progress, the removal of sin, and grace tends to recede into the background. Progress according to the scheme is the reality, grace appears as something of a theological addendum to make it Christian, a kind of "anti-Pelagian codicil."[16]

Faith born of the imputation of total righteousness, however, will see the truth of the human condition, the reality and persistence of human sin; it will see that concupiscence indeed remains and that it is sin, but that God nevertheless does business with sinners. Such faith will see the fantastic magnitude of the divine act and actually begin, at least, to love God from the heart, to hate sin, and to hope for that righteousness which it knows full well cannot be attained by any human power either with or without the help of what the Scholastics called grace. Such faith makes a "beginning" precisely by believing the imputation of God which goes so contrary to all empirical evidence, will cry to God "out of the depths,'' and actually begin to hunger and thirst after righteousness.

One should note carefully here that when Luther speaks in this vein, he speaks of actual affections: love, hope, hatred (of sin and "the body of death"), not about theological abstractions. The radical nature of the divine imputation which sets the *totus iustus* against the *totus peccator* kindles the first beginnings of actual hope and love for God and his righteousness, whereas before there had been only hypocrisy or despair. There is no contradiction between the *simul* and the *partim* once the presuppositions are changed, once, that is, one no longer thinks *ad modum Aristotelis*.

But what sort of progress is then put in the place of the older scheme? Is there a certain growth in which one arrives at one stage and goes on to the next? Is the *transitus* no longer from nothing to all, at once beginning and end? Could it mean that one does not constantly have to return to "point zero"? Does one "become" so that the admonition "become what you are" could here find its rightful home? Does one attain to a certain approximation of the goal?

Much as such a scheme might suggest itself, it does not do justice to the full intent of Luther's thought on the matter. If progress is envisaged according to the ordinary ways of thinking, it would mean progressive emancipation from the divine imputation. The more one progresses, the less grace would be needed. Imputed righteousness would be only the starting point which one leaves progressively behind until it recedes into the background as an outmoded stage, perhaps something like a temporary loan which is no longer needed once one gains capital of one's own.

This of course would be a serious mistaking of Luther's intention and would destroy the whole edifice. The imputed righteousness is not a mere beginning point which can be allowed to recede into the background; it is the perpetual fountain, the constant power of whatever formal righteousness we may acquire. To look upon it as a stage which could be left behind or as something we gradually need less of would be to deny it altogether. We cannot understand what Luther means by progress unless all ordinary human perceptions of progress are completely reversed, stood on their head, so to speak. The progress Luther has in mind is not our progress towards the goal, but the goal's movement in upon us. This has already been indicated in the idea that imputed righteousness is eschatological in character and that a battle is joined in which the *totus iustus* moves against the *totus peccator*. The progress is therefore the coming of the kingdom of God among us. That is why for Luther complete sanctification is always the same as imputed righteousness. Complete sanctification is not the goal, but the source of all good works. The way is not from the partial to the whole, but always from the whole to the partial. "Good works do not make man good, but a good man does good works." [17] The imputed righteousness is thus not a legal fiction, without reality, but a power, indeed, *the* power of God unto salvation which attacks sin as a total state and will eventually reduce it to nothing. It is always as a whole that it attacks its opposite: either hypocrisy or despair. Good works are not building blocks in the progress of the Christian edifice; they are the fruits of the "good tree."

The expulsion of sin is thus quite other than a morally conceivable process of sanctification. In such a process the person remains more or less constant and only the properties are changed. One supposedly "puts off sin," as Luther sarcastically remarks, as though one were peeling paint from a wall or taking heat from water. [18]

The sanctification resulting from imputed righteousness, however, does not merely take sin away and leave the continuously existing moral subject intact, but rather takes the person, heart, mind, soul, and affection *away from sin*. There is a death and a new life involved that proceeds according to no moral scheme.

> Human righteousness . . . seeks first of all to remove and to change the sins and to keep man intact; this is why it is not righteousness but hypocrisy. Hence as long as there is life in man and as long as he is not taken by renewing grace to be changed, no efforts of his can prevent him from being subject to sin and the law. [19]

Sanctification viewed as progress in partialities, changing of properties, or removing of sins, would, for Luther, lead only to hypocrisy. Sanctification comes always from the whole, the penetration of the divine imputation into time, and involves the death of the old, not its progress. The "beginning" is the first fruit of the resurrection. [20]

In sum, for Luther the idea of progress is stood on its head. Precisely and only because justification is imputed or forensic, a total reality invading the old realm of sin, it is effective. Whatever sanctification there is comes from a divine imputation that is the eschaton breaking into our time.

5. Justification and Continuity in Reformation Theology

The fundamental problem for the Reformation view of justification is therefore that of law and the continuity of the self under the law. If grace is understood as entering into what might be called a positive synthesis with existing human nature and its capacities under law, it can become pernicious. For if one does not perceive oneself actually to have made or to be able to make the progress demanded, talk about "grace" does not work. Indeed, the more one exalts such grace—the more one makes it "free," and even at least verbally excludes all semi-Pelagianism and the like—the worse it can get. The grace to progress is free, it is said. It comes before, during, and after all movement. But if I do not seem to move or get anywhere, I can only conclude either that I have somehow frustrated the grace or that God has decided not to give it. The I is caught between questioning its own sincerity or preparation and the terrors of predestination. The result of the attempt to construct a positive synthesis between grace and natural human capacity under law is the anxious conscience.

Seen in this light, justification by faith is a polemical doctrine. It posits a break with all schemes purporting to effect a positive synthesis with grace. The imputed or forensic righteousness is an eschatological reality which breaks in, indeed, negates the old. The "polemical assertions" so disconcerting to ordinary perception are quite consistent once this is understood: whoever does what is in him commits mortal sin; no free will can carry one across the break; the end of the law; and so on.[21] If one is going to maintain a *sola fide, sola gratia,* then a forensic or imputed righteousness follows, and with it a break in continuity, a dying to the old and a rebirth to the new in the Spirit. The fundamental systematic problem posed by this eschatological understanding of forensic justification is that while on the one hand it avoids the possibility of being called a legal fiction or ineffective, on the other hand it brings with it a break in continuity with existing systems of law and progress which people are apparently very reluctant to surrender. In other words, speaking humanly, forensic justification is not "cheap"; it may just be too dear, too effective to be readily accepted.

Historically Lutherans themselves have not always understood this very clearly. Forensic or imputed righteousness was accepted generally as the mark of Orthodoxy, but the fatal attempt was made to combine it with a scheme of law and an anthropology which presupposed the continuity of the "I." Thus the attempt was made to do what Luther had insisted could not be done: to synthesize the imputed righteousness with thinking *ad modum Aristotelis*. The result, as Hans Joachim Iwand points out, could only be a theology which always carries within itself a profound inner contradiction.[22] Forensic righteousness cannot easily coexist with progress and continuity *ad modum Aristotelis*. The attempt to put them together could only mean that forensic justification would have to be isolated and antiseptically separated from "progress" in sanctification as a completely "objective" fact over against the continuity of the subject. Thus in order to retain the forensic justification at all it was necessary to maintain a strict and careful separation between justification and sanctification. The point is that a break in the continuity must come somewhere. If it does not come as eschatological reality in the death of the old and the resurrection of the new being in faith, then it must come somewhat artificially and abstractly in the theological system. But the result of that is a fracture of the understanding of the Christian life which could not escape spawning a host of other problems: arguments about the "necessity of good works," antinomianism, the third use of the law, and so forth (witness the controversies which gave rise to the Formula of Concord).

A further systematic difficulty was that the forced, stringent isolation of forensic justification as an objective fact over against a continuously existing subject meant that theologians were faced with the question of mediation all over again. How was this completely objective, *extra nos* justification to be appropriated by the individual subject? One would have to provide, so to speak, a theological "shuttle service" between the objective and the subjective which would not disturb the continuity of the subject. The result was the evolution of the so-called order of salvation (*ordo salutis*). The first steps were taken already by Melanchthon with the idea that one moves from knowledge of the objective fact to assent and finally to trust (*notitia, assensus, fiducia*).[23] Such beginnings seem virtually to demand further development. How do assent and trust arise out of knowledge of the objective fact? Thus later dogmaticians spoke of a more full-blown "order" involving such things as call, illumination, conversion, regeneration, renovation, and mystical union, although there was often no agreement about either the number or sequence. In so doing they

. . . seek to collect, under one general topic, all that is to be said concerning what God, or, more accurately, the Holy Ghost, does, in order to induce fallen man to accept of salvation through Christ, and what takes place in order to bring about the designed change in man.[24]

The outcome of this development was to reinforce a fundamental split between the objective means of salvation coming from God and the subjective means of appropriation on the part of the believer, with the subsequent tendency to turn from the objective to the subjective.[25]

> The merit of Christ waits before the closed door of the heart like an immovable object, even though it carries in it the entire salvation of mankind. Only some action from within the heart can open the door and permit the salvation treasure to enter the existence of man. Even if one seriously takes into account the fact that faith was correctly evaluated as a gift of the Holy Spirit, did it not nevertheless lead to an understanding of faith as an independent means, and, finally as the merit of pious inwardness? . . . One can also diminish the merit of Christ by appealing to the Holy Spirit, especially if one reduces this merit to a dead, heavenly "thing" no longer capable of action, as Lutheran Orthodoxy has already done. . . . The so-called objective fact of salvation thus really forms only something like a common foundation. It represents a basis on which the so-called subjective fact is only then able to begin the really decisive action. It almost seems as if God had to be reconciled anew through faith.[26]

For the Orthodox fathers the problem of discerning the parts of the order was of course a purely analytic task. The order was to be understood as instantaneous, not a temporal succession. But after all, the medieval Scholastics had said the same. Thus once again we are back at square one. Once the analysis was made, the way was open for temporalization and psychologization of the order. This is what in fact happened in many forms of Pietism. A "dead" Orthodoxy could be vitalized only in the same way as an "arid" Scholasticism: turn it into a "way" with certain steps or stages in the religious progress of the subject. Therewith the fate of forensic justification as an eschatological power invading this age is more or less sealed. A temporalized or psychologized order of salvation is all too easily rationalized as a "pure practical religion" shorn of all objective or theoretical elements (Kant), or distilled as a religion of pious feeling (Schleiermacher), stretched out as salvation history (*Heilsgeschichte*), universalized as the history of the unfolding of the spirit (*Geistesgeschichte*) (Hegel), and finally perhaps secularized as a revolution (Marx and Engels). In all of that, forensic justification could not but get lost. The development illustrates the difficulty of attempting to maintain both forensic justification and continuity under the scheme of law. The either/or seems to remain in effect: either justification or the scheme will recede into the background as more or less a pious fiction without real dynamic. Most generally, of course, it is justification that falls victim to the "reality" and "seriousness" of progress according to the scheme of law.

One can only conclude from all this, it would seem, that justification, if it is to mean anything at all in the Lutheran tradition, must be forensic in character. Lutheran Orthodoxy and even Pietism should not be faulted for that. That was their finest achievement. The fact that such forensic justification has managed to survive in churchly circles in spite of critical attack from more academic and secular circles has been one of the sole redeeming features of the tradition. The problems in the tradition are not with forensic justification as such. The problem arises because of the attempt to combine such justification with a continuous scheme of law and progress and the anthropology which that presupposes. One is faced with a fundamental either/or: either justification as a divine judgment is the final reality, the creative possibility for human existence, or human achievement (i.e., works—by whatever aid one can muster) is "the real." For Luther there can be no doubt that the former is the only real alternative for human beings. Imputed or forensic justification is a creative, eschatological reality that opens the possibility for new life. Thus it is clear that, for Luther at least, the old stand-off between a forensic and an effective justification is obviated. Justification can be effective only when it is forensic, imputed, a judgment of God that breaks in upon human life ending the old and beginning the new. If it is not forensic in that sense, it becomes merely an attempt to alter or augment already existing possibilities and will lead either to hypocrisy or despair. That is to say, justification is effective because and to the degree that it is forensic and announced or proclaimed as such to the ears of faith. That is what the tradition and the debate about it have failed to appreciate.

But that means that justification brings with it a break in continuity of the "I" and the schemes of possibility it presupposes or proposes. No doubt this is the most sensitive systematic issue with which to deal. No doubt continuity and discontinuity are always dialectically related in some fashion. Perhaps it is fair to say that the issues involved can be handled in either of two ways. If one assumes some sort of natural continuity, i.e., that one is, however tenuously, "on the right track" and is only impeded or weakened, then grace can be conceived to enter into some kind of positive synthesis with whatever is left of human capacity. Grace works to repair what is lacking. One can then debate about the degree of repair needed. Discontinuity is a matter of degree and will tend to be somewhat carefully hidden or even disguised in theological distinctions.

If, however, one finds that to be theologically and experientially questionable and concludes from the nature of the gift of grace itself that one is actually "on the wrong track," then grace posits initially at least a radical and complete break, a discontinuity with the track one is on. One has then, so to speak, to be put back on the right track, in this case, to be put to death in order to be reborn *sola fide*. Then, however, one might begin to see "by faith" another continuity, the continuity of the work of the Triune God, continuity with the created life God intended but which one has lost. By faith one is given back the created life lost in the fall. Grace reveals the depth and totality of the sin and bondage at the same time as it gives new life and hope to faith. The radical discontinuity with what we are brings faith into a different continuity between what was intended and what we shall be. The continuity, however, is not a human achievement, but is carried precisely by faith in the Triune God. The God who created us is one with him who redeems and the Spirit who sanctifies. But one can grasp that only *sola gratia, sola fide*.

Where one wants to preserve natural continuity of some sort, the mark of having received grace would be expressed in terms of transformation perhaps, or conversion, or progress, or even merit. The mark of having received grace would then be indicated by the degree to which sin is said to have been lessened or removed. Otherwise there would be no reality to the activity of grace. To say that sin remains would be tantamount to saying that grace is not "real."

Where grace and faith mean a fundamental discontinuity with the way things are in a fallen world, however, the mark of having been grasped by such grace would be quite the opposite: the confession to being a sinner saved by grace alone, by the unconditional gift of the Triune God. The new as absolute gift reveals the old to be completely lost and fallen—simultaneously. Sin is truly recognized in both its depth and ultimate powerlessness in the moment of its overcoming. Such a faith would also be protected from Manichaean dualism and pessimism. That the Creator has preserved his creation in spite of the fall and sin will appear precisely as the miracle for which prayer, praise, and thanksgiving are due.

The traditional questions raised between Lutherans and Roman Catholics about the sin remaining after justification stem, it would seem, from this kind of difference with regard to continuity and discontinuity. The question it raises for us is the degree to which this difference can be mediated.

6. The Uses of the Law

If forensic justification proposes a profound discontinuity in the Christian life so that it cannot be viewed as a steady "progress" according to a moral scheme or law, the resulting systematic question is that of the place of law in the theological scheme. For it is usually the view of law or its equivalent that provides the major structural backbone of a theological system. What is law for if it is not the measure by which justice is to be attained and judged? Put otherwise: if justification is by faith alone, what is the use of the law? Lutheranism has met this question by proposing that a proper distinction between law and gospel should be the major theological task of a truly evangelical theology. If justification by faith is the proposal of dogma which the Lutheran Reformation made to the church catholic, then the proper distinction between law and gospel is its major methodological proposal. It is a distinction that is to be applied to all doctrines and their use in the church.

> The proper function of the doctrine of justification is that of giving a true significance to all other doctrines. But it can only be understood as Luther saw it if it is identical with what is implied by the distinction between the law and the gospel as the basic guiding principle of theological thought, and therefore as the decisive standard of theological judgment.[27]

Since justification is forensic, imputed for Christ's sake and received by faith alone, and since that entails a fundamental discontinuity with all human attempts to achieve righteousness, the first premise for a proper distinction between law and gospel is that the law is not a way of salvation. It does not designate a possibility for human beings; it rather indicates an impossibility, a way that has been forever lost. As such, it does not promise, but accuses. The gospel, the imputation of justice by forensic decree, on the other hand, does not accuse, but promises. Indeed, the major point in defining justification as a forensic decree is precisely that it must simply be decreed, proclaimed.

For Lutheran theology, therefore, the terms law and gospel can be defined on two levels: the level of content and the level of function.

On the level of content, law means demand and gospel designates promises given in Christ. On the level of function, however, the words law and gospel designate functions: the accusing and comforting character of the living word of God. The task of theology is to learn not merely to define the words, but to use the word in such a way that faith is created. Faith is created out of the encounter with the word which attacks and slays the sinner and raises up the believer. The word, that is, "does" the discontinuity to its hearers as old beings and gives the new continuity by incorporating them into the story of Jesus Christ. The word of God is therefore not mere information to which the subject relates in some fashion out of its own capacity but as living word is creative in accomplishing its eschatological goal. God's word is the same as God's deed.[28]

The crucial question in this regard is therefore that of what the word does, the question of its function in the living present, or as Luther repeatedly said, its *usus*. On the level of content the word is also, of course, a conveyor of information. But it is that when the moment of living address has past and when it has become congealed in written form and is only a memory. If it were to remain only that, the word becomes something about which we must do something. In other words, it would remain merely demand, law. The distinction between law and gospel is the attempt to recover the present tense, the creative address character of the word, the proper *usus*. The word is to be used not merely to convey information but to do something to us.

This is perhaps the crucial issue in all discussions about the Reformation doctrine of justification, and the one most poorly understood and usually overlooked. The question is whether the theology in question is so constructed or disposed as to foster a proclamation as present, unconditional address which actually *delivers* the new reality and does not undermine its own cause by merely talking, however correctly, *about* it. Merely to exalt grace and exclude all works and Pelagianism in the theological system is not to guarantee a *practice* and a preaching that *actually* does so. The question is not merely one of what the words say but what they actually do to the hearers.

Thus the Lutheran insistence on a functional understanding of law. The Lutheran Confessional writings often speak of law in this sense. ". . . [T]he law always accuses and terrifies consciences."[29] ". . . [T]he law was given by God first of all to restrain sins. . . . However, the chief function or power of the law is to make original sin manifest and show man to what utter depths his nature has fallen and how corrupt it has become."[30] Especially articles 5 and 6 of the Formula of Concord concern themselves with the functional understanding of law and gospel. Both the Epitome and the Solid Declaration speak of the "office" of the law and define it functionally over against sin.

> Everything that preaches about our sin and the wrath of God, no matter how or when it happens, is the proclamation of the law. On the other hand, the Gospel is a proclamation that shows and gives nothing but grace and forgiveness in Christ. At the same time it is true and right that the apostles and the preachers of the Gospel, just as Christ himself did, confirm the proclamation of the law and begin with the law in the case of those who as yet neither know their sins nor are terrified by the wrath of God, as he says in John 16:8, "The Holy Spirit will convince the world of sin because they do not believe in me." In fact, where is there a more earnest and terrible revelation and preaching of God's wrath over sin than the passion and death of Christ, his own Son? But as long as all this proclaims the wrath of God and terrifies man, it is not yet the Gospel nor Christ's own proclamation, but it is Moses and the law pronounced on the unconverted.[31]

This passage is especially interesting because it demonstrates that not content but function decides what law or the office of law is. Everything, no matter how or when it is done, that attacks, accuses, and exposes sin is "Moses" and performs the office of law. Even, indeed especially, the passion and death of Christ, which would hardly be accounted as law according to content, nevertheless functions as law as long as it proclaims wrath and terrifies. Here it can clearly be seen that "law" designates a function of the word of God.

The full-blown Lutheran doctrine speaks of two and sometimes three functions or uses of the law. The first use is the civil use: to restrain evil and maintain order in a fallen world. The law holds the world in readiness for the gospel. This is accomplished for the most part by God's "left hand" work: earthly institutions such as family, economic order, government, and the like. The second is the theological use: to accuse and convict of sin. The third and somewhat disputed use among Lutherans is the use of the law by the reborn as a guide to Christian living. The reason such a third use is disputed is because it proposes a view of law which survives the eschatological break and maintains a kind of continuity.

The roots of this functional understanding of law lie deep in the hermeneutical tradition, the age-old problem of letter and spirit and its checkered history. St. Paul in 2 Cor. 3:6 began the debate with the pronouncement that "the letter [written code, law] kills, but the Spirit give life." In general the tradition, following early interpreters like

Origen, took this in a Platonizing sense; the letter, since it belongs to the sensible and perishing world, is insufficient. One must transcend it by penetrating into the intelligible world of "spirit" where there is life. This could be accomplished by "spiritual" interpretation: in terms of doctrine (allegory), morals (tropology), and eternal hope (anagogy). The problem of transcending mere dead letter was therefore understood to be a problem in interpretation. The accomplished interpreter could get beyond or above the letter which "kills." This understanding of the letter/spirit dichotomy, however, created profound turmoil in the interpretive tasks of the church.[32]

The basic problem with the hermeneutic which tried to move from letter to spirit by means of interpretation was not simply its temptation to allegorical fancy and excess, but rather its root theological and anthropological presuppositions. The method presupposed that the move from letter to spirit was possible for human "spirit." The human spirit, since it is rational and free, can transcend the realm of mere letter, and the text becomes only the jumping-off place for the human spirit in its flight, the material upon which it works in its freedom.

This root problem had actually already come to light in the battle between the Pelagians and Augustine. In the crucial treatise, *On the Spirit and the Letter*, Augustine already saw that if the letter which kills means simply the inadequacy or obscurity of the literal, one's relationship to the text would be a Pelagianizing one. Furthermore the inner secret of the method of interpretation is exposed: it is basically a defense mechanism against the claims of the text because it enables one to translate the text into one's own story. That is the secret of allegory. Thus Augustine suggests that the letter which kills should not be taken to mean the obscurity of the letter but rather the law, the written code, which kills by its accusing voice. If that move were made, the "escape hatch" for Pelagianism would finally be closed. For then one could no longer translate the text into one's own story; rather the text would take the believer into *its* story.[33]

Unfortunately Augustine's insight was not taken up or made much of either by Augustine himself or subsequent tradition. Therefore the problem festered until it came to a head again in the early days of the Reformation. In wrestling with the Scriptures and his own conscience Luther found the spiritual flight prescribed by the tradition to be not only unscriptural but personally destructive. In this regard Luther's move was simple yet far-reaching in its implications. He took 2 Cor. 3:6 to mean just what it says: "The law kills, but the spirit gives life."

Though the passage has profound implications for interpretation, it is basically about proclamation and ministry. The letter, the written, literal, history kills and *through* that gives life. The letter is not therefore merely "dead" because it belongs to the sensible world. Rather, it is powerful because it is deadly. The passage speaks of the function of the word, not merely the content. If the letter has the power to kill, it can by no means be taken lightly or circumvented by spiritual interpretation. The letter, the whole long history of God's struggle with his people, spells eventually one thing for the "old Adam": death. The hermeneutic itself takes the form of the cross and the resurrection; the letter kills the old so the spirit can raise up the new by faith alone. The word functions to conform its hearers to itself. The spirit is not a secret inner sphere to be reached by clever interpretation. The spirit is the Holy Spirit who comes precisely through the letter—the concrete history and the proper proclamation of it—to kill and make alive. With that move the hermeneutical foundation for the Reformation is laid. The literal, historical sense of Scripture is affirmed as the only legitimate sense, but beyond that it is a question of function and *usus*, what the word does to the hearer. The word of God is living and active; it does what it says.

The understanding of the law as functional evolves quite naturally out of this hermeneutical development. Luther's writings against Emser provide a classic statement of this. Luther there insists that letter and spirit do not indicate two levels of meaning, but rather two kinds of preaching, one of the Old Testament (letter) and one of the New Testament (spirit).

The letter is nothing but divine law or commandment which was given in the Old Testament through Moses and preached and taught through Aaron's priesthood. It is called "letter" because it is written in letters on stone tablets and in books. It remains letter, and does not yield more than that, because no man improves through the law; he only becomes worse. Thus the law does not help, nor does it grant grace; it only commands and orders something done which man is neither able nor willing to do. But the Spirit, the divine grace, grants strength and power to the heart; indeed, he creates a new man who takes pleasure [in obeying] God's commandments and who does everything he should do with joy. . . . Everything which does not have the grace of the living Spirit is dead, even though external obedience to the whole law glitters. That is why the Apostle says of the law that it kills, gives no one life, and holds one eternally in death if grace does not arrive to redeem and give life.

These then are the two ways of preaching: the priests, preachers, and sermons of the Old Testament deal with no more than the law of God. The

Spirit and grace are not yet openly preached. But in the New Testament only Spirit and grace, given to us through Christ, are preached. For the New Testament preaching is but an offering and presentation of Christ, through the sheer mercy of God to all men. . . . Thus St. Paul here calls the New Testament preaching the "ministry of the Spirit" (2 Cor. 3:6), that is, the office of preaching whereby God's Spirit and grace are offered and put before all those who are burdened by the law, who are killed, and are greedy for grace. He calls this law "a ministry of the letter," that is, the office of preaching whereby no more is given than the letter or law. No life flows from it, the law is not fulfilled by it, and man can never satisfy it. That is why it remains letter, and in the letter it can do no more than kill man, that is, show him what he should do and yet cannot do. Thus he recognizes that he is dead and without grace before God and that he does not fulfil the commandment, which, however, he should fulfil.

From this it is now clear that the words of the apostle, "The letter kills, but the Spirit gives life," could be said in other words: "The law kills, but the grace of God gives life."[34]

Luther insists on taking Paul's words about letter and spirit in their context, that of ministry and preaching. The fact that the letter kills translates directly into "the law kills" and is a specific preaching office. The fundamental problem with the tradition then and now is a failure to grasp this point. One can exclude all Pelagianism *formally* in the interpretation and in the theological system, but that is of little avail if the preaching does not actually do it by exercising this office. The point is directly related, moreover, to the anthropological question of one's free will before God.

Those who want to emphasize their good works and boast about free will do not allow all human works to be sin. They still find something good in nature, just as the Jews and our sophists, together with the pope, do. They are the ones who do not want to let Moses' face shine clearly. They put a veil over the law and do not really look it in the face. They refuse to let everything belonging to them be either sin or death before God; that is, they do not really want to know themselves or to be humble. They only strengthen their pride. They flee the letter and a true understanding of it, just as the Jews fled the face of Moses. That is why their mind remains blind and they never come to the life of the Spirit. Therefore it is impossible for someone who does not first hear the law and let himself be killed by the letter, to hear the gospel and let the grace of the Spirit bring him to life. Grace is only given to those who long for it. Life is a help only to those who are dead, grace only to sin, the Spirit only to the letter. No one can have the one without the other.[35]

Nor are those who are already of the New Testament beyond such preaching:

> But even though we are already in the New Testament and should have only the preaching of the Spirit, since we are still living in flesh and blood, it is necessary to preach the letter as well, so that people are first killed by the law and all their arrogance is destroyed. Thus they may know themselves and become hungry for the Spirit and thirsty for grace. . . . These then are the two works of God, praised many times in Scripture; he kills and gives life, he wounds and heals, he destroys and helps, he condemns and saves, he humbles and elevates, he disgraces and honors. . . . He does these works through these two offices, the first through the letter, the second through the Spirit. The letter does not allow anyone to stand before his wrath. The Spirit does not allow anyone to perish before his grace. Oh, this is such an overwhelming affair that one could talk about it endlessly.[36]

It is thus only in this "dialectic" with gospel that the law will receive its due. Without the gospel the law will not be taken seriously. One will only attempt to construct one's own defenses against it, cover it with a "veil." Only when the law is carefully distinguished from the gospel will it function properly, and only then will one come to love the law. When law and gospel are mixed or confused, both will suffer and eventually be lost. But since it is an eschatological dialectic, it is not permanent. The gospel is the last word, the final end of the law.

> Thus we want to finish this [discussion] now with St. Augustine's fine comment regarding Psalm 17, in which he defines nicely and briefly what the letter is. He says, "The letter is nothing but LAW WITHOUT GRACE." We, on the other hand, may say that the Spirit is nothing but GRACE WITHOUT LAW. Wherever the letter is, or the law without grace, there is no end to making laws, to teachings and to works. And yet they are of no avail; no one becomes better through them, everything remains dead in the letter. On the other hand, wherever the Spirit of God exists, there is freedom, as St. Paul says (2 Cor. 3:17); there no teaching or law is needed; everything happens as it should happen. It is just like the man who has healthy, good vision; he does not need anyone to teach him how to see. His vision is unhindered, and he has more than any teaching could help him get or give him. But if his vision is not healthy, he is no longer free, and there is not enough teaching to help and protect him. He will have to worry about every single glance and have a rule about it in order to see.[37]

Against the background of this hermeneutical discussion it can quite readily be seen how and why law is understood in a functional sense and that this involves a fundamental break in the continuity of the law. Law is not a continuous way offering the possibility of salvation. Law belongs to "this age." Its use is to restrain evil and to expose sin. The gospel, the sheer goodness and favor of God in Christ, grants possibility to human existence. The law was "added because of the trespass." It accuses and kills. It reminds the world it has fallen from its true destiny. But the law is not just "laws," it is "the letter," the more or less empty shell of a world which has lost the Spirit. It is the darkness of a world that can no longer see and must have rules about it. The very existence of law means that what it points to is gone and no amount of "law" preaching will bring it back. Insofar as it brings knowledge, it brings knowledge not of the good but of sin:

> . . . not knowledge of that which should happen, but knowledge of that which has already happened; not knowledge of open, but of excluded and lost possibilities. . . . Whether one is a Jew, or a sinner, or heathen; whether pious or godless; every mode of existence is like others in spite of all differences in that it is existence under the law. Every religion or worldview, even the atheistic, but also a Christianity which has been perverted out of faith into an ideology—has the common structure of law. They are all against faith. For "*lex est negatio Christi*" (law is the negation of Christ).[38]

The law does not open the future, it closes it. It only reveals what should or might have been when it is too late and the future is sealed, unless there is another possibility. To live under the law is always to be attempting to repair or atone for yesterday; thus yesterday always controls tomorrow. The law kills and brings death, not life, for yesterday is always yesterday. Grace, the gift of God's eschatological kingdom in the promise of the gospel, is humanity's tomorrow. Since that is the case, the law *must* function to cut off every human attempt to create its own tomorrow. The letter, the literal history, must do its work to cut off every form of metaphysical or religious escape. We do not have some transcendent scheme of meaning which somehow protects us from history, rather we are cast *into* history with nothing but faith, to wait and to hope. The dialectic makes us historical beings. "If we have died with him, we shall also live with him" (2 Tim. 2:11).

The law and its office or function is therefore strictly limited to this age. It is an accuser. That is its chief function, its office. As accuser it stands inviolate, unrelenting, without any "veil," until that to which it points arrives. As long as sin and death remain, the law remains. Unfaith, sin, death, and the law are inseparable partners. Until the ultimate triumph of the eschatological kingdom, the law will sound.

All of this raises the inevitable question about whether there is not a more "positive" use of the law in Lutheran theology. Here it should be remembered that Lutherans do speak of the "civil use" of the law, the so-called first use. But that use, too, it should be noted, was a use restricted to "this age." In its civil use the law restrains evil and establishes order for the care of human society. God uses the law in this sense to hold the world in readiness for the gospel and keep it from collapsing into the chaos which threatens it. Under the civil use of the law it is quite possible to speak of the goodness and "civil righteousness" of human activity even though it does not reach beyond this age. If this use of the law is overextended, however, if one begins to take the law into one's own hands in order to bring in one's own version of the kingdom, tyranny results and resistance must be mounted. Precisely the proper distinction between law and gospel limits and humanizes the law. The purpose of the law in its civil use is to take care of the world and of human beings, not to tyrannize them.

7. The Law and the Christian Life

A more persistent question in the Lutheran and Protestant tradition generally has been that of a more positive role for the law in the life of the Christian. Does the law always accuse even the "reborn" Christian? What about the admonitions one finds in the New Testament? Does not the Christian too need the law? This is the question about the so-called "third use" of the law, the use of the law as a guide to Christian living for the reborn Christian. Most interpreters would agree that Luther himself did not explicitly teach a third use of the law, but many would argue that there is some such use implicitly in his writings, especially in the catechisms. It is in some ways a semantic debate; much depends on what one means by a third use. Without going into the particulars of the intra-Lutheran debate, it can be fairly said that the issue once again is the problem of continuity versus eschatology. A "third" use of the law presupposes that law somehow survives the eschatological break and that the reborn Christian as well has already been translated into the eschatological kingdom where law no longer restrains or threatens but is a rather gentle and quiescent "guide." If such is what a third use proposes, it would have to be rejected in the light of the views developed here. There can be no continuity in a law that survives the eschatological break, nor is the Christian one who has already crossed over it. One participates in the eschatological kingdom only by faith; for the rest one remains in this age under the law. Thus one *does* indeed still need the law but not as reborn believer in a "third" use. Rather, precisely the believer would see that law is needed in exactly the same way as the rest of fallen humanity needs it; to restrain from presumptive and evil ways and to convict of sin. The Formula of Concord is ambiguous on the matter in its article on the third use (article 6). It seems to approve a third use, but then goes on to define it as though it were actually just a repetition of the first and second uses. It declares that the law is indeed to be preached to Christians but only because they are not yet truly Christian. But that simply means that the Christian needs the law in the same way as everyone else.

The rejection of a third use in this sense simply underscores that the Christian is *simul iustus et peccator* until the end, and the end *is* the end of the law. The view is fired by the eschatological vision: when the kingdom comes, there will be no more law; when love is given, no one needs to be told how to do it; when sight is restored, no one needs rules about how to see. When the goal is reached, the office of the law is over; it has then been fulfilled. The truth in the idea of the third use is that the Christian does indeed know something about law that others do not know. But what the Christian knows is not a different law or a different use of it, but precisely the difference between law and gospel. The Christian knows about the end of the law and waits for it in faith. Precisely because of this faith, this waiting, this hope, the idea that law should continue or be reintroduced on the other side must be rejected.

But this rejection involves precisely a more serious consideration about the place of the law in the life of the one who believes, waits, and hopes for the end. It means that for the time being the law remains in force, there is no watering down, no shift to a third use. It is the sinner who must die and be made new, not the law that must be watered down or changed. Thus we return to what was said earlier in connection with the *simul*. As *totus peccator* the sinner is attacked by the law unto death until the new being arises who actually loves the law as an expression of the will of God. Luther knows of only two possibilities over against the law: either it is an enemy or a friend, but never a more or less neutral guide to a more or less converted sinner. That is simply to say that the will of God for us is either law in the full sense or gospel in the full sense, but never a third something which is neither.[39]

The same interpretation would no doubt apply to the New Testament admonitions. It can hardly be maintained that the exhortations of the New Testament taken according to the letter are any sort of weakening of the demand of God. If anything the stakes are raised just because of the gospel. Now believers are even exhorted to arise from the dead! But how can we do that? The exhortations and admonitions are either bad news or good news; between these two our actual lives as *simul iustus et peccator* resonate until that day when Christ shall be all in all.

To be true to a view of the Christian life rooted in forensic justification, one must then arrive at a different understanding of the relationship between law and the Christian life. One cannot view it as an ascent into rarified spiritual air via the law or some other continuous scheme which mediates possibility. Rather, it must be viewed as a descent into the world of service and love. Luther tried to express this with his idea that the gospel reigns in the conscience while the "flesh" still stands under the law. The conscience is ruled and captivated and protected by the gospel of the imputed righteousness breaking in through God's eschatological judgment. The "flesh," the empirical life I live in this age, however, remains under the law. And that is true in a double sense; both in the sense that law attacks the flesh as inimical to the will of God and also in the sense that under the impulse of the spontaneity and joy fostered by the gospel in the conscience, the empirical life I live in this age is to become the actual fulfillment of the will of God. Because the gospel reigns absolutely in the conscience, the Christian is free so that the true battle can be joined in the flesh. The new being is not therefore a kind of mystical theologoumenon without substance but is to be incarnated in concrete earthly fashion in the vocation of the Christian in this world. In this battle the commandments of God can be seen ultimately not as an enemy nor as a mere emasculated guide but as a real friend. The commandments of God for Luther do not lead us to heaven, but rather into the world of the neighbor. One should make no mistake about it, the law of God is to be and will be fulfilled— not, however, by our powers, not by human moral progress, but by the power of the righteousness imputed by God for Jesus' sake.

16

JUSTIFICATION BY FAITH AND THE NEED OF ANOTHER CRITICAL PRINCIPLE

Carl J. Peter

The purpose of this essay is twofold. First, attention will be called to a fact that has received relatively little notice despite its significance. It is this. When justification by faith is described as *a* or even *the* criterion for judging all churchly discourse and practice, the language employed is frequently that of unconditionality.[1] Second, a case will be made that when justification by faith is so understood, the meaning of unconditionality needs to be unpacked with the aid of a second principle or criterion.[2]

Justification as a Norm

By 1980 the members of the Lutheran-Roman Catholic Dialogue in the U.S.A. were well into their discussion of justification by faith. The latter had been described repeatedly as more than one doctrine among others, as more even than the chief and foremost of all the doctrines. It was proposed as nothing less than a criterion to be used in judging all that the church says and does. Of everything from buttresses to boycotts, from catechesis to chant, from decretals to dogma, one question had to be asked: "Is it conducive to bringing people to put their trust and hope in the God of Jesus Christ *alone*?" With an affirmative answer, the test was passed; with a negative, the result was failure; if the issue was in doubt, caution was advised. Only in its attachment to this criterion could Lutheranism be understood as a reform movement in the church catholic.

Tillich, Justification, and the Protestant Principle

However great the differences, there are family resemblances between this criterion and what Paul Tillich called the Protestant principle. Those similarities are worth noting.

The principle so designated is the stimulus in the name of which Protestant theology objects when "our ultimate concern" is identified with any of the church's creations.[3] Among the latter are the Scriptures, given the fact that their witness is " . . . also a *conditioned* expression of their own spirituality."[4] The adjective *conditioned* is crucially important for understanding the critical role Tillich attributes to the Protestant principle.

Later in the same first volume of his *Systematic Theology*, the topic under discussion is the jealousy shown by the God of Abraham, Isaac, and Jacob. Yahweh's refusal to tolerate rivals is not to be thought of as an instance of the "demonic," that is, it does not involve " . . . the claim of something *conditioned* to be *unconditioned*."[5] It is rather a claim made in the name of the *universality* and *ultimacy* of covenantal justice.[6] The "exclusive monotheism" of Israel is for Tillich the prophetic principle, which the Protestant principle restates " . . . against a self-absolutizing and consequently demonically distorted church."[7]

Later, in the third volume, Tillich has recourse once more to the Protestant principle. One very important context in which he does so is the Roman Catholic-Protestant dispute about the relation between faith and love. Acts of the latter are not to be understood " . . . as conditioning the act by which the Spiritual Presence takes hold of man."[8] The Protestant principle is there to prevent this: God's act doing part and thus being conditioned by human love that does the rest.[9]

In another context Tillich refers to the principle of justification by grace through faith as the " . . . first and basic expression of the Protestant principle itself."[10] The act by which God designates as just the person who is unjust is unconditional; divine acceptance of one who is midway between sin and justice would be conditioned; divine goodness gives itself unconditionally.[11] The Protestant principle understood as justification by grace through faith holds suspect and challenges pretensions to unconditionality on the part of anything creaturely.

Roman Catholic teaching does not, according to Tillich, permit one who has been brought to the state of holiness or sanctification to doubt the church's teachings. The authority of the church is to be accepted unconditionally. To this the Protestant principle reacts negatively. The reason is clear enough. The conditioned is confused with the unconditioned.[12]

For Tillich the Protestant principle is not the exclusive property of the churches of the Reformation. It transcends any individual church.[13] When the demonic does not triumph in a church, it is because of the power of this principle, which will not let humans boast unchallenged about their laying hold of the God who instead grasps them.[14]

Tillich had of course no intention of writing his Systematics as a commentary on the Lutheran Confessions. Indeed he had much earlier declared that he found scarcely any way to make justification by faith intelligible to modern human beings.[15] Given this breakdown in tradition, he said it would not be easy to " . . . resume our connection with the Reformation again."[16] Still he did more than call the principle of justification by grace through faith " . . . the first and basic expression of the Protestant principle."[17] He regarded it as a criterion for judging what intellectual good work may be imposed on the believer and in that sense as " . . . the universal principle of Protestant theology."[18] He translated justification by grace through faith into the terms of the contemporary problem of despair over life's meaninglessness. There are those who do not find the translation adequate. But this much is undeniable. Tillich did regard justification by grace through faith as an important critical principle, and in the process of its articulation he employed the language of unconditionality.[19]

Justification as Critical Principle and the Language of Unconditionality

Not all, by any means, who propose justification by faith as a needed criterion for judging what the church does and says do so in terms of Tillich's Protestant principle. George Lindbeck prefers to designate as a "metatheological rule" what Lutherans have meant when speaking of justification as a criterion of all doctrines. This rule prescribes that for justification one should not trust anything " . . . except God's unconditional promises in Jesus Christ."[20] Luther saw baptism, the Lord's Supper, and absolution as " . . . the supremely unequivocal proclamations of the unconditional character of the promise on which faith depends."[21] Episcopal and papal structures must be " . . . in the service of God's unconditional promises in Jesus Christ."[22] Lindbeck also sees the "unconditional character of God's free gift in Jesus Christ" as a reason for Gerhard Ebeling's opposition to substantialist metaphysics.[23] Again one notes a nexus between justification by faith and the language of unconditionality.

For Robert Jenson and Eric Gritsch the divine promise of forgiveness is unconditional because in his resurrection Jesus has satisfied the one condition (death) that might keep any other human from fulfilling a promise he or she makes.[24] In fact the crisis faced by the Reformers in their experience of sin was one of meaning, which was under threat from all sides. Themselves affected, the traditional practices of Christian piety and ecclesiastical institutions could not be looked to for the assurance, support, and consolation that were needed.[25] Luther and his followers found their answer in God's unconditional affirmation or promise that human life has worth and value no matter what.[26] That most certainly included sin! A promise or an affirmation involving a condition dependent on human status or cooperation would have been no answer at all. Precisely as conditional it would have reintroduced doubt—threatening meaning and value. One would always wonder whether the condition was really fulfilled. The church's preaching, teaching, witness, liturgy, and the like, must be tested by this criterion: "Do they engender or strengthen conviction that God gives human life meaning no matter what?"[27] But this is the linguistic stipulation (norm) of justification by faith, and again it is articulated in the language of unconditionality.

Other examples could be cited.[28] For their part the essays presented in this dialogue and the discussions that ensued made one thing very clear indeed. Some Lutheran scholars find the language of unconditionality very helpful in an effort to describe God's promise of forgiveness and justification because of Jesus Christ. Sometimes justification by faith is proposed as a metatheological rule and sometimes as a linguistic stipulation. There may be no reference at all to Tillich's Protestant principle and perhaps even a reluctance to have the one compared with the other. But the nexus between justification by faith as a criterion of churchly discourse and practice and recourse to the language of unconditionality is a fact that deserves attention and further consideration. Why this is the case may not be immediately clear. Perhaps another allusion to Tillich's problematic may be helpful.

Catholic Substance

Tillich had been concerned that the Protestant principle not be considered without its demand or need for what he called the *Catholic substance*.[29] To stress this point he called attention to the fact that his treatment of the church was one of the longest in his whole theological system.[30] In the prayer life, preaching, witness, and teaching of that church were to be found the embodiment of God's presence, the entire corpus of tradition inherited from the past, and thus the subject matter or substance on which the Protestant principle was to be brought to bear. Without that Catholic substance and with the Protestant principle alone there would be danger of reducing or eliminating the sacramental mediation of God's Spirit.[31] Indeed, Tillich was at pains to let his readers know that out of fear of demonization he would not so stress the Protestant principle that God's presence became overly intellectualized, moralized, or mysticized.[32]

In his interpretation of Luther's Reformation Jaroslav Pelikan too made use of *Catholic substance*. He had it refer to the traditions, worship, authoritative teaching or Confession, and leadership functions as well as offices that the sixteenth century inherited from the early church. These Luther encountered in the Roman Catholic Church in which he had grown up.[33] That substance Luther wished to purify and reform, not abolish.

Not all Lutherans may wish to designate with the term *Catholic substance* their confessional commitments to the church's ancient creeds, the administration of baptism, the regular celebration of the Lord's Supper, the encouragement of the practice of private absolution, and the office of the ministry. But that commitment is real and in no wise diminished in those who make justification by faith a metatheological rule or linguistic stipulation rather than the Protestant principle.

In what follows it will be argued that the health and well-being of the church call for another critical principle in addition to that of justification by faith—another critical principle precisely for the sake of the preservation of the Catholic substance. The principle in question is needed in a special way to unpack—without enfeebling—the language of unconditionality used in the articulation of justification by faith as norm, rule, or linguistic stipulation.

The Need of Another Critical Principle

Tillich was right in asserting that the Protestant principle needs the Catholic substance. Perhaps, however, he did not go quite far enough. It may be that both need something else as well, namely, another critical principle. To argue that this is the case is not to ignore the wisdom contained in the adage known as Ockham's razor. Substances are not multiplied at all, nor are principles, without sufficient reason. There is in fact a very good reason to assert the need of a critical principle distinct from both the Catholic substance and justification by faith as principle, rule, norm, or stipulation with regard to churchly discourse and practice. The Catholic substance is in need of protection because it is in danger of being mutilated, be it out of fear of demonization or of works-righteousness.

Is there anything so holy that it cannot be ridiculed and made to look tawdry? One has to answer in the negative. But what does this imply? Perhaps it is the following conclusion.

The criterion of justification by faith alone is an imperative to keep the churches from idolatry. But that is not the only temptation the churches face. They need another critical principle to warn them that they may run the risk of blasphemy. Out of a desire to avoid confusing the creaturely with the Creator and to realize that no work of a sinful creature can win God's forgiveness, they may regard the sacred as something religiously indifferent or even sinful. To fail to recognize the divine where it is in fact being mediated or embodied because the mediating agency or embodying symbols are touched by sin may well involve both insolence and arrogance with regard to the divine. Christian churches need to avoid both idolatry and blasphemy in their attitudes and stances toward the Catholic substance. Justification by faith alone helps as a safeguard against the former; another critical principle is needed to assist in avoiding the latter.

An Attempt at Formulation

Be not so prone to expect sin and abuse that you fail to recognize God's grace where it is at work. That is one way in which this other critical principle may be formulated.[34] Whether it be liturgy, moral or doctrinal teaching, canon law, programs of evangelization or catechesis, preaching, or witness, all these do need to be tested. Of them it may and must be asked: "Are they or is this or that one of them conducive to leading people to put their *ultimate* trust and hope in the God of Jesus Christ *alone*?" Quite appropriately this question (often by preference formulated without the qualifying adjective *ultimate*) is pressed by Lutherans. A more united church will have to allow for the exercise of the reforming criterion such questions articulate.[35]

But another question is no less important. It is this: "Do ultimate hope and trust in God alone imply and ground a warranted if penultimate trust in ecclesial ordinances, rites, and offices?''[36] Or to put it in a somewhat different fashion: ''Is a desire to trust and hope *ultimately* in God *alone* leading people to refuse to trust or even disdain ecclesial institutions where God has promised through Jesus Christ to be present and operative with His Spirit and grace?'' One ought not to call the holy profane; what God has made clean one ought not to regard as unclean.[37]

Where abuse exists, it should be criticized and corrected. But a function, rite, office, or institution should not be amputated and lost from the Catholic substance simply because of its openness to possible and actual abuse. *Abusus non tollit usum!* Mutilation is the alternative. Have such losses been suffered by the Catholic substance? A responsible reply is ecumenically necessary; this requires recourse to another principle in addition to that of justification by faith. Perhaps it might be called the ''Principle of Respect for the Divine in its Concrete Realizations.''

In an attempt to be more specific, it may help to raise the neuralgic issue of prayer for the dead. Abuse of the latter can still lead to gross superstition and unwarranted reliance on human works rather than the promise of salvation in Jesus Christ. As a result the practice will continue to need the critique of justification by faith alone. But the fostering of such prayer (rather than its abandonment) is also important for inculcating trust in the power of the risen Christ which is at work in the prayers of his followers on earth for their deceased sisters and brothers.[38] Examples such as this might be multiplied to show that the integrity and well-being of the Catholic substance call for another principle in addition to that of justification by faith alone. There is, however, one current usage that does this in a particularly striking fashion.

The Language of Unconditionality and the Need of Another Critical Principle

With very good reason and benefit to other Christians, Lutherans describe God's promise of forgiveness as operative on behalf of the sinner in a fashion akin to that of a last will and testament. At times, it will be recalled, one becomes an heir not by fulfilling certain conditions that merit it but simply by being named one. This kind of will is unconditional; so is God's promise to forgive. The point this comparison is intended to make is clear enough. God forgives because of his promise to do so in Jesus Christ and not because of any natural attainment or half-goodness (even one brought about by grace) in the sinner on the way to justification.

Lest there be any doubt about it, according to official Roman Catholic teaching neither the faith nor the works that precede justification are conditions sufficient to win forgiveness for the sinner. Divine acceptance is not conditioned by the previous attainment of an acceptability that merits it.[39] But does the promise of forgiveness exclude all conditions: antecedent, simultaneous, and subsequent?

This much is beyond dispute. For Lutheran scholars, basing their position on that of their Confessions, the unconditionality of the promise does not exclude word and sacraments. Here one might ask whether the importance attributed to word and sacraments would be less likely to be missed if a more qualified unconditionality were attributed to the divine promise, to God's love for sinners, to justification. Might another critical principle be in even more need of affirmation if unconditionality is affirmed without the users unpacking its meaning? An affirmative answer seems warranted in both cases.

God's promise provides for word and sacraments and guarantees their indefectibility in Christ's church for the sake, among other things, of the forgiveness of sins. Their role is unquestionably similar to what in other contexts is that of conditions. Might designating these divine works of salvation as *subsequent conditions* and results of the divine promise enhance rather than detract from the sovereignty, effectiveness, and faithfulness of the One who promises? Are word and sacraments so liable to be pretenders to divinity and temptations to works-righteousness that they may not be called the conditions through which God justifies sinners because of Jesus Christ alone?

Eschatological concerns too deserve mention. For both Lutherans and Roman Catholics, conversion on earth is not to be identified with the attainment of heaven or final salvation. Moreover, for both the latter is the fulfillment of a divine promise in Jesus Christ as well as a gift dependent on faith. Might ultimate trust in God alone imply and ground a trust that God's grace will preserve one in the faith that is a condition for life everlasting? Again an affirmative answer seems warranted and another critical principle is at work to bring about recognition of what it is that one receives in the gift of faith.

At times the promotion of the right kind of preaching is closely connected with the Lutheran affirmation that God's promises in Christ are unconditional. The gospel is to be proclaimed in such a way that trust and hope in God will be fostered. Good preaching will enable the sinner to avoid both unwarranted self-reliance and despair. Those who need forgiveness will not be helped if the preacher appeals to their freedom and natural goodness despite their fallen state. What they must rather hear is God's unconditional promise. This will relieve them of the torment that comes from trying to determine whether they have or have not fulfilled any and all conditions dependent on them.

To be sure, from a Roman Catholic perspective as well, a good preacher will avoid giving false impressions to a congregation. Those who are brought to recognize their sinfulness must not be left to think God's readiness to forgive depends on something they do or refrain from doing. That readiness is independent of either. Whether they respond appropriately or not to the divine call to repentance, God is graciously disposed toward them because of his promise in Jesus Christ and nothing can change this. In this sense the divine promise is unconditional. But the divine call to repentance comes not to stones or beasts; it comes to human beings. And in those human beings sin has not shown itself stronger than divine compassion; its potential for ultimate destructiveness has not been realized—because of God's forbearance. Traces of the divine image and likeness have not been completely effaced. Human beings are not totally bereft of free choice, however much the latter is inhibited by habit and vice, conditioned by relevant antecedents, and in need of radical empowerment if its subject is to relate properly to the God of Jesus Christ. That sin has not wrought the devastation that it could and should have is the result and the subsequent condition of God's unconditional promise to be gracious and ready to forgive for the sake of Jesus Christ alone.

But that promise has other effects as well. With strength derived from that same source the sinner comes slowly and on other occasions in a conversion of dramatic swiftness to justification. But that path—long or short—is not traversed by anyone without his or her really walking it. The journeying, the passage, is God's work and at the same time a subsequent condition required for the truth of God's promise to forgive because of Jesus Christ.

To preach that God's promise has prevented the destruction of the last vestige of the divine image and freedom in the sinner need not lead to an anxious conscience. Nor does any and all reference to human freedom in conversion necessarily reduce itself to works-righteousness.

It might well be, for example, that one hears the gospel of forgiveness preached Sunday after Sunday with little or no change in the way one lives the rest of the week. Such a person might think that either God is not disposed to give the grace needed to be victorious over sin or that he or she has failed to do all that is possible and required. The theological alternatives might then appear to be either double predestination or semi-Pelagianism. The net result of this lack of progress despite hearing the promise of forgiveness might well be despair.

Good preaching might be looked to in an effort to bring about a different outcome. The preacher might call attention to the goodness that is to be found from time to time in even the most hardened sinner and to the freedom that must not be *presumed* to be completely extinct in even the weakest. Such preaching might seek to inculcate this conviction. Only God knows infallibly what lies within the realm of the possible for an individual at each and every given moment. To assume one must always be able to assess this in one's own case is to aspire to make judgments that are properly divine. Progress in overcoming the sin in one's life may be impossible to detect; grace may still be at work slowly strengthening human beings for future victories through present defeats. Reference to human dignity and goodness despite the repeated successes of sin, to freedom despite habitual succumbing to temptation, to grace despite recurring falls, might well lead to a renewed ultimate hope in God alone and penultimate hope in self as never lacking divine assistance. But that would be preaching influenced by an important critical principle in addition to that of justification by faith.

One final example may be helpful. The language of unconditionality is also used to articulate the rule or linguistic stipulation of justification by faith when the latter is brought to bear on the question of life's meaning. Because humans are tempted to despair that life has any ultimate meaning, God promises in the death and resurrection of Jesus that life is unconditonally meaningful. In this context too another critical principle may have something important to add. Whatever the future may hold in store for the human race, God has irrevocably and unconditionally promised that human life is endowed with a meaning. Precisely because this is true, grace-assisted works to make life meaningful are imperative and will never be lacking. Those works are the effects and the subsequent condition of the divine promise. Trusting ultimately in God alone leads one to trust that they will never cease to make a needed contribution to the quality of human existence. Faith must work itself out through charity because God's promise of a meaningful life for humans is unconditional. God's unconditional promise of the meaningfulness of human life is grasped only in a faith that communicates the freedom which is to be engaged in a new obedience. Here too the language of unconditionality has been unpacked by the aid of another critical principle that does not replace justification by faith.

Justification by Faith Alone, the Need of Another Critical Principle, and Lutheran-Roman Catholic Unity

Roman Catholics have been asked whether their church could accept a reforming principle that would judge all things ecclesial with the purpose of determining whether and to what degree they are conducive to bringing people to put their ultimate trust in the God of Jesus Christ alone. The answer proposed in this essay is a "Yes, but." It is an affirmative but on the condition that another critical principle, however the latter may come to be designated, be allowed to call for efforts to recognize grace and its renewing effects already present in the Catholic substance that is prized by both Lutherans and Roman Catholics.

Lutherans will have to decide whether the unconditionality involved in the criterion of justification by faith excludes all kinds of conditions and therefore this one as well or only certain kinds and therefore perhaps not this one. The answer may be that the additional critical principle is indeed needed and that this admission is compatible (or at least not incompatible) with the criterion of justification by faith.

Hopefully both principles may be acknowledged as needed in a more united church embracing Lutherans and Roman Catholics. A case can be made that each could be fruitfully brought to bear even now on obstacles alleged to stand in the way of closer union. Justification by faith might reveal that not all of these obstacles which are at times said to be insurmountable because of the gospel or word of God are so in fact. But there is a second principle as well, one that this paper has proposed as necessary. Whether it be called a catholic principle or a principle calling for acknowledgment of the divine where it is at work, that principle too might make a contribution and help to break the contemporary ecumenical logjam. Conscientiously applied, that second principle might lead many to a conclusion that deserves consideration. It is this. The progress that has already been made toward greater understanding and shared values on the part of Christians who are still denominationally divided results from a divine promise that must be allowed to have its effects and subsequent conditions in the unity for which Jesus prayed.

Neither in its entirety nor in any of its parts should this essay be taken as calling into question the contention that justification by faith need no longer divide Lutherans and Roman Catholics. The intent is precisely the opposite; suggestions have been offered to make the case for this contention more persuasive.

In particular those Lutherans who choose to speak of justification by faith existentially have not been heard with metaphysical ears and then told to change their mode of discourse or forego chances of closer union with the Roman Catholic Church. Nevertheless, something of a *caveat* has been uttered. It comes to this. There are those who will hear existential language about justification by faith and unpack its meaning metaphysically in ways the speakers do not intend unless greater care is used with regard to the language of unconditionality. This is true not only when justification by faith is proposed as a doctrine but as well when it is presented as a norm, rule, principle, or linguistic stipulation. Room left for a second critical principle might make it a great deal easier to avoid such misunderstanding.

It might do something else as well. It might remove a potential obstacle that would keep Lutherans and Roman Catholics from coming to grips with a serious contemporary challenge both would do well to face together. Are teaching and preaching that aim at convicting of sin and convincing of God's grace in Jesus Christ more likely than not to fall victim to Nietzsche's critique of Christianity as cultivating guilt-consciousness?[40] Or might they, among other redeeming values, give expression to the religiously healthy notion that at least in some societies at present the emotion of guilt is often given a "bum rap"?[41]

NOTES

Part I. Justification by Faith (Common Statement)

1. Lutherans and Catholics in Dialogue, 6 vols. 1. *The Status of the Nicene Creed as Dogma of the Church* (1965); 2. *One Baptism for the Remission of Sins* (1966); 3. *The Eucharist as Sacrifice* (1967); 4. *Eucharist and Ministry* (1970); 5. *Papal Primacy and the Universal Church* (Minneapolis: Augsburg, 1974); 6. *Teaching Authority and Infallibility in the Church* (Minneapolis: Augsburg, 1980). Vols. 1-4 were originally published by the Bishops' Committee for Ecumenical and Interreligious Affairs, Washington, D.C., and the U.S.A. National Committee of the Lutheran World Federation, New York, N.Y. Vols. 1-3 have been reprinted together in one volume by Augsburg Publishing House (n.d.), as has vol. 4 (1979).
2. The common statement of the Joint Study Commission appointed by the Lutheran World Federation, Geneva, and the Secretariat for Promoting Christian Unity, "The Gospel and the Church," was published in *Worship* 46 (1972) 326-51; and *Lutheran World* 19 (1972) 259-73. The text of it in German and English, along with position papers which were discussed over five years, can be found in H. Meyer, ed., *Evangelium—Welt—Kirche: Schlussbericht und Referate der römisch-katholisch/evangelisch-lutherischen Studienkommission "Das Evangelium und die Kirche," 1967-1971* (Frankfurt am M.: O. Lembeck/J. Knecht, 1975). The final drafting of the statement was done in San Anton, Malta (1971), whence the commonly used name for it. See especially section 26; L/RC 2:61-68, 74-75, 82, where the topic of justification by faith is also briefly mentioned.
3. For an assessment of the treatment of justification in the Malta Report and the view that fuller treatment is needed, see *Ecumenical Relations of the Lutheran World Federation: Report of the Working Group on the Interrelations between the Various Bilateral Dialogues* (Geneva: Lutheran World Federation, 1977) 117-23, 131-32. Further, *Lutheran-Episcopal Dialogue. Report and Recommendations. Second Series, 1976-1980* (Cincinnati: Forward Movement Publications, 1981) 22-24.
4. A complete list of the essays and when they were discussed is found in this volume, 10-12.

316

5. William G. Rusch, "How the Eastern Fathers Understood What the Western Church Meant by Justification," in this volume, 131-42.
6. Augustine, *De Spiritu et Littera* 26, 45: "*Quid est enim aliud, justificati, quam justi facti, ab illo scilicet qui justificat impium ut ex impio fit justus*" ("What does the word 'justified' mean except 'made just,' i.e., by him who justifies the ungodly so that one who was ungodly becomes just"). This meaning of *dikaioun/justificare* can also be found in Greek writers. See John Chrysostom, *In ep. ad Rom. hom.* 8.2 (PG 60:456): ". . . *dynatai ho theos ton en asebeia bebiōkota touton exaiphnēs ouchi kolaseōs eleutherōsai monon, alla kai dikaion poiēsai . . .*" (". . . God is able of a sudden not only to free someone who has lived in impiety from punishment, but even to make him righteous") (Chrysostom's comment on Rom. 4:5). See also John Chrysostom, *In ep. II ad Cor. hom.* 11.3 (PG 61:478).
7. These concerns are summarized in Jaroslav Pelikan, *The Christian Tradition, Vol. 1: The Emergence of the Catholic Tradition* (Chicago: University of Chicago Press, 1971) 280-86.
8. Modern studies have argued that Pelagius' concerns were not totally contrary to those of Augustine. His appeal to human responsibility was not intended to belittle God's initiative but to encourage human response. See R. F. Evans, *Pelagius. Inquiries and Reappraisals* (New York, Seabury, 1968), and G. Greshake, *Gnade als konkrete Freiheit. Eine Untersuchung zur Gnadenlehre des Pelagius* (Mainz: Matthias-Grünewald, 1972).
9. This does not mean that the accusers were consistently Augustinian and lacking in Pelagian tendencies. See A. E. McGrath, "Augustinianism? A Critical Assessment of the So-Called 'Medieval Augustinian Tradition' on Justification," *Augustiniana* 31 (1981) 247-67.
10. The situation was complex due to the context of a sophisticated Scholastic theology and was further complicated by several historical factors. Knowledge of the so-called semi-Pelagian controversy and of the important decisions of the regional Council of Orange (A.D. 529) was for the most part lost after the Carolingian period. Only in the mid-sixteenth century did the texts of Orange reappear and start to be used. See H. Bouillard, *Conversion et grâce chez S. Thomas d'Aquin* (Paris: Aubier, 1944) 99-123; M. Seckler, *Instinkt und Glaubenswille nach Thomas von Aquin* (Mainz: Matthias-Grünewald, 1961) 90-133. Furthermore, Pelagius' own commentary on the Pauline Epistles circulated under orthodox names in only slightly revised form and was widely read; see the *Introduction* to the critical edition by A. Souter, *Pelagius' Expositions of Thirteen Epistles of St. Paul* I (Texts and Studies 9; London: Cambridge Univ. Press, 1922); also H. A. Frede, *Ein neuer unbekannter Paulustext und Kommentar* (Vetus Latina, Aus der Geschichte der lateinischen Bibel 7; 2 vols.; Freiburg: Herder, 1973-74). Finally, rising monastic-ascetic fervor as well as the humanism of the late Middle Ages reinforced not only Eastern soteriological accents but also a general confidence in the powers of human nature.

11. The shift to new accents of this kind cannot be traced easily in the development of justification language itself. The term was not important and was
discussed incidentally within various other contexts such as the doctrines
of grace, of the work of Christ, and of the sacrament of penance. (Cf.
Karlfried Froehlich, "Justification Language in the Middle Ages," in this
volume, 143-61.) Nor do the medieval treatments of sin or faith reveal much
of the shift, because the Augustinian notion of original sin and the patristic
understanding of faith with its emphasis on an assent to credal content (*fides
quae*), which is completed by being active in love (cf. Gal. 5:6), remained
normative.

12. Augustine, *De praedestinatione sanctorum* 3, 7 (PL 44:964).

13. For the following, see the accounts in O. H. Pesch and A. Peters, *Einführung
in die Lehre von Gnade und Rechtfertigung* (Darmstadt: Wissenschaftliche
Buchgesellschaft, 1981) 15-54; P. Fransen, "Dogmengeschichtliche Entfaltung der Gnadenlehre," in *Mysterium Salutis* (ed. J. Feiner and M. Löhrer; Einsiedeln: Benziger, 1973) 4/2:631-772.

14. Peter Lombard, *Sent.* I. d. 17, c. 1 and 6.

15. See H. de Lubac, *Surnaturel: Études historiques* (Paris: Aubier, 1946); B.
Stoeckle, *Gratia supponit naturam. Geschichte und Analyse eines theologischen Axioms* (Rome: Herder, 1962).

16. The distinction between *gratia creata* and *gratia increata* first appears in
the commentaries on I. *Sent.* d. 17. See J. Auer, *Die Entwicklung der
Gnadenlehre in der Hochscholastik* (Freiburg: Herder, 1942) 1:86-123. The
systematic use of the term *habitus* probably goes back to Philip the Chancellor (12th century); a first official reference to grace as habit occurs at
the Council of Vienne in 1312 (DS 904). See Fransen, "Dogmengeschichtliche Entfaltung," 672-79.

17. This is certainly the intention of Aquinas' doctrine of grace. See Pesch and
Peters, *Einführung,* 64-107 (cited above, n. 13).

18. After the Council of Trent the technical term for the infused habit of grace
was "sanctifying" grace.

19. Sometimes *gratia gratis data* meant a gift bestowed by God on one person
for the sake of assisting others on the way to salvation. At other times the
term was used more widely to include what is today called actual grace,
i.e., a transient divine assistance moving an individual toward a salutary
operation. Thomas Aquinas knew how to combine both meanings (*De Ver.*
q. 24, a. 15, c.) when he asked about the need of grace to prepare oneself
for sanctifying grace (*gratia gratum faciens*).

20. *Ex suis naturalibus* or *ex puris naturalibus* referred in the *via moderna* to
the natural abilities remaining in fallen human beings and should not be
confused with the later concept of *natura pura* introduced by Cajetan. Cf.
de Lubac, *Surnaturel,* 105 (cited above, n. 15).

21. Paul Vignaux, *Justification et Prédestination au XIVe Siècle* (Paris: Presses
Universitaires de France, 1934), esp. 97-175 on William of Ockham and

Gregory of Rimini. For Ockham's understanding of Pelagianism and consequent denial that he favored that heresy, see 126-27.

22. ". . . *cum Deus coronat merita nostra, nihil aliud coronet quam munera sua,*" Augustine, Ep. 194:5, 19 (CSEL 57:190).

23. The term "congruous" merit seems to have its root in the Porretan school of the late 12th century. "Condign" merit (cf. Rom. 8:18) appears at about the same time. See B. Hamm, *Promissio, Pactum, Ordinatio: Freiheit und Selbstbindung Gottes in der scholastischen Gnadenlehre* (Tübingen: Mohr-Siebeck, 1977) 445-62.

24. See A. M. Landgraf, *Dogmengeschichte der Frühscholastik* (Regensburg: Pustet, 1952) 1/1:238-302; Auer, *Entwicklung der Gnadenlehre*, 1:229-61.

25. *In IV Sent.*, d. 17, q. 1, a. 2, sol. 1, c.; *De Ver.* q. 24, a. 15, c.

26. *In IV Sent.*, d. 15, q. 1, a. 3, sol. 4, c: ". . . *ex merito congrui dicitur aliquis mereri aliquod bonum per opera extra caritatem facta. . . .Quia tamen hoc meritum non proprie meritum dicitur ideo magis concedendum est quod hujusmodi opera non sint alicujus meritoria quam quod sint.*"

27. See W. Dettloff, *Die Lehre von der acceptatio divina bei Johannes Duns Scotus mit besonderer Berücksichtigung der Rechtfertigungslehre* (Franziskanische Forschungen 10; Werl: Dietrich-Coelde Verlag, 1954); *Die Entwicklung der Akzeptations- und Verdienstlehre von Duns Scotus bis Luther mit besonderer Berücksichtigung der Franziskanertheologen* (Beiträge zur Geschichte der Philosophie und Theologie des Mittelalters 40/2; Münster: Aschendorff, 1964); "Die antipelagianische Grundstruktur der scotistischen Rechtfertigungslehre," *Franziskanische Studien* 48 (1966) 266-70.

28. Ap 4:19-20; BS 163; BC 109-110.

29. DS 387.

30. Both the monk Gottschalk in the 9th century (DS 621) and probably the presbyter Lucidus in the 5th century (DS 330-42) taught double predestination; they were condemned.

31. *In I Sent.*, d. 41, a. 1, q. 1c.

32. Ibid., q. 2c.

33. *In I Sent.*, d. 41, q. 1, a. 3, c. and ad 2; *In II Sent.*, d. 27, q. 1, a. 4, c. and ad 4.

34. "*Et sic impossibile est quod totus praedestinationis effectus in communi habeat aliquam causam ex parte nostra*" (S.T., I, q. 23, a. 5). "*Sed quare hos elegit in gloriam et illos reprobavit, non habet rationem nisi divinam voluntatem*" (ad 3).

35. *Ordinatio* I, d. 40, c.

36. *Ordinatio* I, d. 44, c.

37. Heiko Oberman, *The Harvest of Medieval Theology* (Cambridge: Harvard Univ. Press, 1967) 185-96, esp. 189-92, discusses the role of foreseen merits in predestination for Gabriel Biel in relation to William of Ockham. It should be noted that for these authors and for the many late medieval theologians who agree with them, God does in some exceptional cases, such as those

of St. Paul and the Virgin Mary, elect to eternal life apart from foreseen merits, but ordinarily (*regulariter*) God requires "that one must do his very best" (192).

38. McGrath, "Augustinianism?" (see above, n. 9) 256-266.
39. McGrath, "Augustinianism?" (see above, n. 9).
40. See A. Zumkeller, "Erbsünde, Gnade und Rechtfertigung im Verständnis der Erfurter Augustinertheologen des Spätmittelalters," *Zeitschrift für Kirchengeschichte* 92 (1981) 39-59.
41. P. Vignaux, *Luther, Commentateur des Sentences* (Livre I, Distinction XVII) (Paris: J. Vrin, 1935).
42. Cf. K. Froehlich, "Aspects of Justification Language in the Middle Ages," in this volume, 143-61.
43. See §§22-28 below.
44. See §§29-63 below.
45. See §43 below.
46. See n. 22 above.
47. The *sola*, added by Luther in his translation of Rom. 3:28, was to express the exclusion of good works in justification. See *On Translating*, 1530 (WA 30/2:636, 11-638,22; LW 35:187-89). On Luther's doctrine of faith, see Walter von Loewenich, *Luther's Theology of the Cross* (Minneapolis: Augsburg, 1976), ch. 2. Melanchthon regarded the *sola* as an "exclusive particle" denying "trust in the merit of love or works" (Ap 4:73-74; BS 175; BC 117).
48. CA 3:4; BS 54; BC 30; CA 5:2; BS 58; BC 31.
49. Cf. CA 4, where "alone" is implied rather than expressed (BS 56; BC 30).
50. See SA 2/1:1-5; BS 415; BC 292.
51. ". . . *quia isto articulo stante stat Ecclesia, ruente ruit Ecclesia*," *Exposition of Ps. 130:4*, 1538 (WA 40/3:352, 3). Luther used similar formulations elsewhere. This statement and similar ones caused later Lutheran theologians to call the article of justification by faith "the article on which the church stands and falls" ("*articulus stantis et cadentis ecclesiae*"). Valentin E. Löscher seems to have been the first to employ this phrase in his anti-pietist essay, *Timotheus Verinus* (Wittenberg, 1718). See Friedrich Loofs, "Der *articulus stantis et cadentis ecclesiae*," *Theologische Studien und Kritiken* 90 (1917) 345.
52. FC SD 5:20-21; BS 958-59; BC 561-62.
53. Luther expounded these views in the *Disputation Against Scholastic Theology*, 1517 (WA 1:221-28; LW 31:9-16); in the *Ninety-Five Theses*, 1517 (WA 1:233-38; LW 31:25-33), and in *The Heidelberg Disputation*, 1518 (WA 1:353-74; LW 31:39-70). See also Thomas N. Tentler, *Sin and Confession on the Eve of the Reformation* (Princeton: Princeton Univ. Press, 1977) 351-63. On the influence of Staupitz on Luther, see David C. Steinmetz, *Luther and Staupitz* (Duke Monographs in Medieval and Renaissance Studies 4; Durham, N.C.: Duke Univ. Press, 1980) 141-44.

54. Letter of October 31, 1517 (WA Br 1:111, 37-46; LW 48:47).

55. WA 1:233-38; LW 31:25-33.

56. See, for example, Thesis 25 in *The Heidelberg Disputation*, 1518 (WA 1:364, 1-16; LW 31:55-56). Luther had already dealt with justification in his *Lectures on Romans*, 1515-16. See Karl Holl, "Die Rechtfertigungslehre in Luthers Vorlesung über den Römerbrief mit besonderer Rücksicht auf die Frage der Heilsgewissheit" in *Gesammelte Aufsätze zur Kirchengeschichte, I: Luther* (4th and 5th eds; Tübingen: Mohr, 1927: reprinted, Darmstadt: Wissenschaftliche Buchgesellschaft, 1965) 111-54.

57. In much of the Scholasticism of the day *caritas* was understood as a divinely infused virtue whereby the believer is brought into union with God. The formula *fides caritate formata* was meant to interpret the Vulgate version of Gal. 5:6, "*fides quae per caritatem operatur*," transposing it into Aristotelian thought categories: "faith formed [in the Aristotelian sense of formal causality] by charity," i.e., a faith animated by love. The Greek of Gal. 5:6 is usually translated "faith working through love" (RSV), but another possible meaning is "faith inspired by [God's] love [toward us]." Contemporary Scholastic usage is indicated by the statement of Johannes Altenstaig, *Vocabularius theologiae* (Hagenau, 1517) I: Fol. XXXI: "Charity . . . is the form of the virtues inasmuch as through charity the act of virtue is made perfect, because through charity they [the acts of the virtues] are referred to their last end, which is God. For it is more perfect for an act to be related to God than to any other end." Altenstaig is here speaking of infused charity, poured into the human heart by God.

58. See Jared Wicks, *Cajetan Responds. A Reader in Reformation Controversy* (Washington, D.C.: Catholic University of America, 1978) 56-58 et passim. In greater detail see J. Wicks, "Roman Reactions to Luther: The First Year (1518)," *Catholic Historical Review* 69 (1983) 521-62, esp. 549-50; also Gerhard Hennig, *Cajetan und Luther. Ein historischer Beitrag zur Begegnung von Thomismus und Reformation* (Arbeiten zur Theologie 7; ed. Alfred Jepsen et al.; Stuttgart: Calwer, 1966) 67-69.

59. DS 1025-26.

60. See Luther's own account of the Proceedings at Augsburg, 1518 (WA 2:7, 29-34; LW 31:261). For Cajetan's view see n. 58 above. For a review of this encounter in the context of Luther's doctrine of justification, see Ernst Bizer, *Fides ex auditu: Eine Untersuchung über die Entdeckung der Gerechtigkeit Gottes durch Martin Luther* (Neukirchen-Vluyn: Verlag der Buchhandlung des Erziehungsvereins, 1958) 115-23.

61. Cf. Cajetan, *Opuscula* (Lyons, 1562) 111a: "*Hoc enim est novam ecclesiam construere.*" Quotation translated in Wicks, *Cajetan Responds*, 55; cf. 22-23.

62. Luther summarized his view of the papacy in thesis 13. See the *Leipzig Debate*, 1519 (WA 2:161, 35-38; LW 31:318). Cf. the analysis of Scott H.

Hendrix, *Luther and the Papacy: Stages in a Reformation Conflict* (Philadelphia: Fortress, 1981) 81-85.

63. DS 1451-92.

64. See WA 6:202-76; LW 44:21-114. WA 6:381-469; LW 44:123-217. WA 6:497-673; LW 36:5-126. WA 7:49-73; LW 31:333-77.

65. See A. Kluckholm et al., eds., *Deutsche Reichstagsakten unter Karl V* (Göttingen: Vandenhoeck & Ruprecht, 1962 [reprint]) 2:647, 1-3. English text in DeLamar Jensen, *Confrontation at Worms* (Provo, Utah: Brigham Young Univ., 1973) 86-87. For a detailed account of events, see E. Gordon Rupp, *Luther's Progress to the Diet of Worms* (New York: Harper, 1964). On Luther's trial, see Daniel Olivier, *The Trial of Luther* (tr. John Tonkin; St. Louis: Concordia, 1978); Remigius Bäumer, ed., *Lutherprozess und Lutherbann* (Corpus Catholicorum 32; Münster: Aschendorff, 1972).

66. These reforms were started by Luther. See *The Basic Liturgical Writings*, 1523-26 (WA 12:35-37, 205-20; 18:417-21; 19:72-113; LW 53:5-90); *The Large and Small Catechisms*, 1529 (BS 501-733; BC 337-461).

67. Translation of Latin text (BS 56; BC 30). Compare the German text of this article.

68. "The dispute and dissension are concerned chiefly with various traditions and abuses" (Conclusion of Part I; BS 83d,5; BC 48:2).

69. Text in *Melanthonis Opera*, CR 27:6-244. See also Herbert Immenkötter, *Die Confutatio der Confessio Augustana vom 3. August 1530* (Corpus Catholicorum 33; Münster: Aschendorff, 1979). English translation in J. M. Reu, ed., *The Augsburg Confession: A Collection of Sources with An Historical Introduction* (Chicago: Wartburg Publ. House, 1930; reprinted, St. Louis: Concordia Seminary Press, 1966) *348-83.

70. ". . . ex *diametro pugnat cum evangelica veritate opera non excludente*," *Confutatio* 6, 3 (CR 27:99; Immenkötter, *Confutatio*, 90, 18-21; Reu, *The Augsburg Confession*, 352).

71. For a detailed analysis of these negotiations, see Vinzenz Pfnür, *Einig in der Rechtfertigungslehre? Die Rechtfertigungslehre der "Confessio Augustana" (1530) und die Stellungnahme der katholischen Kontroverstheologie zwischen 1530 und 1535* (Wiesbaden: Franz Steiner, 1970). Cf. J. Raitt, "From Augsburg to Trent," in this volume, 200-17.

72. Ap 4:2-8; BS 158-60; BC 107-08.

73. "Die höchste Kunst im Christentum," Sermon on Gal. 3, January 1, 1532 (WA 36:9, 28-29).

74. Ap 4:382; BS 232; BC 165.

75. Ap 4:252; BS 209; BC 143.

76. Ap 4:227; BS 209; BC 139.

77. Ap 4:229; BS 204 ("*summum opus legis*"); BC 139.

78. CA 5:2; BS 58; BC 31.

79. "Things that make no difference," or things neither commanded nor prohibited; "things in the middle" (*Mitteldinge*). The concept originated in

Stoic philosophy referring to ethically neutral matters not necessary for true wisdom. Lutherans used the concept as an equivalent for items which fall under the heading of *ius ecclesiasticum*. See FC SD 10:5-9; BS 1055-57; BC 611-12. See also Arthur C. Piepkorn, "*Ius Divinum* and *Adiaphoron* in Relation to Structural Problems in the Church: The Position of the Lutheran Symbolical Books," L/RC 5:123-26; and Bernard J. Verkamp, "The Limits Upon Adiaphorist Freedom: Luther and Melanchthon," *Theological Studies* 36 (1975) 52-76.

80. CA 26:39; BS 106; BC 69.

81. Recommendations of a select committee of nine cardinals and prelates to Pope Paul III. See Colman J. Barry, ed., *Readings in Church History* (Westminster: Newman, 1965) 2:96-102. Barry gives 1538 as the date of this document, though some others date it a year or two earlier.

82. See, for example, the notions of the supremacy of Scripture in the works of Kaspar Schatzgeyer (1463-1527), Johann Dietenberger (d. 1534), and Ambrose Catarinus Politi (1484-1553). Cf. George H. Tavard, *Holy Writ and Holy Church* (New York: Harper and Row, 1959) 173-84.

83. See, e.g., Hubert Kirchner, *Luther and the Peasants' War* (Facet Books, Historical Series 22; Philadelphia: Fortress, 1972). On the "left wing" in general, see George H. Williams, *The Radical Reformation* (Philadelphia: Westminster, 1962), esp. chs. 4 and 13.

84. Mensing, *Antapologie* (Frankfurt/Oder, 1533), fol. 13, r.v.; cited by Pfnür, *Einig in der Rechtfertigungslehre* . . . , 328 (cited above, n. 71). Mensing, a Dominican adversary of Luther, received his licentiate in theology at Wittenberg in 1517, became provincial of Saxony in 1534, and suffragan bishop of Halberstadt in 1539. He died about 1541.

85. See above, §27.

86. SA 2/2:10; BS 419; BC 294.

87. SA 2/4:7; BS 429; BC 299.

88. Appendix to SA; BS 464:7; BC 316-17.

89. The text of the "Regensburg Book" (*Liber Ratisbonensis*) can be found in *Melanthonis Opera*, CR 4:190-238. The colloquy met from April 17 to May 31, 1541. For a detailed account of Luther's influence on the Regensburg meeting, see Walter von Loewenich, *Duplex iustitia: Luthers Stellung zu einer Unionsformel des 16. Jahrhunderts* (Veröffentlichungen des Instituts für europäische Geschichte, Mainz 68; Wiesbaden: Franz Steiner, 1972) 23-55. On the problems generated at Regensburg, see Vinzenz Pfnür, *Die Einigung bei den Religionsgesprächen von Worms und Regensburg 1540/ 41: Eine Täuschung?* (Schriften des Vereins für Reformationsgeschichte 191; Gütersloh: Gerd Mohn, 1980).

90. CR 4:201.

91. Hubert Jedin, *A History of the Council of Trent* (tr. Dom E. Graf; London: Nelson and Sons, 1954) 1:382.

92. Letter to John Frederick, May 10 or 11, 1541 (WA Br 9:406, 8). See also Loewenich, *Duplex iustitia*, 54. The Protestant participants submitted their objections to the Catholic side on May 31, 1541. See *Melanthonis Opera*, CR 4:348-76.

93. This was the principal condition of the Smalcald League. Luther had proposed the condition during a meeting with the papal emissary Paul Vergerio in Wittenberg in 1535. See *Melanthonis Opera*, CR 2:987.

94. DS 1515. Cf. Augustine, *Ctr. duas ep. Pelagianorum,* bk. 1, ch. 13, #26 (CSEL 60:445; PL 44:562).

95. DS 1523.

96. DS 1532. Heiko Oberman maintains that the verb *promeretur* (translated in our text as "truly merits") indicates the council *did not exclude* that acts of the sinner posited with divine grace may prepare for or merit justification congruously, i.e., not in the strict sense (*de condigno*), but in a lesser or partial way (*de congruo*). If so, this passage does not exclude (though it also does not endorse) the Ockhamist thesis. See H. Oberman, "Das tridentinische Rechtfertigungsdekret im Licht spätmittelalterlicher Theologie," *Zeitschrift für Theologie und Kirche* 61 (1964) 251-82 (tr., "The Tridentine Decree on Justification in the Light of Late Medieval Theology," *Journal for Theology and the Church* 3, *Distinctive Protestant and Catholic Themes Reconsidered* [ed. R. W. Funk; New York: Harper & Row, 1967] 28-54, esp. 38-39). Thus the text, in Oberman's opinion, leaves room for justification to be *partim* a work of God and *partim* a work of the still unjustified human being. Oberman thinks that Roman Catholic scholars are themselves divided in the way they interpret *promeretur* in this context and knows that not all concede his reading as plausible. Lutherans may fear that failure to exclude any and all types of merit prior to justification will engender false confidence and works-righteousness. Catholics may suspect that this fear discounts Trent's insistence on the prevenience of God's grace and its description of human cooperation in terms of a failure to do what humans could do by their own devices (namely, reject the grace and thus sin). For a Catholic reaction to Oberman's article, see Eduard Schillebeeckx, "The Tridentine View on Justification," in F. Böckle, ed., *Moral Problems and Christian Personalism* (Concilium 5, 1965) 176-79.

97. DS 1525.

98. DS 1526.

99. DS 1529.

100. Ibid. The council is here quoting Augustine, *De Trinitate*, bk. 14, ch. 12, #15 (PL 42:1048).

101. DS 1532, with quotations from Roman Ritual *Ordo Baptismi* n. 1 and from Heb. 11:6.

102. DS 1530-31.

103. DS 1535.

104. DS 1540.
105. DS 1540, 1565-66.
106. DS 1548. Cf. Augustine, quoted in n. 22 above.
107. DS 1549.
108. DS 1546.
109. DS 1582.
110. See §27 above.
111. FC SD 1-6; BS 843-99; BC 508-68. See also Eric W. Gritsch and Robert W. Jenson, *Lutheranism* (Philadelphia: Fortress, 1976), ch. 5.
112. "Forensic" (from Latin *forum*, the marketplace where judicial and other business was conducted) is a designation used by Luther and other Reformers to emphasize the justification (*Rechtfertigung*) of the sinner on account of Christ rather than on account of merit by fulfilling God's law (*Recht*) through good works. In this sense "forensic" denotes the *pronouncing* or *declaring* righteous of the sinner who stands before God's judicial tribunal without, however, excluding the necessity of good works as the fruit of justification. Luther used the designation in analogy to old German judicial practices. See Werner Elert, "Deutschrechtliche Züge in Luthers Rechtfertigungslehre," *Zeitschrift für systematische Theologie* 12 (1935) 22-35. See also Melanchthon, Ap 4:252-53; BS 209; BC 143. FC SD 3:32; BS 925; BC 544. Cf. G. Forde, "Forensic Justification and the Law in Lutheran Theology," in this volume, 278-303.
113. FC SD 3:32; BS 925; BC 544-45. These statements were directed against such theologians as Andreas Osiander, who spoke of justification as the "indwelling" (*Einwohnung*) of the divine nature in the believer. See FC SD 3:54; BS 932-33; BC 548-49.
114. FC SD 2:60-62; BS 864-65; BC 519.
115. FC SD 5:27; BS 961; BC 563.
116. FC SD 6:20; BS 968; BC 567.
117. FC SD 11:28; BS 1071; BC 620. FC SD 11:91; BS 1089-90; BC 631-32.
118. *De servo arbitrio*, WA 18:600-787; LW 33:15-295. Cf. also Luther's "Preface to the Epistle of St. Paul to the Romans" 1546 (1522), WA DB 7:22-25; LW 35:378: "In chapters 9, 10, 11 he teaches of God's eternal predestination . . . in order that our salvation may be taken entirely out of our hands and put in the hand of God alone. . . . But you had better follow the order of this epistle. Worry first about Christ and the gospel. . . . Then, when you have reached the eighth chapter and are under the cross and suffering, this will teach you correctly of predestination in chapters 9, 10, and 11, and how comforting it is."
119. Martin Chemnitz, *Examen Concilii Tridentini* I-IV (ed. Eduard Preuss; Leipzig: Hinrichs, 1975) Part I, Locus Eighth, sec. I, art. 1-3, pp. 147-99 (*Examination of the Council of Trent* [tr. Fred Kramer; St. Louis: Concordia Publ. House, 1971], Eighth Topic, Concerning Justification, Sec. I, art. 1-3, 1:465-92).

120. A. Hasler, *Luther in der katholischen Dogmatik* (Munich: Max Hueber Verlag, 1968) 58-98.
121. This is the judgment of critical analysts of Lutheran Orthodoxy. See, for example, Wilhelm Dantine, *The Justification of the Ungodly* (tr. Eric W. Gritsch and Ruth C. Gritsch; St. Louis: Concordia Publ. House, 1968), chs. 1-2, esp. 24. Hans E. Weber, *Reformation, Orthodoxie und Rationalismus* (2nd ed.; Gütersloh: Gerd Mohn, 1937; reprinted, Darmstadt: Wissenschaftliche Buchgesellschaft, n.d.) I/1:126.
122. DS 1997, 2008, 2509-10, 2564-65. The controversy is referred to as *"de auxiliis (divinae gratiae)"* ["on the aids (of divine grace)"].
    A position similar to the Molinist view was taken by the Danish Lutheran Bishop Erik Pontoppidan in his explanation to Luther's Small Catechism, *Truth unto Godliness (Sanhed til gudfrygtighed . . . forklarung over Luthers Liden catechismo*, 1737); in answer to question 548, "What is election?," he wrote, "God has appointed all those to eternal life who He from eternity has foreseen would accept the offered grace, believe in Christ, and remain constant in this faith unto the end" (as cited from the "Madison Agreement" among U.S. Norwegian Lutheran groups, in R. C. Wolf, ed., *Documents of Lutheran Unity in America* [Philadelphia: Fortress, 1966] document 100, p. 233). On the ongoing influence of Pontoppidan's formulation, cf. T. R. Skarsten, "Erik Pontoppidan and His Asiatic Prince Menoza," *Church History* 50 (1981) 33-34.
123. DS 2005-06.
124. DS 2438, 2464.
125. DS 2123. *Fides late dicta*, a term coined by Juan Ripalda, s.j. (1594-1648), means faith based on the so-called "natural" revelation of God through the created order. Ripalda held that such faith, in the case of the unevangelized, could be justifying provided it was elicited in response to divine grace. The condemnation was apparently directed at Gilles Estrix, s.j., who is reported to have taught Ripalda's opinion at Louvain in 1670. The Holy Office did not state that Ripalda was in error but that Estrix's thesis in the form quoted was "at least scandalous and harmful in its practical effects" (DS 2166). See S. Harent, art. "Infidèles (salut des)," DThC 7:1759-60, 1792-98.
126. See *Ascent of Mount Carmel*, II, ch. 9, in Kieran Kavanaugh and Otilio Rodriguez, eds., *The Collected Works of St. John of the Cross* (Washington, D.C.: Institute of Carmelite Studies, 1973) 129-30. On Bérulle and his classical work, *Discours de l'état et des grandeurs de Jésus* (1623), see Fernando Guileen Preckler, *Bérulle aujourd'hui. Pour une spiritualité de l'humanité du Christ* (Paris: Beauchesne, 1978).
127. Henri-Marie Boudon (1624-1702), *Oeuvres completes* (Paris: Migne, 1856) 1:406; similar expressions recur in all his writings. Jean-Martin Moye (1730-1793), *Lettres* (Gap, 1962) 59; see Georges Tavard, *L'Expérience de Jean-Martin Moye. Mystique et mission* (Paris: Beauchesne,

1978) 67-68, 145. Other formulations along the same lines will be found in many authors of the period, e.g., in Jean-Pierre de Caussade, *L'Abandon à la providence divine* (Paris: Desclée de Brouwer, 1966), composed between 1730 and 1740; in English: *The Sacrament of the Present Moment* (tr. Kitty Muggeridge; San Francisco: Harpe. & Row, 1981). See also the prayers from Teresa of the Child Jesus, from Claude de la Colombière, and from the Roman Liturgy (collect for the Fifth Sunday after Epiphany) cited in H. Küng, *Justification: The Doctrine of Karl Barth and a Catholic Reflection* (tr. T. Collins, E. E. Tolk, and D. Granskou; New York: Thomas Nelson, 1964; 2nd ed., Philadelphia: Westminster, 1981) 274.

128. See, for example, the Pietist August Hermann Francke (1663-1727) in Gerhard Müller, *Die Rechtfertigungslehre. Geschichte und Probleme* (Studienbücher, Kirchen und Dogmengeschichte; Gütersloh: Gerd Mohn, 1977) 81, cf. 77-83 (bibliography).

129. See, for example, the Lutheran theologian Johann Salomo Semler (1725-91), in Müller, *Rechtfertigungslehre*, 85, cf. 83-88 (bibliography) (cited above, n. 128).

130. Friedrich Schleiermacher, *The Christian Faith* (English tr. of the 2nd German edition, 1830; ed. H. R. Mackintosh and J. J. Stewart; Philadelphia: Fortress, 1976) 478-505, 484; justification is treated as part of regeneration. Albrecht Ritschl, *The Christian Doctrine of Justification and Reconciliation* (ed. and tr. H. R. Mackintosh and A. B. Macaulay; Library of Religious and Philosophical Thought; Clifton, N.J.: Reference Book Publishers, Inc., 1966), chs. 1-3: "The Conception of Justification and Its Relations." How Ritschl influenced later theologians, among them Wilhelm Herrmann (1846-1922) and Adolf von Harnack (1851-1930), is shown by Walther von Loewenich, *Luther und der Neuprotestantismus* (Witten: Luther-Verlag, 1963) 111-29. For a summary of Schleiermacher's and Ritschl's treatments of justification, see Müller, *Rechtfertigungslehre*, 89-100 (cited above, n. 128).

M. Kähler, *Die Wissenschaft der christlichen Lehre von dem evangelischen Grundartikel aus im Abrisse dargestellt* (3 vols.; Erlangen: Andreas Deichert, 1883).

P. Althaus, *The Theology of Martin Luther* (tr. Robert C. Schultz; Philadelphia: Fortress, 1966), esp. 224-50; *Die christliche Wahrheit: Lehrbuch der Dogmatik* (3rd ed.; Gütersloh: Bertelsmann, 1952), esp. section 61.

W. Elert, *Der christliche Glaube. Grundlinien der lutherischen Dogmatik* (2nd ed. rev.; Hamburg: Furche Verlag, 1960); on Elert, see Müller, *Rechtfertigungslehre,* 107-12 (cited above, n. 128). R. Prenter, *Creation and Redemption* (tr. Theodor I. Jensen; Philadelphia: Fortress, 1967); *Spiritus Creator* (tr. John M. Jenson: Philadelphia: Muhlenberg, 1953).

G. Aulén, *The Faith of the Christian Church* (tr. E. H. Wahlstrom and G. E. Arden; Philadelphia: Muhlenberg, 1948).

P. Tillich, *Systematic Theology* (3 vols. in one; Chicago: University of

Chicago Press, 1967) I:49-50, 222-28; K. Barth, *Church Dogmatics*, 4: *The Doctrine of Reconciliation*, Part I (tr. G. W. Bromiley; Edinburgh: Clark, 1956) 514-642.

For an overview see Ernst Kinder, ed., *Die evangelische Lehre von der Rechtfertigung* (Quellen zur Konfessionskunde, Reihe B, Protestantische Quellen 1; Lüneburg: Heliand-Verlag, 1957) 12-13, 83-105; A. Peters, in O. H. Pesch and A. Peters, *Einführung in die Lehre von Gnade and Rechtfertigung* (Darmstadt: Wissenschaftliche Buchgesellschaft, 1981) 284-365; Robert Bertram, "Recent Lutheran Theologies on Justification by Faith: A Sampling," in this volume, 241-55. H. G. Pöhlmann, *Rechtfertigung: Die gegenwärtige kontroverstheologische Problematik der Rechtfertigungslehre zwischen der evangelisch-lutherischen und der römisch-katholischen Kirche* (Gütersloh: Gerd Mohn, 1971). Arthur B. Crabtree, *The Restored Relationship: A Study in Justification and Reconciliation* (Valley Forge, Pa.; Judson, 1963) 160-86. Vittorio Subilia, *La Giustificazione Per Fede* ("Biblioteca Di Cultura Religiosa"; Brescia: Paideia Editrice, 1976) (in German: *Die Rechtfertigung aus Glauben: Gestalt und Wirkung vom Neuen Testament bis heute* [tr. Max Krumbach; Göttinger theologische Lehrbücher; Göttingen: Vandenhoeck & Ruprecht, 1981]).

131. J. A. Möhler, *Symbolism, or Exposition of the Doctrinal Differences between Catholics and Protestants as Evidenced by Their Symbolical Writings* (first German ed., 1832; tr. James B. Robertson; 5th English ed.; London: Gibbins and Co., 1906), ch. 3, "Opposite Views on the Doctrine of Justification."

John Henry Newman, *Lectures on the Doctrine of Justification* (Westminster, Md.; Christian Classics, 1966; first ed. 1838; reprint of ed. of 1900) 348, 278.

M. J. Scheeben, *The Mysteries of Christianity* (first German ed. 1865; tr. Cyril Vollert; St. Louis: B. Herder, 1946) 625-628; *Nature and Grace* (first German ed., 1861; tr. C. Vollert; St. Louis: B. Herder, 1954).

On K. Rahner, see below, I. D. 2, "Catholic Theology since World War II," §79.

H. Küng, *Justification* (cited above, n. 127). Cf. also George Tavard, "Catholic Views on Karl Barth," *Christian Century* 76, 5 (February 4, 1969) 132-33; Müller, *Rechtfertigungslehre*, 100-106 (cited above, n. 128).

For developments among Catholic theologians, see also Wilfried Joest, ed., *Die katholische Lehre von der Rechtfertigung und von der Gnade* (Quellen zur Konfessionskunde, Reihe A. Römisch-Katholische Quellen 2; Lüneburg; Heliand-Verlag, 1954); and Avery Dulles, "Justification in Contemporary Catholic Theology," in this volume, 256-77.

132. A. Schlatter, *Gottes Gerechtigkeit: Ein Kommentar zum Römerbrief* (Stuttgart: Calwer, 1935; 3rd ed. 1959) 42-43, 117. Schlatter's son Theodor felt constrained to explain in the preface to the 4th ed. that the commentary's

aim was not criticism of Luther's interpretation but to "go beyond Luther forward to Paul" in order to show how Paul saw God's saving work. R. Bultmann, *Theology of the New Testament* (tr. K. Grobel; New York: Scribner's 1951) 1:270-85: "*Dikaiosyne Theou*," *Journal of Biblical Literature* 83 (1964) 12-16. A different approach was offered by Krister Stendahl, who warned against narrowing the gospel to an introspective interpretation of justification but has subsequently shown his interest to be not against justification so much as in favor of a salvation-history approach. Cf. his "The Apostle Paul and the Introspective Conscience of the West," *Harvard Theological Review* 56 (1963) 199-215; reprinted in *Ecumenical Dialogue at Harvard* (ed. S. H. Miller and G. E. Wright; Cambridge, Mass.: Harvard Univ. Press, 1964) 236-56; and most recently in Stendahl's *Paul Among Jews and Gentiles* (Philadelphia: Fortress, 1976) 78-96; cf. 23-40 and 129-32.

E. Käsemann, "The 'Righteousness of God' in Paul," in *New Testament Questions of Today* (Philadelphia: Fortress, 1969) 168-82. Note also the dissertations done under Käsemann: Christian Müller, *Gottesgerechtigkeit und Gottes Volk: Eine Untersuchung zu Römer 9-11* (FRLANT 86; Göttingen: Vandenhoeck & Ruprecht, 1964); and Peter Stuhlmacher, *Gerechtigkeit Gottes bei Paulus* (FRLANT 87; Göttingen: Vandenhoeck & Ruprecht, 1965).

See further n. 200 below for Catholic exegetes such as Lyonnet and Kertelge.

133. *Dei verbum* 5 implies such a broader definition when it describes the obedience of faith as one "by which man entrusts his whole self freely to God offering 'the full submission of intellect and will to God who reveals' [Vatican I] and freely assenting to the truth revealed by Him." The Council of Trent had already referred to faith as *fundamentum et radix omnis justificationis* (DS 1526) but in the sixth chapter of its decree on justification it described faith rather as the gift whereby we believe the truth of what God has revealed and promised (DS 1532). Trent, therefore, favored a more strictly intellectual concept of faith than that which prevailed at Vatican II.

134. *Lumen gentium* 48.

135. Ibid., 14.

136. Ibid., 48.

137. Ibid., 49.

138. In addition to the text just quoted, see *Ad gentes* 7 and *Lumen gentium* 8, 14, 28, 41, 60, and 62.

139. *Sacrosanctum concilium* 5.

140. Ibid., 7.

141. On bishops, see *Lumen gentium* 25 and *Christus Dominus* 12. On presbyters (priests), see *Lumen gentium* 28 and *Presbyterorum ordinis* 4.

142. *Sacrosanctum concilium* 9.

143. Ibid., 10.
144. Ibid., 59.
145. Ibid., 10.
146. Ibid., 11.
147. See Vilmos Vajta, "Renewal of Worship: *De sacra Liturgia,*" in *Dialogue on the Way* (ed. G. Lindbeck; Minneapolis: Augsburg, 1965) 101-128, esp. 108-113.
148. *Lumen gentium* 8.
149. Ibid.
150. *Unitatis redintegratio* 6.
151. "For in the sacred books, the Father who is in heaven meets His children with great love and speaks with them; and the force and power in the word of God is so great that it remains the support and energy of the Church, the strength of faith for her sons, the food of the soul, and pure and perennial source of spiritual life" (*Dei verbum* 21).
152. Ibid.
153. *Dei verbum* 10.
154. Ibid. 9. In 21 it is noted that the Scriptures "impart the word of God Himself without change." In 24 it is stated: "The sacred Scriptures contain the word of God and, since they are inspired, really are the word of God; and so the study of the sacred page is, as it were, the soul of sacred theology."
155. According to *Lumen gentium* 25 all definitions by popes and councils will win acceptance in the church "on account of the activity of that same Holy Spirit, whereby the whole flock of Christ is preserved and progresses in unity of faith." The Catholic doctrine of the assistance promised to the hierarchical *magisterium* was discussed in volume 6 of this dialogue, L/RC 6:26-27, 44-45.
156. See, for example, L. Bouyer, *The Spirit and Forms of Protestantism* (tr. A. V. Littledale; Westminster, Md.: Newman, 1956); H. Küng, *Justification* (cited above, n. 127); H. U. von Balthasar, *The Theology of Karl Barth* (tr. John Drury; New York: Holt, Rinehart and Winston, 1971); G. Söhngen, *Gesetz und Evangelium* (Freiburg and Munich: K. Alber, 1957); P. Fransen, *The New Life of Grace* (tr. G. Dupont; New York: Herder and Herder, 1972). For other references see A. Dulles, "Justification in Contemporary Catholic Theology," in this volume 256-77.
157. K. Rahner, *Foundations of Christian Faith* (tr. W. Dych; New York: Seabury [Crossroad], 1978) 359-69. Cf. his "Questions of Controversial Theology on Justification," *Theological Investigations* (tr. K. Smyth; Baltimore: Helicon, 1966) 4:189-218.
158. ". . . [N]ot only the grace of divinization, but even the acceptance of this gift must according to all theological sources be characterized as grace. Hence the acceptance of the divine gift of justification is itself part of the

gift. . . . '' (Rahner, ''The Word and the Eucharist,'' *Theological Investigations* 4:257).

159. ''This word of God (as inner moment of the salvific action of God on man and so with it and because of it) is the salutary word which brings with it what it affirms. It is itself therefore salvific event, which, in its outward, historical and social aspect, displays what happens in it and under it, and brings about what it displays. It renders the grace of God present'' (ibid., 259-60). For a sampling of recent Catholic ''word'' theology, see *The Word: Readings in Theology* (compiled at The Canisianum, Innsbruck; New York: P. J. Kenedy, 1964).

160. E. Schillebeeckx, *Christ: The Experience of Jesus as Lord* (tr. John Bowman; New York: Seabury [Crossroad], 1980) 838.

161. J. L. Segundo, ''Capitalism—Socialism: A Theological Crux,'' in *The Mystical and Political Dimension of the Christian Faith* (ed. C. Geffre and G. Gutiérrez; Concilium 96; New York: Herder and Herder, 1974) 122.

162. L. Boff, *Liberating Grace* (tr. John Drury; Maryknoll, N.Y.: Orbis, 1979) 151-52.

163. Earlier in Germany important discussions on justification had taken place between Roman Catholic and Lutheran theologians. Cf. esp. the essays in *Pro Veritate* (ed. H. Volk and E. Schlink; Münster: Aschendorff, 1963) by P. Brunner, pp. 59-96, and H. Volk, pp. 96-131.

164. *A Study Document ''On Justification,''* prepared by the Commission on Theology for the Lutheran World Federation Assembly in Helsinki, July 30–August 11, 1963 (New York: National Lutheran Council, n.d.).

165. *Proceedings of the Fourth Assembly of the Lutheran World Federation Helsinki, July 30–August 11, 1963*, published by the Lutheran World Federation (Berlin and Hamburg: Lutherisches Verlagshaus, 1965). Cf. ''Helsinki 1963,'' *Lutheran World* 11 (1964) 1-36, esp. 4-10.

166. *Proceedings*, ¶¶77 and 83 for the quotations from an address by Gerhard Gloege; 95, cf. ¶¶97 and 89 for that by Helge Brattgård, who refers to FC SD 3:41; BS 928; BC 546, ''*sola fides est, quae apprehendit benedictionem sine operibus, et tamen numquam est sola*'' (cf. Luther, WA 43:255, 38; LW 4:166).

167. '' 'Justification Today,' Document 75—Assembly and Final Versions,'' *Lutheran World* 12, 1, Supplement (1965) 1-11. The supplement includes ''The Meaning of Justification 1958-1963,'' by Jorg Rothermund, ''The Discussion since Helsinki,'' and ''Questions for Further Study and Discussion.'' On the development of the Helsinki texts on justification, see also Peter Kjeseth and Paul Hoffman, ''Document 75,'' *Lutheran World* 11 (1964) 83-86.

168. ''Justification Today,'' 1.

169. Cf. Henning Graf Reventlow, *Rechtfertigung im Horizont des Alten Testaments* (Beiträge zur evangelischen Theologie 58; Munich: Kaiser, 1971).

170. A. R. Wentz, "Lutheran World Federation," in *The Encyclopedia of the Lutheran Church* (ed. Julius Bodensieck; Minneapolis: Augsburg, 1965) 2:1428-29, for this and the following quotations. For a summary of further, subsequent interpretation, see Albrecht Peters, "Systematische Besinnung zu einer Neuinterpretation der reformatorischen Rechtfertigungslehre," in *Rechtfertigung im neuzeitlichen Lebenszusammenhang. Studien zur Neuinterpretation der Rechtfertigungslehre* (ed. W. Lohff and C. Walther; Gütersloh: Gerd Mohn, 1974) 107-25; and in Pesch and Peters, *Einführung*, 332-33 (see n. 130 above).

171. K. Holl, "Luthers Bedeutung für den Fortschritt der Auslegungskunst," *Gesammelte Aufsätze* (cited above, n. 56) 1:544-82. Gerhard Ebeling, "Die Anfänge von Luthers Hermeneutik," *Zeitschrift für Theologie und Kirche* 48 (1951) 172-230; "The New Hermeneutics and the Young Luther," *Theology Today* 21 (1964) 34-45. Cf. also James S. Preus' study of Luther's hermeneutic, *From Shadow to Promise* (Cambridge, Mass.: Harvard Univ. Press, 1969).

172. Ap 4:42-43; BS 168; BC 113. This unconditionality of the promise, to be sure, does not exclude "the Word and sacraments" (see below, §92).

173. *Luther and Erasmus: Free Will and Salvation* (ed. E. G. Rupp and D. Watson; Library of Christian Classics 17; Philadelphia: Westminster, 1969) 143.

174. Cf., e.g., FC SD 2:20-21; BS 879-80; BC 524-25. This passage, pieced together from a number of Luther's writings, was a favorite target of Catholic controversialists. See Hasler, *Luther* (cited above, n. 120) 175-76.

175. Ap 4:73-74; BS 175; BC 117.

176. Advent Postil, 1522, WA 10/1, 2:48,5; WA 7:475, 14-18; WA 18:638; LW 33:70.

177. For Luther's view that these saints were saved by faith despite their errors on justification, see WA 40/1:687; LW 26:459-60; WA 39/2:107-8; 7:774; 8:451-2. Cf. John M. Headley, *Luther's View of Church History* (New Haven: Yale Univ. Press, 1963) 191, 212, 220-1.

178. In speaking of the state of historical humanity Pope John Paul II has recently used the phrase, "*status naturae lapsae simul et redemptae*" (*L'Osservatore Romano*, Eng. ed., Feb. 18, 1980, p. 1).

179. Thomas Aquinas, S.T., I, q.1, a.8, ad 2.

180. "Catholic theologians also emphasize in reference to justification that God's gift of salvation for the believer is unconditional as far as human accomplishments are concerned" (MR #26).

181. According to Trent (DS 1528-30) the infusion of grace, the forgiveness of sins, and sanctification are simultaneous. For St. Thomas the process of justification, of its nature, requires that in the justified person liberation from sin precede the attainment of justifying grace. But he holds that in relation to God, who justifies, the order is reversed. "*Et quia infusio*

gratiae et remissio culpae dicuntur ex parte Dei iustificantis, ideo ordine naturae prior est gratiae infusio quam culpae remissio. Sed si sumantur ea, quae sunt ex parte hominis iustificati, est e converso; nam prius est naturae ordine liberatio a culpa, quam consecutio gratiae iustificantis'' (S.T., I-II, q. 113, a.8, ad 1).

182. SA 3/3:43-45; BS 448; BC 310. See also Ap 4:48; BS 169; BC 114.
183. Council of Trent, Session VI, chap. 5 (DS 1515).
184. Ibid., can. 23 (DS 1573).
185. Ibid., ch. 11 (DS 1537).
186. Ibid.
187. Karl Rahner in particular has emphasized that created grace is "a consequence" rather than "the basis" of uncreated grace, i.e., of God's communication of himself (*Theological Investigations* 1 [tr. Cornelius Ernst; Baltimore: Helicon, 1961] 325).
188. Luther, Small Catechism, 2 (Creed) 6; BS 512; BC 345. Luther spoke of faith as the power which "unites the soul with Christ as a bride is united with her bridegroom." He called this communion "a joyous struggle and exchange" (*fröhlicher Streit und Wechsel*), WA 7:25,34; 55:8; LW 31:351. See also *Lectures on Galatians*, 1535, where Luther speaks of faith "consummating the Deity" (*consummat divinitatem*) not in the substance of God but in us, WA 40/1, 360:24-25; LW 26:227. A comparable notion appears in FC SD 8 (Person of Christ), 96: ". . . that our flesh and blood have in Christ been made to sit so high at the right hand of the majesty and almighty power of God" (BS 1049; BC 610).
189. DS 1531. See above §54.
190. A contemporary Lutheran, Robert W. Jenson, has coined the term "anti-Pelagian codicil" to describe the efforts of medieval theology to evade the Pelagian consequences he holds to be implicit in the Scholastic doctrine of cooperation. See Gritsch and Jenson, *Lutheranism* (cited above, n. 111) 39; also R. W. Jenson, "On Recognizing the Augsburg Confession" in *The Role of the Augsburg Confession* (ed. J. A. Burgress et al.; Philadelphia: Fortress, 1980) 160-62. In a parallel way some Catholics seem to find something resembling an anti-Manichaean or anti-Antinomian codicil in certain formulations of Lutheran Orthodoxy. See Avery Dulles, "Luther's Theology: A Modern Catholic Reflection," unpublished paper for the convocation on Luther and the Modern World held at the Lutheran School of Theology at Chicago, October 20, 1980; manuscript p. 19.
191. Ap 4:366; BS 229; BC 163.
192. Ap 4:194; BS 198; BC 133; cf. Ap 4:365-69; BS 229-30; BC 163. See also M. Luther, *Rhapsodia seu Concepta in Librum de loco Iustificationis* (1530), WA 30/2:670; and his *Wochenpredigten über Matt. 5–7* (1530/32), WA 32:543; LW 21:292-94.
193. CA 12:6; BS 67; BC 35. Cf. Ap 12:45-46, 164-66, 174; BS 260, 288, 290; BC 188, 208, 210.

194. Ap 12:168; BS 288; BC 209. See H. Fagerberg and H. Jorissen, "Penance and Confession," in *Confessing One Faith: A Joint Commentary on the Augsburg Confession by Lutheran and Catholic Theologians* (ed. G. W. Forell and J. F. McCue; Minneapolis: Augsburg, 1982) 234-61, esp. 244-47.

195. See in this connection the statement of the Lutheran/ Roman Catholic Joint Commission, *The Eucharist* (Geneva: Lutheran World Federation, 1980), especially the fourth Supplementary Study, "The Mass as Sacrifice for Atonement for the Living and the Dead *ex opere operato*," by Vinzenz Pfnür, 76-80 and the fifth Supplementary Study, "The Eucharist as a Communal Meal," by Harding Meyer, 81-83.

196. See §41 above.

197. MR #29.

198. See L/RC 5:21-3, 31-3; 6:32, § 42.

199. Fuller discussion of the New Testament material which bears on the topic of justification by faith has been provided in the volume developed within the dialogue, *"Righteousness" in the New Testament: "Justification" in Lutheran-Catholic Dialogue*, by John Reumann, with responses by Joseph A. Fitzmyer, s.j., and Jerome D. Quinn (Philadelphia: Fortress; New York: Paulist, 1982). This material was discussed by dialogue members in the plenary sessions. It is cited above with the sections of the book indicated by the symbol ‡. See also Jerome D. Quinn, "The Scriptures on Merit," and Joseph A. Burgess, "Rewards, But in a Very Different Sense," in this volume, pp. 82-93 and 94-110.

200. E.g., A. Schlatter, *Gottes Gerechtigkeit* (cited above, n. 132) 35-39, 117; E. Käsemann, " 'The Righteousness of God' in Paul," (cited above, n. 132); *Commentary on Romans* (Grand Rapids, Mich.: Eerdmans, 1980) 21-32 et passim; P. Stuhlmacher, *Gerechtigkeit Gottes bei Paulus* (cited above, n. 132); K. Kertelge, *"Rechtfertigung" bei Paulus: Studien zur Struktur und zum Bedeutungsgehalt des paulinischen Rechtfertigungsbegriffs* (Neutestamentliche Abhandlungen ns 3; Münster in W.: Aschendorff, 1967); S. Lyonnet, "De 'iustitia Dei' in epistola ad Romanos," *Verbum Domini* 25 (1947) 23-34, 118-21, 129-44, 193-203, 257-63; K. Kertelge, *"Dikaiosyne*, etc.," *Exegetisches Wörterbuch zum Neuen Testament* (Stuttgart: Kohlhammer, 1980) 1:784-810. Other literature is cited in *"Righteousness" in the New Testament*.

201. See Luther's *Preface to the Complete Edition of the Latin Writings*, 1545 (WA 54:185-86; LW 34:336-37). Luther ascribed "the formal or active righteousness . . . with which God is righteous and punishes the unrighteous sinner" to "all the teachers" (WA 54:185; LW 34:336). On Luther's "tower experience" (*Turmerlebnis*), reference to which follows in his *Preface*, see also the Table Talk passage, WA TR 3: Nr. 3232a, b, c; LW 54:193-94; further, in O. Scheel, ed., *Dokumente zu Luthers Entwicklung* (2nd ed.; Tübingen: J. C. B. Mohr [Paul Siebeck], 1929) 91, and K. G.

Hagen, "Changes in the Understanding of Luther: The Development of the Young Luther," *Theological Studies* 29 (1968) 472-96, esp. 478-81. Joseph A. Fitzmyer, "Brief Remarks on Luther's Interpretation of Pauline Justification" (unpublished paper).

202. Literally, "the righteousness which matters (or holds up, or is valid) before God"; thus in the Luther Bible at Rom. 1:17; 3:21; 2 Cor. 5:21. Cf. the literature cited in n. 201.

203. Heinrich Denifle, O. P., *Die abendländischen Schriftausleger bis Luther über "Justitia Dei"* (*Rom. 1, 17*) *und "Justificatio"* (vol. 1, part 2; 2nd ed.; Mainz: F. Kirchheim, 1905). Karl Holl, "Die *iustitia dei* in der vorlutherischen Bibelauslegung des Abendlandes" (1921), reprinted in *Gesammelte Aufsätze, III: Der Westen* (1928; reprinted 1965) 171-88. Gordon Rupp, *The Righteousness of God: Luther Studies* (New York: Philosophical Library, 1953) 123-26.

204. See esp. Phil. 3:9: "the righteousness from God that depends on faith." Cf. 2 Cor. 5:21: ". . . so that in him [Christ] we might become the righteousness of God"; if not pre-Pauline (see above, §128), then it is Paul's own phrase expressing what Luther means by "*die Gerechtigkeit die vor Gott gilt.*" On the righteousness of God as "gift," see esp. R. Bultmann, *Theology* and "*Dikaiosyne Theou,*" as cited above in n. 132.

205. See esp. Rom. 3:5 and Käsemann, as cited above in n. 127; *Righteousness* ‡‡93, 381.

206. See above, n. 57.

207. Burgess, "Rewards . . . ," p. 104 in this volume.

208. See "*Righteousness*" *in the New Testament*, ‡‡280-83, cf. 413-14, and contrast 275; to the dissenting literature there cited can be added P. Stuhlmacher, "Schriftauslegung in der Confessio Augustana," *Kerygma und Dogma* 26 (1980) 201-202 (the texts, Stuhlmacher holds, cannot be reconciled; instead there must be a more systematic relating to the mission and death of Jesus for sinners from a Pauline perspective), and Jürgen Roloff, *Neues Testament* (Neukirchen-Vluyn: Neukirchener, 1977) 165-66. Cf. D. Lührmann, "Glaube," *Reallexikon für Antike und Christentum* 11 (1979) 78; *Glaube im Frühen Christentum* (Gütersloh: Gütersloher Verlagshaus Gerd Mohn, 1976).

209. Merit language appears frequently in the texts of the Roman liturgy, but words such as "*meritum,*" "*dignus,*" and "*iuste*" are often used in vague and poetical senses that do not lend themselves to precise theological interpretation. For example, the *praeconium paschale* in the Easter Vigil praises the sin of Adam "*quae talem ac tantum meruit redemptorem*" ("which merited such and so great a redeemer"). On Good Friday the wood of the cross is hailed for being "*digna ferre mundi victimam*" ("worthy to bear the victim of the world") (hymn, "*Pange lingua*" in the *Missale Romanum*, commonly called the Tridentine missal). In many of the old Roman collect prayers God is petitioned to grant favors in view of the

merits of the saints. Very frequently God or Christ is acknowledged as the giver of all our merits and is implored to grant us merits we do not have. Frequently also the faithful confess their own lack of merits, their unworthiness, and their need of mercy, as they do, for instance, in the *"Domine, non sum dignus"* ("Lord, I am not worthy") regularly recited before the reception of Holy Communion. There are also some texts in which God is acknowledged as justly giving to sinners and saints the rewards of their respective deeds.

Illustrative texts from the contemporary Roman liturgy would include the following: ". . . *et omnium sanctorum tuorum; quorum meritis precibusque concedas, ut in omnibus protectionis tuae muniamur anxilio"* (". . . and of all your saints; may their merits and prayers gain us your constant help and protection" [or more literally, ". . . and of all your saints; grant that through their merits and prayers we may be fortified by your protection in all things"]); Prex Eucharistica I, *Missale Romanum* (Editio typica; Typis Polyglottis Vaticanis, 1971) 448. The first translations given are those of ICEL (International Commission on English in the Liturgy) in *The Sacramentary* (New York: Catholic Book Publishing Co., 1974), followed by a more literal rendering *"Non aestimator meriti sed veniae quaesumus largitor admitte"* ("Do not consider our merits but grant us your forgiveness" [or "Receive us, we beg, not as a judge of merit but as a giver of mercy"]); ibid., 455. *"Gratias agentes quia nos dignos habuisti astare coram te et tibi ministrare"* ("We thank you for counting us worthy to stand in your presence and serve you"); Prex Eucharistica II, ibid., 458. Other texts: First Sunday of Advent, Opening Prayer: *Missale Romanum*, 129; Ash Wednesday, Prayer after Communion: ibid., 180; Wednesday of First Week of Lent, Opening Prayer: ibid., 188; Friday of Second Week of Lent, Opening Prayer: ibid., 198. Also pertinent is the final antiphon of the Blessed Virgin Mary starting with Saturday after the octave of Pentecost: *"Ora pro nobis, sancta Dei Genetrix, ut digni efficiamur promissionibus Christi"* ("Pray for us, holy Mother of God, that we may be made worthy of the promises of Christ"); *The Hours of the Divine Office in English and Latin* (Collegeville, Minn.: Liturgical Press, 1964) 3:4 of the supplementary material.

Regarding the collect which became the opening prayer for the fifth Sunday in Ordinary Time, A. Baumstark (*Comparative Liturgy* [Westminster, Md.: Newman, 1958] 61) observes that it was precisely the Pelagian and semi-Pelagian controversies that marked such collects in the ancient sacramentaries, particularly in the season after Pentecost. Some texts indicating a convergence between Catholic and Lutheran prayer language have been listed in L/RC 4:18-19. For additional texts consult the liturgical concordances such as Andre Pflieger, *Liturgicae Orationis Concordantia Verbalia: Prima Pars, Missale Romanum* (Freiburg: Herder, 1964); Thaddeus A. Schnitker and Wolfgang A. Slaby, *Concordantia Verbalia Missalis Romani* (Münster: Aschendorff, 1983).

210. Examples in recent American Lutheran hymnals, *The Lutheran Hymnal* (1941, LH); *Service Book and Hymnal* (1958, SBH); and *Lutheran Book of Worship* (1978, LBW), include the following: Luther (*"Aus tiefer Not,"* v. 3), *"Darum auf Gott will hoffen ich, auf mein Verdienst nicht bauen"* (LBW 295, 3, "It is in God that we shall hope, and not in our own merit"); (*"Nun Freut Euch,"* 3), *"Mein guten Werk die galten nicht, es war mit ihn' verdorben"* (LBW 299, 3, "My own good works all came to nought, No grace or merit gaining"); LBW 374, 3, ". . . forgiveness and salvation/ Daily come through Jesus' merit" (LH expanded trans. of Luther's *"Wir Glauben All"*). Paul Speratus (*"Es ist das Heil,"* 1523, v. 11), *"Der woll mit Gnad erfüllen, was er in uns angfangen hat"* (LBW 297, 5, "The God who saved us by his grace, all glory to his merit"). J. Major (*"Ach Gott und Herr,"* 1613, v. 3), *"Zu dir flieh ich; verstoss mich nicht, wie ichs wohl hab verdienet"* (LH 317, 3, "Lord, Thee I seek, I merit nought"). E. C. Homberg (*"Jesu, Meines Lebens Leben,"* 1659, v. 1), *"in das aüsserste Verderben, nur dasz ich nicht möchte sterben"* (LBW 97, 1 [tr. Catherine Winkworth], "Through your suff'ring, death, and merit/Life eternal I inherit"). J. Neander (*"Gott ist gegenwärtig,"* 1680), as translated in LH 4 and SBH 164, v. 3, "trusting only in thy merit."

Isaac Watts (Congregationalist; "Blest is the man," 1719), "He pleads no merit of reward/And not on works but grace relies" (LH 392, 2). Edward Mote (Baptist; ca. 1834), "My hope is built on nothing less/Than Jesus' blood and righteousness; No merit of my own I claim, But wholly lean on Jesus' name" (LBW 294, 1). J. M. Neale (Anglican; "Blessed Savior, who hast taught me," 1842), "Resting in my Savior's merit" (LH 333, 3; SBH 290, 3). K. J. P. Spitta (Lutheran; *"Wir sind des Herrn,"* 1843), trans. C. T. Astley (Anglican), "We are the Lord's. His all-sufficient merit . . . this grace accords" (LH 453, 1; LBW 399, 1). H. W. Baker (Anglican; "Ransomed, Restored, Forgiven," 1876), "Not ours, not ours the merit" (LH 32, 2); ("O Perfect Life of Love," 1875), "Thy works, O Lamb of God, I'll plead, Thy merits, not mine own" (LH 170, 6). LH 437, 3, "Who Trusts in God," ". . . Until we stand at Thy right hand/ Thro' Jesus' saving merit."

For many more examples, see E. V. Haserodt, *Concordance to The Lutheran Hymnal* (St. Louis: Concordia, 1956) 404-5, *s.v.* "merit, merits," noun and verb.

211. Quinn, "Merit," 89-90; Burgess, "Rewards . . . ," 107-108 in this volume.

212. *Dei verbum* 18.

213. *Breviloquium*, prol., n. 2. See George H. Tavard, *Transiency and Permanence. The Nature of Theology according to St. Bonaventure* (St. Bonaventure, N.Y.: Franciscan Institute, 1974); Renato Russo, *La Metodologia del sapere nel sermone di S. Bonaventura, Unus est Magister Vester Christus* (Grottaferrata: Collegio S. Bonaventurae, 1982).

214. Luther used the German phrase (sometimes translated "what inculcates Christ," LW 35:396) to indicate that the "genuine, sacred books" always

preach and teach Christ; Preface to the Epistles of St. James and St. Jude, 1546 (1522); WA DB 7:385, 27; LW 35:396. Such preaching and teaching must be normed by justification, i.e., by the way in which Christ made right the relationship between God and sinners (Rom. 3:21; 1 Cor. 2:2, quoted ibid.). *"Treiben"* is an old German verb which may have been widely used by seafarers. It may have been related to *"propellere—*to drive, to propel" and to *"trudere—*to thrust, to impel"; see Friedrich Kluge, *Etymologisches Wörterbuch der deutschen Sprache* (21st ed.; Berlin: de Gruyter, 1975) 788.

215. The disagreement over the canonical status of the so-called Aprocrypha or deuterocanonical books of the Old Testament is irrelevant to our present topic because, with the exception of a single passage (2 Macc. 12:42-45) purportedly referring to the tangential question of purgatory, these books have not been cited in the disputes relating to justification.

216. L/RC 6:37, 52-56 deals with the question of the acceptance of all church dogmas as a condition for church union. Page 54, §46, takes note of the limited eucharistic sharing that can exist between Roman Catholics and Orthodox notwithstanding the nonacceptance by the Orthodox of certain Roman Catholic dogmas such as papal infallibility and the Immaculate Conception.

217. MR #27.

218. S.T., II-II, q.18, a.4, ad 2. For discussions of the parallelism between Thomas Aquinas and Martin Luther on the assurance of salvation (ascribed by the former to hope and by the latter to faith), see S. Pfürtner, *Luther and Aquinas—A Conversation: Our Salvation, Its Certainty and Peril* (tr. Edward Quinn; New York: Sheed & Ward, 1965) and, more briefly, O. H. Pesch, *Theologie der Rechtfertigung bei Martin Luther und Thomas von Aquin: Versuch eines systematisch-theologischen Dialogs* (Walberger Studien der Albertus-Magnus Akademie, theologische Reihe 4; Mainz: Matthias-Grünewald, 1967) 262-83, 748-57.

Part II. Background Papers

1. Fitzmyer

1. "Gedanken zum Theologischen Wörterbuch zum Neuen Testament," a four-page insert that accompanied vol. 7 of TWNT (Stuttgart: Kohlhammer, 1964). It was not translated in TDNT.

2. Edited by J. Blank, R. Schnackenburg, E. Schweizer, and U. Wilckens (Einsiedeln: Benziger; Neukirchen-Vluyn: Neukirchener Verlag, 1969—).

3. Edited by J. Botterweck and H. Ringgren (Stuttgart: Kohlhammer, 1970—); translated as *Theological Dictionary of the Old Testament* (4 vols. to date; Grand Rapids: Eerdmans, 1977—).

4. Edited by H. Balz and G. Schneider (3 vols.; Stuttgart: Kohlhammer, 1978-83).

5. "The Office of Teaching in the Christian Church according to the New Testament," *Teaching Authority & Infallibility in the Church* (ed. P. C. Empie, T. A. Murphy, and J. A. Burgess; Minneapolis: Augsburg, 1980) 186-212.

6. "Teaching Office in the New Testament? A Response to Professor Fitzmyer's Essay," ibid., 213-31.

7. "On the Terminology for Faith, Truth, Teaching, and the Spirit in the Pastoral Epistles: A Summary," ibid., 232-37.

8. His paper was entitled, " 'Justification by Grace through Faith' as Expression of the Gospel: The Biblical Witness to the Reformation Emphasis" (see n. 13 below).

9. My response was entitled, "The Biblical Basis of Justification by Faith: Comments on the Essay of Professor Reumann" (see n. 13 below).

10. "The Pastoral Epistles on Righteousness" (see n. 13 below).

11. See pp. 82-93 below.

12. See pp. 94-110 below.

13. (Philadelphia: Fortress; Ramsey, N.J./New York: Paulist, 1982). Reumann's material appears on pp. 1-192, mine on pp. 193-227, and Quinn's on pp. 229-38. References are made in the common statement to this book; the symbol ‡ indicates the marginal paragraph numbers of this book.

14. Edited by P. C. Empie and T. A. Murphy (Lutherans and Catholics in Dialogue 5; Minneapolis: Augsburg, 1974).

15. Edited by R. E. Brown, K. P. Donfried, and J. Reumann (Minneapolis: Augsburg; Paramus, N.J./New York/Toronto: Paulist, 1973).

16. Ibid., 5; emphasis in the original.

17. A similar task force was commissioned to work on *Mary in the New Testament: A Collaborative Assessment by Protestant and Roman Catholic Scholars* (ed. R. E. Brown, K. P. Donfried, J. A. Fitzmyer, and J. Reumann; Philadelphia: Fortress; Ramsey, N.J./New York/Toronto: Paulist, 1978). This assessment was based on discussions by P. J. Achtemeier, M. M. Bourke, R. E. Brown, S. Brown, K. P. Donfried, J. A. Fitzmyer, K. Froehlich, R. H. Fuller, G. Krodel, J. L. Martyn, E. H. Pagels, and J. Reumann. Likewise sponsored by the national Roman Catholic-Lutheran dialogue, its assessment will serve as a basis for the work of the eighth series of the dialogue, dealing with "Mary and the Saints."

2. Quinn

1. P. Chantraine, *Dictionnaire étymologique de la langue grecque* (Paris: Klincksieck, 1968) I:94 (see 2 Cor. 4:17). The Latin **mer-* means *prize, price, value, earned salary, to receive one's share* and is to be compared with the Greek *meiromai/meros* (A. Ernout and A. Meillet, *Dictionnaire étymologique de la langue latine* [Paris: Klincksieck, 1958] 399).

   For essays and bibliography to which this study is indebted, see E. Lohse and G. Bornkamm, *"Verdienst," Religion in Geschichte und Gegenwart,* 3rd ed., 6:1261-66; *"Retribution"* by the editors of *Dictionnaire de la Bible, Supplément* 10 (fascicle 56, 1982) 582-86; Claude Wiener, "Reward," *Dictionary of Biblical Theology* (2nd ed.; ed. X. Leon-Dufour; New York: Seabury, 1973) 505-508; P. E. Davies, "Reward" and G. Barrois, "Wages," *Interpreter's Dictionary of the Bible* 4:71-74, 795; W. S. Towner, "Retribution," *Interpreter's Dictionary of the Bible, Supplementary Volume* 742-44; K. Seybold, *"gāmal," Theological Dictionary of the Old Testament* 3:23-33; K. Koch, *"ḥaṭa'," Theological Dictionary of the Old Testament* 4:309-19.

2. Many of the texts will be cited below; for further detail, see the articles cited in n. 1.

3. Cf. 1 Sam. 16:6-7 with Luke 1:25, 46-48, 52-53; 1 Cor. 4:4-5.

4. Thus Gen. 4:6, 10-15 on Cain; see G. Mendenhall, "The 'Vengeance' of Yahweh," *The Tenth Generation* (Baltimore: Johns Hopkins, 1973) 69-104, with the qualification by M. Greenberg, *Biblical Prose Prayer* (Berkeley: University of California Press, 1983) 13; 61, n. 6.

5. Ex. 21:23-24; Lev. 24:19-20; Deut. 19:21; J. Pritchard, *Ancient Near Eastern Texts* 175, #200, #219; 417 (c).

6. See Ex. 20:5-6; 34:6-7; Deut. 5:9-10 and all of ch. 28.

7. Tob. 11:15; 13:2, 5-6; Job 38:1–40:2; Eccl. 2:9-17; 9:1-6; Sir. 51:30.

8. Wis. 2:22 (cf. 1 Clem. 6:2; Rom. 6:23); Wis. 5:15-16 (cf. Manual of Discipline [1QS] 4:6-8). The effects of good deeds are stored with God in his heavenly home just as material treasures—gold, silver, and clothing—are deposited for safekeeping in his earthly temple. The goods are truly the property of the deity; they are truly the produce and property of the one who deposits them.

9. See 2 Cor. 5:15, "And he died for all, that those who live might live no longer for themselves but for him who for their sake died and was raised." In the argument of Rom. 5:9-10 it is thus expressed: "Since therefore we are now justified by (*en*) his blood, much more will we be saved by him (*di' autou*) from the wrath of God. For if while we were enemies we were reconciled to God by the death (*dia tou thanatou*) of his Son, much more, now that we are reconciled, shall we be saved by his life (*en tēi zōēi autou*)." The instrumental prepositions are integral to the argument (E. Käsemann, *Commentary on Romans* [Grand Rapids: Eerdmans, 1980] 138). See also

Rom. 5:3-5, with its use of *katergazetai* (cf. 2 Cor. 4:17) and the assertion that Christian hope will not be put to shame in the final judgment.

10. See 2 Cor. 8:9; Col. 3:16; Rom. 2:4; 9:23; 11:12, 33-36 for applications of the terminology for wealth to God and Christ.

11. Cf. Eph. 2:8-9 with Heb. 6:1; 9:11-14; 1 Pet. 1:14-19 on our dead works and futile ways. Good works are to our own works as merit is to simply human merit.

12. See J. Quinn, "Parenesis and the Pastoral Epistles," *De la Tôrah au Messie: Mélanges H. Cazelles* (ed. J. Doré; Paris: Desclée, 1981) 495-501.

13. The *-ma* suffix "denotes the result of *charis* viewed as an action with no sharp distinction from this term" (H. Conzelmann, *TDNT* 9:403; see also F. Blass, A. Debrunner, R. Funk, *A Greek Grammar of the New Testament and Other Early Christian Literature* [Chicago: University of Chicago, 1961] §109.2).

14. Contrast "the fruitless works (*erga akarpa*)" of Eph. 5:11. In Titus 3:14 the *akarpoi* are contrasted with those who take the lead in fine deeds (*kala erga*). In 2 Pet. 1:8 the *akarpoi* are synonymous with the *argoi*, i.e., the *a-ergoi*.

15. See J. Quinn, "The Spirit and Biblical Anthropology: Flesh and Spirit," *Credo in Spiritum Sanctum: Atti del Congresso Internazionale de Pneumatologia* (Rome: Libreria Editrice Vaticana, 1983) 2:865-871.

16. See K. J. Dover, *Greek Popular Morality* (Berkeley: University of California Press, 1974) 232. On all that follows, also see V.C. Pfitzner, *Paul and the Agon Motif* (Leiden: Brill, 1967) and the evocative essay by L. Gernet, "The Mythical Idea of Value in Greece," *The Anthropology of Ancient Greece* (Baltimore: Johns Hopkins, 1981) 73-111.

17. On the needless problems that persons bring on themselves by competition and ambition, see Menander, fragment 620.12-13, as in *Menandri quae supersunt* (ed. A. Koerte; Leipzig: Teubner, 1953) 2:198, or F. Sandbach, *Menandri reliquiae selectae* (Oxford: Clarendon, 1976) 320.

18. See J. Quinn, "The PE on Righteousness," in J. Reumann, *"Righteousness" in the NT* (Philadelphia: Fortress, 1982) 238.

19. Hermas, Sim. 9.21.2 contrasts *erga nekra* with words that live. I have not encountered the phrase "living works (*zōnta erga*)" in biblical Greek or documents of Hellenistic Judaism or of early Christianity.

20. For the *hōs* construction here, see Rom. 12:3; 1 Cor. 3:5; 7:17.

3. Burgess

1. Ap 4:24; BS 164-65; BC 110; Ap 4:194; BS 198; BC 133; Ap 4:375, cf. 366-67; BS 227, 229; BC 161, 163.

2. E. E. Kellett, "Rewards and Punishments," *Encyclopedia of Religion and Ethics* 10 (1919) 761-62.

3. Klaus Koch, "Gibt es ein Vergeltungsdogma im Alten Testament?" *Zeitschrift für Theologie und Kirche* 52 (1955) 37-39.

4. Peter Stuhlmacher, *Gerechtigkeit Gottes bei Paulus* (FRLANT 87; Göttingen: Vandenhoeck & Ruprecht, 1965) 46-50, 113-15; Wolfgang Harnisch, *Verhängnis und Verheissung der Geschichte* (FRLANT 97; Göttingen: Vandenhoeck & Ruprecht, 1969) 78-79, 154-55; Klaus Koch, ed., *Um das Prinzip der Vergeltung in Religion und Recht des Alten Testaments* (Wege der Forschung 125; Darmstadt: Wissenschaftliche Buchgesellschaft, 1972).

5. Klaus Koch, "Wesen und Ursprung der 'Gemeinschaftstreue' im Israel der Königszeit," *Zeitschrift für Evangelische Ethik* 5 (1961) 81, 90.

6. Martin Hengel, *Judaism and Hellenism* (Philadelphia: Fortress, 1974) I:120-21, cf. 115-20 (emphasis in the original).

7. Inge Lönning, *"Kanon im Kanon"* (Forschungen zur Geschichte und Lehre des Protestantismus, Ser. 10, vol. 43; Munich: Kaiser; Oslo: Universitets Forlaget, 1972) 220-22.

8. Johannes Beumer, "Die Kanonfrage und ihre katholische Lösung in den Versuchen der Aufklärungszeit und der Theologie der Gegenwart," *Catholica* 18(1964) 268-69.

9. Paul Althaus, "Verdienst Christi," *Religion in Geschichte und Gegenwart* 6 (3rd ed., 1962) 1270-71.

10. Michael Schmaus, *Dogma*, vol. 6, *Justification and the Last Things* (Kansas City: Sheed & Ward, 1977) 138; cited in Dulles, n. 60, below.

11. For the material in 1-10 above, see: Herbert Braun, *Gerichtsgedanke und Rechtfertigungslehre bei Paulus* (Untersuchungen zum Neuen Testament 19; Leipzig: J. C. Hinrichs'sche Buchhandlung, 1930) 14-31, 89-92; Karl P. Donfried, "Justification and Last Judgment in Paul," *Zeitschrift für die neutestamentliche Wissenschaft* 67 (1976) 90-110; Floyd V. Filson, *St. Paul's Conception of Recompense* (Untersuchungen zum Neuen Testament 21; Leipzig: J. C. Hinrichs'sche Buchhandlung, 1931) 128-31; Ernst Käsemann, *Commentary on Romans* (tr. G. Bromiley; Grand Rapids: Eerdmans, 1980) 53-61; Ulrich Luz, *Das Geschichtsverständnis des Paulus* (Beiträge zur evangelischen Theologie 49; Munich: Kaiser, 1968) 314-15; Lieselotte Mattern, *Das Verständnis des Gerichtes bei Paulus* (Abhandlungen zur Theologie des Alten und Neuen Testament 47; Zürich: Zwingli Verlag, 1966) 212-15; for a careful criticism of Mattern, see Luz, *Geschichtsverständnis*, 316: "For Paul what is essential is not the *idea* of judgment, but the way judgment functions in his proclamation"; K. Oltmanns, "Das Verhältnis von Röm 1,18–3,20 zu Röm 3,21ff," *Theologische Blätter* 8 (1929) 110-16; Heikki Räisänen, *Paul and the Law* (Wissenschaftliche Untersuchungen zum Neuen Testament 29; Tübingen: Mohr, 1983) 266-68; Calvin J. Roetzel, *Judgement in the Community* (Leiden: Brill, 1972) 1-13; E. P. Sanders, *Paul, the Law, and the Jewish People* (Philadelphia: Fortress, 1983) 105-6, 118-19; Ernst Synofzik, *Die Gerichts- und Vergeltungsaussagen bei Paulus* (Göttinger Theologische Arbeiten 8; Göttingen: Vandenhoeck & Ruprecht, 1977) 9-12, 105-10, 152-54.

12. Raymond E. Brown et al., eds., *Peter in the New Testament* (Minneapolis: Augsburg; New York/Paramus/Toronto: Paulist, 1973) 168; Raymond E. Brown et al., eds., *Mary in the New Testament* (Philadelphia: Fortress; New York/Ramsey/Toronto: Paulist, 1978) 294.

13. See August Strobel, *Erkenntnis und Bekenntnis der Sünde in neutestamentlicher Zeit* (Arbeiten zur Theologie, ser. 1, vol. 37; Stuttgart: Calwer, 1968) 21-22, 38-55, and literature cited there.

14. "Flesh" can also be used in a neutral sense, as in 1 Cor. 15:39, or as body, as in Phil. 1:22-24 and perhaps 1 Cor. 5:5. On this whole subject, see E. Schweizer, "*sarx*," TWNT 7:123-45; TDNT 7:124-144.

15. Small Catechism, Lord's Prayer, Fifth Petition; BS 514; BC 347; cf. Large Catechism, Lord's Prayer, Fifth Petition; BS 683; BC 432.

16. SA 3, 343-45; BS 448-49; BC 310.

17. WA 56:70; LW 25:63.

18. Werner G. Kümmel, *Römer 7 und das Bild des Menschen im Neuen Testament* (Theologische Bücherei 53; Munich: Kaiser, 1974; reprint of the ed. of 1929) 1-138.

19. WA 40/1:233; LW 26:133.

20. Luz, *Geschichtsverständnis*, 282-86.

21. Cf. Nils A. Dahl, "In What Sense is the Baptized Person 'simul iustus et peccator' according to the New Testament?" *Lutheran World* 9 (1962) 219-231; against Wilfried Joest, "Paulus und das Luthersche Simul Iustus et Peccator," *Kerygma und Dogma* 1 (1955) 271, 291.

22. H. Schlier, "*eleutheros*," TWNT 2:494; TDNT 2:498.

23. H. Schlier, *Der Römerbrief* (Herders theologischer Kommentar zum Neuen Testament 6; Freiburg/Basel/Vienna: Herder, 1977) 182.

24. WA 7:445.

25. Strobel, op. cit., 55.

26. Paul Althaus, *Paulus und Luther über den Menschen* (3rd ed.; Studien der Luther-Akademie 14; Gütersloh: Bertelsmann, 1958) 94-95; it is simply false to imply, as Althaus does (ibid., 57-60), that in Paul the sinner continues to be God's creature, but in Luther this is not the case (Strobel, op. cit., 55). Joest's attempt to affirm a genuine agreement between Paul and Luther on the actuality of sin on the one hand while positing on the other hand disagreement between Paul and Luther because Luther has made a dogmatic system out of sin's inevitability fails to take into account either Paul as a consistent although not systematic thinker or Luther as a creative thinker using personalistic categories (Joest, op. cit., 319).

27. Käsemann, op. cit., 58.

28. Ibid.

29. Günther Bornkamm, "Der Lohngedanke im Neuen Testament," *Studien zu Antike und Unchristentum. Gesammelte Aufsätze* (Beiträge zur evangelische Theologie 28; Munich: Kaiser, 1959) 2:89-91; in typical, paradoxical fashion Luther wrote: "If you consider worthiness, there is no merit and

no reward. . . . If you consider consequence, there is nothing either good or evil that does not have its reward" (WA 18:693-94; LW 33:152).

30. Other Pauline passages that say the same are: 1 Cor. 3:7; 2 Cor. 4:7; 5:18, 21; Gal. 2:20; Phil. 1:6; 3:12.

31. Eberhard Jüngel, *Paulus und Jesus* (2nd ed.; Hermeneutische Untersuchungen zur Theologie 2; Tübingen: Mohr, 1964) 69-70.

32. Rom. 2:1-11; 14:10-12; 1 Cor. 3:8; 5:5; 2 Cor. 5:10; 9:6; Gal. 6:7-8; Sanders, *Paul, the Law, and the Jewish People*, 132, makes the telling statement: "Nevertheless, even when one considers that Paul is not always consistent, that he not infrequently incorporates and makes use of material which he did not coin, and that he often draws on Diaspora synagogue traditions in discussing behavior, Romans 2 still stands out. It stands out because it deals directly with salvation and makes salvation dependent on obedience to the law. What is said about the law in Romans 2 cannot be fitted into a category otherwise known from Paul's letters. . . . "

33. Rom. 6:4; 14:1; 1 Cor. 3:1-3, 6; 8:7-9; 2 Cor. 10:15; cf. Joest, op. cit., 280-82.

34. Cf. rest (Heb. 4:1); possession (Heb. 10:34); reward (Heb. 11:26).

35. H. Conzelmann, *A Commentary on the First Epistle to the Corinthians* (tr. J. W. Leitch; Philadelphia: Fortress, 1975) 76-77; a further question is whether the proclaimer of the gospel, the "apostle," is to receive a special reward for proclaiming the gospel. Reicke has pointed to possible Old Testament parallels for this possibility in Isa. 40:10-11 and 62:11; New Testament indications might be Rev. 14:3-4; John 4:36; Luke 6:35, 38; and 1 Pet. 2:12; 3:1-2 (Bo Reicke, "The New Testament Conception of Reward," *Aux sources de la tradition chretienne* [Festschrift Goguel; Neuchatel/Paris: Delachaux & Niestlé, 1950] 200-201; cf. Filson, op. cit., 107-8); W. Pesch has developed this thesis, particularly on the basis of 1 Cor. 3:8, 14-15 (Wilhelm Pesch, "Der Sonderlohn für die Verkündiger des Evangeliums," *Neutestamentliche Aufsätze* [Festschrift Josef Schmid; ed. J. Blinzler et al.; Regensburg: Pustet, 1963] 199-206; see also 1 Cor. 4:5; 9:17-18; Gal. 2:2; Phil. 2:16; 4:1; 1 Thess. 2:19-20; 3:5). At stake in this debate is whether the apostle as the place of Jesus' epiphany is separate from the rest of the body of believers (cf. Erhardt Güttgemanns, *Der Leidende Apostel und sein Herr* [FRLANT 90; Göttingen: Vandenhoeck & Ruprecht, 1966] 94-97, 195-98, 323-28). Paul, at least, does not make this distinction, for he expects converts to be imitators of him (1 Cor. 4:16; 11:1; Gal. 4:12; Phil. 3:17; 1 Thess. 1:6; 2:14), and he uses "apostle" in a broad sense (Luz, *Geschichtsverständnis*, 385).

36. R. Bultmann, *Der zweite Brief an die Korinther* (Kritisch-exegetischer Kommentar über das Neue Testament, Sonderband; Göttingen: Vandenhoeck & Ruprecht, 1976) 99.

37. Conzelmann, op. cit., 282.

38. U. Luz, "Rechtfertigung bei den Paulusschülern," *Rechtfertigung* (Festschrift Käsemann; Göttingen: Vandenhoeck & Ruprecht, 1976) 371-75.

39. Ibid., 376-82.

40. Wolfgang Schrage, "Der Jakobusbrief," *Die "Katholischen" Briefe* (11th ed.; Das Neue Testament Deutsch 10; Göttingen: Vandenhoeck & Ruprecht, 1973) 34.

41. Albrecht Peters, *Glaube und Werk. Luthers Rechtfertigungslehre im Lichte der Heiligen Schrift* (2nd ed.; Arbeiten zur Geschichte und Theologie des Luthertums 8; Berlin and Hamburg: Lutherisches Verlagshaus, 1967) 229-35.

42. Ernst Dassmann, *Das Stachel im Fleisch. Paulus in der frühchristlichen Literatur bis Irenäus* (Münster: Aschendorff, 1979) 316-20; Andreas Lindemann, *Paulus im ältesten Christentum* (Beiträge zur historischen Theologie 58; Tübingen: Mohr, 1979) 396-403.

43. E. P. Sanders, *Paul and Palestinian Judaism* (Philadelphia: Fortress, 1977) 552.

44. Hans Hübner, "Pauli Theologiae Proprium," *New Testament Studies* 26 (1980) 472-45; cf. Lindemann, op. cit., 403.

45. Luz, "Rechtfertigung," 383.

46. A. N. Wilder, *Eschatology and Ethics in the Teaching of Jesus* (2nd ed.; New York: Harper & Brothers, 1950) 88-90.

47. H. Preisker, "*misthos*," TWNT 4:724; TDNT 4:718; cf. F. Berrouard, "Le mérite dans les Évangiles synoptiques," *Istina* 3 (1956) 197; Bornkamm, op. cit., 78; Martin Wagner, "Der Lohngedanke im Evangelium," *Neue kirchliche Zeitschrift* 43 (1932) 135; Wilder, op. cit., 96-97.

48. Reicke, op. cit., 196; cf. G. de Ru, "The Conception of Reward in the Teaching of Jesus," *Novum Testamentum* 8 (1966) 217-18.

49. Pesch, op. cit., 139.

50. de Ru, op. cit., 219; Preisker, op. cit., 717-19; Wilder, op. cit., 108.

51. Preisker, op. cit., 718.

52. Bornkamm, op. cit., 72-73.

53. For the five interpretations, see de Ru, op. cit., 203-210.

54. U. Luz, "Die Erfüllung des Gesetzes bei Matthäus (Mt 5, 17-20)," *Zeitschrift für Theologie und Kirche* 75 (1978) 434-35.

55. Wagner, op. cit., 129-32.

56. Ap 4:372; BS 230; BC 164.

57. FC SD 11:52-53; BS 1079; BC 625.

58. Ap 4:364; BS 229; BC 162-63.

59. FC SD 11:92; BS 1090; BC 632.

4. Eno

1. A longer version with full documentation will be found in *Recherches Augustiniennes* 19 (1984) 3-27.

2. Origen, *Comm. in Rom.* 4.1 (PG 14:965).

3. Marius Victorinus, *Comm. in Gal.* 2:15-16 (ed. A. Locher; Bibliotheca Teubneriana, Latin vol. 245; Leipzig: B. G. Teubner, 1976) 26.
4. Marius Victorinus, *Comm. in Gal.* 5:6, ibid., 61.
5. Marius Victorinus, *Comm. in Eph.* 5:1, ibid., 190.
6. Ambrosiaster, *Comm. in Rom.* 3:24 (ed. H. J. Vogels; CSEL 81/1; Vindobonae: Hölder-Pichler-Tempsky, 1966) 119.
7. Ambrosiaster, *Comm. in Titum* 3:7, ibid., CSEL 81/3:332.
8. Ambrosiaster, *Comm. in Rom.* 3:21, ibid., CSEL 81/1:117.
9. Ambrosiaster, *Comm. in Rom.* 2:15, ibid., CSEL 81/1:77.
10. Ambrosiaster, *Comm. in Gal.* 5:6, ibid., CSEL 81/3:55.
11. Ambrosiaster, *Comm. in Gal.* 3:12, ibid., CSEL 81/3:34.
12. Pelagius, *Comm. in Rom.* 3:24. *Expositiones XIII Epist. Pauli* (ed. A Souter; Texts and Studies 9, 2; Cambridge, England: Cambridge University Press, 1926) 32.
13. Pelagius, *Comm. in Rom.* 4:6, ibid., 37.
14. Pelagius, *Comm. in Eph.* 6:23, ibid., 386.
15. John Chrysostom, *Encomium on St. Paul* 6.9 (ed. A. Piédagnel; SC 300; Paris: Editions du Cerf, 1982) 278.
16. John Chrysostom, *Hom. in Rom.* 11:1 (PG 60:483).
17. John Chrysostom, *Hom. in Rom.* 14:6 (PG 60:531).
18. Augustine, *De perfectione iustitiae hominis* 5.11. *Oeuvres de Saint Augustin* (ed. G. de Plinval and J. de la Tullaye; Bibliothèque augustinienne 21; Paris: Desclée de Brouwer, 1966) 142.
19. Augustine, *De gratia Christi* 9.10 (BA 22:72).
20. Augustine, *Tractatus in Johannem* 26.1 (BA 72:482).
21. Augustine, *Sermo* 170.10 (PL 38:932).
22. Augustine, *De spiritu et littera* 32.56 (ed. S. Kopp; *Schriften gegen die Pelagianer I;* Würzburg: Augustinus Verlag, 1971) 408.
23. Augustine, *Comm. in Gal.* 44.4 (ed. J. Divjak; CSEL 84; Vindobonae: Hölder-Pichler-Tempsky, 1971) 118.
24. Augustine, *Sermo* 162A.4 (*Sermo* Denis 19), *Miscellanea Agostiniana Sancti Augustini Sermones post Maurinos reperti I* (ed. G. Morin; Rome: Tipografia Poliglotta Vaticana, 1930) 101.
25. Augustine, *Sermo* 158.5 (PL 38:864).
26. Augustine, *De perfectione iustitiae hominis* 8.19 (BA 21:158).
27. Augustine, *Sermo* 169.13 (PL 38:923).
28. Augustine, *De perfectione iustitiae hominis* 3.7 (BA 21:134).
29. Augustine, *Sermo* 158.4 (PL 38:864).
30. *2 Clement* 1:3; Polycarp *Ep.* 1:2-3, alluding to Eph. 2:8. *The Apostolic Fathers* (ed. K. Lake; Loeb Classical Library; Cambridge, Mass.: Harvard University Press, 1965, reprint of 1912 ed.) 128, 282, 284.
31. Tertullian, *Adversus Marcionem* 5.13 (ed. E. Evans; Oxford Early Christian Texts; Oxford: Oxford University Press, 1972) 594.

32. Origen, *Contra Celsum* 3.69 (ed. M. Borret; SC 136; Paris: Editions du Cerf, 1968) 158.
33. Cyprian, *Ad Donatum* 4 (ed. M. Simonetti; CCL 3A; Turnholt: Brepols, 1976) 4-5.
34. Ambrose, *Ep.* 73.11 (PL 16:1254).
35. *1 Clement* 33:1, 7 (Loeb 1:62,64).
36. Cyprian, *De oratione* 12 (ed. C. Moreschini; CCL 3A:96).
37. Cyprian, *De opere et eleemosynis* 2 (ed. M. Simonetti; CCL 3A:55-56).
38. Cyril of Jerusalem, *Catechesis* 4.2 (PG 33:456).
39. Gregory the Great, *Hom.* 14.3 (PL 76:1129-30); Ignatius of Antioch, *Eph.* 14.1 (Loeb 1:188).
40. Tertullian, *De exhortatione castitatis* 3 (ed. A. Kroymann; CCL 2:1019).
41. Ambrose, *De Jacob* 1.6.23 (ed. C. Schenkl; CSEL 32/2; Vindobonae: Tempsky-Freytag, 1897) 18.

5. Rusch

1. Eric W. Gritsch and Robert W. Jenson, *Lutheranism: The Theological Movement and Its Confessional Writings* (Philadelphia: Fortress, 1980) 40.
2. G. W. H. Lampe, *A Patristic Greek Lexicon* (Oxford: Clarendon, 1961) 370-71.
3. Gritsch and Jenson, op. cit., 42-44.
4. George A. Lindbeck, "Article IV and Lutheran/Roman Catholic Dialogue," *Lutheran Theological Seminary Bulletin*, Gettysburg, Pa., 61 (Winter, 1981) 5.
5. Ibid.
6. Panagoitis N. Trembelas has assembled a considerable amount of material on justification as a concept in the Greek Fathers in his *Dogmatique de l'Église Orthodoxe Catholique*, vol. 2. The problem with Trembelas' presentation is that it implies a systematic presentation of this topic in Eastern patristic literature. This is not true; see his *Dogmatique* (tr. P. Dumont; Chevetogne: Desclée de Brouwer, 1967) 2:288-377. See further: G. Bardy, "Divinisation, II and III," *Dictionnaire de spiritualité, ascetique et mystique* 3 (1957) 1375-98; P. B. T. Bilaniuk, "The Mystery of theosis or divinization," *Orientalia Christiana Analecta* 195 (1973) 337-59; O. Faller, "Griechische Vergöttung und Christliche Vergöttung," *Gregorianum* 6 (1925) 405-35; M. Farantos, "Die Gerechtigkeit bei Klemens von Alexandrien," (dissertation, Bonn, 1972); Jules Gross, *La Divinisation de Chrétien d'après les peres grecs* (Paris: Gabalda, 1938); M. Lot-Borodine, "La doctrine de la deification dans l'Église grecque jusqu' au XIe siècle," *Revue de l'histoire des religions* 105 (1932) 5-43; 106 (1932) 525-74; 107 (1933)

8-55; A. Schmitt, "Dikaiosynē Theou," *Natalicium. Johannes Geffcken* (Festschrift Geffcken; Heidelberg: C. Winter, 1931) 111-31.
7. See V. Capanaga, "La deification en la soteriologia augustiniana," *Augustinus Magister* (Supplement of L' Année Théologique Augustinienne; Paris: Études Augustiniennes, 1954) 2:745-55.

6. Froehlich

1. This essay appears here in an abbreviated form without its documentation. The complete, annotated text will be published elsewhere in the near future.
2. Only a few general studies can be mentioned here. Roman Catholic: J. Rivière, "Justification," DThC 8 (1924) 2042-2227; J. Auer, *Das Evangelium der Gnade. Kleine katholische Dogmatik* (vol. 5; 2nd ed.; ed. J. Auer and J. Ratzinger; Regensburg: Pustet, 1970); P. Fransen, "Dogmengeschichtliche Entfaltung der Gnadenlehre," *Mysterium Salutis* (ed. J. Feiner and M. Löhrer; Einsiedeln: Benziger, 1973) 4/2:631-765; G. Greshake, *Geschenkte Freiheit: Einführung in die Gnadenlehre* (Freiburg/Basel/Wien: Herder, 1977); O. H. Pesch and A. Peters, *Einführung in die Lehre von Gnade und Rechtfertigung* (Darmstadt: Wissenschaftliche Buchgesellschaft, 1981). Protestant: A. Ritschl, *Die christliche Lehre von der Rechtfertigung und Versöhnung. Erster Band: Die Geschichte* (4th ed.; Bonn: Marcus und Weber, 1908); J. Bauer, *Salus Christiana. Die Rechtfertigungslehre in der Geschichte des christlichen Heilsverständnisses. Band 1: Von der christlichen Antike bis zur Theologie der deutschen Aufklärung* (Gütersloh: Mohn, 1968); G. Müller, *Die Rechtfertigungslehre: Geschichte und Probleme (Studienbücher Theologie*; Gütersloh: Mohn, 1977). For some time the British scholar A. E. McGrath has announced a comprehensive monograph on the history of justification, to be published by James Clarke, Cambridge. His volumes are not yet available.
3. See J. de Ghellinck, "Pierre Lombard," DThC 12:2 (1935) 1954-59. On the place of the work in the development of the Gloss, see B. Smalley, *The Study of the Bible in the Middle Ages* (Oxford: Blackwell, 1952) 64. The commentary on Romans has been reprinted from Josse Bade's Paris edition (1535) in a usable, though not always reliable form by Migne PL 191:1298-1534; the title *Collectanea* is not original. I will cite the Migne edition by column and section.
4. The history of the theme is surveyed in two excellent fascicles of the *Handbuch der Dogmengeschichte* (ed. M. Schmaus, A. Grillmeier, L. Scheffczyk, and M. Seybold; Freiburg/Basel/Vienna: Herder, since 1951): L. Scheffczyk, *Urstand, Fall und Erbsünde von der Schrift bis Augustin* (vol. 2/3a, pt. 1, 1981), and H. Köster, *Urstand, Fall, und Erbsünde in der Scholastik* (vol. 2/3b, 1979). Other important literature includes A. M. Landgraf, *Dogmengeschichte der Frühscholastik* (Regensburg: Gregorius-Verlag, 1953) 1/2:204-81; 4/1-2 (1955-56); J. N. Espenberger, *Die Elemente*

der Erbsünde nach Augustin und der Frühscholastik (Forschungen zur christlichen Literatur und Dogmengeschichte 5/1; Mainz: F. Kirchheim, 1905); R. M. Martin, *La controverse sur le péché originel au début du XIVe siécle* (Louvain: Louvain University, 1930); J. Gross, *Geschichte des Erbsündendogmas: Ein Beitrag zur Geschichte des Problems vom Ursprung des Übels* (vols. 1-3; Munich/Basel: Reinhardt, 1960-71); L. Hödl, "Theologische Neuansätze zum Verständnis des peccatum originale im 12. Jahrhundert," *Sapientiae Doctrina* (*Mélanges H. Bascour;* Louvain: Abbaye de Mont-César, 1980) 119-36. One of H. Rondet's comprehensive studies is available in English: *Original Sin. The Patristic and Theological Background* (Shannon, Ireland: Ecclesia Press, 1972).

5. In addition to the literature mentioned in n. 2, and Landgraf, *Dogmengeschichte* 1/1-2, the important studies include: J. Schupp, *Die Gnadenlehre des Petrus Lombardus* (Freiburger Theologische Studien 35; Freiburg: Herder, 1932); J. Auer, *Die Entwicklung der Gnadenlehre in der Hochscholastik* (vols. 1-2; Freiburg: Herder, 1942-51); E. Iserloh, *Gnade und Eucharistie in der philosophischen Theologie des Wilhelm von Ockham* (Wiesbaden: F. Steiner, 1956); B. Lonergan, *Grace and Freedom: Operative Grace in the Thought of St. Thomas Aquinas* (New York: Herder and Herder, 1971); B. Hamm, *Promissio, Pactum, Ordinatio: Freiheit und Selbstbindung Gottes in der scholastischen Gnadenlehre* (Tübingen: Mohr-Siebeck, 1977).

6. The problem with the term "Pelagianism" is well stated by H. A. Oberman: "Here we touch on one of the most difficult, as yet insufficiently explored, aspects of medieval thought: the flavor of the accusation, 'Pelagian,' and its concomitant verb, 'to pelagianize,' shifted from author to author, just as opinions varied considerably with regard to the position Pelagius actually took" (*Forerunners of the Reformation. The Shape of Late Medieval Thought Illuminated by Key Documents* [New York/Chicago: Holt, Rinehart and Winston, 1966] 126). In addition to Oberman's various studies and Landgraf, *Dogmengeschichte* 1/1 (1952) 144-48, see also H. McSorley, *Luther: Right or Wrong? An Ecumenical-Theological Study of Luther's Major Work, The Bondage of the Will* (New York: Newman; Minneapolis: Augsburg, 1966) 7-215, for an instructive and well-documented survey of Pelagianism in the Middle Ages. The understanding of medieval "Augustinianism" is in great flux today. Special interest concentrates on a *schola moderna Augustiniana* and its place in late medieval thought; see D. Trapp, "Augustinian Theology of the Fourteenth Century. Notes on Editions, Marginalia, Opinions, and Book Lore," *Augustiniana* 6 (1956) 146-274; A. Zumkeller, "Die Augustinerschule des Mittelalters: Vertreter und philosophisch-theologische Lehre (Übersicht nach dem neuesten Stand der Forschung)," *Analecta Augustiniana* 27 (1964) 167-262. Zumkeller's detailed studies of individual theologians in numerous journals have shed considerable light on what developed, especially in the Augustinian order. For a recent assessment, cf. H. A. Oberman, "Augustinrenaissance im späten

Mittelalter," *Werden und Wertung der Reformation* (Tübingen: Mohr-Sie-beck, 1977) 82-140. A. E. McGrath, "Augustinianism? A Critical Assess-ment of the So-Called 'Medieval Augustinian Tradition' on Justification," *Augustiniana* 31 (1981) 247-67, stresses the diversity of combinations which defies any neat classification.

7. Important studies on this topic include: J. Rivière, "Mérite," DThC 10 (1928) 574-785; Landgraf, *Dogmengeschichte* 1/1 (1952) 238-302; 1/2 (1953) 75-110; W. Dettloff, *Die Lehre von der acceptatio divina bei Jo-hannes Duns Scotus mit besonderer Berücksichtigung der Rechtfertigungs-lehre* (Franziskanische Forschungen 10; Werl: Dietrich Coelde, 1954); *Die Entwicklung der Akzeptations- und Verdienstlehre von Duns Scotus bis Lu-ther mit besonderer Berücksichtigung der Franziskanertheologen* (Beiträge zur Geschichte der Philosophie des Mittelalters 40:2; Münster: Aschendorff, 1964); O. H. Pesch, "Die Lehre vom 'Verdienst' als Problem für Theologie und Verkündigung," *Wahrheit und Verkündigung* (Festschrift M. Schmaus; vol. 2; ed. L. Scheffczyk and W. Dettloff; Paderborn: F. Schöningh, 1967) 1865-1907; Hamm, *Promissio* (n. 5 above); A. Solignac, "Mérite," *Dic-tionnaire de la Spiritualité* 10 (1980) 1040-51.

8. Important studies: Landgraf, *Dogmengeschichte* 1/1 (1952) 141-201; 238-302; 1/2 (1953) 7-40; two fascicles of *Handbuch der Dogmengeschichte*: I. Escribano-Alberca, *Glaube und Gotteserkenntnis in der Schrift und der Patristik* (Bd. 1/2a, 1974), and E. Gössmann, *Glaube und Gotteserkenntnis im Mittelalter* (Bd. 1/2b, 1971); G. Englhardt, *Die Entwicklung der dog-matischen Glaubenspsychologie in der mittelalterlichen Scholastik* (Beiträge zur Geschichte der Philosophie und Theologie des Mittelalters 30:4-6; Müns-ter: Aschendorff, 1933); M. Seckler, *Instinkt und Glaubenswille nach Thom-as von Aquin* (Mainz: Matthias-Grünewald-Verlag, 1961).

9. B. Hägglund, *The Background of Luther's Doctrine of Justification in Late Medieval Theology* (Philadelphia: Fortress, 1971) 10.

10. For this section, see especially the valuable essay by H. Bornkamm, "*Ius-titia Dei* in der Scholastik und bei Luther," *Archiv für Reformationsge-schichte* 39 (1942) 1-46; also H. A. Oberman, " 'Justitia Christi' and 'Justitia Dei.' Luther and the Scholastic Doctrine of Justification," *Harvard Theological Review* 59 (1966) 1-26.

7. Gritsch

1. Evidence on Luther's early years has been collected by Otto Scheel, *Martin Luther. Vom Katholizismus zur Reformation* (3rd. ed. rev.; 2 vols.; Tüb-ingen: Mohr, 1917-21). Literature on both Luther's relation to late medieval thought and the date of his "conversion" is extensive. Overviews have been presented by Bernhard Lohse, ed., *Der Durchbruch der reformato-rischen Erkenntnis bei Luther* (Wege der Forschung 123; Darmstadt: Wis-senschaftliche Buchgesellschaft, 1968). A rather convincing approach is

offered by Otto H. Pesch, "Zur Frage nach Luthers reformatorischer Wende," ibid., 445-505. By the same author, "Neuere Beiträge zur Frage nach Luthers 'reformatorischer Wende,' " *Catholica* 4 (1983) 259-87. On Luther's relationship to nominalism and mysticism see Bengt Hägglund, "The Background of Luther's Doctrine of Justification in Late Medieval Theology," *Lutheran World* 8 (1961) 24-46 (reprinted as Facet Book [Philadelphia: Fortress, 1971]). A survey of issues and answers is presented by Bernhard Lohse, *Martin Luther. Eine Einführung in sein Leben und Werk* (Munich: Beck, 1981) 157-60. See also Marilyn J. Harran, *Luther on Conversion. The Early Years* (Ithaca and London: Cornell University Press, 1983).

2. CA, Conclusion 5; BS 134; BC 95.

3. The phrase is derived from Luther's Smalcald Articles, 1537, 2, 1:5; BS 415; BC 292. There he linked *sola fide* to the "office and work" of Christ, whose justification of sinners is the "first and chief article." The phrase appears for the first time in Valentin E. Löscher's anti-Pietist essay, *Timotheus Verinus* (Wittenberg, 1718) 342. See Friedrich Loofs, "Der *articulus stantis et cadentis ecclesiae*," *Theologische Studien und Kritiken* 90 (1917) 323-420; on the phrase, 345. On Luther's conviction that the article of justification was the basic condition for unity, see Scott H. Hendrix, *Luther and the Papacy. Stages in a Reformation Conflict* (Philadelphia: Fortress, 1981) 149. At issue was Lutheran participation at the Council of Trent in 1545.

4. For a summary of the history and problems see Gerhard Müller, *Die Rechtfertigungslehre* (Studienbücher Theologie, Kirchen- und Dogmengeschichte; Gütersloh: Mohn, 1977); and Vittorio Subilia, *Die Rechtfertigung aus Glauben. Gestalt und Wirkung vom Neuen Testament bis heute* (tr. Max Krumbach; Göttinger theologische Lehrbücher; Göttingen: Vandenhoeck & Ruprecht, 1981) ch. 3. On the significance of justification for contemporary Catholicism see Otto H. Pesch, *Gerechtfertigt aus Glauben. Luthers Frage an die Kirche* (ed. Karl Rahner and Heinrich Schlier; Questiones Disputatae 97; Freiburg/Basel/Vienna: Herder, 1982).

5. Luther has been called a professor of Old Testament; see Heinrich Bornkamm, *Luther and the Old Testament* (tr. Eric W. and Ruth C. Gritsch; Philadelphia: Fortress, 1969) 7.

6. Lohse, *Martin Luther*, 157.

7. For a detailed evaluation of the evidence see Leif Grane, *Modus Loquendi Theologicus. Luthers Kampf um die Erneuerung der Theologie* (1515-1518) (ed. Torben Christensen et al.; tr. Eberhard Grötzinger; Acta Theologica Danica 12; Leiden: Brill, 1975) chs. 1-3.

8. Luther recalled his quest for a gracious God in the "Sermon on Baptism" (WA 37:661.20-26).

9. On the influence of Staupitz see David C. Steinmetz, *Luther and Staupitz. An Essay in the Intellectual Origins of the Protestant Reformation* (ed.

Arthur B. Ferguson et al.; Duke Mc .ographs in Medieval and Renaissance Studies 4; Durham, N.C.: Duke University Press, 1980) esp. 141-44. See also Eric W. Gritsch, *Martin—God's Court Jester. Luther in Retrospect* (Philadelphia: Fortress, 1983) 11-12.

10. "Preface to the Complete Edition of Luther's Latin Writings," 1545 (WA 54:185.17-20; 186.3-9; LW 34:336-7. Emphasis added.

11. "Two Kinds of Righteousness," 1519 (WA 2:145.9-12; 146.36-147.3. LW 31:297; 299).

12. "On Translating," 1530 (WA 30/2:636.11-638.22; LW 35:187-89).

13. Especially in the "Disputation Against Scholastic Theology," 1517 (WA 1:221-28; LW 31:9-16). See also Grane, *Modus Loquendi*, 133-35.

14. *The Heidelberg Disputation*, 1518 (WA 1:361.32-362.3; LW 31:40). Translation mine. See also Walter von Loewenich, *Luther's Theology of the Cross* (tr. Herbert J. Bouman; Minneapolis: Augsburg, 1976) part 1.

15. WA 1:362.18-19; LW 31:53.

16. *Lectures on Galatians*, 1535 (WA 40/1:589.25-28; LW 26:387).

17. *"Die hoechste Kunst im Christentum."* Sermon on Gal. 3, January 1, 1532 (WA 36:9.28-29).

18. Gerhard Müller, *Die Rechtfertigungslehre*, 56.

19. Disputation of 1537 on 1 Cor. 13:10 (WA 39/1:241.11-22).

20. Disputation on Matt. 22:1-14, 1537 (WA 39/1:283.18-19).

21. See the interpretation of Eph. 5:31-32 in *The Freedom of a Christian*, 1520 (WA 7:55,8-14, 24-27; German ibid., 25.34; LW 31:351-52).

22. Small Catechism, 1529. The Creed, Second Article, 4; BS 511; BC 345.

23. Luther called Paul and John "two high commanders" who are on his side in his fight against "freedom of the will." *The Bondage of the Will*, 1525 (WA 18:757.9-10; LW 33:247). On Luther's Christology see Marc Lienhard, *Luther's Witness to Jesus Christ* (tr. Edwin H. Robertson; Minneapolis: Augsburg, 1982).

24. See Wilhelm Maurer, "Die Anfänge von Luthers Theologie," *Kirche und Geschichte. Gesammelte Aufsätze*. Vol. I: *Luther und das evangelische Bekenntnis* (ed. Ernst-Wilhelm Kohls and Gerhard Müller; Göttingen: Vandenhoeck & Ruprecht, 1970) 28-32.

25. See Regin Prenter, *Spiritus Creator* (tr. John M. Jensen; Philadelphia: Muhlenberg, 1953) 288-305.

26. See the title of Luther's incomplete attempt to write a treatise on justification: *Rhapsodia seu Concepta in Librum de loco Iustificationis*, 1530 (WA 30/2:657).

27. *Commentary on Gal.* 3:12, 1535 (WA 40/1:27.21).

28. Smalcald Articles, 1537, 2, 1:5; BS 415; BC 292.

29. Letter of May 15, 1530, to Elector John (WA Br 5:319.6-9; LW 49:297-98).

30. This is the real intention of the Augsburg Confession if read from the viewpoint of Melanchthon's Apology of the Augsburg Confession; see Robert W. Jenson, "On Recognizing the Augsburg Confession," in *The Role of the Augsburg Confession. Catholic and Lutheran Views* (ed. Joseph A. Burgess; Philadelphia: Fortress, 1980) 153.

31. 2:2; BS 54; BC 29.

32. Jenson, "On Recognizing the Augsburg Confession," 153.

33. 5:2; BS 58; BC 31.

34. BS 84; BC 48.

35. Conclusion of part I: 1; BS 83d; BC 47.

36. "Table Talk," 1530s, no. 4780 (WA TR 4:495.7-9).

37. 4:1; BS 56; BC 30.

38. BS 60; BC 31-32. Emphasis added.

39. *Confutatio* 6:3; CR 27:99; Herbert Immenkötter, *Die Confutatio der Confessio Augustana vom 3. August 1530* (Corpus Catholicorum 33; Münster: Aschendorff, 1979) 90, 18-21; English translation in J. M. Reu, ed. and tr., *The Augsburg Confession: A Collection of Sources with an Historical Introduction* (Chicago: Wartburg Publishing House, 1930; reprinted, St. Louis: Concordia Seminary, 1966) 352.

40. BS 158-233; BC 107-68.

41. Otto H. Pesch, *Die Theologie der Rechtfertigung bei Martin Luther und Thomas von Aquin: Versuch eines systematisch-theologischen Dialogs* (Walberger Studien der Albertus Magnus Akademie, theologische Reihe 4; Mainz: Matthias Grünewald, 1967) 956. Translation mine.

42. Cardinal Jan Willebrands, "Gesandt in die Welt," *Lutherische Rundschau* 20 (1970) 459. Speech at the Assembly of the Lutheran World Federation in Evian. Translation mine. The German text reads "*gemeinsamer Lehrer,*" which was translated "we could all learn from him" in the English version (see *Lutheran World* 17 [1970] 351).

43. This was the view of Joseph Lortz, *The Reformation in Germany* (2 vols.; tr. Ronald Walls; New York and London: Herder, 1968) 1:200.

44. Hans J. Iwand, *Rechtfertigungslehre und Christusglaube. Eine Untersuchung zur Systematik der Rechtfertigungslehre Luthers in ihren Anfängen* (Theologische Bücherei 14; Munich: Kaiser, 1961) 1.

45. Gerhard Müller, *Die Rechtfertigungslehre,* 60.

46. Gerhard O. Forde, *Justification by Faith—A Matter of Death and Life* (Philadelphia: Fortress, 1982) 18.

47. George H. Tavard, *Justification. An Ecumenical Study* (New York: Paulist Press, 1983) 67.

48. Ibid., 112-13.

49. *Lectures on Galatians,* 1535 (WA 40/1:181, 10-13; LW 26:99).

8. Bertram

1. Ap. 4:2; BS 159; BC 107.
2. Ap 4:1; BS 158; BC 107.
3. Ibid.
4. Quoted in BC 107, n. 8. See *Confutatio Pontificia,* Part I, Article VI, in J. Michael Reu, ed., *The Augsburg Confession: A Collection of Sources* (Chicago: Wartburg Press, 1930) 352; CR 27:99-100; Herbert Immenkötter, *Die Confutatio der Confessio Augustana vom 3. August 1530* (Corpus Catholicorum 33; Münster: Aschendorff, 1979) 91, 93.
5. Quoted in BC 137, n. 9; BS 202, n. 1; in Reu, op. cit., 351. Emphasis added. See also Johann Eck, *Four Hundred and Four Articles,* in Reu, op. cit., 97-121, esp. the articles "Against Faith" (186-191), "Against Works" (192-202), "Against Merits" (203-205), and "Against Love" (206-212).
6. Ap 4:381; BS 231-32; BC 165.
7. Ibid.
8. Ap 4:382; BS 232; BC 165.
9. Ap 12:59; BS 263; BC 190.
10. I am indebted for this word count to my former assistant, Pastor Richard Kraemer.
11. See especially Robert Stupperich, "Die Rechtfertigungslehre bei Luther und Melanchthon, 1530-1536," in Vilmos Vajta, ed., *Luther und Melanchthon: Referate des Zweiten Internationalen Lutherforscherkongresses* (Göttingen: Vandenhoeck & Ruprecht, 1961) 73-88; also Martin Greschat, *Melanchthon neben Luther: Studien zur Gestalt der Rechtfertigungslehre zwischen 1528 und 1537* (Witten: Luther-Verlag, 1965) esp. 50-79.
12. WA Br 5:500.
13. Ibid. 560.
14. WA 30/2:657-676.
15. WA 30/2:643; LW 35:198.
16. WA 40/3:361.
17. Stupperich, op. cit., 76, 74.
18. Ibid., 81.
19. WA 40/1:368, 27; LW 26:232.
20. WA 40/1:367, 20-21; LW 26:232.
21. WA 40/1:367, 27-28; LW 26:232. Emphasis added.
22. WA 40/1:371, 33-372, 16; LW 26:235.
23. WA 40/1:373, 13-14; LW 26:235.
24. WA 40/1:373, 16-17; LW 26:236.
25. WA 40/1:376, 27, 23-24; LW 26:238.
26. WA 40/1:377, 13-14; LW 26:238.
27. WA 40/1:376, 16; 375, 30-31; LW 26:238.
28. WA 40/1:377, 13-14; LW 26:238.
29. WA 40/1:376, 23-24; LW 26:238.

30. WA 40/1:376, 24; LW 26:238. Emphasis added.
31. WA 40/1:323, 33-34; 324, 11; 323, 25-26; LW 26:198.
32. WA 40/1:376, 24-377, 13; LW 26:238. Emphasis added.
33. WA 40/1:377, 13-18; LW 26:238.
34. WA 40/1:371, 30-33; LW 26:234-35.
35. WA 40/1:364, 31-365, 13; LW 26:230. Emphasis added.
36. WA 40/1:361, 26; LW 26:228.
37. WA 40/1:376, 28-377, 13; LW 26:238.
38. WA 40/1:376, 27; LW 26:238. Emphasis added.
39. WA 40/1:376, 23-24; LW 26:238. Emphasis added.
40. WA 40/1:207, 11; LW 26:115. Emphasis added.
41. WA 40/1:202, 23-24; LW 26:112.
42. WA 40/1:206, 27-28; LW 26:115.
43. WA 40/1:204, 11ff.; LW 26:113.

9. Johnson

1. FC Ep 3:1; BS 781; BC 472.
2. FC SD 3:6; BS 916; BC 540; WA 31/1:255; LW 14:37. Cf. Luther: "The first and chief article is this, that Jesus Christ, our God and Lord, 'was put to death for our trespasses and raised again for our justification' (Rom. 4:25). . . . Nothing in this article can be given up or compromised" (SA 2,1, 1-3; BS 415; BC 292).
3. FC Ep 12:31; BS 827; BC 500.
4. FC SD, Rule and Norm, 9; BS 83, 836-37; BC 505.
5. FC SD 3:67; BS 936; BC 551.
6. CA 21; BS 83 c-d; BC 47.
7. CA 4; BS 56; BC 30.
8. Ap 4, n. 8; BS 158-59; BC 107. The Roman Confutation declared the Lutheran ascription of justification to faith alone to be diametrically opposed to the truth of the gospel by which works are not excluded.
9. The Apology has been called a companion volume to Melanchthon's *Loci Communes* of 1521, a theological dissertation rather than a Confession.
10. Ap, Preface 9-10; BS 143; BC 99.
11. Ap 4:2; BS 159; BC 107.
12. FC SD, Rule and Norm, 6; BS 835; BC 504.
13. This was patently a return to the Roman notion of infused grace (*iustitia infusa*) as the basis for justification.
14. It was, of course, granted that such virtues were infused by the Holy Spirit.
15. Each prince was given the right to decide which religion would be established in accordance with the principle of one government, one religion (*cuius regio, eius religio*).

16. The Preface to the Solid Declaration refers to grievous and dangerous schisms which had arisen in the Evangelical churches (FC SD Preface, 7; BS 831-32; BC 502).

17. Melanchthon made several changes in the *Augustana.* The amended edition came to be known as the Variata. The Formula clearly receives the unaltered edition (FC SD, Rule and Norm, 4; BS 835; BC 504).

18. FC SD 12:40; BS 1100; BC 636.

19. Cf. Albrecht Ritschl, *Die christliche Lehre von der Rechtfertigung und Versöhnung* (3rd ed.; Bonn: Adolph Marcus, 1889) 1:235-40, for a fuller presentation of Osiander's teaching. Lutheran dogmaticians speak of the indwelling of Christ in the believer as the *unio mystica,* a consequence, not a cause of forensic justification.

20. Melanchthon insisted that by faith in Christ the sinner is justified, not merely prepared to become just, by the indwelling of God.

21. Ap, Preface, 15-16; BS 143-44; BC 99.

22. Cf. SA 2, 1, 1-5; BS 415-16; BC 292.

23. Ap 4:2; BS 159; BC 107.

24. Of the forty paragraphs comprising article 20 the doctrine of faith is treated in nineteen, while the doctrine of works is treated in but eight. This reflects Melanchthon's conviction that the doctrine of faith must ever be and remain the chief teaching in the church since it is by faith that the Holy Spirit is received and hearts are renewed to do good works (CA 20:29-30; BS 80; BC 45).

25. The Council of Trent later defined faith as the beginning of salvation (*initium salutis*). In the *Loci Communes* Melanchthon had written: *Hoc est Christum cognoscere, beneficia eius cognoscere,* meaning that genuine faith knows the saving work of Christ in existential appropriation of its benefits. In the Apology Melanchthon speaks of knowing in a saving way the purpose of the history, to wit, the forgiveness of sins. Cf. Robert Stupperich, ed., *Melanchthons Werke in Auswahl* (Gütersloh: Bertelsmann, 1952) 1:7.

26. FC SD 4:7-14; BS 941-42; BC 552-53; WA DB 7:10; LW 35:370.

27. Ap 4:4-7; BS 159-60; BC 108. Melanchthon asks: "Since we obtain justification through a free promise, however, it follows that we cannot justify ourselves. Otherwise why would a promise be necessary?" (Ap 4:43; BS 168; BC 113).

28. FC SD 5:20; BS 958; BC 561.

29. FC Ep 3:1-4; BS 781-82; BC 472-73.

30. Lutheran theologians have utilized various terms in defining how the sinner is put in possession of the objective salvation won by Christ. *Ordo salutis* is the order of salvation; *applicatio salutis a Christo acquisitae* is the appropriation of salvation; *via salutis* is the way of salvation. While the Formula does not offer a dogmatic system, it does take up conversion, justification, sanctification (inner renewal), and good works (FC SD 3:41; BS 927-28; BC 546).

31. FC SD 3:66; BS 936; BC 550.
32. Ap 4:5; BS 159; BC 108; cf. 4:40-44; BS 167-68; BC 112-13; 4:62; BS 172; BC 115; 4:102; BS 181; BC 121; 4:183-86; BS 196-97; BC 132.
33. Ap 4:45; BS 168-69; BC 113. *Fides personalis* does not refer to a special promise made by God to the sinner, but to special or personal appropriation of a general promise, to wit, the grace of God in Christ for all sinners (*gratia universalis*). Melanchthon also stresses that faith must always go back to the promise (gospel) of mercy and forgiveness in Christ (Ap 4:164; BS 193; BC 129).
34. Ap 4:51-56; BS 170-71; BC 114. In the Augsburg discussion with Cajetan Luther defined faith as trust in Christ's promise (*der Vertrau–Glaube an die Zusage Christi*) (Klaus Peter Schmid, *Acta Augustana* [Augsburg: FDL Verlag, 1982] 14).
35. FC SD 3:10; BS 917; BC 541.
36. Dogmaticians speak variously of the object of saving faith as Christ, the gospel, the grace of God, the God who raised Jesus from the dead, or the promise of mercy. One does not exclude the other. Lutheran systematicians also speak of justifying faith as actual faith (*fides actualis*) in order to emphasize the category of relation. Faith justifies not as a work, but as instrument. Saving faith does not justify because it is a gift of the Spirit (which it, of course, is), but inasmuch as it stands in relation to Christ (*quatenus habet se correlative ad Christum*).
37. Ap 4:227; BS 203; BC 138-39.
38. Ap 4:86; BS 178; BC 119.
39. Ap 4:72; BS 174; BC 117.
40. Ap 4:62; BS 172; BC 115.
41. Ap 4:117; BS 184; BC 123. When discussing the necessity of good works, the Apology equates being justified with being righteous and being reborn to do the works required (Ap 4:348-49; BS 227; BC 160; Ap 386; BS 232; BC 166).
42. Ap 4:252; BS 209; BC 143.
43. Ap 4:305-306; BS 219; BC 154. In his lectures on the Psalms, delivered 1513-15, Luther viewed justification in the Augustinian sense as a way by which the sinner is cleansed from sin. God first makes a person righteous and then declares him to be righteous. Luther later understood justification as a forensic act (*actus forensis Dei*).
44. FC SD 3:6-9; BS 916-17; BC 540-41.
45. FC SD 3:17; BS 919-20; BC 541-43.
46. FC Ep 3:8; BS 783; BC 474.
47. FC SD 3:41; BS 927-28; BC 546.
48. FC SD 3:50; BS 931; BC 548.
49. Though categories of causality are employed by them, later Lutheran theologians stress that in the article on justification both justification and sanctification, as internal renewal, occur simultaneously.

50. Ap 4:76-78; BS 175; BC 117.
51. Ap 4:86; BS 178; BC 119.
52. Ap 4:307; BS 219; BC 154; cf. 4:163; BS 193; BC 129.
53. Ap 4:43; BS 168; BC 113; cf. 4:263; BS 212; BC 145.
54. FC SD 3:4; BS 914-16; BC 540.
55. This is sometimes expressed as a vicarious satisfaction or atonement (*satisfactio vicaria Christi*). Christ sacrificed his holy life (*obedientia activa*) and his sufferings and death (*obedientia passiva*) for us.
56. FC SD 3:14-16; BS 918-19; BC 541.
57. FC SD 3:55-58; BS 933-35; BC 549-50. The Formula states that this is the teaching of the Augsburg Confession.
58. FC SD 3:54; BS 933; BC 549.
59. Ap 4:44-45; BS 168-69; BC 113.
60. Ap 4:110-111; BS 183; BC 123. This is the *fides caritate formata*, sometimes understood as faith animated by love.
61. Lutheran systematicians stress that renewal to do good works is always a consequence of justification. Melanchthon writes: "Faith precedes while love follows (Ap 4:141; BS 188; BC 126; cf. 4:111; BS 183; BC 123; 4:122-25; BS 185; BC 124).
62. Ap 4:125; BS 185; BC 124.
63. Melanchthon's basic attitude toward the law of God is that it "always accuses" the sinner before God. Apart from justification and the Holy Spirit, one cannot correctly keep the law at all.
64. Ap 4:177-78; BS 195; BC 131.
65. Ap 4:189; BS 197; BC 133; cf. 4:214; BS 201; BC 136.
66. Ap 4:194; BS 198; BC 133. The Apology quotes 1 Cor. 3:8: "Each should receive his wages according to his labor."
67. Ap 4:275; BS 214; BC 148; cf. 4:356-77; BS 227-31; BC 161-65.
68. Ap 4:372; BS 230; BC 164.
69. FC SD 3:13; BS 918; BC 541.
70. FC SD 3:41-43; BS 928-29; BC 546-47; WA 43:255; LW 4:166.
71. Lutherans sometimes speak of the *forma* of good works as the law of God, but good works please God only because their *forma* is faith in Christ.
72. Luther's *Preface* to Romans is cited, in which Luther describes the dynamic character of faith; it is impossible for faith not to be constantly doing what is good (FC SD 4:10; BS 941-42; BC 552-53; WA DB 7:10; LW 35:370).
73. FC SD 3:36-43; BS 926-27; BC 545-47; cf. Ap 4:183ff.; BS 196ff.; BC 132ff.
74. On the basis of Eph. 2:10 and 1 John 3:14, Lutheran systematicians have spoken of the good works of the justified as an external witness of the Holy Spirit (*testimonium Spiritus Sancti externum*).
75. Ap 4:389; BS 232; BC 166.
76. Ap 4:398; BS 233; BC 167.
77. Ap 4:389; BC 232; BC 166.

10. Raitt

1. Herbert Immenkötter, Introduction, *Die Confutatio der Confessio Augustana vom 3. August 1530* (Münster: Aschendorff, 1979) 25.
2. CR 2:170.
3. Immenkötter, *Confutatio*, 29.
4. Ibid., 37.
5. Ibid., 39.
6. James McCue, "Roman Catholic Responses to the Augsburg Confession on Justification: 1530 and 1980." An unpublished paper delivered at the Concordia Academy, Wartburg Seminary, n.d.
7. See below, p. 205; cf. also, R. Jenson's unpublished paper for this dialogue on article 4 of the Apology.
8. For the Roman Catholics these were: the Bishop of Augsburg, Christopher von Stadion; Duke Henry of Braunschweig; Bernhard Hager, Chancellor of the Archbishop of Cologne; Jerome Vehus, Chancellor of the Margrave of Baden; and the three theologians, John Eck, Conrad Wimpina, and John Cochläus. For the Lutherans the collocutors were: Duke Frederick of Saxony; Margrave George of Brandenburg-Ansbach; the above princes' two chancellors, Gregor Brück and Sebastian Heller. The Protestant theologians were Philip Melanchthon, John Brenz, and Erhard Schnepf (from Vinzenz Pfnür, *Einig in der Rechtfertigungslehre: Die Rechtfertigungslehre der Confessio Augustana (1530) und die Stellungnahme der katholischen Kontroverstheologie zwischen 1530 und 1535* (Wiesbaden: Franz Steiner Verlag, 1970) 252. I have read the documents in CR 2 and concur with Pfnür's analysis.
9. George Spalatin, *Annales Reformationis oder Jahr-Bücher von der Reformation Lutheri* (Leipzig: J. L. Gleditsch, 1718) 163.
10. For this interpretation, compare J. Eck's *Enchiridion locorum communium adversus Lutherum et alios hostes ecclesiae (1525-1543)* (ed. P. Fraenkel; Münster: Aschendorff, 1979) 96-102, esp. 100, and Melanchthon's *Loci Theologicae,* CR 21:43-46, 183-84.
11. Pfnür, 263.
12. Ibid., 265-266.
13. Ibid., 266.
14. Hubert Jedin, *A History of the Council of Trent* (tr. Dom E. Graf; London: Thomas Nelson and Sons, Ltd., 1957) 1:259.
15. Ibid.
16. Ibid.
17. CR 2:282-83.
18. CR 2:283-84; 299-300.
19. CR 2:340; cf. 355-56.
20. CR 2:373-78.
21. Jedin, 274.

22. Ibid., 345.
23. SA 3:13; BS 460-61; BČ 315.
24. Peter Matheson, *Cardinal Contarini at Regensburg* (Oxford: Clarendon Press, 1972) 23-35. These pages provide a history of the political maneuvering of Charles V and Granvelle, the pope and his legate, Morone, and the forces at work at Hagenau and Worms.
25. The original draft of the Regensburg book, probably by Gropper, was discovered in the Marburg state archive by Max Lenz and published in 1878; cf. Max Lenz, *Briefwechsel Landgraf Philipps des Grossmütigen von Hessen mit Bucer* (3 vols.; Publicationen aus den K. Preussischen Staatsarchiven 5, 28, and 47; Leipzig: G. Herzel, 1880, 1887, 1891) esp. vol. 5:293-294 and vol. 47:31-72.
26. Matheson, 79.
27. Ibid., 97.
28. Ibid., 103-104.
29. Ibid., 93-96.
30. Ibid., 71.
31. Ibid., 84.
32. Ibid., 101. Cf. the rest of this chapter with regard to Granvelle's direction of the collocutors' work.
33. CR 4:414.
34. Matheson, 107 with n. 37. I do not endorse Matheson's analysis of the agreement on justification. See T. L. Parker's review of this point in *The Journal of Theological Studies* 24 (April 1973) 303-305. Parker appears to me to err in the opposite direction.
35. CR 4:190-238. My analysis is based on this text edited by Melanchthon. The portion on justification is found on 198-201.
36. Matheson, 132-135; 137.
37. Jedin 1:382 with n. 2.
38. WA Br 9:441 ##3629 and 3630; cf. 445-46. See also Vinzenz Pfnür, "Die Einigung bei den Religionsgesprächen von Worms und Regensburg 1540-41," in *Die Religionsgesprächen der Reformationszeit* (ed. G. Müller: Schriften des Vereins für Reformationsgeschichte 191; Gütersloh: Güttersloher Verlaghaus Gerd Mohn, 1980) 64-68.
39. Jedin, 386.
40. From an unpublished paper read by Luther Pederson at a session of a meeting of the American Society of Reformation Research at Western Michigan University, Kalamazoo, May 1979.
41. CR 7:48-62 sic (misnumbered; it should be 64).
42. CR 7:215-221: *Ultima sententia Consiliariorum de Adiaphoris in Cellesi*.
43. CR 7:62: ". . . und is wahr, dass das ewige Leben gegeben wird um des Herrn Christi willen aus Gnaden, und dass zugleich Erben sind ewiger Seligkeit alle, die sich zu Gott bekehren, und durch Glauben Vergebung der Sünden und heiligen Geist empfangen."

44. CR 7:51.
45. Ibid.
46. The "four judgments" refer to:
    Iudicium I. de libro Interim, April 1, 1548 (CR 6:839-42).
    Iudicium II. de libro Interim, April 13, 1548 (CR 6:853-57).
    Iudicium III. de libro Interim, April 24, 1548 (CR 6:865-74).
    Iudicium IIII. de libro Interim, June 16, 1548 (CR 6:924-42).
47. CR 7:62: ". . . die *sich* zu Gott *bekehren*, und durch Glauben Vergebung der Sünden und heiligen Geist empfangen." Emphasis added.
48. CR 6:215-21. The Leipzig Interim is found in CR 7:258-64, which also refers the reader to Melanchthon's Pegau statement for the section on justification and good works.

11. Peter

1. "Justification by Faith," part I of this volume.
2. This they did when referring to: (*a*) the relationship between the forgiveness of sins and the transformation wrought by grace ("Justification by Faith," part I of this volume, n. 181); (*b*) concupiscence and sin in the justified (ibid., n. 183); (*c*) the avoidance of venial sin (ibid., nn. 184-85); (*d*) the need of daily prayer for forgiveness (ibid., n. 186); (*e*) the need for love to qualify faith if the latter is to unite believers perfectly to Christ (ibid., n. 189). See too the Tridentine position which they describe as their own conviction and with which they begin their treatment of merit (ibid., §109).
3. What would have happened if this decree had come earlier, perhaps from the Fifth Lateran Council (1512-17), and really become part of the life of the church? Adolf Harnack answered this question by saying it is doubtful that the Reformation would have developed; cf. *History of Dogma* (tr. N. Buchanan; New York: Dover, 1961) 7:57. He then went on to say the decree resulted from a set of circumstances in which the Roman Catholic Church found itself under the simultaneous influence of Augustinianism and Protestantism; that will never happen again! So he assured his readers over eighty years ago (ibid.). He concluded by saying it is really not so important *what* was actually taught in the Tridentine decree on justification. The content was, in his view, clearly subordinate to the decisive operative principle, namely, " . . . the use and wont of the Roman Church is the supreme law" (ibid., 58). For the members of the Lutheran-Roman Catholic Dialogue, the decree in question was not the occasion for: (*a*) speculating on a *might-have-been*; (*b*) succumbing to the temptation of the historian playing prophet; or (*c*) introducing an explanatory principle supported by neither text nor context. It was all three for Harnack, and this in the space of two pages.
4. What theological weight was the conciliar usage of the term *anathema* intended to give to the exclusion of these propositions? The answer depends

on historical research into the debates that led to the approval of the canons in their final form. Pius IV saw the council's conclusion, approved its decrees, and planned for publication of its *Acta*. With his death things changed. Free access to the *Acta* of the council, preserved in the Vatican Archives, came only in the nineteenth century with Leo XIII; for details cf. Owen Chadwick, *Catholicism and History—The Opening of the Vatican Archives* (Cambridge: Cambridge University Press, 1978), esp. "The Minutes of the Council of Trent," 46-71. That was too late to prevent a widespread but false assumption that any proposition anathematized by the Council of Trent was rejected as heretical in the strict sense, namely, as a denial of the word of God or of "divinely revealed truth." A concern of churchmen for secrecy had made it needlessly difficult for scholars to discover that Trent's usage of *anathema* was far more subtle than indicated by such an oversimplification. Sometimes (though to be sure not always) the use of *anathema* meant that the council judged the willful affirmation of such a condemned proposition to be a serious act of disobedience. The latter was seen as putting one so much at odds with the Church's practice (and indirectly perhaps with the teaching underlying that practice) that it warranted an excommunication (*anathema*) incurred (when the conditions of culpability were present) without the intervention of any ecclesiastical authority. To say that embracing a position involves serious disobedience worthy of excommunication falls considerably short of saying it involves a denial of God's revealing word. When the Tridentine *anathema* means the first and when the second must be determined in individual instances from context and other indications. Cf. Heinrich Lennerz, s.J., "Notulae Tridentinae, Primum Anathema in Concilio Tridentino," *Gregorianum* 27 (1946) 136-42; Piet Fransen, s.J., "Réflexions sur l'anathème au Concile de Trente," *Ephemerides Theologicae Lovanienses* 29 (1953) 657-72; A. Lang, "Der Bedeutungswandel der Begriffe 'fides' und 'haeresis' und die dogmatische Wertung der Konzilsentscheidungen von Vienne und Trient," *Münchener Theologische Zeitschrift* 4 (1953) 133-46; Fidel García Martinez, "Una novíssima interpretación de los cánones Tridentinos," *Rivista Española de Teologia* 15 (1955) 637-54; Hubert Jedin, *Geschichte des Konzils von Trient* (Freiburg-Basel-Wien: Herder, 1970) 3:517-8; Carl J. Peter, "Auricular Confession and the Council of Trent," *The Jurist* 28 (1968) 280-97; Carl J. Peter, "Integrity Today?" *International Catholic Review: Communio* 1 (1974) 60-82.

5. Some of those propositions involved "tendentious summarizations." Others were taken only by "extremists" or "eccentrics." Cf. A. G. Dickens, *The Counter Reformation* (New York: Harcourt, Brace, and World Inc., 1969) 114. In the fifth century Ephesus may well have misunderstood Nestorius while condemning a position deserving of just such treatment. Later the Augsburg Confession may have misunderstood Catholic doctrine regarding the Mass (CA 24:21; BS 93; BC 58); nevertheless the opinion it repudiated

merited rejection and by more than Lutherans. The canons of Trent on justification may have misunderstood Luther, Melanchthon, and the Lutheran Confessions; the positions those canons anathematized must nevertheless be said to have distorted God's word about forgiveness. Lutherans and Roman Catholics today have passed from *anathema* to dialogue. Each side must still learn to avoid caricaturing the other's theology. For Roman Catholics it may well be that by learning just this they will come to realize they are not faced with the choice of repudiating Trent's teaching on justification or questioning the Christian faith of their Lutheran sisters and brothers.

6. Cf. CA 2: BS 53; BC 29: DS 1510-16.
7. DS 1513, 1515.
8. DS 1510.
9. DS 1513.
10. DS 1515.
11. The grace of God in Jesus Christ is absolutely indispensable because of original sin; so Trent in its first three canons (DS 1511-13). That same grace of Christ is available in baptism to meet the needs of children as well as adults (DS 1514, canon 4). And finally Christ's grace in baptism is stronger than sin (DS 1515, canon 5). The concupiscence that remains after baptism has its source in sin and leads to sin but is not itself sin in the proper sense of the term; otherwise Christ's grace in baptism is not truly effective. Here the decree on original sin maximizes Christ's importance precisely because it will not have baptism less than victorious over sin. For a comparison between Trent, the Augsburg Confession, and the Apology on this issue of the relation of concupiscence to sin, cf. Wilhelm Breuning and Bengt Hägglund, "Sin and Original Sin," in *Confessing One Faith* (ed. George Forell and James F. McCue; Minneapolis: Augsburg, 1982) 94-115.
12. DS 1551.
13. DS 1552-53.
14. DS 1525.
15. DS 1532.
16. Heiko A. Oberman, "Das tridentinische Rechtfertigungsdekret im Licht spätmittelaltlicher Theologie," *Zeitschrift für Theologie und Kirche* 61 (1964) 251-82 (tr., "The Tridentine Decree on Justification in the Light of Late Medieval Theology," *Journal for Theology and the Church* 3, *Distinctive Protestant and Catholic Themes Revisited* [ed. R. W. Funk: New York: Harper and Row, 1967] 28-54).
17. "Justification by Faith," n. 96.
18. DS 1545.
19. DS 1513.
20. Cf. what is said of perseverance; DS 1541.
21. DS 1523-24.
22. DS 1524.

23. DS 1526.
24. These objections were discussed by members of the dialogue. The answers proposed here were part of an essay the author presented; they remain his sole responsibility.
25. DS 1525. In the agreement reached at Regensburg in 1541 God was said to reward the good works of the just because (among other reasons assigned) those works proceed from the indwelling divine Spirit and with the concurrence of free choice as a partial agent (. . . *concurrente libero arbitrio tanquam partiali agente*) (cf. CR 4:201). Trent spoke of free choice as a *partial agent* neither in the grace-assisted process leading to justification nor in the meritorious works performed by the justified.
26. Ibid.
27. It is not that God has first made the sinner acceptable and then accepts him or her in justification. It is rather that even though prepared by grace, the sinner does not deserve acceptance but is nevertheless accepted by God because of the merits of Jesus Christ.
28. DS 1528.
29. Ibid.
30. DS 1529.
31. Later Roman Catholic theology would speak of this as uncreated grace or God's self-communication, without which there is no justification.
32. DS 1529.
33. Ibid.
34. Ibid.
35. Ibid.
36. DS 1530.
37. DS 1526.
38. DS 1529.
39. DS 1530.
40. DS 1532.
41. Ibid.
42. *Concilium Tridentiunum: Diariorum, Actorum, Epistularum, Tractatuum Nova Collectio* (ed. Soc. Görresiana; Freiburg im Breisgau: B. Herder, 1911) Tom. 5, Pars Altera; 731, 734.
43. Ap 4:71-72; BS 174; BC 116-17.
44. DS 1545-49; 1581-82.
45. DS 1545.
46. DS 1546.
47. In 1949 and again in 1963 (with an important introductory note indicating significant research that had appeared in the meanwhile) Peter Brunner suggested his own interpretation of the meaning of merit in Trent; cf. "Die Rechtfertigungslehre des Konzils von Trient," in *Pro Veritate: ein theologischer Dialog* (Festschrift L. Jaeger and W. Stählin; ed. E. Schlink and Hermann Volk; Münster: Aschendorff, 1963) 141-69. According to Brunner

the view of Seripando on *duplex iustitia* may have escaped Trent's censure. Brunner posits in the justified person two created "justices": (*a*) the *iustitia inhaerens* bestowed on and in that sense belonging to each individual; (*b*) the justice of Christ precisely as communicated, filtered through, and making up for the deficiencies of the *iustitia inhaerens*. This, he argues, is compatible with Trent's teaching. Christ's communicated justice is in the justified. No *new* application on his part is needed to make up for the deficiencies of the *iustitia inhaerens* which would otherwise keep the works of the justified from being truly meritorious. In reply one notes that the created justices Brunner posits in the justified are two. Would not the communicated justice of Christ vie with or coalesce with the *iustitia inhaerens* for the role of formal cause? But Trent said the formal cause was *unica* (one and one alone) and identified it with the *iustitia inhaerens*. For his part Hubert Jedin says Trent rejected without formally condemning the doctrine of a twofold justification. Cf. *Reformation and Counter Reformation, History of the Church* (tr. Anselm Biggs and Peter W. Becker; New York: Seabury, 1980) 5:470.
48. DS 1547.
49. DS 1548.
50. DS 1583.

12. Lindbeck

1. Revised in consultation with Dr. Kenneth Hagen but on the sole responsibility of the author.
2. Peter Brunner, "Die Rechtfertigungslehre des Konzils von Trient," *Pro Ecclesia, Gesammelte Aufsätze* (Berlin & Hamburg: Lutherisches Verlagshaus, 1966) 2:141-169; Wilfrid Joest, "Die Tridentinische Rechtfertigungslehre," *Kerygma und Dogma* 9 (1963) 41-69. A shorter version appeared in *Lutheran World* 9 (1962) 204-18. In what follows, references are to the English version.
3. Karl Rahner, *Theological Investigations* (Baltimore: Helicon, 1966) 4:189-218.
4. The possibility of caricature is recognized by Carl Peter in n. 5 of his essay, "The Decree on Justification in the Council of Trent," in this volume.
5. For the prevalence of these charges against Luther, see August Hasler, *Luther in der katholischen Dogmatik* (Munich: Max Hübner Verlag, 1968) 58-98.
6. For a Roman Catholic treatment which reaches the conclusion that Luther's basic intentions (though not his "exaggerated" early formulations) are reconcilable with Roman Catholic dogma, see Harry McSorley, *Luther, Right or Wrong?* (Minneapolis: Augsburg, 1969).
7. Ibid., 359-362. For the problem of the *promerere*, see Carl Peter, above, 220-22.

8. Carl Peter, above, 223 and 226 respectively.

9. Luther's understanding of *Heilsgewissheit* has been discussed from the Roman Catholic perspective by S. Pfürtner and O. Pesch, and most recently by J. Wicks, "Fides sacramenti—Fides specialis: Luther's Development in 1518," *Gregorianum* 65 (1984) 53-87. See his nn. 1-4 for references to the earlier literature.

10. Cf. DS 1548: "Far be it that a Christian should either trust or glory in himself and not in the Lord." In the light of this affirmation, the condemnations of the *sola fides* in DS 1533 and 1562 can be taken as opposing reflexive "faith in faith," i.e., the notion that justification is through confidence that one has faith, rather than the Reformation insistence that justifying faith ultimately relies on God's promises in Christ alone. For the Reformer's rejection of a reflexive understanding of faith, see Wicks, op. cit., p. 82, and O. Hof, "Luthers Unterscheidung zwischen dem Glauben und der Reflexion auf den Glauben," *Kerygma und Dogma* 18 (1972) 294-324.

11. Vinzenz Pfnür, *Einig in der Rechtfertigungslehre?* (Wiesbaden: Franz Steiner, 1970) 253-56, 391-93, and W. Breuning & B. Hägglund, "Sin and Original Sin," in *Confessing One Faith* (ed. G. W. Forell and J. F. McCue; Minneapolis: Augsburg, 1982) 94-116.

12. Pfnür, op. cit., 189, n. 325. Cf. CR 4:32, 86.

13. DS 1515.

14. Bruening and Hägglund, op. cit., 108-12.

15. Herbert Jedin, *A History of the Council of Trent* (Edinburgh: Nelson, 1961) 2:134, 143-52.

16. Edmund Schlink, *The Coming Christ and the Coming Church* (Philadelphia: Fortress, 1961) 89-95; Otto Pesch, *Theologie der Rechtfertigung bei Martin Luther und Thomas von Aquin* (Mainz: Matthias Grünewald, 1967) 946-48. These texts provide a stimulus rather than a source for what I say here.

17. Ap 4:43-45; BS 168-69; BC 106.

18. DS 1575.

19. *Contra Latomus*, WA 8: esp. 58-90; LW 32: esp. 160-204.

20. WA 8:79-80; LW 32:190.

21. WA 8:89-90; LW 32:204; Augustine is cited from *Letter* 167.4 (PL 33:739).

22. WA 8:89; LW 32:204.

23. August Hasler, op. cit., 156-160, has a useful summary of the inapplicability of traditional Catholic charges against Luther on this point. His n. 43, 156-57, supplies a lengthy bibliography on the subject.

24. As will become apparent in the next section, Luther's *simul* involves more than the Augustinian "imperfection of love" (see also n. 28 below).

25. DS 1528.

26. Joest, op. cit., 210.

27. Ibid., 206. The citation is from M. Schmaus, *Katholische Dogmatik* (5th ed.; Munich: Hübner, 1956) 3/2:116-17.

28. For this formulation, see Wilfrid Joest, *Ontologie der Person bei Luther* (Göttingen: Vandenhoeck & Ruprecht, 1967) 233-74, esp. 233-38, 269-74.

29. It should also be observed that in a nonsubstantialist in contrast to a substantialist ontology, it is not contradictory to conceive of a person as simultaneously wholly justified and wholly sinful; the justified are, so to speak, simultaneously and entirely bi-located in Christ and in themselves. If this argument holds, the full force of Luther's *simul* can be consistently asserted only in a nonsubstantialist conceptual context. Further, Trent can be interpreted as rejecting the legitimacy of the *simul* within a substantialist framework but not necessarily outside such a framework (for it never raised this question). If one absolutizes substantialism (as was done by neo-Scholasticism), or nonsubstantialism (as existentialists and a Lutheran theologian such as Gerhard Ebeling tend to do), the conflict over the *simul* becomes irresolvable. The absolutization for theological purposes of either of these philosophical outlooks was in effect rejected by Lutherans in the sixteenth century (for the Formula of Concord selectively uses Aristotelian substantialist categories when, for example, it asserts against Flacius that sin is an "accident" of the good human "substance" [FC SD 1:54-62; BS 861-66; BC 517-19]), and by Catholics in the twentieth (for Vatican II deliberately refrained from recommending that any one philosophy, such as Thomism, be officially preferred to others in theological studies. See *Presbyterorum ordinis* 15 and the commentary by Joseph Neuner on the place of Thomism in *Das zweite Vatikanische Konzil, Lexikon für Theologie und Kirche* [2nd ed.; Freiburg: Herder, 1967] Supplement, 2:339-40).

30. Ap 2:27-37; BS 152-54; BC 103-105.

31. For a fuller discussion of the Lutheran problem with the "*sola gratia* codicil," see Robert Jenson, "On Recognizing the Augsburg Confession," in *The Role of The Augsburg Confession* (ed. J. A. Burgess et al.; Philadelphia: Fortress, 1980) 160-62.

32. For a discussion of this approach, see Pesch, op. cit., 648-59.

33. C. Peter, above, 227-28.

34. See esp. Otto Pesch and Albrecht Peters, *Einführung in die Lehre von Gnade und Rechtfertigung* (Darmstadt: Wissenschaftliche Buchgesellschaft, 1981) 64-118. For Trent on justification, see 169-221.

35. DS 1531; cf. canon 32, DS 1582.

36. DS 1582.

37. This recasts rather than summarizes the argument (in Reinhard Koesters' "Gerecht und Sünder zugleich," *Catholica* 18 [1964] 193-217), but does not, I think, do violence to his thought. Koesters, it should be noted, claims the support of a substantial number of recent Roman Catholic theologians, including Scheffczyk, Boros, and Rahner, for his "single judgment" view, although applying this to Trent seems to be original with him. See Koesters, op. cit., 215-217. All other authors seem to assume a "double judgment" interpretation of Trent (see, e.g., Joest, article cited in n. 2, 209).

38. For an interpretation of the Reformation doctrine of justification that emphasizes its performative character, see Eric Gritsch and Robert Jenson, *Lutheranism* (Philadelphia: Fortress, 1976) 7-10, 36-44, et passim.

13. Bertram

1. Krister Stendahl, *Paul Among Jews and Gentiles* (Philadelphia: Fortress, 1976) 26-27, 39-40 (emphasis in text).
2. Wolfhart Pannenberg, *Reformation zwischen gestern und morgen* (Gütersloh: Gerd Mohn, 1969). "Protestant Piety and Guilt-Consciousness" and "A Search for the Authentic Self," unpublished lectures presented in Chicago, Saint Paul, Berkeley, and Saint Louis in October and November 1980. Pannenberg also contributed an essay, "The *Confessio Augustana* as a Catholic Confession and a Basis for the Unity of the Church," which in its English translation appears in *The Role of the Augsburg Confession* (ed. J. A. Burgess; Philadelphia: Fortress, 1980), but this essay deals with justification by faith only in the context of sixteenth-century polemics, then very briefly, and not at all with reference to the question of doctrinal centrality.
3. Paul Tillich, *The Protestant Era* (Chicago: The University of Chicago Press, 1957) 196, 201, x.
4. Anders Nygren, *Commentary on Romans* (Philadelphia: Fortress, 1949) 65-96.
5. Anders Nygren, *Agape and Eros* (Philadelphia: Westminster, 1953) 681-91, 739-41.
6. Werner Elert, *Outline of Christian Doctrine* (Philadelphia: United Lutheran Publication House, 1927) 14.
7. Werner Elert, *The Christian Faith: An Outline of Lutheran Dogmatics* (Columbus, Ohio: Trinity Lutheran Seminary Bookstore, 1974) 298.
8. Regin Prenter, *Creation and Redemption* (Philadelphia: Fortress, 1967) 190.
9. Gustav Wingren, *Creation and Gospel: The New Situation in European Theology* (New York: Edwin Mellen Press, 1979) 146, 159, 48, 61-69.
10. Gerhard Ebeling, *Word and Faith* (Philadelphia: Fortress, 1963) 10-11.
11. Gerhard Ebeling, *The Nature of Faith* (Philadelphia: Fortress, 1961) 120, 126-27, 150 (emphasis added).
12. Gerhard Müller, *Die Rechtfertigungslehre: Geschichte und Probleme* (Gütersloh: Gerd Mohn, 1977) 115.
13. Carl Braaten, "The Christian Doctrine of Salvation," *Interpretation* 35 (1981) 129.
14. Eric Gritsch and Robert Jenson, *Lutheranism* (Philadelphia: Fortress, 1976) 42-43 (emphasis in text).
15. G. Müller, op. cit., 115.
16. SA 2, 1:1-5; BS 415-16; BC 292; Ap 4:185; BS 196-97; BC 132; Ap 4:269; BS 214; BC 147; Ap 4:372; BS 230; BC 164; FC SD Summary Formulation 1-13; BS 833-39; BC 503-506.

17. Horst Georg Pöhlmann, *Rechtfertigung: Die gegenwärtige kontroverstheologische Problematik der Rechtfertigungslehre zwischen der evangelischlutherischen und der römisch-katholischen Kirchen* (Gütersloh: Gerd Mohn, 1971) 25-39.
18. Ibid., 23, 31 (emphasis in text).
19. Ibid., 31, 33.
20. Ernst Käsemann, *Commentary on Romans* (Grand Rapids: Eerdmans, 1980) 96.
21. SA 2, 1:1-5; BS 415-16; BC 292.
22. Pöhlmann, op. cit., 29 (emphasis added).
23. SA 2, 1:4; BS 415; BC 292.
24. Rudolf Bultmann, *Theology of the New Testament* (New York: Scribner's, 1951, 1955) 1:314-24.
25. Ibid., 319.
26. Ibid., 315, 287 (emphasis in text).
27. Helmut Thielicke, in *Kerygma and Myth* (tr. and ed. R. Fuller; London: S.P.C.K., 1953) 148. See also H. Thielicke, "Reflections on Bultmann's Hermeneutic," *The Expository Times* 67 (1956) 154-57, 175-77.
28. Ernst Kinder, *Ein Wort Lutherischer Theologie zur Entmythologisierung* (Munich: Evangelischer Presseverband für Bayern, 1952).
29. Carl Braaten and Roy Harrisville, *Kerygma and History* (Nashville: Abingdon, 1962).
30. See also R. Fuller, *The New Testament in Current Study* (New York: Scribner's, 1962) 17; F. Gogarten, *Demythologizing and History* (London: SCM Press, 1955) 49.
31. Ernst Käsemann, *Perspectives on Paul* (Philadelphia: Fortress, 1971) 75, 83-84, 89, 93.
32. Francis Pieper, *Christian Dogmatics* (Saint Louis: Concordia, 1951) 2:438.
33. Carl Braaten (n. 13 above), 117, 122, 124, 127, 130 (emphasis added).
34. Dietrich Bonhoeffer, *The Cost of Discipleship* (rev. ed.; New York: Macmillan, 1963) 47-48, 53, 55-56.
35. W. Elert, *The Christian Faith*, 297-98, 302-305 (emphasis in text).
36. R. Prenter, op. cit., 101-111.
37. Ibid., 444-45 (emphasis in text).

14. Dulles

1. In the twelve hundred pages of R. P. McBrien's two-volume *Catholicism* (Minneapolis: Winston, 1980), the word *justification* is indexed as appearing on only three pages. In each case the reference is to the historic Protestant-Catholic controversy. By contrast, Michael Schmaus gives a rather complete and ecumenically sensitive treatment to the question of justification in his *Dogma*, vol. 6, *Justification and the Last Things* (Kansas City: Sheed &

Ward, 1977). M. Flick and Z. Alszeghy, *Il Vangelo della Grazia* (Florence: Editrice Fiorentina, 1967), divides the treatise on grace into three main parts: the preparation for justification, justification itself, and the life of the justified person. But justification is here understood not in the forensic sense but simply as "the passage from the state of sin (original or personal) to the state of righteousness" (p. 23).

2. K. Rahner, "Questions of Controversial Theology on Justification," *Theological Investigations* (Baltimore: Helicon, 1966) 4:201-202. For Küng's view see his "Justification and Sanctification according to the New Testament" in D. J. Callahan et al., eds., *Christianity Divided* (New York: Sheed & Ward, 1961) 309-35, esp. 331-33; cf. H. Küng, *Justification: The Doctrine of Karl Barth and a Catholic Reflection* (New York: T. Nelson, 1964) 268-70.

3. P. Fransen, *The New Life of Grace* (New York: Herder and Herder, 1972) 55.

4. H. Volk, "Imputationsgerechtigkeit," *Lexikon für Theologie und Kirche* (2nd ed.; Freiburg: Herder, 1960) 4:641-42. Cf. Heinrich Fries, "Die Grundanliegen der Theologie Luthers in der Sicht der katholischen Theologie der Gegenwart," in E. Iserloh et al., *Wandlungen des Lutherbildes* (Würzburg: Echter-Verlag, 1966) 157-91, esp. 168-72.

5. R. Franco, "Justification," *Sacramentum Mundi* (New York: Herder and Herder, 1969) 3:239-41.

6. K. Rahner, "Some Implications of the Scholastic Concept of Uncreated Grace," *Theological Investigations* (Baltimore: Helicon, 1961) 1:328.

7. P. Fransen, *New Life*, 89-90; T. M. McDonough, *The Law and the Gospel in Luther* (London: Oxford University Press, 1963) 164.

8. According to Charles Moeller and Gérard Philips, "At the present moment, theology is moving in the direction of a synthesis between the doctrine of indwelling, and that of created grace, the latter being understood in the light of the great scholastics of the thirteenth century" (in *The Theology of Grace and the Oecumenical Movement* [London: Mowbray, 1961] 23).

9. Rahner, "Some Implications," 319-46.

10. Three articles by M. de la Taille, originally published in 1925-29, have been collected and translated under the title, *The Hypostatic Union and Created Actuation by Uncreated Act* (West Baden Springs, Ind.: West Baden College, 1952).

11. Fransen, *New Life*, 91.

12. K. Rahner, "The Theology of the Symbol," *Theol. Inv.*, 4:327.

13. E. Mersch, *The Theology of the Mystical Body* (St. Louis: B. Herder, 1951) 325-74. See also Schmaus, *Justification*, 76-80.

14. K. Rahner, "What is a Sacrament?," *Theol. Inv.* (New York: Seabury, 1976) 14:144.

15. K. Rahner, "Introductory Observations on Thomas Aquinas' Theology of the Sacrament in General," *Theol. Inv.*, 14:158.

16. K. Rahner, "Anonymous Christians," *Theol. Inv.* (Baltimore: Helicon, 1969) 6:390-98; "Anonymous Christianity and the Missionary Task of the Church," *Theol. Inv.* (New York: Seabury, 1974) 12:161-78; "Observations on the Problem of 'Anonymous Christianity,' " *Theol. Inv.*, 14:280-94.

17. K. Rahner, "The Word and the Eucharist," *Theol. Inv., 4*:253-86.

18. Cf. O. Semmelroth, *The Preaching Word* (New York: Herder and Herder, 1965); H. Volk, *Zur Theologie des Wortes Gottes* (Münster: Verlag Regensberg, 1962). See also the compilation *The Word: Readings in Theology* (New York: P. J. Kenedy, 1964).

19. R. A. Duffy, "Justification and Sacrament," *Journal of Ecumenical Studies* 16 (1979) 672-90. Some of this material appears in briefer form in Duffy's book, *Real Presence* (San Francisco: Harper & Row, 1982).

20. Ibid., 687.

21. Ibid., 686.

22. According to some interpreters the Council of Trent left open the possibility that the grace of justification might be merited in some broad or improper sense, though not strictly, by morally good acts, even when such acts are performed without the help of actual grace. E. Schillebeeckx regrets that the Council did not clearly exclude this hypothesis, which he regards as erroneous. See his "The Tridentine Decree on Justification: A New View," *Concilium* (New York: Paulist, 1965) 5:176-79.

23. K. Rahner, "Nature and Grace," *Theol. Inv.*, 4:180. Rahner attributes this view to Juan Martinez de Ripalda (d. 1648).

24. B. Lonergan, *Grace and Freedom: Operative Grace in the Thought of St. Thomas Aquinas* (New York: Herder and Herder, 1971).

25. B. Lonergan, *Method in Theology* (New York: Herder and Herder, 1972) 107.

26. Ibid., 241.

27. K. Rahner, "Theology of Freedom," *Theol. Inv.*, 6:195.

28. Rahner, *Foundations of Christian Faith* (New York: Seabury, 1978) 360.

29. Ibid., 359-60; cf. Rahner, "The Word and the Eucharist," 257-58.

30. Küng, *Justification*, 249-63.

31. Küng, "Justification and Sanctification," 322.

32. Rahner, "Questions of Controversial Theology," 202.

33. Rahner, *Foundations*, 361.

34. L. Bouyer, *The Spirit and Forms of Protestantism* (Westminster, Md.: Newman, 1956) 102-3.

35. O. H. Pesch, *Theologie der Rechtfertigung bei M. Luther und Thomas von Aquin* (Mainz: Matthias-Grünewald, 1967) 736.

36. These and other scriptural texts are mentioned by E. Schillebeeckx, *Christ: The Experience of Jesus as Lord* (New York: Seabury/Crossroad, 1980) 531.

37. Lonergan, *Method*, 107.

38. Fransen, *New Life*, 226, 236-44. For a later defense of this position see Fransen's "Das neue Sein des Menschen in Christus," in *Mysterium Salutis* (ed. J. Feiner and M. Löhrer; Einsiedeln: Benziger, 1973) 4/2:954-58.

39. J. Fuchs, *Human Values and Christian Morality* (Dublin: Gill and Macmillian, 1970) 109. Fuchs' chapter 4, "Basic Freedom and Morality" (92-111), contains an excellent discussion of what other authors call the "fundamental option."

40. Fransen, *New Life*, 274.

41. K. Rahner, "Considerations on the Active Role of the Person in the Sacramental Event," *Theol. Inv.*, 14:177.

42. See, for example, Rahner's articles on "Contrition" in *Sacramentum Mundi* (New York: Herder and Herder, 1968) 2:1-4 and on "Penance" in *Sacramentum Mundi* 4 (1969) 385-99.

43. K. Rahner, "The History of Penance," *Theol. Inv.* (New York: Crossroad, 1982) 15:16.

44. The question of the "supernatural formal object" is one to which Rahner returns frequently. For a rather full discussion, with ample references to the historical opinions, see his *De Gratia* course (*ad usum auditorum*) (5th ed.; Innsbruck, 1959-60) 329-38.

45. Rahner, "Nature and Grace," *Theol. Inv.*, 4:178. Cf. Fransen, *New Life* 282-85.

46. Fransen, *New Life* 285-92.

47. K. Rahner, "Reflections on the Experience of Grace," *Theol. Inv.* (Baltimore: Helicon, 1967) 3:86-90; "The Experience of God Today," *Theol. Inv.* (New York: Seabury, 1974) 11:149-65; "Religious Enthusiasm and the Experience of Grace," *Theol. Inv.* (New York: Seabury, 1979) 16:35-51.

48. P. Fransen, "Towards a Psychology of Divine Grace," *Cross Currents* 8 (1958) 211-32.

49. H. U. von Balthasar, *The Theology of Karl Barth* (New York: Holt, Rinehart, and Winston, 1971) 271-84; K. Rahner, "Justified and Sinner at the Same Time," *Theol. Inv.*, 6:218-30.

50. Küng, *Justification*, 236-48; O. H. Pesch, "Gottes Gnadenhandeln als Rechtfertigung des Menschen," *Mysterium Salutis* 4/2, esp. 886-91; O. H. Pesch, *Hinführung zu Luther* (Mainz: Matthias-Grünewald, 1982) ch. 11, 189-202.

51. Von Balthasar, *Barth*, 278.

52. O. H. Pesch, "Existential and Sapiential Theology: The Theological Confrontation between Luther and Thomas Aquinas," in J. Wicks, ed., *Catholic Scholars Dialogue with Luther* (Chicago: Loyola Univ., 1970) 70.

53. See Rahner, "Penance" (supra, n. 42); also K. Rahner, "Punishment of Sins," *Sacramentum Mundi* (New York: Herder and Herder, 1970) 6:92-94; also his "A Brief Theological Study on Indulgence," *Theol. Inv.* (New York: Herder and Herder, 1973) 10:150-65.

54. K. Rahner, "On the Official Teaching of the Church Today on the Subject of Indulgences," *Theol. Inv.*, 10:166-98.

55. Rahner, *Foundations*, 79.

56. J. L. Segundo, *The Liberation of Theology* (Maryknoll, N.Y.: Orbis, 1976) 143.

57. R. R. Roach, "Tridentine Justification and Justice," in *The Faith That Does Justice* (ed. J. C. Haughey; New York: Paulist, 1977) 181-206.

58. L. Boff, *Liberating Grace* (Maryknoll, N.Y.: Orbis, 1979), quotation from 154.

59. Fransen, "Das neue Sein" (supra, n. 38), 977.

60. Fransen, *New Life*, 201-30. According to Schmaus (*Justification*, 138): "Because of God's transcendence and the resultant inequality between God and man, merit in the strict sense of the word cannot occur in man in his relationship to God."

61. Fransen, "Das neue Sein," 978.

62. Fransen, *New Life*, 216; "Das neue Sein," 979. Thomas Aquinas had already made the point in *S. Theol.* 1-2.114.1c: "*Meritum hominis apud Deum esse non potest nisi secundum praesuppositionem divinae ordinationis.*"

63. Fransen, *New Life*, 228.

64. Rahner, "Questions of Controversial Theology," 209, n. 12.

65. Ibid.

66. Küng, *Justification*, 274. See also K. Rahner, "The Comfort of Time," *Theol. Inv.*, 3:144, who quotes a prayer also quoted by Küng, loc. cit.

67. Quoted in Küng, *Justification*, 274.

68. Pesch, "Existential and Sapiential Theology," 66-67. See also his *Hinführung zu Luther*, 128-33.

69. Pesch, *Theologie der Rechtfertigung*, 31-32, 74-76. McDonough likewise sees the law-gospel doctrine as the heart of Luther's system: *Law and Gospel*, 1.

70. G. Söhngen, *Gesetz und Evangelium* (Freiburg and Munich: Alber, 1957) 6.

71. W. Kasper, "Law and Gospel," *Sacramentum Mundi* (New York: Herder and Herder, 1969) 3:297.

72. Report of the Joint Lutheran-Roman Catholic Study Commission, "The Gospel and the Church," *Lutheran World* 19 (1972) 259-73.

73. J. A. Fitzmyer, "The Kerygmatic and Normative Character of the Gospel," in *Evangelium—Welt—Kirche* (ed. H. Meyer; Frankfurt: Lembeck; Frankfurt: Knecht, 1975) 111-28, esp. 122-25. One is reminded in this connection of Alfred Loisy's rather acerbic response to Harnack: "Here again the importance attached by Protestant theology to the idea of sin and justification accounts for what, from the point of view of historical criticism, is nothing but a preconceived determination to find in the gospel nothing but the essentials of one's own religion. Christ nowhere confounds the kingdom

with the remission of sins, which is only the condition of entrance into the kingdom" (*The Gospel and the Church* [New York: Scribner's 1912] 65-66).
74. Augustine, *De Spiritu et littera,* 19.34 (ML 44:221). For discussion see Söhngen, *Gesetz und Evangelium,* 91-103.
75. Kasper, "Law and Gospel," 298.

15. Forde

1. See, for instance, Albrecht Ritschl, "Die Rechtfertigungslehre des Andreas Osiander," *Jahrbücher für deutsche Theologie* 2 (1857) 785-829; also Emanuel Hirsch, *Die Theologie des Andreas Osiander und ihre geschichtliche Voraussetzung* (Göttingen: Vandenhoeck & Ruprecht, 1919).
2. Karl Holl, *Gesammelte Aufsätze* (7th ed.; Tübingen: J. C. B. Mohr [Paul Siebeck], 1948) 1:119, 125; 3:532. For a reply see F. Brunstäd, *Theologie der Lutherischen Bekenntnisschriften* (Gütersloh: C. Bertelsmann Verlag, 1951) 76.
3. WA 34/2:140, 6.
4. Ap 4:305; BS 219; BC 154.
5. Heinrich Schmid, *The Doctrinal Theology of the Evangelical Lutheran Church* (3rd ed.; tr. C. Hay and H. E. Jacobs; Minneapolis: Augsburg, n.d.) 424-25.
6. Thomas Aquinas, *S. T.* I IIae, Q. 113. Art. 6.
7. Martin Luther, *Lectures on Romans,* WA 56:268-69; LW 25:257-58.
8. Ibid., WA 56:273; LW 25:261.
9. For an excellent recent treatment see Leif Grane, *Modus Loquendi Theologicus: Luthers Kampf um die Erneuerung der Theologie (1515-1518)* (tr. E. Grötzinger; Leiden: E. J. Brill, 1975).
10. Wilfred Joest, *Gesetz und Freiheit* (2nd ed.; Göttingen: Vandenhoeck & Ruprecht, 1956) 58-59.
11. Ibid., 60-62.
12. WA 56:486; LW 25:478.
13. WA 39/1:542,6: "Law is to be taught without discrimination as much to the pious as the impious because the pious are partly just and partly sinner."
14. WA 40/2:351; LW 12:327: "It is not enough that this sin is forgiven through grace, for through our infirmity we fall right back into sin. Therefore we want sin not only to be forgiven, but to be completely removed."
15. Luther, *Lectures on Romans*, WA 56:275; LW 25:262.
16. Eric W. Gritsch and Robert W. Jenson, *Lutheranism: The Theological Movement and Its Confessional Writings* (Philadelphia: Fortress Press, 1976) 39-40.
17. *Freedom of a Christian*, WA 7:61; LW 31:361.
18. Luther, *Lectures on Romans*, WA 56:335; LW 25:323.
19. Ibid., WA 56:334-35; LW 25:323.

20. Joest, op. cit., 95.
21. In this light one would have to caution against recent attempts to downplay the "polemical exaggerations" of the early Reformation days for the sake of more irenic later statements, such as one finds in the otherwise informative and useful work of Vinzenz Pfnür, *Einig in der Rechtfertigungslehre?* (Wiesbaden: Franz Steiner Verlag, 1970). Removing the "polemical exaggerations" for the sake of more immediate consensus simply drives an illegitimate wedge between earlier and later Reformation teaching and obscures the fact that justification by faith involves a break in continuity.
22. Hans J. Iwand, *Um den Rechten Glauben. Gesammelte Aufsätze* (ed. K. G. Steck; Theologische Bücherei 9; Munich: Chr. Kaiser Verlag, 1959) 17-18.
23. Cf. Jaroslav Pelikan, "The Origins of the Subject-Object Antithesis in Lutheran Theology," *Concordia Theological Monthly* 21 (1950) 94-104.
24. Schmid, op. cit., 407.
25. Ibid., 408.
26. Wilhelm Dantine, *Justification of the Ungodly* (tr. Eric and Ruth Gritsch; Saint Louis: Concordia Publishing House, 1969) 32-33.
27. Gerhard Ebeling, *Luther: An Introduction to His Thought* (tr. R. A. Wilson; Philadelphia: Fortress Press, 1972) 113.
28. WA 3:152, 7: "God's works are his words. 'For he spoke and it was so:' the doing and the speaking of God are the same."
29. Ap 4:38; BS 167; BC 112.
30. SA 3,2:1, 4; BS 435-36; BC 303.
31. FC SD 5:12; BS 955-56; BC 560; WA 15:228.
32. For a more complete account of Luther's understanding of the problem of letter and spirit as it relates to law and gospel, see especially the work of Gerhard Ebeling, *Lutherstudien 1* (Tübingen: J.C.B. Mohr [Paul Siebeck], 1971); James S. Preus, *From Shadow to Promise* (Cambridge, Mass.: The Belknap Press of Harvard University Press, 1969); and my article, "Law and Gospel in Luther's Hermeneutic," *Interpretation* 37 (1983) 240-52.
33. Augustine, *On the Spirit and the Letter*, 4.6.
34. WA 7:653-55; LW 39:182-83. The contrast between Old and New Testaments in passages such as these raises problems for modern exegetes. One should note carefully, however, that Luther is not referring to certain sets of books or even a given content, but to kinds of preaching, offices, functions. Testament in this context means for Luther "will," as in "last will and testament." Preaching is the publication of the *will* of God, not merely conveying information *about* him. For a fuller treatment of this problem, see my article, "Law and Gospel in Luther's Hermeneutic," op. cit., 250-52.
35. WA 7:656; LW 39:185.
36. WA 7:658-59; LW 39:188.
37. WA 7:659-60; LW 39:189.

38. Gerhard Ebeling, "Erwägung zur Lehre vom Gesetz," *Wort und Glaube* (Tübingen, J.C.B. Mohr [Paul Siebeck], 1960) 291. The quotation is from Luther's Galatians commentary of 1531 (WA 40/2:18; LW 27:16).
39. Joest, op. cit., 190ff.

16. Peter

1. A precedent for recourse to the language of unconditionality is found in the fourth article of the Apology of the Augsburg Confession (4:41-42). There Melanchthon assures his reader that God's promise to forgive and to justify is to be trusted and not to be thought of as conditioned by human merit. The Tappert edition of *The Book of Concord* states it clearly once and then repeats that the promise is not *conditional* upon our merits (BC 112-13). The Latin text twice excludes merits as a condition for justification and forgiveness (BS 168). The conditionality which Melanchthon excludes here is clearly that of merit winning from God the forgiveness of sin and justification. It is not clear that his words must be taken to exclude all mention of any kind of condition when there is talk of the divine promise to forgive because of Jesus Christ.
2. For an earlier effort on the part of the author to do the same thing, cf. "Justification and the Catholic Principle," *Lutheran Theological Seminary Bulletin,* Gettysburg, Pa., 61 (1981) 16-32. The printed text was made available to the members of the Lutheran-Roman Catholic Dialogue in the USA at their request. In retrospect it seems that the indefinite article *a* might have been preferable before *Catholic principle*. What is more, a less ambiguous term than *Catholic* might have been employed since it was surely not implied that only Roman Catholicism has made use of the critical principle that was and still is being proposed. Hence the modification in the title of the present essay!
3. Paul Tillich, *Systematic Theology* (Chicago: University of Chicago Press, 1956) 1:37.
4. Ibid. Italics mine.
5. Ibid., 227. Italics mine.
6. Ibid.
7. Ibid.
8. Paul Tillich, *Systematic Theology* (Chicago: University of Chicago Press, 1963) 3:135.
9. Ibid.
10. Ibid., 223.
11. Ibid., 226.
12. Ibid., 238-39.
13. Ibid., 245.
14. Ibid.

15. Paul Tillich, *The Protestant Era* (4th impression; Chicago: University of Chicago Press, 1957) 196.
16. Ibid.
17. Paul Tillich, *Systematic Theology* 3:223.
18. Ibid., 224.
19. In the preface to his book *Obedient Rebels* (New York: Harper and Row, 1964), Jaroslav Pelikan thanks Paul Tillich for teaching him to speak of "Catholic substance and Protestant principle." Later he asks why Luther was excommunicated whereas Erasmus was not. A theological answer is said to be found in the fact that Luther's reformation had ". . . as its central Protestant principle the doctrine of justification by faith alone. . ." (ibid., 17).
20. "Article IV and Lutheran/Roman Catholic Dialogue: The Limits of Diversity in the Understanding of Justification," *Lutheran Theological Seminary Bulletin,* Gettysburg, Pa., 61 (1981) 6.
21. Ibid., 10.
22. Ibid., 13.
23. Ibid., 8. For Lindbeck's reaction, cf. his review of the first volume of Ebeling's *Dogmatik des Christlichen Glaubens*: "Ebeling: Climax of a Great Tradition," *The Journal of Religion* 61 (1981) 309-14.
24. Robert Jenson and Eric Gritsch, *Lutheranism: The Theological Movement and Its Confessional Writings* (Philadelphia: Fortress, 1976) 44.
25. Ibid., 38, 40.
26. Ibid., 41.
27. Ibid., 43.
28. See Eric W. Gritsch, *Martin—God's Court Jester* (Philadelphia: Fortress, 1983) 170-77.
29. Paul Tillich, *Systematic Theology* 3:6, 245.
30. Ibid., 6.
31. Ibid., 122.
32. Ibid.
33. Jaroslav Pelikan, *Obedient Rebels*, op. cit., 13.
34. Carl J. Peter, "Justification and the Catholic Principle" op. cit., 22. There the formulation of the principle was in the context of what the Roman Catholic members of the dialogue had said earlier about the papal office in *Papal Primacy and the Universal Church* (Lutherans and Catholics in Dialogue 5; ed. Paul Empie and T. Austin Murphy; Minneapolis: Augsburg, 1974) 37. The principle in question may be operative without being recognized or articulated.
35. Cf. Robert Jenson, "On Recognizing the Augsburg Confession," in *The Role of the Augsburg Confession* (ed. J. Burgess; Philadelphia: Fortress, 1980) 163; Carl J. Peter, "Justification and the Catholic Principle," op. cit., 20.

36. Carl J. Peter, "Dialog der Kirchen in den USA," *Evangelische Kommentare* 17 (1984) 140.
37. "Justification and the Catholic Principle," op. cit., 25.
38. Ibid., 23-24.
39. A Roman Catholic view of the preparation for justification has been dealt with at length in the essay entitled "The Decree on Justification in the Council of Trent," part II, ch. 11 in this volume.
40. For Wolfhart Pannenberg's fear in this regard, cf. "Protestant Piety and Guilt Consciousness," *Christian Spirituality* (Philadelphia: Westminster, 1983) 13-30.
41. Dr. Willard Gaylin is Clinical Professor of Psychiatry at Columbia University's College of Physicians and Surgeons and President of the Hastings Center. For his observations on an underdeveloped sense of guilt, cf. "A Conversation with Willard Gaylin: The Emotion of Guilt Has Been Given a Bum Rap," *U.S. News and World Report* 96 (April 30, 1984) 84.

LIST OF PARTICIPANTS

Catholics

The Most Rev. T. Austin Murphy
Auxiliary Bishop of Baltimore, Maryland
The Rev. Avery Dulles, s.j.
Catholic University of America, Washington, D.C.
The Rev. Robert B. Eno, s.s.
Catholic University of America, Washington, D.C.
The Rev. Joseph A. Fitzmyer, s.j.
Catholic University of America, Washington, D.C.
The Rev. John F. Hotchkin
Director, Bishops' Committee for Ecumenical and Interreligious Affairs, Washington, D.C.
The Rev. Kilian McDonnell, o.s.b.
President, Institute for Ecumenical and Cultural Research, Collegeville, Minnesota
The Rev. Carl J. Peter
Dean, School of Religious Studies, Catholic University of America, Washington, D.C.
The Rev. Msgr. Jerome D. Quinn
The St. Paul Seminary, St. Paul, Minnesota

Dr. Jill Raitt
Chairwoman, Department of Religious Studies, University of Missouri–Columbia, Columbia, Missouri
The Rev. George H. Tavard, A.A.
Methodist Theological School, Delaware, Ohio

Lutherans

Dr. H. George Anderson
President, Luther College, Decorah, Iowa
Dr. Robert W. Bertram
Christ Seminary–Seminex Professor of Historical and Systematic Theology, Lutheran School of Theology at Chicago, Chicago, Illinois
Dr. Eugene L. Brand
Director, Office of Studies, USA National Committee of the Lutheran World Federation, New York, New York (until December 1981)
Dr. David G. Burke
Director, Office of Studies, USA National Committee of the Lutheran World Federation, New York, New York (beginning January 1983)
Dr. Joseph A. Burgess
Executive Director, Division of Theological Studies, Lutheran Council in the U.S.A., New York, New York
Dr. Gerhard O. Forde
Professor of Systematic Theology, Luther Northwestern Theological Seminary, St. Paul, Minnesota
Dr. Karlfried Froehlich
Professor of Ecclesiastical History, Princeton Theological Seminary, Princeton, New Jersey
Dr. Eric W. Gritsch
Professor of Church History, Lutheran Theological Seminary, Gettysburg, Pennsylvania
Dr. Kenneth G. Hagen (beginning February 1982)
Professor of Theology, Department of Theology, Marquette University, Milwaukee, Wisconsin
Dr. John F. Johnson
Senior Pastor, Our Savior Lutheran Church, St. Petersburg, Florida

Dr. Fred Kramer (until February 1982)
Professor Emeritus of Systematic Theology, Concordia Theological Seminary, Springfield, Illinois
Dr. George A. Lindbeck
Professor of Historical Theology, Yale University Divinity School, New Haven, Connecticut
Dr. Warren A. Quanbeck (until February 1979)
Professor of Systematic Theology, Luther Theological Seminary, St. Paul, Minnesota
Dr. John Reumann
Professor of New Testament, Lutheran Theological Seminary, Philadelphia, Pennsylvania